# The
# GIRLS
# NEXT
# DOOR

Bringing the Home Front
to the Front Lines

KARA DIXON VUIC

Harvard University Press

Cambridge, Massachusetts
London, England
2019

First printing

*Library of Congress Cataloging-in-Publication Data*

Names: Vuic, Kara Dixon, 1977– author.
Title: The girls next door : bringing the home front to the front lines / Kara Dixon Vuic.
Description: Cambridge, Massachusetts : Harvard University Press, 2019. |
Includes bibliographical references and index.
Identifiers: LCCN 2018013648 | ISBN 9780674986381 (alk. paper)
Subjects: LCSH: Women and war—United States—History—20th century. | United States.
Army—Military life—History—20th century. | Soldiers—Recreation—United States—
History—20th century. | World War, 1914–1918—War work. | World War, 1939–1945—War
work. | Korean War, 1950–1953—War work. | Vietnam War, 1961–1975—War work. |
Military morale—United States—History—20th century.
Classification: LCC JZ6405.W66 V85 2019 | DDC 355.1/230973—dc23
LC record available at https://lccn.loc.gov/2018013648

Book design by Chrissy Kurpeski
Typeset in Arno Pro

*For Jason*

# Contents

===

# THE GIRLS NEXT DOOR

# Introduction

At a United Service Organizations (USO) benefit in October 2008, President George W. Bush boldly declared, "The moment things began to turn around in Iraq is when the USO deployed Jessica Simpson."[1] While the president's attribution of military success to a pop singer might seem illogical or even cavalier, military and civilian leaders throughout the twentieth century argued that American women provided essential symbolic support and moralizing influences that contributed to soldiers' positive performance and overall success. In every war in the twentieth century—and now into the twenty-first—the military has turned to organizations such as the Young Men's Christian Association (YMCA), the Red Cross, and the USO to send women entertainers to war zones. These women opened canteens where soldiers could find a friendly face, coffee, and doughnuts; performed on stage, played games, and engaged in conversation; and, when possible, brought a momentary reprieve from the war to battlefield soldiers. Designed to domesticate the military environment, recreation programs variously sought to combat prostitution, remind soldiers of their mothers or sweethearts, and symbolize a supportive American home front.

Much of American memory of these women's work is colored in sepia tones and drenched in nostalgia. Popular culture, for example, celebrates women like the Andrews Sisters, who boogie-woogied their way into the hearts of American GIs fighting in World War II. The blonde bombshell herself, Marilyn Monroe, shimmied into the lore of military history when she crooned her famously sultry tunes for thousands of American men stationed in Korea. Far less well known are the many more women from home who volunteered to fry doughnuts and warm hot chocolate for doughboys in World War I, or those who jitterbugged with lonely men in the Red Cross clubs that dotted all of World War II's theaters. In all of the Cold War's hot conflicts, the military, the Red Cross, and the USO hired civilian women to open recreation centers where military personnel could find a touch of home and, most importantly, average American girls next door. Yet, these women too are similarly absent from most Americans' knowledge of the extensive work women have done to bring a bit of the home front to the front lines of war.

*The Girls Next Door* looks behind the stage and through the doughnuts to provide a fuller, more expansive history of women's work in military entertainment. The armed forces developed formal recreation programs during World War I, when the YMCA and the Salvation Army deployed women to France, Britain, and postwar occupied Germany. There, the women served snacks, organized musical events and dances, and made small talk with soldiers. During the unprecedented military buildup of World War II, the USO began what would become a long history of sending famous starlets and budding performers to sing and dance around the globe. The Red Cross also mobilized young women to operate service clubs throughout Europe, Asia, and Africa and to entertain the troops in new mobile canteens that allowed the women to take refreshments and amusements to forward locations. Although entertainment programs proved smaller during the more limited deployments of the Korean and Vietnam Wars, the US Army's Special Services, the Red Cross, and the USO continued to dispatch women to perform and socialize in far-off war zones. Formal recreation programs staffed exclusively by women ended shortly after the Vietnam War as the armed forces incorporated increasing numbers of family members and servicewomen, though recent wars in the Middle East have revitalized the central place of women in military entertainment.

To be sure, women have been but one part of a continually expanding array of recreational and entertainment options provided for wartime soldiers. Always concerned with morale, the military's branches and civilian organizations have ensured that deployed troops have had access to everything from decks of playing cards to baseballs and bats, radios, books, magazines, and ways of communicating with home. But, however many other options for amusement GIs enjoyed, officials attributed greater significance to American women than they did to anything else. As women joined in card games and listened to the radio with the troops, they imbued wartime entertainment with its meaning as a symbol of home front support and comfort. A cozy club in which to relax was one thing, but as officials from World War I to the First Gulf War understood, the women who welcomed the men and made them feel at ease are what made it meaningful.

These women were not sideshows to American wartime and military experiences. They played a central part in national efforts to construct wartime gender roles, maintain an effective fighting force, mobilize home front support, render the military and its work palatable to the American public, and manage the American military presence in foreign countries. In its examination of the official rationales for and the nature of wartime entertainment, this book traces the evolution of wartime gender ideologies and connects women's work for the military to their changing place in the nation. It reveals how, even as the military mobilized women as conventionally feminine symbols, women worked within the confines of the ideologies imposed on them to create new wartime roles and meanings for their work. But this story is about more than the women themselves. Military entertainment highlights the central role gender and sexuality played in GI culture and masculinity. Civilian and military officials relied on women both to bolster men's soldiering efforts and to counter the all-male environment of war, all the while positioning women as symbols of the domestic life for which soldiers fought and to which they would return. Intended to boost morale, heighten desire, and comfort spirits, Salvation Army Lassies, Red Cross Donut Dollies, Special Services club women, and USO dancers bridged public work and private desires in the service of the state.

Much of the actual work women performed in clubs and on stages remained constant throughout the twentieth century, but a closer examination reveals that it also evolved with each war to reflect changing concerns about sexuality and gender. During World War I, military and civilian officials drew on prevalent ideas about the moralizing and tantalizing nature of femininity as they designed entertainment programs to lure soldiers away from vice and foreign women. In later wars, few officials expected American women to uplift servicemen morally, though they did insist that the right kind of woman boosted soldiers' morale in politically significant ways. During the increasingly controversial war in Vietnam, for example, unit commanders depended on eligible young women to offer support for soldiers and the war effort. Amid the political and cultural turmoil of the era, military entertainment utilized both conventionally feminine and explicitly sexualized images of women to bolster soldiers' commitment to the war. Even as the military altered the precise objectives with which it charged women in each war, it continually insisted that they were essential to the effort.

The changing objectives and nature of entertainment work also exposes the fault lines of gender, race, nation, and sexuality. While racially segregated entertainment upheld popular connections between race and womanhood during World War I and World War II, racial integration in the Cold War posed complicated questions for program officials about interracial sexual appeal. Ties between gender and race proved especially complicated in the Pacific theater in World War II and in the Korean and Vietnam Wars, where officials employed a language of racial domesticity to distinguish American and Asian women. By characterizing American women's entertainment as legitimate and wholesome in the face of the prostitution and unsanctioned entertainment that blossomed around military bases, officials held up American women as symbols of appropriate gender roles, both for soldiers and for the women in whose nations they served. *The Girls Next Door* thus highlights entertainment as an important part of the American military's foreign presence by showing how sexuality and gender shaped its interactions with local populations around the world.

Military commanders also relied on women to help them ensure that servicemen were the right kind of men. While officials continually enlisted women as physical reminders of soldiers' manly obligations, they also relied on women to regulate masculinity according to the situation. Especially in non-Western theaters and isolated posts, military commanders pleaded for Red Cross and USO women who, they believed, civilized an otherwise savage and barbaric environment. At the same time, until the mid-twentieth century, military and civilian officials called for women to feminize the all-male military environment, which they feared would otherwise result in homosexual activity among the troops. Women from home, officials assumed, affirmed soldiers' sense of heterosexual manhood by symbolizing domestic gender relations and reminding them of the women who waited for them at home. More than simply abating men's loneliness, the proper young women who accompanied military personnel to war zones were to remind the men of why and for whom they fought.

As a constant thread of women's wartime work, military entertainment provides a fruitful tool for analyzing the connections between the complex ways the armed forces have utilized women and the fundamental changes of the twentieth century. In many ways, entertainment work drew upon conventional notions of women's wartime work—it used them as symbols of a supportive home front, and it employed them as agents of morality and heterosexual desire. But, though the military and civilian organizations intended women to symbolize staid domestic gender roles, and though women performed traditionally feminine roles, many embraced their wartime service as a symbol of their burgeoning self-assurance and of women's expanding place in the nation. Even conventional work as a hostess proved expansive and transformative for women who credited their wartime experiences with having a progressive meaning for their lives. By contrasting the prescribed versions of gender and sexuality in recreation programs with the women's interpretations of their work, *The Girls Next Door* highlights the ways American women and institutions negotiated the character and the pace of gender change.

Women's perspectives highlight many contrasts between institutional and personal experiences and reveal a fundamental tension in the mobilization of their sexuality. Although military and civilian leaders always carefully couched the women's work in a language of respectability, and although they expressly forbid women from engaging in any activity that even hinted at immorality, sexual appeal remained the underpinning of programs in which women served as symbols of men's hopes and desires. Wartime recreation and entertainment called upon women not only to lure men away from prostitutes and to exhibit friendly camaraderie but also to symbolize both sexual desire and familial love. Maintaining a balance between these related yet divergent tasks proved a difficult balance for women, whose work placed them in precarious and sometimes dangerous situations from which they had to maneuver.

For all of these reasons, the military's use of women as wartime entertainment is essential to understanding the history of the military and gender—separately and together—across the twentieth century. The history of women's entertainment work is important for military historians interested in the ways the armed forces regulate soldier life, in the ways commanders seek to maintain morale and moderate the difficulties of deployments, and in the ways the military manages relations with foreign peoples. It has much to say to women's historians about the ways the state enlists women's bodies during wartime and the ways morale work has framed notions of women's citizenship. And it has much to say to gender historians about the central ways that the military and wars framed both masculinity and femininity, not only during wartime but also during peacetime. For all of us, women's work entertaining the military is an important lens through which to understand the relationship between the military and civilian society. As the US military integrates women completely into all specializations and grapples with appalling reports of sexual harassment, this history of women's entertainment work offers important insights into the fundamental ways that gender and sexuality have shaped military policies and culture and the place of women in the nation.

# 1

≡

# A New Kind of Woman Is Following the Army

CANTEENING ON THE WESTERN FRONT

On April 3, 1918, a young woman from Montclair, New Jersey, boarded a ship headed for the war in France. Only twenty-six years old, Emma Young Dickson was both excited and nervous about her impending adventure. Her parents had accompanied her as she traveled from home to the New York City dock, where they made their final good-byes, and now she was on her own for the first time in her life. Feeling "very lost and teary," she managed to gather her courage and board the SS *Espagne*. "We left the harbor at 3:45 in a drizzily rain," she noted in her diary, and then confessed, "I buried my face in the lavender sweet peas and orchids that Graham sent me while I watched the New York skyline fade from view." Pining for her sweetheart, she wrote: "I knew he was somewhere behind the barbed wire fence on the pier and I almost wished I had stayed at home." She continued: "When I could see no more between my tears and the rain, I went down to my cabin where I met my roommate."[1] Dickson did not spend too much time feeling sorry for herself, however. She quickly developed a stalwart attitude about the dangers that surrounded her. A week into her voyage, she remarked that four convoys had arrived to escort the *Espagne* into the French harbor, but wryly observed that it would take them a half hour to reach the ship if it were torpedoed. "It seems so silly to be scared," she assured herself. "One can only die once anyway."[2]

From the earliest days of US involvement in the Great War, Dickson had sought out ways to contribute to the effort. Like many women, she volunteered in local relief agencies and took Red Cross first aid courses. But her extensive volunteer work did not satiate her longing for a more direct way to serve. Nearly every house in Montclair displayed a service flag in the window, she later explained, and as she watched young men "go out to fight for the freedom of the world," she too wanted to play a part. Like the daring young woman in Howard Chandler Christy's famous Navy recruitment poster, Dickson proclaimed that "I wished that I too had been a man to have a small part in this great conflict."[3] After a few months of her "rolling eternally long bandages for the Red Cross," the Young Men's Christian Association (YMCA) accepted her into its canteen program, and she embraced the chance to serve overseas.

After she arrived in France, the YMCA charged Dickson with establishing a canteen for the Seventh Machine Gun Battalion of the American Expeditionary Force's (AEF) Third Division near the small village of Valdelancourt, west of Chaumont. Although Dickson welcomed the opportunity to take a more active role in the war than she had been able to do at home, she quickly learned that providing refreshments and amusements for doughboys required her to perform many of the same, conventionally feminine roles. She rose early each day to prepare hot chocolate and other treats for soldiers eager for a brief reprieve from war and the chance to speak with an American woman. Dickson tried to make the men feel at home and spent her days playing the violin for them, organizing activities and dances, and teaching them rudimentary French. As she explained to the men in her canteen, while her task was "a much bigger job" than she ever dreamed it would be and she felt "very little and incompetent measured up beside it," she was there to do "a thousand little things that your own mothers and sisters would do for you if they only had the chance."[4]

Although Dickson characterized herself as a substitute for the men's mothers and sisters, she knew that doughboys held more complicated understandings of her and the work she performed. One or another soldier fell in love with her, she often noted in her diary, and she developed ways of deflecting their attention without offending them. Such skills proved invaluable one evening when two Marines took her and a friend for a stroll by a river. "It is a most romantic spot," Dickson quipped, "so we didn't linger long."[5] Another doting soldier frequently rode his motorcycle to visit her. She considered the handsome officer a friend but dreaded one particular visit when she knew he planned, as she put it, "to tell me something." She had heard it before, from plenty of other men and the captain, and though she "wasn't crazy to hear it," she felt that "as long as he was on his way to the front . . . he might as well get it off his chest." After patiently listening to yet another marriage proposal, she "kidded him along," and told him she was "entirely too busy to get married right now."[6]

With heightened awareness of the ways her work as a hostess demanded that she exhibit a friendly and charming demeanor, Dickson created boundaries between herself and the many admiring men who surrounded her, revealing the tension between casual friendships and romantic relationships that women in her position managed daily. This balance was not always easy. As Dickson learned after receiving a "lecture about flirting with the officers," YMCA officials took seriously their insistence that canteen women project a respectable image and demeanor, even as they called on women to interact with men in ways that they never would have condoned outside the war. Still, Dickson took offense at the reprimand and angrily retorted to her diary, "Being nice to lonely men was not flirting with them." She was unable to stew in her anger for long, however, because the war, as usual, interrupted her night. "About 12:30," she recorded, "we heard the shells whistling and one landed just up the street with a big 'bang.'"[7]

In only a few months the young woman who had wept as her ship left the New York harbor began feeling more self-assured. "I am getting so independent," she warned her mother, "you won't know me when I come home."[8] In fact, in late May 1918, when the Third Division moved to Château-Thierry to defend against the last major German offensive of the war, Dickson was upset that she could not move forward with them. Infuriated at what she considered an unfair policy that prevented women from doing their part, she complained, "I hate this watchful waiting. Why can't we help too?"[9] Like many women in her position, she boasted that she had found her "niche at last." Contrasting her new existence to her comfortable life before the war, she wrote, "I couldn't be happy having hot baths and plenty to eat and enjoying myself, when I could be doing something useful."[10]

Over the course of World War I, approximately 3,500 women like Dickson opened YMCA and Salvation Army huts and canteens for soldiers and sailors across France and Britain. Some remained after the war with the American forces that occupied the German Rhineland. Typically in their late twenties and early thirties, single, and overwhelmingly white, these women also worked in Leave Areas, former resorts operated by the American military and the YMCA for soldiers granted a week's leave from the war. When conditions permitted, a select few operated "rolling kitchens" that brought refreshments and a reprieve from the war to soldiers behind the lines. Some women patrolled large cities at night, seeking out men whom they could steer away from illicit activities and into more wholesome environs. More than 500 traveled throughout the war zone entertaining soldiers with theatrical and musical performances. When not performing, they too spent time serving coffee, doughnuts, tobacco, and hot chocolate; organizing musical events and talent shows; and making small talk with men eager to be near women from home.

Recreation work required women to walk a fine line between a friendly, inviting manner that comforted and encouraged servicemen and an alluring charm that would draw them from other, less wholesome activities. This tension underlay all aspects of the work, from its genesis as an attempt to entice soldiers away from vice, to the careful selection of wholesome and attractive women, to the organizations' efforts to impart a sense of respectability to the women through regulations and uniforms, and to the frequently awkward attempts to appease men's longing for intimate contact with women as well as the reformers' desire to provide morally uplifting entertainment. For their part, women frequently felt torn between the expectations that they be both surrogate mother and comely dance partner, although many women also embraced the newfound freedom that they experienced in their wartime roles. Eager to be of service as close to the war as possible, women advocated to move forward with soldiers they grew to see as comrades and chafed at what they felt were unduly restrictive rules based on archaic ideas about women's delicate natures. Embracing both the excitement and the danger of the war, women ascribed significant meaning to the relationships they formed with doughboys, which in turn imbued their work with national, wartime significance. Even menial tasks such as cleaning huts or preparing snacks and drinks held great meaning for women who interpreted such labor as their equivalent of fighting.

Lonely doughboys across the Western Front welcomed warm drinks and friendly conversation with eager YMCA girls and Salvation Army "Lassies," but the military did not merely seek to provide soldiers with friendly faces. Canteens and huts grew out of Progressive Era concerns about the potentially corrupting influence of military service and a belief that upstanding women could defuse such problems. Linking women's wartime work to their moral status, military and civilian officials created a patriotic role for women that neither upset common gender norms nor challenged popular notions of sexual respectability. And yet, even while drawing on historical notions of women as guardians of men's—and the nation's—morality, the canteen programs created new opportunities for women at a time of expanding notions of women's citizenship and public roles. In both their reliance on conventional gender norms and their expansion of wartime opportunities for women, canteen programs offer a valuable window into the rapidly evolving relationship between women and the state at a crucial moment in US women's history.[11]

## SEX, SOLDIERING, AND RECREATION

The United States' entry into World War I transformed public perceptions of military service and, relatedly, understandings of the relationship between martial masculinity and American womanhood. In the early twentieth century, most Americans believed that military camps were dirty, degrading environments that introduced men to a host of peculiar temptations and vices. Civil War encampments had been notoriously rife with disease, while more recent forays into the western frontier and extended engagements in the Caribbean and the Philippines had produced no less shocking accounts of soldiers engaging in sanctioned lewd behavior.[12] Most Americans were willing to grant soldiers a certain degree of latitude when it came to such things as drinking and sex. Soldiers were, the thought went, hardscrabble men who did thankless work and should be permitted to exercise their lustful passions. In the early twentieth century, however, when Progressive reformers linked social vices (particularly prostitution) to public health, the American public and military officials grew less willing to accept venereal disease as simply an undesirable but tolerated facet of military life. Public and military fears compounded in 1916 when Mexican revolutionary Francisco "Pancho" Villa crossed into New Mexico and the Army deployed ten thousand men to the border.

When reports of a lax moral environment on the Mexican border surfaced, Secretary of War Newton D. Baker dispatched noted reformer Raymond B. Fosdick to investigate the conditions, while the YMCA sent its sex education director Max Exner to do the same.[13] In their separate reports, Fosdick and Exner horrified progressives and government officials by revealing that soldiers often drank to excess in their off-duty hours and frequented houses of prostitution. Nearly 30 percent of the men tested positive for a venereal disease.[14] Perhaps even more troubling, commanding officers in the region expressed little concern about the situation and even regulated brothels for soldiers' use. Military culture held that "men were men," Fosdick discovered, "and 'sissies' were not wanted in the army."[15] Whatever problems prostitution might bring, officers believed its benefits outweighed its costs. Men "made poor soldiers if they did not have women," they maintained, reflecting the long-held belief that sexual activity bolstered martial masculinity.[16] Moreover, they cautioned that restricting soldiers' sexual activity could have serious, even national, repercussions. "If prostitution were not provided," one high-ranking cavalry officer warned, "these men would disobey orders, go to Mexican villages and get mixed up with the women and thereby possibly bring on war."[17] Additionally, they insisted that regulated prostitution was the best way to control the spread of costly venereal diseases. The military establishment, as Exner warned, believed prostitution "necessary for the contentment and well-being of the men, or, at least, that it is inevitable."[18]

The following year, however, as the United States prepared to send soldiers to France—a nation widely assumed to be teeming with debauchery—neither the public nor the government was willing to turn a blind eye to the military's toleration of prostitution.[19] The Selective Service Act mobilized a cross-section of American men, and government officials steadfastly assured the public that their sons would be kept safe from the dangers that had seemed so inconsequential among a small cadre of professional soldiers. In particular, Secretary Baker argued that the government needed both to repress evil and to provide alternatives to it. Repressing illicit vices near military training camps in the United States was a fairly straightforward matter, at least on paper. Sections 12 and 13 of the Selective Service Act prohibited the sale of alcohol and prostitution in "moral zones" around military camps. Local officials who refused to enforce the mandate, Baker warned, would find the camps—and soldiers' wallets—removed from their towns.[20] As a practical matter, though, Baker knew that soldiers' sexual desires could not be eliminated "by either proclamation or prayer" and maintained that healthy alternative activities must be offered.[21] To that end, in April 1917 the government created the Commission on Training Camp Activities (CTCA) and charged it with operating a wholesome recreation program in and near domestic military camps to fill the soldiers' free time.

The creation of the CTCA signaled a broader shift in Americans' thinking about the services that should be provided for soldiers. No longer content to leave soldiers to their own devices, reformers successfully lobbied for the extension of recreation facilities, entertainment, religious programs, educational courses, and other amenities. Throughout the war, the CTCA organized a host of activities for soldiers—from sporting events to religious services, musical concerts, and dances. In huts and canteens built near training camps, soldiers could find a quiet place to read a book, write a letter, or meet with visiting family members. The CTCA also sponsored an extensive social welfare program designed to increase military efficiency by educating soldiers about the dangers of venereal disease. These efforts advocated a progressive vision of American society by promoting social hygiene, modern gender norms, and urban, middle-class notions of citizenship.[22] Civilian organizations such as the YMCA and the Salvation Army embraced similar aims in their development of recreation services for the AEF. Charged with providing services for doughboys overseas, they maintained that moral behavior worked "not only for the purpose of beating Germany but also for the purpose of strengthening citizenship."[23] These were lofty goals to be sure, and they met with approval at the highest levels. "The Federal Government has pledged its word," President Woodrow Wilson promised, that "the men committed to its charge will be returned to the homes and communities that so generously gave them with no scars except those won in honorable conflict."[24]

As AEF commander General John J. Pershing sailed to France in June 1917, he contemplated how to reconcile this new vision for a moral Army with the military's—and his own—history of regulating prostitution. Previously, General Pershing had approached the problem of prostitution rather pragmatically. Embracing the pervasive belief that soldiers needed sex, he established brothels and ordered medical inspections of the prostitutes in an attempt to prevent them from passing disease to soldiers. The system reduced the venereal disease rate, Pershing boasted, and was "the best way to handle a difficult problem."[25] This was the policy that the French military employed for its soldiers throughout World War I and that Premier Georges Clemenceau offered the American forces upon their arrival.[26] The French government maintained that sexual release was "beneficial if not essential to health" and operated state *maisons de tolérance* in which registered prostitutes underwent regular medical inspections.[27] Although largely effective in controlling disease, the policy seemed reckless and dangerous to Johns Hopkins Hospital urologist Dr. Hugh Hampton Young, who joined Pershing on the journey to France and would soon be named the AEF's chief urologist.

As they sailed to France, Young presented a series of harrowing lectures to Pershing on the dangers that venereal disease would pose to the war effort if infected soldiers were unable to perform their duties. Convinced, Pershing ordered that soldiers attend sexual hygiene lectures to warn them of the dangers of prostitution and that any soldier who engaged in sexual activity had to report for prophylaxis treatment which, although unpleasant, generally blocked the transferal of disease. Those who contracted a venereal disease were court-martialed and forfeited their pay.[28] Later, Pershing explicitly deemed brothels off-limits and—in an attempt to enforce this unpopular policy—held commanding officers responsible for the health of their soldiers.[29]

In adopting a strict policy against sexual license, the military broke with its prior understanding of the relationship between manly soldiering and sexual activity. Contrary to earlier theories that men needed to exercise their passions to develop manhood, social welfare organizations drew on contemporary studies of human sexuality and argued instead that manhood had to be preserved through sexual continence.[30] These ideas took hold in the military, where the Army Medical Department linked martial power with soldiers' sexual restraint. "Energy dissipated in one way is lost to another," one Medical Corps officer vividly warned. "There is less reserve to draw upon in emergency."[31] In an attempt to bolster this new approach to sexuality, the YMCA referenced images of rapacious German soldiers that were being propagated in the press and suggested that a man who turns to women to "gratify his lustful desires" is no different than "the Hun who ravages women."[32] The new military had no place for the "old type of soldier" who was "turned loose sporadically to vent his passions in animal excesses."[33]

Having decided on a policy of sexual continence for its soldiers, the AEF faced a difficult challenge in enforcement. Without the jurisdiction to simply outlaw vice as it could in the United States, the War Department turned to recreation facilities and activities to fill the doughboys' free time, much like the CTCA was doing in training camps at home. The YMCA anticipated this need; several Y officials had been working with Allied forces since the war's outbreak and saw firsthand the critical role that healthy amusement could play in diverting men's attentions from vice. Only days after the United States declared war on Germany, the Y volunteered to organize welfare work

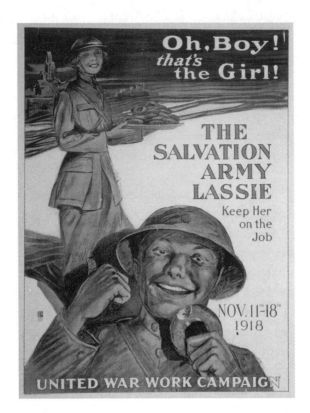

The United War Work Campaign raised the public donations that allowed organizations like the Salvation Army and the YMCA to send American women to France during World War I. Women like this "Lassie" cheerily serving doughnuts offered the American public a new, reassuring image that their soldiers were being cared for while away at war.

with the AEF. "In view of the serious menace of prostitution to the physical life and general morale of fighting men," the Y representative in France pledged, "the YMCA will concentrate its efforts against this evil, with every possible form of direct and indirect attack."[34] Wilson accepted the Y's offer and charged it with keeping the American doughboys free from disease and fit to fight.[35]

To accomplish this goal, the YMCA coordinated recreation activities throughout France, England, and postwar occupied Germany.[36] It opened huts for soldiers where doughboys could gather, see films, attend religious services, purchase miscellaneous items from the canteen, participate in athletic events, and talk with well-meaning Y officials from home. General Pershing later granted permission to the Salvation Army, the Knights of Columbus, and the Jewish Welfare Board (JWB) to build huts and clubs of their own, and together, the four organizations saw to it that doughboys could find a welcoming hut wherever they served, from the ports to the trenches.[37] With the goal of "counteracting the effect of street women" in London and Paris, the YMCA sent women "in the small hours" to look for wayward soldiers they could steer toward lodging or a YMCA for the night. Frequently, they intervened directly to stop soldiers from engaging prostitutes.[38]

Military officials believed that such work was essential to keeping soldiers from engaging in illicit behaviors. "If you wanted to get a firebrand out of the hand of a child," Secretary of War Baker advised, you had to offer "a stick of candy."[39] The Red Cross surgeon-in-chief agreed. Soldiers "must be furnished with healthful amusement," he warned, "or they will turn to . . . the first petticoat they see."[40] Thus, the military intended all recreation activities, whether sporting events or musical concerts, dances or relaxation in a YMCA hut, to "be used to the fullest extent in furthering the practice of continence," according to Pershing.[41] As the YMCA's official history of its war efforts later recorded, its efforts were guided by the assumption that "unless adequate measures are taken . . . a 'sex festival' will be the inevitable result."[42] The work continued even after the Armistice, when military officials called for the YMCA to increase recreation programs in the occupied Rhineland and, particularly, to send women to distract soldiers from the many German women surrounding them.[43]

As government and civilian organizations coordinated entertainment for doughboys, they agreed that American women were the key to success. They believed that men far from home, living in an unfamiliar country and in a regimented, all-male world, needed the influence of women who could impart a sense of domestic normality and prevent the development of "abnormal" men for whom normal "social influences of restraint have ceased to operate."[44] These fears led the military to rely on civilian welfare agencies to provide "opportunities for wholesome comradeship" with American women. "The kind of women he meets every day in the 'Y' huts are the right kind," YMCA officials maintained. "If he wants the other kind he has to hunt for them."[45]

### THE RIGHT KIND OF WOMEN

In early 1918 the YMCA's physical education superintendent, Luther H. Gulick, toured France to study the association's efforts to safeguard the morals of doughboys far from home. He was pleased to find an extensive array of huts available to servicemen, located in such varied spaces as a former convent, a city hall, and a palace. A firm believer in the moral value of recreation for young men, Gulick had spent many years traveling across the United States to promote physical education in schools and to popularize basketball, a game designed at his suggestion to provide healthy activity for young men in the long winter months. Gulick took special pride, though, in his daughter Frances's work in transforming a saloon into a comfortable place for soldiers to relax. "Women have always followed the Army," Gulick told the men in her canteen, referring to a long history of women who had both labored for and offered sexual services to militaries. But as he stood proudly beside his uniformed daughter, he boasted that "a new kind of woman is following the Army." Selected from among the men's "mothers, sisters, sweethearts, and wives," Y women stood as representatives of the men's "own women at home." A proud father of this new kind of woman, Gulick assured his listeners that the reputation and work of canteen women like Frances was beyond reproach. Even as he acknowledged the importance of the many tasks she and her co-workers performed, he clarified that the "main service that these women give is not handing out tea and coffee on a cold day . . . nor is it in selling the men the things they want." The women's primary value and contribution derived simply from the "fact that they are there, and that they are wholesome, attractive women."[46]

Gulick's assessment of canteen women as wholesome and attractive summed up the YMCA's and the Salvation Army's hopes and concerns about this new female wartime role. Women's recreation work drew upon long-standing American beliefs that during wartime, women's primary contribution should be as mothers who maintained the home fires and reared responsible citizens, but relocated those duties to the war zone and deemed them critical to the war effort. And yet, to exert the moralizing influences on soldiers that the AEF believed were necessary to combat vice, women had to be enticing enough alternatives to the temptations that awaited men just beyond their camps. Only the proper combination of moralizing and tantalizing qualifications could create the right blend of regulation and allure that would keep the men from trouble. Moreover, while the women needed to be feminine enough to mark a contrast with the military environment and remind the men of womenfolk at home, they had to be hardy enough to endure the strenuous conditions of war. Strong and soft, wholesome and attractive, women serving with the AEF blended several contrasting and historical images of women into a new, respectable wartime role.

The YMCA began enlisting American women for canteen work in August 1917, drawing its initial workers from women then living in France or working with war relief organizations. Thirty women arrived from the United States in November that year and were followed by groups of thirty to forty women in the first months of 1918.[47] The Y organized the recruitment and selection of canteen workers through its New York headquarters. State and local committees conducted preliminary investigations and interviews and then forwarded successful applicants to New York for participation in a week-long training at Barnard College, where the Y issued a final decision regarding their suitability for wartime work.[48] Demands for women workers grew exponentially. In April 1918, the Y issued a call for 1,000 women workers by September, and although delays in securing passports hindered the organization's ability to send all of the women it had prepared to go, it boasted more than 500 canteen workers in France by August.[49] As the program grew, so did women's efforts to enlist. Applications streamed into the Y offices, with more than 1,200 arriving weekly in July 1918.[50] In all, the YMCA sent 3,401 women to work with the AEF, with the vast majority of them going to stations in France.[51] Among them were 561 professional entertainers and hopeful amateurs the YMCA sent to Europe to stage plays and vaudeville shows, perform concerts, and sing familiar songs from home.[52]

The Salvation Army sent its first workers to France in August 1917, where they received permission from General Pershing to operate canteens along with the YMCA. Operating on a much smaller scale than the YMCA, the Salvation Army faced no need to recruit but instead called up members for overseas service. Still, the organization sought a blend of practicality and feminine appeal. When an officer asked Helen Purviance to join the first group of Salvation Army officers to sail to France, for example, he explained that her work would involve many things: "the conducting of meetings, waiting on tables, cooking, visiting and praying with people." The task, he pressed, "needs a woman of your type, who is full of good horse sense and yet possessing those womanly qualities that are so helpful and attractive."[53] By the war's end, National Commander Evangeline Booth had selected 109 "Lassies" from the organization's membership to serve doughnuts and work in canteens in France.[54]

In the early days before the demand for women grew dramatically, the Y dispatched college graduates and well-to-do clubwomen who could pay their own travel and living expenses. The Y described college alumna as "peculiarly" suited for the work."[55] College-educated women, the Y reasoned, were "more apt to possess the self-reliance needed," while their record of collegiate extracurricular activities would serve as the "safest guide" for evaluation.[56] When Caroline Slade, chair of the Women's Overseas Committee, issued a call to alumnae associations and women's clubs, her action proved fruitful. Six alumnae associations organized and funded units of women; the General Federation of Women's Clubs recruited and financed a contingent of two women from each state; and the Junior League nominated members for canteen work.[57] This "caliber" of women seems to have met the Y's expectations, although it was acknowledged by Elsie Cleveland Mead, who recruited canteen workers in New York before taking charge of the work in France, that the physical operation of a canteen did not require a college education. "There were times when it did seem that we were using very finely tempered steel instruments for work which probably could be done with blunter tools," Mead noted. Nonetheless, she found the class status of college girls—"the finer and higher type of woman," as she described them—a necessary quality that "added just something intangibly better to her canteen."[58]

As the demand for workers grew, the Y began to send women (and men) at its own expense. It paid all workers the same monthly salary of sixty dollars—more if one's living arrangement required it—and it covered the war risk premium on required life insurance policies.[59] Even then, YMCA histories suggest that many women effectively worked as volunteers by donating the equivalent of their salary to the organization.[60] Canteen workers were generally more educated and trained, as well as more urbane, than the average single woman of the era. In a time when few women enjoyed postsecondary education, 31 percent of canteen women were college graduates, and another 26 percent had some kind of postsecondary education, compared to less than 1 percent of conscripted soldiers with college degrees. Two-thirds of women had worked for wages before the war, most in the heavily female fields of clerical work and education. These were not the most elite women, who might have abhorred the physical labor required to run a canteen, nor were they from the lower classes whose labor was required to assist their families and who would have been excluded by the Y's preference for women who exuded middle-class values.[61]

Although the YMCA preferred a particular kind of educated and financially secure woman, it never completely settled on an exact model. The Y advertised that it preferred women between the ages of thirty and forty-five, though the majority of the women it sent to Europe were between twenty-four and thirty-one; and, while the Y accepted a few married women into canteen service, it preferred that they not have dependents.[62] Generally, it believed women in their thirties who "had reached the zenith of their strength but had not passed it" modeled the ideal blend of sisterly camaraderie, motherly assurance, and youthful charm necessary for such work. "Not that the doughboy apparently considered any woman too old or too young," the Y conceded. Still, it maintained that "the woman who could combine some of the attractiveness of the girl with the sage counsel and the steadying influence of the older woman" best embodied its ideal.[63] The Y might have preferred this particular blend of characteristics, but as an internal history of the program noted, "age limits varied with the urgency of the need."[64] As the war progressed, officials in France issued varying calls for women who were matronly, attractive, or skilled in one way or another. In May 1918, for example, Mead complained that just as the college units were ready to sail, officials in Paris requested women who could cook. "I don't suppose the college girls will know anything as useful as that, if I can judge by you," she joked in a letter to her daughter.[65] Six months later, as the war's end seemed imminent, another Y official called for "younger women who are most needed to help give cheer to our boys in France. Not the motherly type, but the real comrade is the type of girl that the American boy wants."[66]

Fluctuating recommendations about the ideal age stemmed in part from understandings that canteen work was both physically and emotionally challenging. Women needed to be young enough to endure long work hours and meager living conditions, yet mature enough to withstand the emotional strain of war and the constant attentions of young men.[67] Gertrude Ely, who directed the canteen program in Paris and had herself worked in a canteen, determined that while "there is a great advantage in youth," women between thirty and fifty "who have done something worthwhile at home in a serious way and yet have remained pretty and attractive and capable of fun, are the ones who will be more useful to us."[68] Blending physical vitality, life experience, and playful appeal, these women possessed the physical and emotional qualities necessary to endure the war and appeal to soldiers. As the Red Cross surgeon-in-chief warned, "we should only have those who are 'steady,' those of well-balanced mental equilibrium. The war zone is no place for emotional flibbity-gibbits."[69]

The doctor's warning about "emotional flibbity-gibbits" reflected a common concern that women who actively sought war work did so out of less than charitable motivations. Women, as Gulick explained to the soldiers at his daughter's canteen, had always followed armies. They did so as wives and daughters, laundresses, sutlers, and sexual companions for soldiers. As the military and civilian organizations attempted to recast the nature of women's war work as wholesome and respectable, however, women suspected to be motivated by the chance to associate with soldiers were immediately turned away.[70] As Elsie Mead explained it, she had to be diligent in her selection because the possibility of "a free ride to the war appeals to the adventurous and sentimental types." In particular, any woman who wore rouge or dyed her hair raised alarms for Mead, who interpreted such frivolities as a signal of promiscuity, or at least a warning that she might be interested in romance more than work. "I may be narrow-minded," she confessed, "but that foolishness indicates something I wouldn't knowingly perpetrate on the army."[71]

Mead's concern about women who applied rouge and dyed their hair betrayed a deeper fear about female sexuality. Government and military officials alike believed that a man in military uniform could undermine nearly any woman's resolve. "There is . . . a fascination in the uniform," an Army Medical Corps officer warned, "which tends to break down the reserve even of pure girls, especially in time of war."[72] Such reasoning about women's lack of self-control had justified the government's regulation of moral zones around home-front training camps, and it explained the Y's careful attempts to weed out any women who might find the attentions of so many soldiers irresistible.[73] Y officials knew that women would be vastly outnumbered—often there was only one American woman among hundreds of doting young men—and sought out canteen workers who could resist the urge to become romantically entangled. As a recruiter in Pittsburgh explained, the Y needed to avoid the kind of adventuresome women "who have flirted when they should have been cooking."[74] This desire accounts in part for the Y's preference for women in their thirties who would have been older than most soldiers and who, the Y supposed, would be equipped to "act as sister or mother as the case required."[75] "Only sincere devotion," Y officials maintained, would allow a woman to "shed the personal tributes without appropriating them, as unconsciously as a duck sheds rain."[76]

Canteen programs also sought women with at least some religious motivation, which officials hoped would protect the women's reputations as they worked and lived among so many men. The YMCA and the Salvation Army, as religious organizations, believed that spiritual guidance played an essential part in the effort to save soldiers from immoral influences. National Commander Evangeline Booth described the Salvation Army's huts as "soul-saving stations" that, while providing the same recreation activities as the Y's canteens, existed for the "sole idea of bringing the men under the refining and restraining influence of my devoted women officers."[77] She did not need to explain that piety was a desired attribute—she selected women from within the ranks who adhered to the organization's strict moral codes. The YMCA demanded that women demonstrate "genuine religious sympathy," but it did not want the women to evangelize.[78] A general religiosity was simply one of many desired attributes that would guard the women against the temptations they would face as they entered "the new relationships to which this service calls them."[79]

Seeking women who could uphold these ideals of sexual respectability, the Y actively opposed the War Department's decision not to grant passports to women whose brothers were serving in the AEF. War Department officials feared that mothers and sisters would create problems as they sought out their loved ones in the war zone. Although the Y conceded that mothers and wives had no place in war, it vehemently disagreed with the characterization of sisters' motivations as meddlesome and selfish. The prohibition "robs us of our best material," Y officials complained, because sisters symbolized the proper platonic relationship between men and women that the organization sought to model. The Y asserted that pure motives guided sisters who were inspired "no doubt by their brothers' example." Pleading with the Army chief of staff to reconsider the ruling, Mead argued that "a sister had the right to be considered a comrade-in-arms."[80] A Red Cross official agreed that sisters were "on a par with the active, vigorous young men in our draft army" and noted that the sibling relationship was devoid of sexual appeal. "A sister combines feminine charm with a good deal of that steadiness and loyalty that exist in the relationships between men," he explained. This camaraderie was "what the boys miss, what they long for."[81] Tellingly, when the War Department reversed the ban, it qualified that any woman who married while abroad would be sent home at the organization's expense.[82] Sisters who used the war to find husbands did not exhibit proper asexual friendliness.

Sisters might have been ideal in many ways, but canteen programs also needed women to be viable alternatives to the very vices they sought to counter. "The praise of the plain, practical woman who can cook, sew, bake, scrub, sweep, launder and do nursing amid the chaos of war has been sung frequently," a Y official in Paris reported. But while "plain, practical" women were necessary, attractive women also had their value. "It does our young American soldiers a world of good to gaze upon pretty girls from back home." He went on to note that "the very fact that they are pretty means so much to the men," explaining that an appealing appearance distinguished canteen women from ordinary "clerks at a country store."[83] Elsie Mead agreed, surmising that "youth and good looks" would "mean a lot in France." She wrote: "I almost feel like advertising: No homely women need apply." But while the Y desired a healthy dose of beauty, it did not want too much. Women did not need to be "necessarily beautiful," Mead explained. But they did need to look good in their uniform. It was "*très chic* [with a] high collar and blue tie *de rigueur*," she wrote to her daughter. "You see the type of girl that is going to look best in that, don't you? You have one or two young Professors at Vassar that are just my ideal."[84]

The military appreciated the Y's affirmation that good looks were essential to women's work. Army Chief of Staff General Peyton March, who had commanded artillery units on the Mexican border and in Europe and knew something of what soldiers wanted, challenged Mead on the necessity of sending American women to work in canteens. "Any French peasant" could cook and wash dishes, he reasoned. But as Mead described the ideal canteen woman, her attention to requisite good looks convinced the general of American women's value and highlighted important ways that even "platonic" sisters symbolized heterosexual desire. As Mead later recounted, her suggestion that canteen women should be attractive resonated with General March, whose "eyes began to twinkle" and who "slapped his hand on his desk, remarking, 'You're right; let us not send any homely old maids to bring

gloom to our soldiers in France.'" Soon thereafter, the Y received notice that the War Department had overturned its ban on soldiers'
sisters.[85] Even the AEF's Senior Chaplain recognized the value of
attractive canteen workers, though he was also careful to emphasize
that excessive good looks could be problematic. After having sailed to
Paris with ninety YMCA women, he reported his approval of the
women he described as "'dangerously attractive,' which is just the
way the A.E.F. likes to have them. Pulchritude helps."[86]

The qualities desired by the Y and Salvation Army reflected the
canteen program's intertwined, if somewhat conflicting, goals of moralizing and uplifting the military environment and enticing lonely
men away from lewd behaviors. Women were to exude both religious
sympathy and appealingly good looks, express youthful enthusiasm
and matronly counsel, and exhibit physical and emotional hardi-
ness and a youthful vibrancy. Balancing these demands proved frustrating and difficult for Y officials charged with recruiting and screening
applicants. The tension between respectability and allure proved
even more difficult for the women charged with maintaining that
permeable line.

## THE REFINING INFLUENCE OF WOMEN

When Katharine Grinnell arrived in Vaiges, France, she was not impressed by the military men who greeted her. A sergeant, "bored
beyond words at the idea of a Y.M.C.A. hostess," escorted her into
the officers' headquarters, a "dreary room" that was "full of officers,
smoke, and stale tobacco." While most of the men ignored her, a colonel confessed that they had not expected her, having long ago given
up hope of having a Y canteen in the area. Determined more than ever
to prove herself to this unwelcoming crowd, Grinnell set to work
transforming an old schoolhouse into a proper canteen. Its broken stairs
and windows seemed to reflect the gloom of the men she found inside. Slumped on boxes and crates, the men were quite unaffected by
her arrival, so much so that "not one of them rose to his feet." Immediately, Grinnell knew she had a big job ahead of her. The men's unit
had been "pretty much up against it," she learned, and since returning
to the rear lines had been living in a depressing environment of

"dirt, mud, drizzle." They even lined up for meals at an old barn "where the yard was inches deep in slime." Understandably, the men were discouraged and tired, but as the cheery new Y woman tasked them with cleaning the canteen, their spirits rose markedly. Suddenly full of energy and excitement, some swept the floors, a few built sofas stuffed with hay, and others constructed flower boxes for the windows. Grinnell, meanwhile, went to a village shop and bought all of the colorful fabric that she could. After hanging curtains and tapestries, arranging flowers on the tables, and moving in a piano, she welcomed the men into her homey canteen. Grinnell and the men had transformed the old schoolhouse into a bright and cozy retreat where for the next few months she served coffee and chocolate and tried her best to provide the men with a brief reprieve from the war.[87]

The daily chores that canteen women like Grinnell performed held many meanings. Serving coffee, making sandwiches, and selling cigarettes were all important tasks for the military, which did not yet operate an organized PX system but relied on civilian organizations to provide the small items doughboys desired.[88] As vital to soldier morale as military officials believed these canteens to be, though, they did not insist that they needed women merely to operate huts. Anyone could clean old schoolhouses and serve drinks and snacks to weary soldiers, but women from home brought a familial and feminine element to the canteen. With each doughnut a woman served, each conversation she initiated, each button she sewed, each dance she danced, a woman reminded men of supportive women from home and encouraged them in their wartime duties. An antidote to the otherwise all-male environment, women exuded a femininity that brightened the gloom of the war and softened its brutality, even as their work reinforced conventional divisions of men's and women's wartime roles.

As surrogate mothers, sisters, or sweethearts, canteen women domesticated the base camps and transportation lines of the AEF by imparting a sense of familial comfort and feminine charm. This domestic ideology justified the women's place in the war zone and worked to ease public fears about the women who labored among so many soldiers.[89] Moreover, as they domesticated the AEF, the women created a familiar image of doughboys that reassured the public that military service had not inalterably militarized their sons. They enjoyed the comforting touch and sympathetic ear of the nation's women, whose huts and canteens exported white, middle-class notions of family, home, and respectability to the Western Front.

Officials argued that women elicited tangible improvements in the men's overall demeanor by countering the less desirable elements of military life. As young men left their families for the military environment, some feared that the absence of women would lead the men to abandon all sense of decorous behavior. "Wherever a number of men are herded together without the presence of refined womanhood," one Y official warned, "there is a strong tendency to degenerate." Women "do more toward toning up the soldiers and keeping the spirit of the army to the proper level of decency and self-respect than any other single influence," he explained. "In a room where one of these fine, frank-faced, trim and attractive girls is sitting no soldier is going to get drunk or profane or otherwise slop into beastliness."[90] Canteen worker Bertha Laurie recalled her encounter with a chaplain who had opposed women's work in canteens before he witnessed firsthand the remarkable difference they made. The chaplain found that women improved not only the "the order and cleanliness" of the canteen, which he described as "a woman's work, of course," but also the men themselves, in "their manner of speaking and their brushed hair and clean hands."[91]

While the women's physical work in the canteen was essential, the YMCA and Salvation Army advocated that their most important task was to positively influence the men around them. "Women should be relieved as far as possible from acting as mere saleswomen," the Y instructed, careful to avoid likening canteen women to the sutlers or camp followers who had performed such work in the past, or even to working-class women at home.[92] Canteen work that facilitated contact with servicemen was fine. But, when the YMCA canteen at the Pavilion Hotel in Paris became so busy that the women workers had no time for "a personal word" with the "throngs of men" eager for attention, the Women's Bureau recommended that men take over the canteen sales to allow the women to mingle more effectively.[93] As a handbook for hut workers explained, "the job of women canteen

workers is a social job—and not one of 'lady cook' or 'dish washer.'"
Canteen workers should employ French help or enlist the services of
Army personnel to accomplish the daily business of running the canteen, preparing food, and scheduling entertainments, so that the
women would be free "to circulate in front of the canteen with the
enlisted men."[94] The Y's policy of keeping canteen women with their
assigned unit also enabled the women to elevate common work to a
greater significance. Gertrude Bray, assigned to the Forty-Second
Infantry Division in France, explained that staying with the men allowed her and the other women to develop relationships with them.
Had the women not been able to move with their unit, they would
have been strangers to each new group and "hardly be more than
waitresses or salesgirls."[95]

As they socialized with soldiers, women domesticated the military
by reminding men of their female family members and by bringing "a
breath of normal and wholesome home life."[96] The organization explained this fundamental purpose in its advertising. "The woman who
can make a home-made pie has her real value in the Hut," it explained,
"as those who can sing, and drive a car, or entertain, have theirs." Even
more desirable, though, was a woman who can "give by her presence
a feeling of home, a bit of encouragement, a helping hand."[97] The Salvation Army characterized its recreation and religious work in similar
domestic metaphors. "We women have made many homes in the
world," Commander Evangeline Booth explained, linking the organization's religious mission with notions of women's public domesticity.
"But we now have the task of changing the world into a home."[98]

Women transformed meager buildings and tents into homelike
huts in part by adding a feminine touch to the surroundings. In the
very least, women and their apparel starkly contrasted the khaki-clad
military. At the Y headquarters canteen in Paris, women wore cherry
red aprons and white caps with black velvet streamers, which canteen
worker Marian Baldwin noted imparted "a splash of color to the room."
More importantly, "the boys love anything that suggests a feminine
touch."[99] In its final estimation, the Y characterized huts as places where
"the touch of woman was apparent in a window drapery," colorful
decorations on the walls, and a "homey corner with a bright fire."[100]

Women's accounts of their work, like Katharine Grinnell's, are full of tales of their efforts to transform rough and downtrodden settings into welcoming respites. Even when stationed in a hut for only a short period of time, women such as Helen Curtis, who "made ice cream and other 'goodies'" for soldiers and "best of all, let them open their hearts to her," made "a bright spot for the men there in that veritable wilderness of hardships."[101]

At times, though, women felt their efforts to feminize the canteens were futile. After cleaning cigar butts from flower vases and catching a "fellow using one of the beautiful chintz runners from the tables with which to wipe the mud off his boots," Katharine Duncan Morse confessed that she wondered "if it really all pays."[102] Even the Y acknowledged that the women did not make the roughly clad huts "really beautiful." Women were, however, "reminders that beauty was real and would one day be again enjoyed; they helped to visualize home."[103] However much or little women could transform the dreariness of the war zone, YMCA officials believed that women's presence was a necessary reminder of the home for which men fought and to which they hoped to return.

The women's preparation of food and treats for soldiers and sailors often blended with their symbolic roles as mothers. Perhaps most famous for the doughnuts its Lassies fried, the Salvation Army used the common sweet as a symbol for its larger familial work. In a fundraising appeal to the "mothers of America," Evangeline Booth assured them that the doughnut girls in France "are passing out to him pies like you used to make and sugared doughnuts, and talking to him at the same time of you."[104] Other women similarly linked food and home. Addie W. Hunton and Kathryn M. Johnson "deliberately planned to make our chocolate so good that [the soldiers] would really come for it . . . and crullers that would 'taste just like home.'" Segregated from most Y facilities, the black soldiers these two women served traveled great distances and waited in long lines for the familiar treats. The women had anticipated that the men would appreciate the gesture but admitted that they "could not even dream of all that it would mean in cheer, comradeship and good will."[105] Whether sewing on buttons, sympathetically listening to a lonely boy's worries, or frying dough-

Salvation Army "Lassies" served countless doughnuts during World War I. While doughboys appreciated the treats and the women who served them, their military commanders hoped that the women would remind soldiers of the comforts of home and the women who remained there.

nuts, canteen women's symbolic maternal love and support meant more than the necessary domestic chores they performed.

Indeed, the AEF went to great lengths to remind doughboys of their mothers, most notably in its very public efforts to encourage men to write home on Mother's Day.[106] For their part, the YMCA and Salvation Army relied on sympathetic images of mothers and homes to tug both the heart and the purse strings in several war-drive fundraising campaigns. The Salvation Army consistently described its Lassies as "little mothers of the battlefields" who supplemented their cooking and sewing with a maternal religious concern.[107] One "motherly-looking woman, wiping the flour from her hands," explained to a *Literary Digest* correspondent that Salvation Army women "thought some one ought to care for the boys as their mothers at home would do." The boys "miss the care and the kindness of home," she reasoned, "and we want to give them a little of something as near like it as possible."[108] Several larger Y huts designated a section "Mother's Corner" where soldiers could have clothes mended and "have heart to heart talks with our older women."[109] A "quiet chat" with a surrogate mother, the Y insisted, countered the dehumanizing effects of military service and "brought to the surface elements of personality almost submerged in the khaki uniformity of the AEF."[110]

Canteen women also adopted maternal language to legitimize the close relationships they formed with soldiers. One Y hostess met a lonely, young soldier who had joined the Army after running away from home. Disappointed that his mother had not responded to any of his letters, the soldier confided his sorrows to the friendly woman at the canteen who was touched by his sad tale and wrote him "the nicest letter I could manage."[111] Reflecting on her wartime work more than a half century later, Salvation Army Lassie Mary Bishop Ryan noted that even though she was only twenty-four-years old at the time, many doughboys called her "little mother" and brought her flowers on Mother's Day. Aware that the men intended their greetings as a sign of respect, she "rather felt complimented" by their actions.[112] One of her cohorts, Elsie Merrifield Corliss, also found that soldiers approached her as a surrogate family member. The men came to her "under the guise of needing a button sewed on or torn clothing mended," she explained, but "they would soon be talking about home and mother and showing us letters and pictures. We soon realized it was torn hearts rather than torn clothing that needed mending."[113]

While steering men away from illicit acts and toward proper manly behavior served to ease the minds of worried American families at home, women also approximated domestic gender relations. Men who socialized with American women in canteens and huts, military and civilian officials reasoned, would fall into their old patterns of proper behavior and be reminded of their duty as soldiers to fight for the protection of these domestic relationships. As one Army medical officer suggested, the women's presence redirected the men's attraction to the women into "chivalrous respect" and protection.[114] Even simple games could produce the desired effect. Women often organized "indoor rough-house games" such as potato sack races, one report noted, which the men played "with an enthusiasm that frequently resulted in broken chairs and furniture." When the women joined in, though, "even the roughest soldiers instinctively moderated their enthusiasm so as always to take proper care of the women."[115]

Canteen women understood this larger significance and embraced it to varying degrees. Soon after opening a hut near St. Amand, one Y woman found herself the object of constant attention. Although frustrated by the ways a small group of men monopolized her time, she insisted that "there is nothing personal in their attentions—I simply represent to them the women they love in America." While it was undoubtedly very easy for a soldier to look at an American woman and be reminded of women he missed from home, this canteen worker intentionally fostered such associations. "I am trying hard to create a homelike atmosphere," she noted, though she admitted the task was sometimes difficult, "owing to the lack of beauty in the canteen." Still, she admitted, women did not have to try very hard to be successful. "As far as I can see," she wrote, "an American woman might be deaf and dumb and cross-eyed, but she would make a hit with Uncle Sam's Army in France. Poor lonely homesick soldiers are not capable of judging a woman's attractions!"[116] Addie W. Hunton and Kathryn M. Johnson, two of the only three African American canteen women stationed in France during the war, felt even more deeply that they represented home to African American soldiers. As representatives of "the womanhood of our race," they wrote, women in canteens "became a trusted guardian of that home back in America."[117]

As symbols of home, canteen women often embraced their charge to exert a motherly and sisterly influence on wayward doughboys. In her work with the Forty-Second Infantry Division, Gertrude Bray took it upon herself to instruct two lonely men in proper, respectable relations with women. One young man with "big brown eyes that see every girl that comes along" used Bray's canteen as a kind of confessional. A self-described wild man, the soldier assured Bray that if she let him spend time in the canteen, he would "try and behave." However, when he showed her a "perfectly disgusting" letter from a girl at home, she instructed him to burn it.[118] Another soldier who frequented Bray's canteen told her about his love interest in a local French woman. Although the two lovers could not speak each other's language, Bray guessed that "their eyes did the talking" and concluded that the infatuated American "sure was in a bad way." Still, she believed the French woman to be a bad influence on the young man and lectured him that "nice girls" were not permitted by their families to associate with soldiers unchaperoned. Bray urged him to forget about the woman and was pleased when a brief assignment to the trenches seemed to cure him of his lovesickness. Although she understood "how terribly lonesome they get and what a girl means to them," Bray was quite pleased with her efforts and noted in her diary that she "felt happier about him that night than I ever had before."[119] Several weeks later, however, Bray's diary reflected the persistent, and often impossible, challenge that canteen women faced in their efforts to keep the doughboys fit to fight. Her lovestruck soldier, she ruefully noted, "has been a back slider from the paths of virtue."[120]

The Y placed great hope on maternal influence when it assigned women to street patrols in London and Paris. Charged with patrolling the city streets at night in search of soldiers who were soliciting (or, as popular understanding had it, being pursued by) prostitutes, women directly intervened to stop any impending illicit act. Even police officers believed the women's maternal influence was more effective than punitive threats and frequently allowed the women to deal with drunk and disorderly soldiers instead of taking them to jail.[121] This kind of work extended well beyond the bounds of what was commonly acceptable for respectable women, but as Y worker Edna Perrin explained to her family, she accepted the task as a challenge. When she failed to keep a soldier from running off with "a devilish little street girl," she wrote to her sister that she hoped she would be able to prevent such a thing from happening again.[122] These kinds of experiences bolstered Perrin's self-confidence. She used to fear drunk men, she confessed to her family, but assured them that she now found them easy to manage even by herself because "a good woman is the most appealing thing in the world to them."[123] Always balancing the "sordidness" she witnessed with reassuring descriptions of wayward men rescued from evil, Perrin concluded that although the work was hard, "it surely has its compensations."[124]

Although the Y only assigned older women who it believed "were usually 'mother' to the men they dealt with" to street patrols, the work raised many eyebrows in the organization.[125] As one Y official noted, street patrols placed women in physical danger and threatened to tarnish the women's reputations. The women wandered the streets, "making friends of disgusting drunks, mixing in street fights and dealing at first hand with the sin that convention forbids any decent woman even to recognize."[126] Although the Y ultimately concluded that "the results more than justified the dangers," the women occasionally faced real threats.[127] When the program expanded to Paris, for example, where prostitution was legal, a lack of support from French gendarmes and "active rioting and attempts on the part of the street women to drive the patrol women from their beat" meant that the women needed the protection of soldier guards.[128] The Y cited the women's danger and the "ill feeling" the patrols sparked between French and American officials as the reason it canceled the patrols before the armistice celebrations, but it seems likely that they also anticipated the patrols would be ineffectual in the face of what was certain to be uncontrollable celebration.[129]

Even if canteen women were not always able to elicit wholesome behavior from the AEF, YMCA and military officials encouraged doughboys to think of themselves as fighting to protect women, and canteen women served as tangible motivation.[130] In a report to Secretary of War Newton Baker and General John Pershing, reformer Raymond Fosdick suggested that women were "in no small degree responsible for the unflagging devotion and inexhaustible patience with which our troops carried forward their high enterprise."[131]

Many women interpreted their wartime work in these conventional ways and actively encouraged men's martial service. Men at an aviation training camp, for example, frequently brought their new wings to the Y woman at the nearby canteen when they were promoted. As she stitched the wings onto their uniforms, her domestic labor symbolized her broader wartime support.[132] YMCA canteen worker Marian Baldwin similarly believed she had a duty to encourage men in their warring efforts in literal and figurative ways. When her friend John's work with a volunteer ambulance corps ended, he considered going home to talk with his family about what he should do next. Baldwin feared that his family would not encourage his return to the war and expressed her opinion "rather strongly concerning a man's duty when his country was at war." John soon decided to join the artillery, a decision that pleased Baldwin, even if she feared its consequences. "I hope I didn't influence him unduly," she admitted, though she insisted that "he will be thankful all his life, if he comes through, that he didn't trot home to Mother, like a slacker."[133] Later, while assigned to the Aix-les-Bains Leave Area, she found that working to make the men's leave "full of the memory of home influences and of home joys" exacted a physical and emotional toll. Nonetheless, she labored on, in this case to make the men temporarily forget their wartime troubles so they would be ready to return to action after their leave. Her encouragement, she believed, was "the most important kind that is being done, outside of the trenches."[134]

Women also felt that part of their purpose in the war was to help men face its consequences. One Salvation Army worker explained that "with a woman's hands" she and her coworkers tried to help soldiers "over the rough spots of homesickness, wounds, or any of the other hurts that come to the fighting man."[135] Katharine Grinnell embraced her task of helping men come to terms with the war's costs, though she confessed it to be quite difficult. When she and the other canteen women arranged a dance for soldiers, "a tall, fine looking lad, now armless" asked her to dance. She never hesitated, she affirmed, and danced "with her hands on that lad's shoulders," but wondered how dancing would help him forget about the war. She recognized, though, that "shattered boys were coming to her" and that it was her job to "help them carry on."[136] When soldiers lost their lives, Y and Salvation Army women felt they had a duty as women to grieve their loss. Two women stationed at a Y hut near an aviation training camp feared the worst when word spread of accidents. After two men died during a training exercise, the women attended the funeral. "I couldn't have borne it not to go," one of them wrote. "It seems somehow as though there should be some *women* at such a funeral."[137]

Helen Purviance and other Salvation Army Lassies similarly embraced the work that women had traditionally performed since the Civil War and decorated the graves of AEF soldiers with "a mass of pink and crimson flowers" before taking pictures of the graves to send to the soldier's family. It "must be some comfort to those at home," Purviance believed, "to know that *his* grave is being cared for by another American woman."[138]

As they prepared snacks and treats for soldiers, provided change at the canteen counter, or repaired a doughboy's uniform, women helped to make the AEF a figurative family that supported soldiers in times of emotional and physical strain and provided them with a visible reminder of the women they left behind. While the whiff of a frying doughnut or the warmth of a cozy canteen might comfort servicemen who found themselves in unfamiliar and emotionally trying situations, the women who prepared the food and decorated the huts had to balance their task to be friendly and inviting to strange men with the necessity of maintaining a professional distance from them. Called upon to remind the men of their mothers and their sweethearts and to serve as a tantalizing alternative to French prostitutes, women found themselves in situations unlike any they had encountered before the war. They were constant objects of attention—both welcomed and undesired—and they juggled their professional and personal lives in a strange world that presented opportunity and danger.

## ALLURING RESPECTABILITY

On a typical day at the Aix-les-Bains Leave Area, Marian Baldwin rose early for breakfast before beginning her work at the canteen. From 9:00 to 10:30 a.m. she sold hot drinks and sandwiches to soldiers undoubtedly more eager for a chat with the young girl behind the counter than for the items they purchased. For the next two hours, she played tennis with three men who had been sent to the region for a week's rest and recuperation. After lunch, she worked another three hours at the canteen. From 5:00 to 7:00 p.m. she escorted soldiers on a walk around the facilities, then from 7:00 to 11:30 p.m. she danced with as many men as possible among the thousands eager to enjoy a few minutes with an American girl from home.[139] "It is as though we were running a mammoth house party," she described, "only we entertain on a schedule." As the winter snow melted and the weather warmed, the pace of Baldwin's work increased. "It has been one endless round of picnics, motor trips, boating, tennis, games, dances and walks." She believed her work to be worthwhile, though emotionally trying at times. "Even if you don't feel like it or cordially dislike some of the men you are dated up with," she noted, "you have to do it just the same and start off with a beaming smile, to laugh, talk and joke yourself and them through three or four hours on end!"

Baldwin knew that while it was her job to be friendly to the men she entertained, it was also her charge to tactfully manage their flirtatious attentions. When two soldiers arrived and "promptly decided" that she was "the 'one and only' lady for them," she tried to deflect their efforts. Exasperated, she described how she "had an awful time keeping them apart" and how she separated the two men when they met in her presence and threatened to fight for her affections. There were "scores of deserving females at home, far superior to me," she futilely assured her competing suitors. After what must have been a very long week, the two men finally left, "each swearing undying devotion and fidelity," and although she admitted they "were nice boys," she found herself "drawing a long sigh of relief!"[140]

As Baldwin's experiences reveal, canteen women's daily duties reframed the rules that had guided their relationships with men in the past.[141] For the predominately white, native-born, Protestant, urban, middle- and upper-class women who worked in huts, their duties required them to be friendly and open to men of backgrounds and social classes with whom they would not have socialized in other circumstances, particularly with the high percentage of poor Southern whites and immigrants who comprised a significant portion of the AEF.[142] YMCA canteen worker Gertrude Bray described the men she worked with as being "made up of all the nationalities on the globe." Many of the men spoke little English, and the differences between the men and the women led to some initial difficulties. However, "just as soon as we gave them to understand they were not in an east side bowery saloon, and that they were to stand in line and act like gentlemen or they wouldn't be waited on," she wrote, "they behaved better."[143] Many women embraced their new experiences with a mix of genuine appreciation and patronizing interest in the exotic, and descriptions of their new associations no doubt shocked family members at home. Whether intended to tease, taunt, or flaunt, women's descriptions of their newfound friendships spoke to the chasm that canteen work bridged, if only for the duration.

Partly a result of the Y's interest in boxing as a healthy athletic venture, canteen women frequently made new "prizefighter friends." One woman assured her parents, "Really, it seems to me that they are quite high-class chaps." The boxers "keep themselves in fine condition, allow themselves no bad habits at all, and they are fine sports." However much she characterized the men as wholesome, though, she reassured her mother that she did not attend their sparring matches.[144] Julia Coolidge Deane wrote similar letters to her parents describing the interesting Irish boxer with "the most enchanting voice" whom she had recently met. Deane happily exclaimed that her new life was "what you might call broadening, and I certainly do love it," though she realized that such a life was possible only because of the war. "Imagine," she jested to her father, "if I started associating with a boxer in Boston."[145]

There were definite limits to the women's willingness to embrace the democratic nature of the AEF, however. Called upon to dance at a party aboard ship en route to France, Katherine Shortall happily participated and had "great fun." Her venture into the "dark, damp, unknown region" of the lower decks, though, betrayed her sense that working with men of a different social class was only a temporary charge. After several months of working with enlisted soldiers, the Y reassigned her to an officers' hut in Chaumont, where she was relieved to be "with cultivated people again."[146] While many white women were willing to embrace new friendships with a charming Irish boxer or a doughboy as a sign of their openness to new experiences, they were much less willing to cross the deepening divides of race. The YMCA generally segregated its huts, though when a hut occasionally serviced both white and black soldiers, military officials overrode the integrated practice and enforced segregation. The only three African American women deployed to France during the war thus found themselves overwhelmed.[147] They noted that when white women were sent to huts for black soldiers, they "gave a service that was necessarily perfunctory, because their prejudices would not permit them to spend a social hour with a homesick colored boy, or even to sew on a service stripe."[148]

Balancing these new and unfamiliar relationships required tact and grace. Julia Coolidge Deane had not even set foot in a Y hut when she realized the complicated balance she would need to maintain in her work. While sailing to Europe she learned that if she did not attend dances with soldiers on the ship's deck, the other passengers decided she was unfriendly, though if she did dance, she risked being labeled too forward.[149] She also had to learn to dismiss the inevitable attentions that came her way. Not long after arriving at her assignment in the Orkney Islands north of Scotland, she wrote to her mother that a naval officer had walked her home on several occasions. The young newlywed is "nothing but a kid and he is terribly lonely," she observed. And while her letters betrayed no romantic interest on her part—she even suspected that she would likely tire of seeing him—their cordial friendship was a bit unusual. "I'm not used to playing with married men," she admitted, "but up here all such rules and regulations go by the board."[150] A few months later, she responded to her mother's concern about the constant attention of the soldiers and sailors with whom she worked. "It is too late. I am spoiled, completely," she confessed. "When you have a whole fleet to play with, all the officers of which will do anything you ask them to, when you have so little time off that you have to fit dates in like puzzles; and when the Admiral takes you to tea and the Captain for automobile rides, then no wonder you begin to think that perhaps you are not awfully unattractive." Careful to maintain her "pretty level head," she assured her mother that she knew a "lack of competition" accounted for the men's advances, even if she knew she would "miss the excitement of all this tremendously" after the war.[151]

Deane's situation was not unusual, and canteen women frequently reminded themselves that men's attentions resulted more from the war's unbalanced sex ratio than individual appeal. Bertha Laurie re-

YMCA canteen worker Emma Young Dickson told the men she worked with that she was their surrogate mother or sister, but these two admiring lieutenants seem to think of her as a surrogate sweetheart instead. Canteen work challenged women to perform all three roles, all while keeping love-struck doughboys at bay.

called two men on a motorcycle who passed her and a friend and yelled, "'Look there, two girls from home; looks good,'" but explained that their "heads would be turning with flattery if we didn't realize what it means to them to talk to an American woman."[152] This mature evaluation was just what the Y hoped its canteen women would exhibit. The Y needed the "very best kind" of women, one woman explained, who were "willing to sacrifice personal pleasure for the great good work they can do." The work was demanding, and many women were bravely "willing to face death, if need be," but, she noted, the women's most difficult task was to be a "cheerful, happy, impersonal friend to hundreds of men when there are so many openings for friendship between one or two."[153] Resisting the men's advances was a necessary, if sometimes difficult, part of the job. "The officers are very polite and thoughtful and we love the men," Marian B. C. Watts admitted. "There is one who is the 'Virginian' come to life, who is a great pet, also a boy from Texas whom no one could help loving, he is only 19 and so kill-ingly southern." Only somewhat in jest, she warned, "I tell you seri-ously it is no place for a young girl!"[154]

Women diffused the sexual nature of their work and assured their own upright motives by affirming soldiers' inherent goodness and characterizing them as children. "Was there ever an army where a girl could live alone in a tent in the middle of an enormous Aviation Camp and feel as safe as a church," Y hostess Mary Lee asked. She assured her *Atlantic Monthly* readers that she was safe and respected, and that the men's benevolent actions were "the greatest of proofs of what we are fighting for." She insisted, "It all seems to be quite natural and de-cent, one girl and fifty men; and it is rather nice to think one lives in a country where it is possible."[155] Describing the men as children allowed women to ease concerns about the nature of this new kind of wartime work. "I play and work with them as though they were children," Kath-erine Shortall noted, "and we have had happy times together."[156] Framing herself as a mother to the boys of the AEF furthered conven-tional and respectable notions of women's wartime obligations and aimed to remove any public fears about sexual impropriety.

The YMCA and the Salvation Army also actively worked to remind women of their professional duties and used militarized uniforms to mitigate the attention women received as they engaged in intimate work with strange men.[157] As one Y official explained, the women "dressed in an appropriate uniform, so that every one knows what they stand for and every one respects them."[158] At the same time, YMCA and military officials expected that the uniforms would evoke a proper sense of professionalism from the women wearing them. When a number of professional entertainers began to acquire a bad reputation, the military ordered that all workers had to be "in full uniform." Don-ning the uniform seemed to help, one Y official believed, and "cut out a great deal" of the entertainers' improper behavior.[159] The organization placed so much trust in the uniform's protective qualities, in fact, that in September 1918 it prohibited women from wearing civilian clothes outside their private residences.[160]

Although some women chafed at uniform regulations—Edna Perrin likened the prohibition against civilian clothes to "almost a death penalty" and complained that YMCA officials were treating women "as if we belonged in a kindergarten"—women workers realized that their uniform allowed them to do their jobs without suspicion.[161] Even Perrin admitted that the uniform protected her while working street patrols in London.[162] "The nice thing about being an American in Paris, and wearing a uniform," another woman explained, is that "you can pick up any U.S. soldier you see and not be thought forward—if you do it in the right way."[163] Marian Baldwin expressed similar thanks for her uniform, which she believed "gives you a more dignified position."[164] Other women took some time to embrace their new apparel. "I don't like women in uniform," Katharine Duncan Morse noted soon after she arrived in France. A uniform hid "a woman's personality," she insisted, explaining that "to really carry off a uniform requires a flair, a dash, a swagger," qualities she felt were "rarely feminine possessions." Nearly a year and a half later, however, during which time she had not "worn white gloves, or silk stockings, or a veil, no, nor even powdered my nose," she concluded that such feminine accoutrements "don't seem to matter any more. Even a uniform, and a homely uniform at that," she finally concluded, "has tremendous advantages as part of a working scheme of life."[165]

Homely uniforms notwithstanding, canteen women on occasion ran afoul of the high expectations set for them. Although neither the YMCA nor the Salvation Army appears to have kept—or at least preserved—detailed records on women's indiscretions, scattered references attest to instances of what the Y called "indiscreet conduct."[166] It attributed such misbehavior to a lack of proper supervision and noted in a postwar investigation that one woman was sent home from England for "immoral conduct" and that thirteen canteen women and six female entertainers were dismissed from service in France.[167] Another report referenced the firing of a dozen professional entertainers stationed with the Third Army in Germany after the armistice.[168] Reports did not list individual reasons for the women's dismissal but noted that intoxication, immorality, and financial dishonesty accounted for most discharges. Any behavior that could be construed as sexual seems to have provoked harsh criticism. An AEF officer, for example, complained to YMCA headquarters about two canteen women he saw "lying up in the arms" of two officers during a train trip to Nice. The women's behavior was bad enough, but the officer took particular offense at the public nature of their actions. Other officers observed the women's "disgusting conduct," he wrote, along with anyone else who happened to pass by their compartment.[169]

The few explicit rules that the YMCA issued for women aimed to curb such public and potentially sexual displays of impropriety. Focusing on behaviors that, though increasingly common among all women, were at least somewhat still deemed disreputable among the reformers in the organization, the Y forbid women from smoking or drinking in public and from traveling in a car unless on official business.[170] The YMCA also admonished women not to devote too much of their time to a small group of men. Hoping to avoid any suggestion that women's work was motivated by romantic interest, a Y bulletin directed that women exhibit "unfailing friendliness" but in an "impersonal and detached" manner "without the suspicion of favoritism."[171] Any woman who allowed personal interest to take precedence over her work with all the men in her hut ran afoul of the Y's intention, as did one woman who, a confidential report concluded, was "not fitted for work with soldiers" because she "spent too much time with one man."[172] Appealing to the women's "deep personal sense of responsibility to each other and to the women at home whose representatives we are," the Y reminded them that one person's missteps would "reflect on all the other women wearing the same uniform."[173]

Relatedly, the Y warned canteen women not to neglect the enlisted men by paying too much attention to officers. Work with officers "is most important and useful," a letter to canteen women allowed before chastising those who spent so much time with their officer friends that they "greatly lessened their influence and usefulness with the enlisted men, whom we have primarily come to serve." While the reprimand aimed to democratize the women's attentions, it also attempted to avoid any presumption that privileged women with officer friends had "come to France for their own amusement, and not because they wished to serve their country."[174] It was a tough balance to strike. "There isn't enough of me to go around," Julia Coolidge Deane confided to her mother, "because the officers want me at the same time as the men."[175] Still, Y materials noted that women should balance their attentions. "Every real man in the army will think more of a canteener who politely refuses agreeable invitations," the manual noted in a reference to officers, if she explained that "her job calls her to give her time to a larger body of enlisted men."[176]

The tension between appeal and respectability was most visible in the AEF's Leave Areas, where for one week soldiers enjoyed—at military expense—a chance to recuperate in one of the world's premiere tourist destinations.[177] Based on military officials' belief that a "period of change and relaxation is essential to health and morale," the Y established Leave Areas as a way to "relax the restraints of military routine and discipline." It leased hotels, chalets, and casinos in places like Chamonix, Cannes, and Monte Carlo where soldiers dined on fine china, toured famous sites, and not once awoke to reveille. But while the military and Y believed this change in routine to be therapeutic, they also feared that "the dangers of such freedom in a foreign country were obvious."[178] Officials quickly discovered that madams were happy to open their *maisons de tolérance* to visiting doughboys, and the Y warned that unoccupied men in Leave Areas could pose a "large problem with regard to women."[179] Ever optimistic, officials nonetheless maintained their insistence that servicemen would choose wholesome "rather than deleterious pleasures," and offered entertainment "late at night, so attractive that no soldier would have a single moment in which he would be at a loss for congenial occupation."[180]

The Y thus offered canteen women as alternatives to the unwholesome attractions awaiting soldiers in French towns. "Picnics and Parcheesi," one official stated simply, "do not quite fill the bill."[181] Soldiers who had "scarcely spoken to a fellow country-woman since leaving home" needed American women with whom they could associate. "Nothing else could have done so much to make the men feel at home," the organization maintained, "and to make them forget the horror and the monotony of their past months."[182] According to one Y secretary at the Grenoble Leave Area, women did not have to work too hard to entertain soldiers who "had not seen an American girl for eighteen months" because the men "were contented just to follow them around and look and listen." The secretary noted, "One common sense wholesome American girl" outperformed the work of fifteen men. "The boys wanted women for companions after so many months of nothing but men."[183]

In its efforts to successfully counter the prostitution awaiting doughboys on leave, the Y placed a greater emphasis on feminine appeal in the Leave Areas than on the matronly counsel it emphasized in huts behind the lines. The Y frequently assigned younger women to work at the Leave Areas, where, as a Y historian put it, "unwearied dancers and picnickers were needed."[184] This policy accounted for Marian Baldwin's transfer to the Aix-les-Bains Leave Area. "I am young," she explained, "and they want all the girls they can get to cheer up the boys and make up to them for not going to Paris," where, presumably, the men could have found all the cheer they wanted.[185] While women like Baldwin engaged in many kinds of work, from canteen duty to accompanying men on walks, the most popular activity at the Leave Areas was dancing. In part, one observer noted, the men desired any activity that was "not rough, harsh, hard—not of their soldier life." Most important, dancing filled the men's desire for intimate contact with women. They were "perfectly happy and content" to dance with American women, but as one Y woman warned, if Y women would not dance with the doughboys, "then others there were, more than plenty, who would jump at the chance."[186] Trying hard to counter the appeal of these "wild women" waiting just beyond the gate, Y women worked long hours and "made it a matter of religion never to admit fatigue while yet one hob-nailed, trench-booted doughboy had a flicker of fancy to dance left in him."[187] Some officials in the Christian organization were not pleased about the men's exuberance for dancing but reluctantly admitted that the alternative could prove disastrous. When Y officials ended Sunday dances at the Nice Leave Area, for example, they found that men left the Y facilities in search of French women. That marked the last attempt to end dancing.[188] *"By all means dance,"* the Y's chief secretary pleaded. *"Hold the men!"*[189]

Dances were not easy events to organize in Leave Areas where soldiers outnumbered women by the thousands, nor were they always enjoyable for the women. "There was no possibility of resting while the orchestra played," the Y noted, "for girls were too scarce, and they were caught from one partner to another often without missing a step."[190] To maintain order and allow dances to "run on the democratic principle," the Y developed a system of tag dancing in which soldiers fastened a colored baggage tag to their collars and could cut in on a dance when a flag of that color was displayed.[191] The system worked as well as could be expected, even if it did not quite satiate the men's desire for more time with the women. The system impressed the women even less. Marian Baldwin described being "literally hurled from one man to another while dozens of eager hands try and snatch her away from him." Although she insisted that she considered herself fortunate to work with soldiers, she admitted that dancing was "pretty rough" and that "one comes out of it every night with black and blue spots."[192] Margaret Mayo similarly described "the long lines of uniforms that penned us in" at dances where men "would seize me . . . snatch me . . . and step on me."[193] Ada Alice Tuttle, who danced countless dances with eager young men in Andernach, Germany, after the armistice, described the "trembling eagerness of these boys for a partner" as "one of the most pathetic things I have seen." When one "nice chap" attempted to cut in on a dance at the same time as another, he lamented that he had been trying for two hours to get a dance.[194] Tuttle frequently found herself in this kind of situation and noted while the "well-bred gentlemen bow and step back," when they tried to cut in at the same time as another man, "the more persistent youths toss coins." One man "got another boy to dance with, and followed me around the floor," just so he could get a closer look at her.[195]

As these women's experiences suggest, dancing held the potential to create conflict among the many men who, as another canteen woman wrote, "want you at the same time."[196] Although women generally insisted that the men were "well behaved, and gentlemanly," dances did elicit some sense of fear. "You would expect that all sorts of disagreeable things might happen to you," Tuttle conceded, "but they don't."[197] Katherine Shortall learned the potential for trouble when she organized a dance at her canteen. Short of enough dance partners, she allowed each of three companies one hour on the dance floor. When the first company, "intoxicated by this taste of fun, refused to leave" and threatened to break up the dance and "take all the girls off" with them, she realized the potential for serious danger. Fortunately, she appealed to the men's sense of fair play and most of them left, allowing their comrades an opportunity to enjoy the women's company.[198] Y officials also understood dances' potential danger. In March 1919, the Y organized a "Flying Squadron" of fifteen "young and deliberately pretty" girls, escorted by two "very far from unattractive" chaperones, to travel wherever doughboys were specifically to dance with them. Women's Bureau officials admitted that soldiers greatly enjoyed the dances but worried that the effort was "fraught with so many dangers, that it could not be considered a solution."[199] As bruised and shaken canteen women discovered in overcrowded dances, their work placed them in tense situations that demanded quick thinking.

Women frequently minimized such precarious situations in their letters and writings to reassure worried minds about the possibility of danger and protect their reputations, even as they conveyed a sense of adventure and excitement about their new experiences. A letter Edna Perrin sent to her mother about her work on street patrols illustrates this balance. One night while on duty, Perrin encountered a Marine who had "imbibed a quart of champagne." When she approached the soldier and shook his hand, he drew her into an embrace and kissed her on the cheek. Perrin acknowledged the inappropriateness of the soldier's behavior—"Did you ever hear of such nerve," she asked—before she deflected its severity with a joke. "It would not be so bad if one just had a chance to pick the ones to do the embracing," she kidded. "Fine recommendation for Y.M.C.A. work. All the girls will want to be coming over."[200]

Although women working with the AEF found themselves in potentially explosive situations, YMCA and Salvation Army records are silent on the real dangers women faced as they lived and worked in such a masculinized and sexualized environment. The Y's official history of its entertainment work, in fact, boasts that all-women's troupes frequently traveled with no "male protector" and that "there was no place in the world" where American women were "safer than in the American army."[201] Undoubtedly countless soldiers did behave honorably toward women. Yet, rules guiding the living arrangements and off-duty hours of other women working for the AEF suggest that women needed to be protected from the men they had come to serve. Clerical workers and telephone operators lived in Young Women's Christian Association (YWCA) houses, where officials monitored their comings and goings and established rules for their off-duty hours. Women were prohibited from being out of the houses after dark, and they had to travel in pairs or groups.[202] Canteen women assigned to huts were often stationed alone or in pairs near encampments of soldiers and thus did not benefit from the security that YWCA houses or groups of women workers could provide.

As canteen women balanced wartime opportunities, challenges, and obligations, they selectively embraced the war's expansion of their lives. Armed with the language of domesticity, women moved into new wartime roles that allowed them to serve alongside the troops. Women juggled expectations that they create intimate relationships with strangers and yet retain an upright demeanor that preserved the good name of the organizations whose uniforms they wore. As both surrogate mothers and symbols of heterosexual desire, canteen women embodied the historical notion that women should mother the nation's warriors who fought for them in return. But in other ways, women advanced new understandings of what their work meant. Even while they performed conventionally feminine tasks, many canteen women developed a progressive understanding of what those tasks symbolized about women's wartime obligations and their place in the nation.

## MILITARIZED WOMEN

Winona C. Martin, a librarian from Rockville Center, New York, arrived in France to begin canteen work in mid-February 1918. Unfortunately, she never made it to a canteen. She had been fully aware of the potential dangers of wartime service, she assured a friend, and insisted that even if she had known her ship would be torpedoed, she would still have gone. Martin's ship was not torpedoed, but she did come down with a case of bronchitis during her voyage. A few weeks later, as she lay in a Red Cross hospital in Paris undergoing treatment, a German bomb struck the hospital and killed her. She was the first YMCA worker to die in the war.[203] Eulogizing her as a "patriot" and the "first woman to die for democracy," the Y ventured that the Germans could have exacted no greater revenge upon the United States than causing the death of a "young woman who had come to offer cheer and what aid a woman's hand and voice could give to our soldiers."[204] Despite the Y's evocation of conventionally feminine images, it proclaimed that her death signaled "the advancing tide of woman's influence." Describing her as "a member of a men's organization" who was "willing to undergo a man's hardship and privations," and had been "prepared to march and labor with men," the Y equated her dedication with that of soldiers. It even termed her final sacrifice "a soldier's death."[205]

Just as the Y ascribed progressive meaning to Martin's war work, canteen women and female entertainers attributed profound personal and national meaning to theirs. Eager to be of service, women volunteered in numbers far outpacing the number of positions available. Once in the war zone, they advocated for the right to work alongside the soldiers they came to see as comrades, even when battle called the men forward to the trenches. They chafed against old-fashioned ideas about women's delicate natures and embraced both the excitement and the danger of the war. In both small and profound ways, the war changed women who framed their service as a symbol of their burgeoning self-assurance and women's expanding place in the nation.

Military regulations held that canteen women could work no closer to the war's front lines than brigade headquarters without the "full and cordial approval of the Commanding Officer in charge."[206] Although the military intended the restriction to protect women from the unpredictable dangers of the war's front lines, women often interpreted it as an unfair limitation on their work. Elsie Merrifield Corliss and a few of her fellow Salvation Army Lassies found some lenient Army officers who escorted them "under shelter of night" to visit the trenches near Sanzey. Their illicit expedition struck Corliss as tantalizingly dangerous, though she reasoned that the rule forbidding women from the front lines was "foolish" because "it was hard to find any sector

YMCA women Elizabeth Baker and M. A. Nash preparing hot chocolate in a "rolling kitchen" for the Third Division in France. Canteen women wanted to be as close to the men at the front as possible and embraced such work as the feminine equivalent of soldiering.

where one could be away from danger."[207] Many women expressed this kind of desire to see the war's front lines regardless of its dangers. When a woman assigned to the First Division was sent back from her assignment near Beaumont on the eve of the St. Mihiel battle, she complained that "the big 'party' is about to begin and the army wouldn't let me stay."[208] The closer she served to the front, she reasoned, the "bigger the chance for service." She expressed little concern about the dangers that might accompany such an assignment but adopted the fatalistic attitude of the men with whom she wanted to serve. If "a shell has my name on it, I shall go," she wrote. Soldiers attributed their chances to luck, but she maintained her fortunes were determined by "something more." Adopting the doughboys' phrase, "if I 'go West,'" she concluded, "well, it is a glorious time to die."[209]

Marian Baldwin spent nearly her entire time in France wishing she were closer to the war. A few months into her tour, she heard that the Y needed women to work in huts behind the trenches. Only twenty-two-years old when she began her work with the YMCA, she was one of the youngest canteen women in France, and officials were reluctant to assign her to such a remote station. Determined nonetheless, Baldwin volunteered for reassignment and explained that though she was young, she was "very old in experience."[210] When she and her friend Alice got the chance to move forward with the 148th Infantry, the two women eagerly traveled with the troops and served them snacks from a small canteen in the evenings. Eventually, however, the men traveled too far for the women to follow, and Baldwin wrote that she and Alice "are champing the bit these days." Baldwin continued, "It seems perfectly criminal to be held away back here when our own regiment may be coming out of the lines any hour and in need of a hundred things."[211] They spent the next several weeks following the men's movements, sometimes without official orders.[212] When finally the women were sent away from the front, they enjoyed "cots with *real sheets* on them" and hot baths, but they longed to be "on the road again following that muddy, disheveled regiment of ours into Belgium!"[213]

As they protested the military's restrictions on how close to the front they could serve, the women developed a sense of camaraderie with the men that they believed united them in ways those at home would not understand. One woman described her time near the front as "days never to be forgotten" because they gave her "an understanding of what the men go through."[214] These kinds of experiences allowed women like Katherine Shortall to feel a part of the military unit they served. "I would be broken-hearted," she noted, "if I had to leave my battalion while they were still in France."[215] Edna Perrin expressed similar feelings of camaraderie and belonging about the Fifty-Ninth Pioneer Infantry. She told her family that she felt as though the "whole regiment was my own personal property." Perrin added, "There is nothing in the world quite like the feeling you have for a lot of dough-boys that you belong to."[216] These wartime bonds would survive even the war itself, Ada Alice Tuttle expected. Contemplating life after the war, she suspected that she and other canteen women would "wish to be back again" where they were bound "by those ties which only those can feel who are in exile."[217]

Women also bonded with doughboys through a mutual frustration with military protocol. When a major came to Katharine Duncan Morse's hut near Gondrecourt and ordered the soldiers to stand at attention, she exerted little effort to hide her contempt at his intrusion into the men's refuge from such regulations. She glared at him when he ordered regular inspection of her canteen's kitchen and established strict rules about when she could open the canteen for business. Thereafter, she refused to sell cigarettes to officers during off hours on the grounds that the major would be upset. She defied his order and aligned herself with the soldiers, however, by selling them whatever they wanted, a sign of her "common bond of sympathy" with the men.[218] Even the Salvation Army Lassies, whose organization modeled military lines, resisted needless protocol. Helga Ramsay was furious when a captain berated two doughboys in her hut for their improper dress. Apparently more familiar with military dress regulations than the captain, she directed her frustration to her own inspection of his uniform. After looking him over, she pronounced the unsuspecting captain to be the one in violation of regulations and then recounted her judgment to the enlisted men the following day. "That," she proudly noted, "they enjoyed!"[219]

Many women embraced their stark living conditions as a symbol of the temporary sacrifices they were making for the war effort. In letters home, one woman likened her filthy sleeping quarters to living "like little pigs."[220] One night she slept on the floor of the Y headquarters, where she lay down with "dirty blankets, gritty with sand" and used a "soiled clothes bag filled with garments" as a makeshift pillow. She "gave a hasty glance about for cock roaches, but happily saw only a few."[221] Having previously indulged in "two baths a day, clean towels and all that goes with it," she embraced her new rugged life as evidence that she was "living close to the big things of life."[222] When a sailor indicated to Julia Coolidge Deane that she would have to spend a lot of time after the war to manicure her hands, she surmised that they must be in a bad state for a man to notice them.[223] A few months later she described them as being in "the most horrid condition, cracked and red," but judged their deplorable condition insignificant compared to her work. "Never mind," she concluded, "I can make doughnuts."[224]

Yet even as canteen women embraced the militarization of their lives, they were also quick to assert that the war had not undermined their essential femininity. "You needn't worry about my getting roughened," Deane reassured her mother.[225] Marian Baldwin greatly enjoyed the rough living she experienced during her work but anticipated that after the war ended she would "never again wear sensible war-like clothes." "No more tailor-made waists and skirts," she declared. "I'll live in chiffon gowns, the sheerest of silk stockings and thin soled pumps!"[226]

As these women chafed against conventional notions of women's wartime service by embracing the war's danger and ruggedness, women also fought more subtle battles for equal treatment. Frances J. Gulick struggled against the limitations of the "oldish bachelor" in charge of her Y hut "who doesn't know what to do with women around." The man believed that "as ladies" the women should not perform manual labor such as washing dishes, nor should they be expected to handle financial transactions. Frustrated by his limited opinion and anxious to "pave the way for other women," Frances and her coworkers worked tirelessly to prove "that we are of use otherwise than as ornaments."[227] Other women expressed similar resolve. Katharine Duncan Morse appreciated the assistance of a man who balanced the canteen's receipts. Sometimes, though, she feared that "it hurts Bill's pride to have to take orders from a lady." When he expressed a "you're-only-a-little-girl-after-all sort of attitude," Morse held her ground, "put on all my dignity and read the riot act to him."[228]

Even women in prominent positions within the YMCA struggled to secure equal treatment for women workers. Caroline Slade, director of the Women's Bureau, insisted that women enjoy the same privileges as men and planned to send canteen women for training at Princeton University where the men received theirs. Only after housing proved problematic did the women's training move to Barnard College—a women's school.[229] From her position as director of the women's work in Paris, Martha McCook felt she was "fast turning into a violent feminist" as she advocated on behalf of canteen women who wanted to work close to the front lines.[230] The Y did not relent, but in November 1918 it directed that all employees, female and male, would be called by the same title of "secretary" as a sign that they were "of one status, irrespective of sex." The title was a progressive move, as was the directive to assign all workers based on their qualifications, but the organization retained some gendered assumptions. Women's assignments should consider "whether their service to the soldiers as women can best be rendered through an administrative channel, or in a more personal, social and intellectual way."[231]

Women's daily struggles for equal treatment signaled a broader effort to give meaning to their wartime work. Moving beyond social and familial expectations proved taxing for many women, though like McCook they held to their conviction that women's work was vital to the war effort. McCook's colleague, Elsie Mead, relied on the encouragement of the husband and college-age daughter she left behind when called to Paris to oversee women's canteen work. Their support gave her the assurance she needed to resist the urges of her parents to return home. Her parents' letters "disturbed me a great deal," Mead admitted, "for it was difficult for me, amidst these war conditions, to remember with proper patience that they belonged to a generation whose axiom was a 'woman's place is in the home.'"[232] Although she wondered "if I'll ever be a lady again," she concluded "I rather enjoy being a hard-working woman."[233] Fourteen months into Katharine Duncan Morse's tour in France, she was offered an opportunity to sail home. The war had ended three months earlier, but as many of the men she worked with were still awaiting their chance to return to the United States, she decided to stay with them. "If I went home now," she explained, "I would feel like a quitter all the rest of my life."[234] Another Y woman wrote her family, "I could not drop this work now and feel right about it." She was healthy, after all, and she loved her work. "While there is a bit for me to do, I *have* to stay with it."[235]

While war work symbolized a growing sense of national belonging and obligation for many women, it also highlighted the ways race continued to exclude African American women from the expanding notions of female citizenship. Years after working as one of the few black women in France, Kathryn Johnson interpreted her wartime service as a symbol of the full citizenship she was still denied. As it had for African American doughboys, serving in France allowed her to see "both the provincialism of America's system of racial subordination and its ability to travel beyond American borders," and she sailed home from the war—on a segregated ship—determined to resist segregation. When a New York theater showed the film *Birth of a Nation* in 1921, she and several other Y women donned their canteen uniforms and sandwich boards to protest the film's racist depictions of African Americans. "We represented America in France," the women's signs declared. "Why Should 'The Birth of a Nation' Misrepresent Us Here?" Dressed in their wartime uniforms, the women publicly equated their canteen work with the national obligations of citizens and demanded equal treatment in return.[236]

On the national stage, women's wartime work—in canteens, hospitals, factories, and military posts—helped to prod President Wilson on the issue of suffrage. Suffragists had drawn much attention and derision to their cause by picketing the White House, but whatever the public thought about the tactic, their message began to have an effect. When Wilson advocated for woman suffrage to the US Senate in September 1918, he adopted the suffragists' charge that American women had proven their dedication to the national cause through wartime service "wherever men have worked and upon the very skirts and edges of the battle itself." Women would continue to support the war effort even without the vote, Wilson insisted, because they "are too noble and too intelligent and too devoted to be slackers." But, just as he would "propose to admit soldiers to the suffrage . . . were they excluded," he encouraged the Senate to extend women the suffrage in recognition of the nation's dependency on their service. Wilson acknowledged that the nation had made women "partners" in the war effort and, in response to the suffragists' charges of hypocrisy, cautioned against admitting women "only to a partnership of suffering and sacrifice and toil and not to a partnership of privilege and right." Women had expanded the conventional ways in which they had served during wartime and had carved out new wartime roles that, in the postwar era, had significant rewards.[237]

In both small and profound ways, the war changed women who framed their service as a symbol of women's expanding place in the nation. But even as they created new wartime roles, soon after the armistice a YMCA official suggested to Major General Edward McGlachlin Jr. that perhaps the military no longer needed women to work with soldiers. The idea struck the First Division commander as nonsensical. Losing the services of women canteen workers "would be the worst blow we could have," he insisted. "I will do without any other thing than give up the women." McGlachlin confessed that he had initially opposed the notion of having women work alongside the soldiers. As "an old regular army man," he explained, he had "never been in favor of welfare work of any kind in the army" and was "more than assured that women had no place in the army." After seeing the positive impact that the women had on his men, however, McGlachlin changed his opinion. "Welfare work has a definite place," he concluded, "and the women have established themselves in a favorable place."[238] Other military officials agreed, and when another, much larger conflict engulfed the world decades later, the military once again turned to civilian welfare agencies to provide the women who would entertain and uplift the nation's soldiers.

# 2

≡

# Take Your Prettiest Dresses and Go

A TOUCH OF HOME IN WORLD WAR II

B. J. Olewiler grew up in Tacoma, Washington, and always felt a bit restless and curious about the world. Even as a child she suspected that the world moved at a quicker place on the East Coast or in California, and she resolved to see new places. Olewiler was also fascinated by stories of what was then called The World War and especially intrigued by stories of the women who worked at the Western Front. She and her brother played soldier games when they were children, and she knew that if another war came, she "didn't want to be left behind."[1] This adventurous spirit shaped Olewiler's purpose for her life. While many of her friends married young, she set her mind on college. Even the Great Depression could not impede her plans, and she used her winnings from a puzzle contest sponsored by Old Gold cigarettes to fund her studies in psychology at the University of Washington in Seattle. After graduation, and without any exciting job prospects on the horizon, she and a friend moved to San Francisco, where they became "real city girls" and impressed themselves with how cosmopolitan they were becoming.[2] None of her adventures in California would compare, however, to how much her life changed once the United States entered the Second World War.

Olewiler moved back home to be near her family after the December 7, 1941, attack at Pearl Harbor and took a job working at a "dull typewriter" for a construction firm. Soon, she began "a quest to get overseas." She considered joining the military but was disappointed that none of the women's services could guarantee an overseas assignment. Even more, she suspected that if she served abroad in the military, it would be "behind a typewriter—way behind the lines. That was not my idea of being in the thick of things." When she saw an article in the local paper about a Red Cross woman who was working overseas, she knew she had found the right position.[3] As an adventurous young woman in her late twenties, with an almost desperate desire to serve overseas, Olewiler was typical of the women who worked in recreation for the Red Cross and the United Service Organizations (USO). She was also exactly what the Red Cross was looking for: a college-educated, experienced worker with a demonstrated sense of vibrancy and independence. After two successful interviews and a send-off dinner with family and friends, Olewiler boarded a cross-country train headed for Washington, DC.

After completing her training, Olewiler was assigned to Clubmobile service in Ireland and England, and later on in France. She relished the work and took special pride in learning to drive and maintain Clubmobiles, converted buses, jeeps, and trucks equipped with doughnut and coffee machines that allowed the women to take their fun and games to remote locations and places closer to the war's front lines. Driving meant a great deal to women like her; she described it as "a precious manifestation of usefulness and independence." However much she enjoyed the unconventional work of driving large trucks across a war zone, she quickly discovered that her main work was with the GIs. Although she had expected difficulty in "learning to accost soldiers even before they had a chance to whistle," she and her co-workers "all gleefully threw off the 'correct upbringing' that was part of our past." In part, she reasoned, their uniforms protected them from "the charge of being 'forward' or 'fast' girls: they proclaimed for us that it was simply our job to be friendly and outgoing." Although not a topic of much conversation, she and other Red Cross women agreed that their new, more forward demeanor "was a new and welcome liberty."[4]

Olewiler insisted that her interactions with GIs were completely respectable and wholesome. Placing the work in the context of mid-1940s culture, she maintained that "there was no thought of such a thing as sexual harassment," explaining that "a little innocent and meaningless flirtation" was a usual part of "inter-sexual communication."[5] Even more, she argued that American GIs held too much respect for American women to entertain the possibility of inappropriate actions. In contrast to their actions around French women, soldiers behaved modestly around American women, she insisted, because they felt that "an American woman speaking the same language stood for home." In fact, when a Clubmobile woman wrote a funny story about the women's efforts to find latrines, the men failed to see anything humorous about it "and were shocked that such a nice girl could write such an essay." Women who represented "a long line of mothers, grandmothers and school teachers," Olewiler believed, reminded the men that "nice American women should be 'above' such ribaldry."[6]

Not all recreation women would have agreed with Olewiler's assessment of the men's actions or intentions, but it meshed neatly with the public image of recreation that the military, the Red Cross, and the newly formed USO hoped to project as they organized programs for soldiers' and sailors' amusement. The extensive nature of the mobilization and the war's duration demanded a much greater effort to provide for creature comforts and well-being than what had been provided by civilian agencies in the previous war. But even as the Army and the Navy formalized Special Services operations that provided GIs with recreation programs and consumer goods, they continued to rely on civilian agencies to supply the women they deemed critical to soldiers' morale.

The Red Cross operated much of the military's recreation overseas, in addition to its extensive service in military hospitals and its efforts to provide for the emergency needs of American personnel. The organization deployed approximately 6,000 women to operate service clubs and hotels in each of the war's theaters, first in cities and towns outside camps and bases, and then, as needs increased, on military posts. They stocked clubs, Clubmobiles, and hotels with newspapers and magazines from home and the latest big band and swing music, as well as the ubiquitous wartime doughnut. At the peak of operations, the Red Cross operated 989 overseas clubs and 319 Clubmobiles. From England to India, Guam to Nigeria, and China to New

Zealand, the Red Cross ensured that GIs enjoyed access to American-style food, magazines, music, and girls.[7]

The USO also provided GIs with what it called a "touch of home," both domestically and overseas. Through its affiliated USO-Camp Shows, the organization sent 5,424 entertainers overseas, where they performed variety shows, musical concerts, vaudeville shows, plays, and a range of individual performances. Although famous starlets such as Marlene Dietrich and the Andrews Sisters captured the headlines, most Camp Shows tours featured unknown talent who hoped that the war would catapult them to stardom.[8]

As they had in World War I, military officials believed that keeping idle hands busy was an important task, but jitterbugging with girls from home and cheering for them as they danced on stage served a much more important purpose than mere diversion. The Red Cross girl and the tantalizing USO performer played central roles in the military's efforts to distract lonely men from war's boredom and brutality and its attempts to craft particular notions of martial masculinity. Military and civilian officials held up women from home as symbols for which the men fought, as representations of ideal femininity and womanhood, and as reminders of the civilian and domestic life to which the men would return. Key components in how the US military motivated men, American women bolstered soldiers' masculine assurance, framed GIs' interactions with local populations, and softened some of the harshness and brutality of the war in a way that suggested soldiers were still normal men, ready for reentry into civilian life. Images of American girls chatting with GIs also projected a reassuring, if not entirely accurate, message for families at home that their boys were not gallivanting with foreign women or prostitutes. Entertainment thus formed a vital part of the wartime experience for soldiers, framed the image of soldiers seen by the home front, and offered a direct way for adventuresome women to participate in the war effort.

Official aims notwithstanding, women's roles changed dramatically during World War II, and entertainment work bridged tradition and progress. In many ways, mobilizing Red Cross and USO women to serve food and dance with GIs reinscribed conventional notions of women's wartime roles, but the women also pushed against these boundaries as they managed expansive supply networks, drove trucks and jeeps across war zones, and endured the harsh living conditions of remote theaters. Similarly, while public officials and ordinary citizens consternated over the ways wartime mobilization and dislocation facilitated a freer sexuality, recreation work called on women to walk a fine line between demure reminders of women from home and blatant sexual appeal. These conflicting yet intertwined tasks meant that women spent their war in a "goldfish bowl," juggling the flattering, if at times wearing and unwanted, attentions of thousands of men along with their own sexual desires and curiosity.[9] The women who signed up for overseas service secured a place for themselves in the war effort while embodying the fluctuating gender ideologies of the era.

## A TOUCH OF HOME

Military and civilian officials began organizing recreation and entertainment programs for the rapidly mobilizing armed forces in 1940. Initially, the military planned to coordinate all morale activities itself, and in 1941 the Army and the Navy established morale divisions to organize athletics, libraries, religious services, educational programs, motion pictures, and service clubs.[10] Although some administrative and War Department officials preferred that government agencies provide all of the military morale work, President Franklin D. Roosevelt directed that private organizations organize supplemental recreation work outside of military camps as a means of maintaining soldiers' ties with civilian communities.[11] Several organizations were already working to organize recreation facilities and activities for servicemen on furlough, and in January 1941, the YMCA, the YWCA, the Salvation Army, the Jewish Welfare Board, the National Catholic Community Service, and the National Travelers Aid Association merged their efforts to form the USO. The USO then coordinated civilian efforts to provide recreation in towns and cities across the country, and its clubs for servicemen and women quickly spread in number and popularity.[12] According to General Frederick Osborne, commander of the Army's Special Services Division, these efforts were greatly appreciated by military officials who were still scrambling to provide sufficient entertainment.[13]

This balance of military and civilian recreation worked well within the United States, where local residents, especially women and girls, volunteered countless hours in USO clubs. When the United States entered the war and began deploying forces overseas, however, the military found itself singly responsible for the recreation and entertainment of a rapidly growing and widely dispersed force. Although officers working hard to establish the newly formed Special Services were wary of inviting a civilian organization to supplement their work, they had no choice but to request assistance.[14] In particular, military officials asked civilian agencies to provide "the right type of recreational woman" to operate service clubs and to add an otherwise absent feminine presence in entertainment shows.[15] As Army Chief of Staff General George C. Marshall expressed early in the US war effort, the Army needed civilian organizations to provide recreation services "where the employment of women is practical."[16]

The military's decision to rely on the Red Cross to provide women for overseas recreation disappointed USO officials who had expected that, because the newly united organization's member agencies had performed morale work during World War I, it would be asked to revive those efforts. When the Red Cross received the charge instead, USO officials found a window of opportunity in providing live entertainment and in early 1941, organized USO-Camp Shows, Inc. to provide civilian entertainment for the military.[17] That October, Camp Shows sent its first tour overseas, featuring comedians Stan Laurel, Oliver Hardy, and Chico Marx, along with Broadway tap dancer and film star Mitzi Mayfair, to entertain troops stationed in the Caribbean.[18]

The organizations learned quickly that military officials valued their women more than anything else. In November 1942, when General Joseph Stilwell requested clubs for servicemen in the China-Burma-India Theater, Red Cross workers began gathering supplies and securing facilities and soon opened seven clubs for the men across the large theater. Despite these herculean efforts to open the clubs so quickly, however, Army officers "left no doubt" that they did not merely want clubs. They wanted clubs staffed by American women. To meet the Army's demands, the Red Cross transferred several female employees in the region to clubs in China, Karachi, New Delhi, and Assam. That the transfer created a serious personnel shortage for the Red Cross mattered very little. Nor did it matter that the women were social workers with no experience or training in recreation work. They were women, and that was all that mattered.[19]

As private, civilian organizations, the Red Cross and the USO cast themselves as representatives of a concerned American public and promised that women would ease GIs' adaptation to military life and temper the militarizing influence of protracted enlistments.[20] USO officials warned that military life might become "so deep-seated that after a year in camp it may be hard for the 'ex-soldier' to take his normal place in his own community."[21] Reaching out to the public as a concerned parent in a radio fund-raising drive, USO benefactor John D. Rockefeller Jr. confessed that he feared that his son might be made "tough by his military training" and would be "abandoned by those influences that make for character." Fortunately, he assured his listeners, the USO saw to it that men could enjoy "a wholesome atmosphere, the companionship of fine women and girls, recreations that are normal and influences that will keep them clean, and worthy."[22] USO President Lindsley Kimball similarly explained, "The military can bring in shows. The military can run canteens, the military can buy doughnuts or make them and sell them." It could not, however, symbolize the support of the American home front, much less the support of American womanhood.[23] In this way, service clubs became more than just gathering places and entertainment shows became more than relaxing diversion; they represented, in the words of civilian personnel, a "home away from home" for lonely GIs.[24] As one Red Cross employee explained, women maintained GIs' ties to home, particularly ties to wives and sweethearts. The women who are "working alongside" soldiers and sailors, she explained, would serve as a "small but important point of contact between those men and the women they left at home" and help the men "readjust themselves to civilian life."[25]

Military officials knew full well that servicemen far from home longed for their wives and girlfriends and insisted—as their predecessors had decades earlier—that servicemen needed contact with

Red Cross Clubmobile women go to great lengths to deliver doughnuts to American soldiers on the Rhine River in March 1945. American women made sure GIs could enjoy a "home away from home" wherever they served.

women from home to abate their loneliness and channel their sexual desires in wholesome directions. At the same time, they feared that too much contact with home could distract men from the task at hand. Red Cross and USO women, then, struck a good balance by providing positive, morale-boosting reminders of supportive women without home-front worries.[26] As Undersecretary of War Robert Patterson noted at an April 1942 USO conference, boys stationed "in the jungle, in the mud and in the dust" were "ready to fight at the drop of a Jap," but had a "critical need for social activity . . . companionship and hospitality." He cautioned, "If American mothers and American families do not see that they get it, those soldiers are going to take it any place they can find it."[27]

Patterson's warning reflected wider military and civilian unease, both on the home front and in the war zones, about what might happen if GIs had to search out female companionship. In many ways, public health officials resurrected World War I concerns that soldiers and sailors needed protection from lewd women who preyed on lonely

men and infected them with debilitating diseases. But while the onset
of another war revived public fears of sexual deviancy, military officials in World War II proffered a more nuanced understanding of wartime sexuality and enacted a more pragmatic response than their
predecessors had. Rejecting the moralistic arguments put forward
by Progressive officials during World War I, military medical officers
understood martial masculinity and sexuality as symbiotic and thus
sought to manage, not restrict, GIs' sexuality.

General George Patton linked manhood to sexuality rather explicitly when he scoffed that "a man who won't fuck, won't fight."[28]
Others, such as Captain Joel T. Boone, a World War I surgeon and senior naval medical officer, more eloquently explained the presumed
relationship between sex and soldiering in a 1941 speech when he
stated that "armies and navies use *men*. Men of the very essence of masculinity. Men in the prime of life." Even if they come from the "best
homes in America," he warned, they will seek out sexual activity
because they "are sexually aggressive" and "they must be if they are
going to be good soldiers and sailors." Moreover, he argued that while
the military could try to prevent men from being "too conscious of
urgings of the flesh," attempts to restrain their sexual proclivities were
futile, even counterproductive. Soldiers' "virile attributes," he argued,
"cannot be sublimated by hard work or the soft whining of Victorian
minds."[29] This belief that soldiers needed sex would prove particularly
troubling in remote, non-Western theaters where officials lamented
the absence of white women. Even more, popular understandings of
sex as essential to good soldiering led some to fear that if men were
not provided sexual outlets, they would resort to rape.[30]

Additionally, many military men like Boone ascribed to contemporary psychological thought that homosexuality could be situ-
ational and that extended periods of time in an all-male environment
could lead some men to engage in homosexual sex.[31] As a 1943 Army
report from an isolated post in Greenland warned, "twelve months of
continence and frustration of normal sexual drives is a long time even
for persons with strong characters to endure." The report continued,
"The longer men are kept from normal channels of satisfaction of their
biological urges, the more likely it is that they will seek out distorted

or perverted outlets if their characters are weak."[32] Even the chief of Army chaplains approved of pinups for men at isolated posts late in the war as a way to affirm the men's heterosexual masculinity.[33] Simply put, military officials believed good soldiers needed to see women, to be around women, and to have sexual interactions with women, though confusingly, they insisted that different women meet these varying needs. In contrast to World War I–era assertions that soldiers should preserve their manhood by abstaining from sex, officials thereby advanced a new understanding of martial masculinity dependent on women to reinforce GIs' heterosexual desires.

Such understandings of sexuality did not mean that military officials adopted a laissez-faire approach to GIs' sexual habits. Military and federal authorities remained preoccupied with sex and particularly with venereal disease (VD), which the chief of the Navy's preventive medicine unit described as the "largest preventive medicine problem confronting the military surgeon."[34] In early 1941, Congress took action to regulate both sex and venereal disease by passing the May Act, which made vice near military camps a federal offense. The act was unenforceable overseas, and military officials found that the average serviceman did not fear VD in any case, particularly after antibiotics and penicillin became available to the military in 1944.[35] Thus, military medical officers collaborated with social hygiene organizations in an education campaign that equated sexual health with victory.[36] "Fool the Axis—use prophylaxis," one poster advocated. Others portrayed attractive and seductive women as tools of the enemy, ready to infect gullible GIs with syphilis or gonorrhea.[37]

Despite these efforts, medical officials admitted that they converted few men to abstinence. "The sex act cannot be made unpopular," one wryly observed.[38] Instead, military officials distributed condoms and prophylaxis kits, established prophylaxis stations across all theaters (many in Red Cross clubs), and stopped punishing those who acquired VD after determining that suspending soldiers' pay dissuaded them from seeking treatment.[39] The military's periodic practice of regulating prostitution further complicated its approach to sexuality. Despite a wide-reaching campaign to suppress prostitution on the home front, military authorities regulated more than a dozen houses of prostitution for troops stationed in Honolulu; monitored the health of prostitutes in the "better" brothels set aside for US soldiers in Italy, Morocco, Algeria, and Liberia in 1943; and briefly opened brothels in France and Italy.[40] While these instances of sanctioned prostitution constituted exceptions to a general prohibition against the practice, they illustrate the widespread contradictions between official proclamations and privately condoned practices. In the words of USO President Lindsley F. Kimball, although officials at higher levels of the military "wouldn't dare" describe sex or venereal disease as inevitable, post commanders generally believed sex was "part of being military."[41]

But while military officials adopted a more pragmatic understanding of servicemen's sexuality than had their predecessors, they echoed earlier suggestions that men who were provided with ample opportunities to associate with women in "normal" situations would be less likely to seek scandalous associations.[42] Speaking at a morale officers' conference, Dr. Joseph Earle Moore, a noted leader in the study of venereal disease, suggested that most men would not seek out "the dance hall, the honky tonk, the street-walker, or the house of prostitution" if provided "more wholesome feminine companionship" and recommended that the military provide clubs staffed by "mature and womanly hostesses" and "a number of personable women of the same age groups as the men themselves." Providing women as alternatives to prostitution for men who, officials believed, needed sex, had the potential for what Moore subtly referred to as "disastrous consequences." Still, in an era when sexual assault and rape were not part of polite conversation, he insisted that the women's patriotism, common sense, and discipline would prevent more than "an occasional unfortunate episode."[43]

Recreation and military officers on the ground concurred with Moore's assessment. In November 1942, Red Cross officials at the US airbase in Natal, Brazil, argued that "there is a crying need for a decent, well-run Club House for the enlisted men" to provide them with an alternative to visiting night clubs in search of women.[44] A year later, after opening a day room, the local military commander credited the Red Cross with the reduced venereal disease rate.[45] The connection proved so convincing that when military activities slowed at the nearby airfield and the men enjoyed more free time, the Red Cross increased its efforts to "occupy the men's leisure time and keep them from going to town."[46] Fears that GIs were "over paid, over sexed, and over here" even threatened American and British relations soon after the "Yanks" arrived in England. In particular, officials worried that insufficient recreation facilities, combined with the GIs' relative wealth, drove the men to "pubs and to the companions one finds there."[47] Even the American high command agreed. In the North African theater, General George S. Patton told Red Cross worker Margaret Chase that he had opposed Red Cross clubs in his command "until he found that the soldiers would go to the clubs instead of bars and brothels and [that] this reduced the VD rate enormously."[48]

As military and civilian officials organized an extensive network of recreation and entertainment programs for GIs, the programs they created reflected a complex set of assumptions about the relationship between militarization and sexuality. With American mobilization drawing unprecedented numbers of men into the armed forces, civilian officials hoped that American women would reassure the public that their boys remained as normal as ever, comforted and supported by good girls from home.[49] As a tangible connection to home, women were physical reminders of a supportive home front and of those the men were fighting to protect. Women would also (and not coincidentally) provide a necessary boost to the men's heterosexual desires—desires that military officials believed were not only essential to good soldiering but also were threatened by the all-male nature of military camps. Recreation and entertainment work thus called on women to embody home and sexual appeal, a tricky set of expectations at a time when women's wartime roles were in flux.

## GI JOE'S BEST GIRL

World War II brought fundamental changes to women's lives. Wives and mothers entered the workforce in record numbers, women joined all branches of the armed forces, and women everywhere assumed greater responsibilities in their families and communities. While women embraced these new opportunities, the public engaged in a good bit of hand-wringing about the ways that these new roles upturned the gender order and threatened contemporary notions of sexual respectability. And yet, despite public concern about a freer, potentially dangerous, women's sexuality, the war effort utilized women as sexual objects in countless ways. Women's magazines insisted that beauty would help win the war. Popular pinup posters wallpapered barracks around the globe, painted nudes adorned aircraft, gridlines over images of women's bodies served as tools for teaching map reading, and *Esquire* editors even convinced the Supreme Court that the magazine's suggestive Varga girls were essential patriotic encouragement for GIs.[50] The public reconciled its trepidation about this mobilization of women's bodies by blaming any unwanted consequences on women and girls who flagrantly violated middle-class notions of sexual respectability. Prostitutes and "victory girls," women who freely engaged in sexual relations with servicemen, the thought went, created gender turmoil, not the average American woman.[51] Still, the line between patriotic, acceptable female sexuality and dangerous sexual transgression was anything but clear, especially for the women expected to remain above reproach.

In this fluid environment, the Red Cross and the USO tried hard to mobilize a comforting, reassuring, and conventional symbol of American womanhood that masked the deeper changes at hand. The organizations enlisted women's bodies and their sexual appeal, to be sure. They needed women who could keep the men from "going to town" but without violating the organizations' image of respectability. Recreation and entertainment women needed to symbolize the men's ideal girl at home, beautiful but not lewd, wholesome not seductive, a "sweetheart" not a lover. The Red Cross and the USO thus projected an image of women that blended beauty and skill with professional qualifications and wartime sacrifice. As a *Los Angeles Times* article put it, Red Cross women were "GI Joe's Best Girl." They were also the "sweetheart[s] of World War II," but they needed to do more than look pretty. They needed to be a "combination hostess, shock absorber and jack-of-all-trades," to supervise club management, parties, and information services. They might be assigned anywhere in the world, but wherever they went, they could "meet one crisis after another." The work would be demanding, and the women would need to improvise and be creative. They "must be prepared for disease, insects, dirt, uncomfortable living quarters and all the perils of modern war," but the article assured women that "it's the greatest adventure" they would ever have.[52]

The Red Cross's personnel demands fluctuated throughout the war. American entry into the war prompted enough women to volunteer that the organization halted recruitment in November 1943. As the number of American military personnel stationed overseas increased, however, so did the number of Red Cross clubs, and overseas directors soon began calling for more staff. Most recruitment occurred locally and informally, even in early 1945 when the organization engaged in an "all-out recruiting campaign" to enlist 1,000 entry-level workers. Most women found their way to the Red Cross after a personal contact suggested that they consider recreation work. Others learned about overseas positions when local or national personnel visited their colleges or universities or when they read newspaper articles about local women stationed in faraway lands.[53] Before May 1943, applicants applied to a regional Red Cross office, then traveled to national headquarters in Washington, DC, for final approval. After the cost of transporting applicants proved prohibitive, all white staff assistants were formally approved or rejected at offices in New York City, San Francisco, Atlanta, St. Louis, and Alexandria, Virginia. Officials at the national headquarters insisted on vetting all African American applicants in person until December 1944.[54]

These women held one of three positions: staff assistant, assistant program director, or assistant club director.[55] Each position required specific work or educational experience, and women could advance to higher paid director positions with time and demonstrated skill. Women who began as staff assistants could, for example, after three years of full-time experience in recreation, advance to assistant program directors, who planned and supervised all aspects of a club's activities. Assistant club directors supervised club operations, including recreation activities, local information services, and the Red Cross's financial loan and emergency communication services.[56] The vast majority of Red Cross women worked as staff assistants, answering questions, playing Ping-Pong and cards, directing games and skits, planning parties and dances, and tending to the many whims of GIs. They earned $150 per month, and the Red Cross carried a $2,000 life insurance policy in their name.[57] The Red Cross later described the typical staff assistant as a twenty-eight-year-old, blue-eyed brunette, of average height and build, who spoke some French, played a little piano, and taught school before going to war.[58] At least two women served as staff assistants in every club, and the larger facilities employed many dozens. Married women could hold any of these positions, but no woman with a child under the age of eighteen was eligible for any of them.[59] The Red Cross expected that all of its employees would serve for the war's duration, though it did not require them to sign a contract binding them to a specified term.[60]

USO-Camp Shows performers fell into two categories: celebrity entertainers and amateurs. Although big-name stars drew the largest audiences and the most public attention, they comprised few of the entertainment programs sent overseas. In 1944, for example, celebrity performers provided less than 3.5 percent of the entertainment.[61] The vast majority of Camp Shows women were amateur singers, dancers, and performers who needed to make a living during the war and who hoped that the exposure might help launch their careers. They auditioned in Chicago, Hollywood, New York City, Cleveland, or Los Angeles.[62] The USO paid their travel expenses, meals, and lodging, along with a salary determined by need. Celebrity performers typically performed in exchange for their expenses alone.[63]

Although both the Red Cross and the USO outlined clear expectations for women workers, balancing professional and personal qualifications proved difficult. The Red Cross, for example, needed women who could manage the activities of service clubs that often saw thousands of visitors daily, and it believed that college graduates with a degree in recreation, social welfare, or education were best prepared to do so. And yet, hiring guidelines noted that "outstanding" candidates without the prescribed educational qualifications could be considered, provided they had appropriate work experience or the right personality.[64] The Red Cross did not standardize evaluation forms or the interview process but allowed evaluators much freedom in determining whether candidates met these somewhat vague qualifications.

This highly subjective system meant that evaluators placed different emphases on candidates' qualifications, in some cases even valuing a pleasing personality over professional preparation.[65] If the selection process seemed inconsistent, however, wartime officials agreed with its flexibility. One supervisor in the China-Burma-India theater recommended that a candidate's "education qualification should be secondary" to other personal attributes and a positive attitude.[66] And while women needed to be adept at organizing activities and working with groups, another official noted, equally important was their ability to make "the serviceman feel at ease." He explained that "friendly outgoing qualities" and a "kindred feeling of warmth towards the enlisted man" were important qualifications whether women possessed these skills through formal training or "by having that all important pleasing personality."[67]

Physical appearance blurred the qualifications even further. Officially, the Red Cross recruiting manual explained that "it is especially important that women have a pleasing appearance, be well groomed, poised, and able to wear a uniform without severity."[68] The directive left much room for interpretation, but military officials knew exactly what they wanted: pretty girls who liked servicemen.[69] Even officials who complained about women "whose only qualification seems to be glamor" treated women's physical appearance as a serious matter.[70] One Red Cross evaluator characterized a twenty-four year-old applicant as "mature for age" and "wholesome looking." She exuded a "charming personality," had "splendid poise," and appeared "very capable but is modest." Overall, she rated an "excellent No. 1 prospect." Another candidate who was twenty-seven received no comments on her work skills. She was, however, "very attractive," with an "open face and wonderful smile and dimples," and impressed the reviewer "as being the wholesome type of American girl that will fit into the work overseas splendidly."[71] Even individuals providing personal references for applicants were asked to evaluate if a candidate had any limitations or failings "in appearance, speech, character, tact, or work habits."[72] These expectations of physical attractiveness shaped the women's understandings of Red Cross work. When Mary Metcalfe Rexford applied, she knew that she had to be "healthy, 'physically hardy,' sociable, and attractive." Attractive, at least in her estimation, did not mean that she had to look like Rita Hayworth or Betty Grable, but she did need to look like a "well-scrubbed, wholesome 'girl next door.' We were all somewhere between dowdy and glamorous," she explained. "We had to look friendly, not seductive."[73]

Most press coverage of the women's work similarly acknowledged that good looks were key to their appeal, but authors were careful to temper their descriptions to avoid disparaging the reputation of the women or programs. "It isn't fair to call them mere glamour girls," a *New York Times* piece insisted, though it admitted that "many of them are as beautiful to look upon as the doughboy or gob [sailor] far from home could wish." Still, the author insisted that the women were chosen for their skills, intelligence, and personality and that "they represent a cross-section of American women."[74] A 1942 *Washington Post* article describing Red Cross worker Gretchen Smith's preparations for her impending deployment noted that skill and beauty worked in tandem. "No matter where her voyage ends," it explained, "she must

Red Cross worker Daisy Pickman serves coffee to a group of young sailors in the Philippines. Young, attractive, and professional, Pickman symbolized the wholesome girl next door for American boys far from home.

be glamorous as well as efficient . . . providing soldiers, sailors, and Marines with a little touch of American fun." The article discussed—in great detail—the clothing and supplies that Smith would need for her work, including evening dresses ("one a red and black crepe and the other a striking gold lame"), dual-duty suede sandals that could be worn with the evening dresses or in the afternoon, "gay bows for her hair," three girdles, and six lipsticks.[75] Nine months later, the journalist struck a different tone. Allowing that "at first glance their jobs seem to be long on glamour and thrills, short on genuine hard work," the author insisted that wartime demands left no room to "bow to a lady's whims" and that the women were expected to endure the conditions of their assignment.[76]

The Red Cross indeed needed women who would have the stamina to work long days and nights on their feet, adapt to ever-changing and often inopportune living conditions, and put forward a smiling face through it all. For many reasons, then, it made sense for club and Clubmobile women to be, in the words of one official, "young and possess an abundance of energy and vitality."[77] Women who performed the managerial roles of assistant program directors and assistant club directors, by contrast, needed experience more than vitality and were required to be between twenty-five and forty, and thirty-five and forty-five, respectively.[78] Their age requirements remained constant throughout the war and elicited little discussion among Red Cross officials. Staff assistants, however, were another matter. The face of the club and Clubmobile, they prepared the food, planned the parties, decorated the clubs, played the music, gathered the supplies, drove the Clubmobiles, talked with the GIs, and danced the jitterbug. They certainly needed to have the physical stamina necessary for their work; personnel in charge of selecting Clubmobile women specifically requested young women who could endure rugged living conditions.[79] And yet, as with other qualifications, more than practicality and physical capability guided the organization's age requirements.

Staff assistants had to be between twenty-five and thirty-five years old. Younger candidates with "outstanding qualifications" or "broad experiences," such as airline hostesses, could be considered, but in August 1945, the organization formally lowered the age requirement to twenty-three and permitted mature applicants between twenty-one and twenty-three.[80] The club operations handbook clarified that "program feature no. 1 is the presence of the A.R.C. girl moving among the soldiers." Soldiers were "hungry," it advised, not for food, coffee, or doughnuts, but "to see and talk to an American girl."[81] Even assistant club directors should be "feminine" and "a good mixer," a Red Cross official explained, "yet know when friendliness passes into familiarity."[82]

This emphasis on youthful appeal reflects a change in public thinking about the role of motherhood in war. While images of mothers dominated patriotic imagery during World War I, by World War II a younger, more sexualized woman had taken their place as the symbolic American woman for whom men fought.[83] World War II's recreation and entertainment women reflected this shift, as the YMCA and the Salvation Army's emphasis on mothers and sisters gave way to the Red Cross and the USO's enlistment of women as attractive, youthful reminders of the romantic relationships waiting for the men at home.

But while the USO and the Red Cross wanted women to symbolize romantic relationships for GIs, they needed women who would neither be overwhelmed by romantic overtures nor use the war as an opportunity to expand their social life. As the recruiting manual explained, "a scarcity of women" often worked alone with "large numbers of men" and needed to appeal to GIs without risking their reputation.[84] How, exactly, to facilitate the right amount of attraction remained an unsettled point, however. Red Cross officials disagreed, for example, over whether or not to assign women to military units for extended periods of time. While extended assignments encouraged familiarity, they also enabled the women to develop relationships that could undermine their larger work.[85] After observing clubs in the Mediterranean and China-Burma-India theaters, film producer and Red Cross advisor Arthur Mayer recommended that "mature women" be sent overseas to provide guidance for young women learning to balance the constant attentions of so many men and to serve as a mother figure or big sister for the men.[86] Sending "girls as young as 21" to war zones, Mayer warned, was "dangerous in the extreme" because they were not mature enough to "correctly gauge and cope with the complications and temptations of the unnatural life on an Army post, where . . . they are courted and pursued nightly by thousands of eager, sex-starved men."[87] The recommendations might have seemed reasonable to many and would have aligned Red Cross overseas clubs with domestic USO clubs, which utilized middle-aged women as pseudo-chaperones for junior hostesses, but not all Red Cross stations welcomed his advice.[88] While officials in the Pacific Ocean area and the China-Burma-India theater began recruiting women to fill this role, officials in Europe, the Philippines, the Middle East, and the Mediterranean theaters declared they did not need the extra staff.[89]

Balancing music, gaiety, laughter, and girls with the USO's goal of providing uplifting influences proved similarly difficult for Camp Shows officials who consistently emphasized that they were very concerned about the "personal character" of performers and would not tolerate "excessive drinking or sexual misbehavior."[90] According to USO President Lindsley F. Kimball, all performers signed a contract pledging they would not divert from an approved performance script, though he admitted that some performances "went sour" when performers became intoxicated or fought with military officials. Such regulations, he explained, derived in part from tensions between "the biblical minded directors . . . and the girls who wanted to give the boys what they wanted to see."[91] Military chaplains sometimes took offense at the bawdy humor of comedians and complained to military and USO officials. Writing to the Army's chief of chaplains, one clergyman complained about the sexual humor of two actors and noted that "there is enough filth and indecency in the Army overseas without importing any from the States at the expense of charitable and patriotic citizens."[92] USO officials were apparently not as biblically minded as Kimball thought but allowed for some artistic license. As Camp Shows Executive Vice-President Lawrence Phillips insisted, comedy could be "risqué" without being "indecent, smutty and obscene."[93]

This balance of sexual appeal and respectability was especially difficult for African American performers. Dick Campbell, who headed the USO's African American branch, initially hesitated to send blues singer Alberta Hunter on tour. Although Hunter kept her sexuality quiet, Campbell knew she was a lesbian and feared she was not attractive enough to appeal to GIs. The solution, he decided, was to also assign Mae Myrtle Gaddy to the tour, a performer who, in his words, "flaunted sexuality." That flaunting went a bit too far, however, when she "sneaked that shake" into her dance routine. Although Gaddy defended her moves as appropriate for jazz music, Hunter and Campbell feared that the moves would be considered too vulgar and lead to trouble for the group and ordered Gaddy to stop the "shake routine dance."[94] In an era in which many whites considered African American music and dancing—even the wildly popular jitterbug—as too sexualized, African American performers faced even more scrutiny than did their white colleagues.

Camp Shows leaders insisted the USO hold performers to strict guidelines and assured the public that military chaplains advised the organization on the content of its shows.[95] Nonetheless, throughout the war, Red Cross and USO officials struggled to find the right mix of appeal and professionalism that would allow women to effectively distract GIs from disreputable activities, maintain symbolic connections to home, and protect their reputations. The women who signed up for this work brought their own mix of motivations and hopes to the work.

## WARTIME MOTIVATIONS

When the United States entered World War II, Jean Holdridge Reeves wanted to contribute in some way. Her father, a farmer, had not been drafted during World War I, and as the only unmarried daughter in a family with no sons, she felt a particular responsibility to serve on behalf of her family. When she joined the Red Cross and departed for a club in New Guinea, her family supported her decision.[96] Janet Mac-Cubbin felt a similar "compulsion" to play a part in the war. She did not want to be "regimented" in the military, nor did she want to miss out on what she expected would be "the biggest thing" of her lifetime. Single and living at her parents' home, she had nothing holding her back and feared that she might later regret it if she did not become directly involved.[97] Reeves and MacCubbin typify many of the reasons women joined the Red Cross and the USO. Like many women of their generation, they believed women could and should contribute to the war effort in some way, and as single women, they were free to commit to overseas service. Their commitment and sense of adventure combined to make work in recreation appealing, even exciting, for women who wanted to be as close to the war as possible.

For some women, the desire to serve in the war was deeply personal. Jean Parnell married her husband Johnny one month before the attack at Pearl Harbor. He was killed in service about a year later. Feeling that she needed to do something for the war effort, she applied for the Red Cross. She was only twenty-four years old, one year shy of the minimum age requirement at the time, but she pleaded her case by arguing that if she could become a war widow at twenty-three, she could work for the Red Cross at twenty-four.[98] The Red Cross offered Nancy Jobson Foster a similar way to cope with loss after her fiancé Bob was killed in the war. She had enjoyed working at a local defense plant but, after he died, turned to overseas service as a way to "get on with my life."[99]

Many women came to recreation work gradually, after being unfulfilled in various other kinds of work or volunteer positions. Like many women at the time, Rosemary Norwalk held a pink-collar retail job when the war broke. With the country at war, she explained, "helping run a luxury store whose main purpose is selling designer clothes, mink coats, Lily Daché hats, and Delman shoes" seemed insignificant. She was not tied down by marriage, she had friends who were already involved in the war, and her career could wait. The Red Cross, she decided, offered her a way to participate in what she described as "the most important event of my life."[100] Even war work paled in comparison to overseas service for some women. Elizabeth Phenix Wiesner worked as a Red Cross nurse's aide and joined the Massachusetts Women's Civilian Defense Corps but grew "increasingly impatient with my dull office work and volunteer activities." She felt a "deep personal need to be of some use somewhere in some capacity, preferably overseas" and applied to the Red Cross.[101] Lillian Jones Dowling left her job as a business teacher at a Milwaukee high school when the war began but, like Wiesner, felt frustrated and underutilized in her civil service office work in Washington, DC. She joined the Red Cross and waited five months before leaving for her post in Australia.[102]

Other women acquired a taste for recreation work by volunteering in USO clubs or soldier recreation in the United States. While managing a retail store in St. Louis, Mary Metcalfe Rexford volunteered one evening each week at an officers' club. Although she found the work "interesting," Rexford said it was "not as rewarding as I had expected." Wanting "to do more," she followed the advice of a friend who was working with the Red Cross overseas and signed up for similar work.[103] Elizabeth Richardson joined the Red Cross with two friends in early 1944 after volunteering as a hostess at a Milwaukee USO club, then worked on Clubmobiles in England and France.[104] One of Richardson's friends, Mary Haynsworth Mathews, also came to Red Cross work through volunteer recreation work at home. She regularly volunteered at GI dances her mother organized. "The boys were like eighteen and nineteen," and she was twenty-seven, but her mother didn't tell them how old she was. Once she learned that the Red Cross preferred women her age with college degrees, she knew she had found the right kind of war work.[105]

While professional aspirations often shaped USO women's reasons for touring on the overseas "Foxhole Circuit," they were also motivated by a desire to contribute to the war effort. As performers, the women understood that GIs wanted to see American women on stage, and they often felt compelled to meet that desire. Broadway starlet Judith Anderson, who toured the South Pacific with USO-Camp Shows, knitted, took first aid courses, sold war bonds, and staged plays for soldiers, but did not feel she was doing enough. One day while walking down a street in Hawaii, a soldier stopped her to say that it had been two years since he had seen a white woman. "I knew that I didn't need an act,'" she explained. The men wanted entertainment and companionship, and as a woman, she could provide both. "Take your prettiest dresses and go," she urged other women. "Take your understanding, your companionship, your warmth and tenderness." Performing for the soldiers would be "the greatest experience that life holds," she promised, "and you will be helping to win the war."[106]

Few club and Clubmobile women joined the Red Cross in hopes of making a career in the organization. Instead, they saw the Red Cross as a respectable and guaranteed way to serve overseas. Ruth White had been teaching physical education at Sophie Newcomb Memorial College in New Orleans, but in April 1945, after the Red Cross lowered its age limit to twenty-three, she and her roommate decided to join. They had not been doing anything for the war effort. Military regulations were not appealing, and the Red Cross promised to put White's education and experience to good use. Even more, she felt, its preference for college graduates made the organization "more elite" and "more trained" than the women's military units. "Plus," she laughed, "I liked the uniforms better, too, and that was important."[107] One Red Cross official concluded that part of what made Red Cross women successful was, in fact, the "highly individualistic tinge" that made military service unappealing. The women are "resourceful, self-reliant and courageous," he observed, and valued "personal independence and freedom from authority."[108] For many women like these three, civilian organizations promised a more direct way to contribute than even the military.

Indeed, one common thread among women's varied motivations was their adventurous spirit. The women wanted to perform wartime service, but home-front work was not enough, and military service seemed too restrictive. Jean M. Bright hoped to combine service with a bit of excitement and initially embraced her work as a clerk in the Adjutant General's office in the newly built Pentagon. She did not like the cramped living quarters in Washington, DC, however, and after a year returned to North Carolina where she organized dances for men at an Overseas Replacement Depot until she learned about overseas Red Cross programs. "Perhaps I shouldn't admit it," she confessed, "but I never felt I was sacrificing anything. I thought it was an adventure to get a chance to see the world."[109] Libby Chitwood Appel would have agreed. When the war interrupted her doctoral studies in French at the University of Wisconsin, she applied to the Red Cross. This kind of work was "right up my alley," she said, "tailor-made for an enthusiastic, adventure-loving, socially inclined Southern gal, who loved male company and could dance, sing, and play the swing tunes of the 20s,

30s, and 40s on the piano by ear." In many ways, her work hardly seemed like work. Instead, she wrote that she "felt like a preacher, called to minister fun and games to lonely GIs . . . I could hardly wait to fulfill my girlhood dreams of high adventure."[110]

A desire for adventure and wartime service proved sufficiently motivating for some women to defy family objections. Rosalie Campbell Jordan had been working as a secretary when her sister told her that the Red Cross was recruiting women for overseas work. But as "the winds of war swirled around my head" and she "became imbued with the spirit of adventure," she knew that her father and mother would not be so overcome. Her father objected to her being so far away from home and to serving overseas. Undeterred, Jordan applied, and after she was offered a position in the Clubmobile program, she called her father again to tell him she had made up her mind about going. It was the first time, she proudly noted, that she had made such a profound life decision entirely on her own.[111]

### LIFE IN A GOLDFISH BOWL

Red Cross and USO women's war work required them to straddle a thin line between wholesome friendliness and suspect behavior. The women knew full well that they reminded men of the female relationships they were missing and that many men redirected their longings toward them. They lived and worked under constant attention from the men, and they developed various strategies of coping with their newfound popularity, as well as the often unwanted and untoward advances that came their way.

The Red Cross intentionally trained and prepared club and Clubmobile women to nurture relationships with GIs and to encourage the men to see them as symbolic substitutes for their romantic partners at home. Women began learning to foster these connections during six weeks of training at American University in Washington, DC. For two weeks they studied the history and philosophy of the Red Cross, the structure of military organization, and the basics of recreation programming before practicing their work for four weeks at a nearby training camp. Throughout their preparation, women studied sports so that they could talk with the soldiers and sailors about their favorite teams; they practiced Ping-Pong, darts, and pool; they honed conversation skills; and they learned to dance.[112] Other lessons more directly taught the women to encourage men's attentions. Mary Thomas Sargent, a club worker in India, was instructed to wear perfume on the job to remind the men of the women they missed.[113] These inviting gestures were not for introverted girls, the handbook on club operations warned. "A new, or bashful, girl must overcome her shyness immediately," it directed, though it insisted that she would not lose her "dignity, charm and loviness" [sic] as she reversed the conventional practice of allowing men to initiate conversation and social interaction. "Our soldiers are hungry for your smile and cheery word," the handbook explained. "It is your stock in trade."[114] Soldiers were also hungry for more direct contact with the women, as Sargent quickly learned. Some women in her training class played chess as a way to engage with soldiers, another analyzed handwriting, and she learned to read palms. "Later when I was a seasoned Red Cross worker," she explained, "I knew that just having a girl holding your hand was what was important, when you were very far from home."[115]

Once at their stations, the Red Cross tasked women with providing a welcoming, relaxed environment for soldiers enjoying a brief escape from military duties. Serving coffee and snacks, playing cards, and dancing with GIs preserved civilian bonds, but some elements of the women's work facilitated more personal connections. A club in the China-Burma-India theater, for example, sponsored a "Blind Date Program," in which a Red Cross woman picked one man from several potential suitors, based on his responses to a series of questions. The club then paid for the couple's transportation and dinner during an evening out.[116] Even without such conscious efforts to arrange dates, women understood dating to be an official part of their duties. Rosemary Norwalk and the other women in her Clubmobile unit dated "a lot," she explained, "since being friendly and congenial is expected of all of us, on or off duty. It's part of our jobs." More pertinent for the Red Cross, she noted that if the women were "unsociable and nasty," their unreceptive behavior reflected badly on the organization and could cost it financial support.[117]

The Red Cross was officially charged with providing recreation for female military personnel, but the sensual undertones of recreation work made such services difficult.[118] As Major Anna Wilson, director of the Women's Army Corps in the European theater, complained, Red Cross programs were geared to men and did not easily adapt to female soldiers.[119] Complicating matters further, inconsistent club policies meant that while some off-post clubs admitted women soldiers, clubs located on military posts frequently did not.[120] The Rainbow Corner club in London, for example, admitted female personnel just as it did men, but women could only attend other London clubs and clubs outside the city as guests of GIs on "special occasions."[121]

When female soldiers did visit Red Cross clubs, they often were surprised to find themselves assigned as dance partners for GIs.[122] Outnumbered and overworked Red Cross women no doubt appreciated the extra help, but the women's presence did not just benefit the men, according to Red Cross officials who were determined to maintain women's access to "the normal relationships between men and women that exist at home." Given widespread rumors about female soldiers' sexuality and fears that military service fostered lesbianism, these dances facilitated heterosexual contacts for the women and thereby helped "avoid the creation of abnormal conditions which otherwise are bound to arise."[123] Ultimately, though, concerns about maintaining "normal" relationships for women were less important than the men's preferences. A report from the Southwest Pacific noted that while some clubs allowed the women to bring dates to dances, the same policy did not apply at other locations, where "the attitude of the men in the unit involved would not permit this generous gesture."[124] Servicemen could accept unaccompanied female soldiers who danced with them but not those who were seemingly unavailable.

The men's possessive attitude did not surprise Red Cross officials, who warned the women that some men would expect to do more than smell their perfume or dance with them. Even the interview process betrayed the organization's concern for finding "women with common sense and a level head" who could handle themselves professionally while deflecting the charms of thousands of men. A "brisk, business-like and thorough" interviewer initially feared that Rosalie Campbell Jordan was "just too pretty," a quality that presumably would have made the inevitable attention all the more intense.[125] Libby Chitwood Appel's interviewer asked directly if she would be able to "hold your own in that morass of sex." After answering affirmatively, she was accepted into the program.[126]

Elma Ernst Fay remembered "long periods of interrogation" on how to "maintain a friendly, but impersonal relationship" with the men they would see on a daily basis.[127] Instructors in Jean M. Bright's fall 1944 training class warned the women not to "misunderstand" their popularity. There would be so few women compared to the men, they cautioned, that even their grandmothers would be "extremely popular and sought after."[128] An instructor in Rosemary Norwalk's training sessions similarly warned the women not to think they were Theda Bara, a popular silent film actress known for her roles as a seductive "vamp." Norwalk had no idea who Bara was, but she did deduce that the women should "be careful not to let our heads be turned by all the attention."[129]

The organization's intent for women to demonstrate a sufficient amount of interest in the GIs also explains its policies regarding marriage. Until May 1945, the Red Cross followed the military's practice of assigning spouses to different theaters. Although the policy was not always enforced in all theaters, for the most part, a woman who married could remain in the service only if she agreed to be assigned to a different station than her husband. If she wanted to remain near him, she could work for the Red Cross only as a volunteer.[130] Generally, the organization explained the practice by noting that it needed personnel who could devote their full attention to their job and be ready to go wherever they were needed.[131] Specifically, though, a Special Services officer explained that women's relationships with GIs "would be less cordial" if their spouse was present in the theater. USO workers, conversely, who traveled through theaters as determined by their schedule, were not subject to prohibitions against serving in the same theater as their spouse.[132]

As the Red Cross prepared women to cultivate relationships with GIs, it also implemented rules intended to guard the women's

reputations. Although it did not forbid drinking alcohol, it did prohibit alcohol in clubs and canteens, and it requested that employees
refrain from drinking in public places while in uniform.[133] The
women were also held to a midnight curfew, earlier if military officials
implemented it or if Red Cross officials decided it was prudent, as
when Commissioner J. Harrison Heckman heard that some women
were staying out late at night in the South Pacific and instated a strict
curfew policy to curb any scandalous notions about their decency.[134]

Even the strictest curfew, however, could not prevent all indiscretions, and over the course of the war, at least fifty-five Red Cross
women became pregnant.[135] Organizational policy dictated that
pregnant women be immediately returned to the United States,
though women more than seven months into their term were to deliver before returning home. Alma Geist Cap, who discovered she
was pregnant while working in the Philippines, did not want to be
sent back to the United States away from her husband and kept her
pregnancy a secret until her seventh month.[136] The Red Cross was
more concerned with "illegitimate" pregnancies, but the female officials in charge of administering assistance to pregnant women took
a very pragmatic approach and treated a woman's pregnancy as "any
other health matter apart from any moral issue."[137] The Red Cross
offered financial loans for three months prior to and after the birth,
for example, reassigned women with positive work evaluations to
new positions in the organization, and meticulously guarded all
pregnant women's confidentiality.[138] This response to what some in
the organization felt should have merited "an attitude of censure and
dismiss" reflected the belief of at least one female official that pregnancies were an undesired but predictable by-product of the war.
While the organization provided "some measure of protection on
hazards of illness," she argued, it did not adequately prepare the
women for the strains of the war. Pregnancy, she felt, simply existed
"on the periphery of the war conditions into which we have sent our
people."[139]

Despite warnings and precautions, the barrage of male attention
disarmed women, and for many, necessitated a readjustment of their

prewar attitudes about proper relations between the sexes. Mary Thomas Sargent's first interactions with GIs confounded her. "After twenty years of being taught not to talk with strangers," she explained, she "needed a mental reshuffle to do it with ease." She felt comfortable when the men initiated the conversation but struggled to "encourage" quiet men to converse. Even her use of the word "encourage" troubled her, as she feared that it implied she welcomed more than conversation. "It was something of a balancing act," she reflected, "to be sincerely friendly without encouraging them."[140] Most men needed little encouragement. As USO performer Frances Langford discovered while performing with an early Bob Hope tour in Sicily, GIs went to great lengths just to look at her, even when she visited the latrine. The men had dug a trench for her and surrounded it with a small picket fence that provided little privacy. The men simply climbed into the surrounding trees for a better view. Their voyeurism unnerved Langford, but she decided not to report them and "got kind of used to it after that."[141] Other women were less disconcerted about the newfound attention they received. Most of the soldiers were "swell guys," Marion Bradley insisted, and she enjoyed their company at dances and parties. Still, she exercised caution. "One has to watch one's heart over here," she admitted, "with so much freedom and so many good looking males."[142]

Whatever they thought of their newfound attention, women quickly learned that reminding men of romantic attachments at home was complicated work. When Marie Coletta Ryan told the Navy's Seabees and sailors that they should think of the club as their home, one man cut straight to the point and asked, "Where is my wife?"[143] The cheeky comment probably got a laugh from other homesick men, but it pointed to a fundamental understanding among many GIs that home meant women. Red Cross worker Virginia Fitzgerald discovered this association thousands of miles away at the Tiger's Den club in China. She and the other three women reminded the men, the *Saturday Evening Post* reported, that "the great, wonderful civilian world of America . . . is more than a dream." One crew chief described her as "Miss America" and reminded his fellow men, "Here's what we're going home to!"[144] Some GIs did not even bother couching their feelings in homesickness. Langford knew that her popular song "I'm in the Mood for Love" made the men think of the romance they were missing. Every time she performed the song, she recalled, someone in the audience would stand up and yell, "You've come to the right place, sister."[145]

However peculiar the women's newfound attention might have seemed, many understood that wartime popularity would not continue at home, where "the man-woman ratio works the other way."[146] Elizabeth Richardson went a step further. "If you have a club foot, buck teeth, crossed eyes, and a cleft pallette [sic], you can still be Miss Popularity," she told a friend from home. "The main thing is that you're female and speak English."[147] As these assessments indicate, GIs often fell for the women. "Lots of the men said they loved us, and maybe they thought they did," Sargent noted. Even though she knew that the men's loneliness and "fear that they would never hold another girl after the next bombing mission" accounted for their amorous feelings, she also knew she needed to encourage their affections. When men received "Dear John" letters, for example, Sargent believed it did no good to assure them that they would find someone else. She had to be that someone else. "Sometimes," she reasoned, "the only thing to do was to let him carry your typewriter and walk home with you after the club closed at night . . . and then maybe kiss him good night and tell him that any girl who'd let such a nice guy get away must be pretty stupid."[148]

Many women struggled to adjust to this newfound popularity. For Hazel Bowman, a twenty-six-year-old woman from Florida, constant male interest diverged starkly from her prewar experiences. While sailing to her post in India, she described being "wined and dined until I feel plumb tuckered out with all the social activity."[149] The attention magnified once she arrived at her club. Not long after beginning her work, she wrote: "We're so popular here that one could have dates with everything from the rank to the file and most any service or nationality. . . . All of us have to pinch ourselves to remember that back home it's 1 man to every 8 women. And the fellows keep insisting that we have beauty, poise, etc. etc. until I'm sure I'll eventually begin to believe it."[150] Her daily work, in fact, demanded that she encourage the men's attentions, even at the cost of her own rest. She had "so many invitations to go dancing or dating," she explained, "that I can hardly find time for sleeping anymore. Here all this social activity is part of the job, and it's nothing to put in 13 hours a day at working and socializing."[151]

Soon, the hours of socializing began to wear on her and changed her opinion of the men she worked with. Early in her tour, she seemed convinced that their intentions were wholesome. "Nicest of all, we aren't bothered with wolves," she insisted, "for they have to behave if they want another date."[152] Several months later, though, she wrote that she liked one man in particular because he "never presumes that just because he was invited over to dinner on Wed. night he'll be welcome again on Thur." Other men, by contrast, "moved in on me because I was kind to them once or twice." Such expectations were common, she explained, and the men "can't understand why, when we've seen them in the club from 11 A.M. to 9:30 P.M. we don't want to spend from 9:30 P.M. to 1 A.M. with them also." Managing their expectations proved "pretty ticklish business sometimes."[153] Moreover, the lack of privacy—what she described as living "in a veritable goldfish bowl"—quickly proved unnerving.[154] Obligated "to ALWAYS be charming to anyone who wants you to entertain them," Bowman grew increasingly frustrated as, regardless of age or marital status, GIs interpreted her obligatory charming ways as an invitation "to smooch." Eventually, despite her charge to be friendly to the GIs at all times, she began to avoid them whenever possible. After a long day of work, she no longer felt "like making inane conversation or fighting off someone."[155]

Bowman was certainly not alone in her exasperation. Rosalie Campbell Jordan greatly enjoyed her work on a Clubmobile in England and wrote to her sister that it was "the grandest experience that any one person can have." But, she allowed, "it is not a normal existence." Regardless of how she felt or how many hours she had worked, she had to "look nice," she explained, "for the men notice every little thing about you; they tell me who I've been out with, what I've been wearing." If "I look the least bit tired or unhappy," she reported, "I immediately hear about it until I change my expression."[156] Working at an enlisted men's club on the other side of the world in Brisbane, Marcia Ward Behr experienced similar aggravations. "Even when you just walk across the room, you must be ready to 'give out,'" she wrote. "The boys do not understand anything else."[157] The men's constant attention derived from what Rosemary Norwalk described as their "especially proprietary and supervisory eyes." If she and her co-workers declined a date with a soldier, the men became even more curious about what they wore and where they went.[158] The incessant attention and expectations to always be upbeat and attentive to GIs' expectations wore so heavily on Elizabeth Phenix Wiesner that she joked she would have to join a convent after her work in North Africa, "just to get away from men."[159]

For many women, spending a war both facilitating and resisting men's attentions prompted a reconsideration of their attitudes about sexuality. Many women considered themselves inexperienced in these matters before the war; as Marcia Ward Behr put it, "I was not particularly smart about men."[160] The war and the military environment quickly changed young women, however, who "had a hard time staying untouched by the coarse and often obscene talk heard all around us." Libby Chitwood Appel insisted that before the war, "a hug was not a proposition. Innuendo was often considered a compliment. The wolf whistle brought smiles to our faces. When the whistles stopped we were considered 'over the hill.'" As the war introduced new people and experiences, however, some women developed "a more lenient wartime moral code" that "became a major concern of our Red Cross supervisors." Associating with men they would not have known outside the war, Appel noted that they "played cards with thugs, learned how to deal with drunks, laughed off propositions, and endured jibes and insults with equanimity." These new experiences made the women "adept at resisting the pawing advances of men of all ranks and ages," but also "hardened" women struggling "to stay afloat in the male military environment."[161] For Rosemary Norwalk, this meant that she came to condone relationships that she would not have approved of before the war, including that of her co-worker and a soldier who were both married to other partners.[162] In Appel's estimation, these new attitudes changed them as women. "Inevitably we lost some of the sweetness, femininity, and refinement of the hometown girl," she lamented, "the very virtues that helped get us into the club service."[163]

### SEXUAL DANGERS

Life in a goldfish bowl was often difficult, and it transformed women's ideas of relationships and sexuality. It could also prove quite dangerous. Organizations' intentions to transfer GIs' romantic longings to recreation women created more problems than officials might have imagined and left the women to manage precarious situations without easy or clear solutions.

The men's persistent attentions illustrated a belief among many GIs and officers that the women were there entirely for their amusement and, worse, a presumption among some that the women would be willing sexual partners. One Red Cross woman discovered this assumption in April 1943 when Admiral William Frederick Halsey Jr. invited her to travel to New Caledonia on his personal plane. When Red Cross official Nyles I. Christensen explained to the admiral that Hall could not go, Halsey, "did not take the explanation in very good part."[164] Rosemary Norwalk found herself in a similarly odd predicament when a port commander asked her to bring some Clubmobile women along on a cruise to the Isle of Wight, ostensibly so they could discuss Red Cross work. In recounting the evening in a letter to her family, she described the tea served and the cucumber sandwiches she ate but did not enjoy. In her journal, however, she was much more candid about the commander's intentions and explained that she censored the evening's events in her letter home because she did not "want the folks dwelling on the thought of me in the bow of the boat with the Port Commander holding my hand and giving me little pats and a serious pitch that didn't sound like Red Cross business at all." Uncomfortable with the commander's unwanted advances, she quickly began "babbling about the long hours we work and how little sleep we manage to get and how demanding my Red Cross duties are" before inventing a story about a fiancé stationed in the South Pacific. Her fake love story seemed to do the trick, as the commander quickly "reverted to a father figure." Feeling as if she had barely scrambled out of a tricky situation, she noted that she "sure was exhausted when we finally docked."[165]

Other women faced more overt and potentially dangerous sexual propositions. When a man came into Ruth White's club in Okinawa, Japan, and asked to make a "sexual date" with one of the women, she took the man into her office and asked him what he would do if someone made the same assumption about his sister. The contrite man began crying, she recalled, and left the club.[166] Not all such situations resolved themselves so easily. Marcia Ward Behr knew that many GIs suspected women "joined [the Red Cross] for men, wine and song" and experienced that presumption firsthand at the Yorkies Knob Officers Rest Home near Cairns, Australia. While the only woman on duty one evening, she listened to the Pianola and played Ping-Pong with a visiting officer before "suddenly his mood changed" and Behr "guessed what he meant." She began crying and recounted that her "tears finally persuaded the officer to stop. . . . The next morning he apologized profusely."[167]

Although the Red Cross insisted that its clubs were respectable institutions and its workers wholesome, its policy of placing prophylaxis stations in some clubs compromised the tense balance of sexual desire and innocent camaraderie that the organization tried so hard to manage. Beginning in March 1943, at the request of military officials concerned with a rising venereal disease rate, some Red Cross clubs permitted the military to operate pro stations in first aid rooms, provided they not be advertised and thereby affect the "present atmosphere" of the clubs. Army medical department officials operated the stations, often housed at large clubs that had overnight accommodations where they could board.[168]

Military surveys of soldiers' opinions confirm that some men believed club and Clubmobile women were promiscuous or even prostitutes, a suspicion rooted, at least in part, in enlisted men's frustrations with officers' privileges and their perception that women were yet another benefit of their status.[169] Officially, the Red Cross insisted that dating was "entirely a matter for individual decision," but instructed women at their training sessions to date only officers.[170] It even permitted the women to wear civilian clothes on dates with officers so that they would not be easily identified as Red Cross employees and thus could enjoy themselves "without fear of criticism from privates that they are neglecting the soldier."[171] Generally, entertainment programs were designed for the benefit of enlisted personnel, and so the dating policy meant that the organization provided GIs with women whom they could look at and even long for, but not date.[172] It positioned women as yet another source of tension between officers and enlisted men, and in many ways, a prize for which soldiers could compete but not win. GIs could engage in friendly conversation with the women, the policy suggested, but only officers could expect something more.[173]

Dating guidelines made some sense given the military's prohibition against fraternization between officers and enlisted personnel and the women's pseudo-officer status that entitled them to officer-level billets and mess.[174] At the same time, however, Red Cross officials worried that too much separation would create too impersonal a relationship between the women and GIs and would exacerbate rumors of the women being "officers' girls."[175] One official suggested that instructing the women to date officers led them to regard enlisted men "as a sort of social case work en masse" and to treat their work as a "9 to 5 proposition."[176] Any perception of such frigidity could harm the organization's reputation, its leaders feared, by contributing to "the development of a prevailing point of view by the G.I.s and their folks back home that our women are not expected to associate with the enlisted personnel." Of all potential allegations that the public could wage against the organization, he felt that none would have as "devastating" an effect.[177]

It was not easy for women to symbolize GIs' sweethearts when they were, or were even suspected of being, someone else's sweetheart. Nancy Jobson Foster appreciated the pragmatic benefits of the prohibition against dating soldiers for without it, "they all would want me to go out and that would be quite impossible." Still, she struggled to manage expectations. When she took a group of GIs to see *As You Like*

*It* at Stratford-on-Avon, the men went to the bar during intermission to get bitters. By the time they returned, an officer Foster knew had stopped to chat and brought her a drink. When he left, the men lectured her "for the rest of the evening about talking to officers (brass as they call them) and accepting their drink while they were battling for my bitter." Foster insisted her intentions were innocent, but she learned quickly that the men expected her to devote her undivided attention to them, not the officers.[178] Clubmobile worker Mary Metcalfe Rexford felt similarly conflicted between her mission to serve enlisted men in remote stations and the officers' expectation that the women dine and attend parties with them. "The last thing I wanted to be accused of was 'officeritis,'" she noted, "because that alienated the GIs. At times I felt very torn and inadequate in handling the complications that arose from this dichotomy."[179]

Although some women disregarded Red Cross preferences and dated whomever they wanted—as Mary Thomas Sargent put it, women at her station "were free to enjoy both worlds"—some women were genuinely more interested in officers who were closer in age to themselves.[180] "If we tended to date Majors and Colonels," explained Margaret Chase, "it was not because of their rank; rather, we thought of them as contemporaries."[181] Class similarities also played a role for Elizabeth Richardson, who described GI dances as "rough," compared to those at officers' clubs, "which are quite civilized" and featured "flowers, good music and wonderful dancing with a miscellaneous assortment of very nice partners."[182] Observing that Red Cross women more often dated officers, USO women like Louise Buckley consciously tried to associate with enlisted men as much as possible. "Dating isn't the point," she insisted, "they appreciate having women pay attention to them instead of officers.[183]

Complicating matters further, many women felt they needed to build relationships with officers to secure support and supplies for Red Cross activities. The Red Cross encountered difficulties in getting supplies, especially in remote theaters. Stationed at the Jorhat Air Base in India, Libby Chitwell Appel struggled to build a recreation program with few supplies. When a "handsome and unattached" officer invited her to a dance, she went because "making a good impression on him was . . . professionally expedient." He was "a handy man to know," she explained, who could procure items she needed for the club, including a "badly needed ping pong table."[184] Frances Langford traded a dance for an airplane while traveling with the Bob Hope tour in the Pacific. When an admiral refused to allow the troupe to continue using a plane for transportation, Hope asked Langford to appeal personally to the admiral. After a round of old-fashioned dancing, in which Langford complained that the admiral "just about broke my back, bending backwards," he allowed them to travel on the plane.[185] Even Red Cross official Eleanor "Bumpy" Stevenson, who served in the Mediterranean theater with her husband, occasionally attended officers' parties to get the equipment she needed—including a generator and a shower—for her club.[186]

Although the women saw these relationships pragmatically as just another part of their job, the expectation of military leaders that the women exchange social pleasantries for essential supplies, equipment, and cooperation constituted, at best, an unequal relationship and, at worst, an egregious abuse of power that placed the women in very difficult situations. One Red Cross official acknowledged the power involved when he described women's interactions with officers as containing "an element of informal coercion." Women might have resented continual requests to attend officers' parties, he explained, but they were also "unwilling to decline party invitations for fear of reprisals." At the same time, Red Cross leaders ignored the potential ramifications of these relationships for the women, but instead, feared that they gave the women too much power. As one Red Cross commissioner complained, women who were able to obtain supplies and favors through high-ranking officers were less "amenable to supervision and discipline."[187]

In this environment of innuendo and expectations, rumors swirled about the women's sexual lives. At best, as Clubmobiler B. J. Olewiler put it, "to a private, a smile that had been flashed on anybody above a sergeant was tainted"; at worst, the men suspected that the women operated as well-paid prostitutes or "legalized whores."[188] One GI in the Mediterranean theater recommended that the organization "obtain a better class of Red Cross girls and send these officers' whores home."[189]

A private first class in Bihar, India, was even blunter. "Either stop them or make them lower their price so we can all afford it," he suggested.[190] Red Cross officials dismissed the men's allegations as "overly sensitive and unduly suspicious," attributing them to their having been away from "normal association with wholesome American girls, exiles in a country where there is only one white woman to several thousand men."[191] Again, officials expected the women to manage an untenable situation while ignoring its deeper cause. Female soldiers and nurses serving in the war faced similar suspicions, but without military rank to protect recreation women, and with their work intentionally positioning them as objects, recreation women endured even more precarious sexual expectations.[192]

These rumors plagued the women throughout their service. Social worker and Red Cross Field Director Jane Hashagen reported early in the war that even though the women followed strict rules and behaved conservatively, "the rumors have been as putrid as if we were right out of the red light district." Hashagen suggested that women be warned that "if they were eighty and harelipped there would still be talk about them."[193] However inevitable rumors might have seemed, they upset women who knew them to be unfounded. When a rumor spread that her underwear had been found in a major's jeep, Mary Thomas Sargent knew they were not hers but was still "pretty upset about the story, and how it made me sound."[194] Rumors followed the women even to the sick ward. When Margaret Chase became ill, she felt that the attending physician had diagnosed her even before examining her. A picture of her boyfriend on the dresser offered all the proof he needed, and he "sneered something to the effect that Red Cross girls were too available to the 'brass.'"[195] Hazel Bowman confronted this kind of suspicion head on when she became sick and was hospitalized. Immediately, she told the staff that she was not pregnant in an effort to prevent "the usual conclusion with the soldier public the minute one of us gets near a hospital."[196]

Virginia C. Claudon Allen went to great lengths to discount a rumor that she was having an affair with an officer. The rumor was "ridiculous," she reasoned, in part because "the only officer we ever saw was a supply officer, and he was a rather uninteresting person." Still, she wanted to put the rumor to rest, so she got medical confirmation to prove that she was not sexually active. Allen then adopted an offensive approach and, like Rosemary Norwalk, fabricated a fiancé to protect herself. A fellow club worker loaned her a ring, and she crafted a story that she knew would meet the approval of the GIs at her club. He could not have "a posh job in the United States," nor could he be an officer. So, Allen made her fake fiancé a sergeant because, as she explained, "GIs always respected their sergeants." Inventing the story "was a terrible thing to do," she confessed, "except that it solved the problem."[197]

Recreation women continually confronted these kinds of situations, by-products of work that required them to be always inviting, and they developed a variety of strategies to manage situations that bordered on dangerous. Hazel Bowman and her coworker Mary Jane frequently felt obligated to invite men to visit in the evenings but never drank and selected only men who "are at least gentlemen," she explained, so that "we can always take care of ourselves."[198] Not all men were gentlemen, though, and as Libby Chitwood Appel explained, "keeping the men off is our biggest problem." She had been "enchanted" with the men's attentions at first, she admitted, but "as the weeks passed and I heard the same old 'lines,' I learned to turn a deaf ear to the proposals and propositions." Appel had left a PhD program to join the Red Cross, and whenever her dance partners got "a little too chummy," she mentioned her graduate degrees, and the "cheek-to-cheek clutch relaxed."[199] Margaret Chase even continued her relationship with her "stuffy" boyfriend Tex, in part because having a steady boyfriend offered "protection and a sense of security."[200]

Even being married did not protect Jane Anne Jack from flirtatious men, so she learned to divert their attentions. "When a new officer arrives and starts looking interested I start talking about my wonderful husband," she assured her concerned spouse. Sometimes, the men lost interest when they learned she was married, but often, she reported, they continued to talk with her and even brought her presents. Having "long since learned that men don't give something for nothing," she told the men that she would give their gifts of candy and cigarettes to other GIs.[201] Several months later, Jack found herself in another awkward situation when a soldier she had agreed to attend a dance with arrived to announce that it had been canceled. Intuitively, she "sensed the next move" and told him that she was too busy that evening to go on a date. After the man finally left, she felt satisfied that she had "very neatly handled" the predicament.[202]

Some Red Cross women learned the hard way that their employer expected them to endure harassing behavior without offending the perpetrating men. In the fall of 1944, Kathleen Roberts and Patricia McDonald left their assignment at the "Shangra Lodge" club in India after growing increasingly frustrated with what a Red Cross official described as "ribbing." Although the Red Cross and military acknowledged that problematic relations between the officers and enlisted men created "exasperating" conditions at the post, Red Cross officials insisted that the women had taken the "so-called insults and disparaging remarks" too seriously, "chose rather to be insulted and offended," and even provoked the men's heckling by limiting their relationships to "a strictly cold business proposition." Instead of addressing the men's behavior, Red Cross officials accused the women of being too sensitive and bringing the attention on themselves, then ordered them back to the United States and discharged them from their jobs.[203] At the China Victory Club the following year, a staff assistant refused to accompany a captain on a date but instead attended an enlisted men's dance at her club. After the rebuffed captain punched her in the jaw and gave her a black eye, she reported the incident to Red Cross personnel officer Norris McClellen, who responded that it was not the right time to mention the incident to the Army. Another Red Cross official expressed outrage at both the incident and McClellen's inaction and warned that failing to address such incidents would not prevent bad publicity. Even more, she warned that the organization's lack of support for the woman would lessen other women's confidence in the organization to protect them and lead the Army to feel that the Red Cross could "be pushed around." Tellingly, she also indicated that the lack of response was not unusual. "One person summarized it well," she explained, "that if a Red Cross girl were raped she would be fired for missing time at the club."[204]

Not all women had negative experiences with soldiers. Publicly, organization officials and women defended the men's honor, and many attributed the sexual underpinnings of their work to the mores of the era. In an essay that appeared in her hometown newspaper, Red Cross worker Elizabeth Phenix Wiesner insisted that the men treated her and her coworkers "with the same teasing protectiveness they would have given a kid sister."[205] Other women even noted that the men policed each other when necessary, while one Red Cross official asserted that the GIs never caused problems for the women.[206] Their flirtations were only meant to be funny, never "fresh," and besides, she claimed, "any level-headed girl could easily develop defensive tactics that were crushingly effective."[207] When dealing with soldiers, Mary Metcalfe Rexford similarly allowed that "sexual innuendos were always present" but maintained that "they were rarely explicit." Acknowledging the potential for sexual harassment, Rexford declared that, "surprisingly," the women did not have "'the problem' that one might have thought we would have." Women were proposed to, propositioned, and tempted, she admitted, but "in most instances," the men respected them. Still, she conceded that "All I could do in any situation was to use my best judgment and hope for the best."[208]

As Rexford's conflicting comments suggest, some women convinced themselves that they were in no real danger, even as they referred to a number of potentially dangerous situations. In an autobiography written fifty years after the war, USO performer Maxene Andrews of the Andrews Sisters insisted that the men "never tried to make advances to any of us" and that "we were never considered sex symbols." At the same time, Andrews describes the experiences of fellow USO trouper Patricia Morrison who noted that the men wanted "to touch your hand or kiss you on the cheek, but that's all." Seemingly unaware of the contradiction, Andrews also noted that Morrison had a guard stationed outside of her billet when she traveled to keep American men from entering.[209] Even Rexford insisted that she and the other women "felt perfectly safe" while also revealing that the Red Cross women's billets were guarded while they were in training at Camp Patrick Henry (after four GIs were discovered prowling nearby) and on duty near Valognes, France.[210]

Throughout the war, the Red Cross and the USO attempted to balance women's appeal and skill, carefully skirting the porous boundary between respectable femininity and disreputable sexuality that took on an elevated importance for women in war zones.[211] The complexities of these sexualized images encapsulated changes in women's lives and public concerns about the ways that the war effected gender and sexual changes. In many ways, women entertainers were one version of the idealized, sexualized American woman. They utilized a version of sexuality that bridged wholesome appeal and tantalizing danger, and that blended with theirs—and their organizations'—"conventional ideals of professionalism, patriotism, decency, and desirability."[212] Moreover, these images worked to fashion an acceptable public image of the American soldier and sailor as "an innocent, starstruck, heterosexual, nonviolent, small-town boy, whose sexual imagination is limited to imagined relationships with 'all-American girls.'"[213] These notions were even more contested by the era's racial contexts.

# 3

≡

# The Difference between Savagery and Civilization

Cotton farming never appealed to Jean Moore Fasse. Like many African American children of the 1930s, she grew up poor, wore the same pair of shoes all year, and longed for something more. Although her father could have afforded to send her to school, he expected that she would—and should—marry, and thus refused to help her attend any schooling beyond what she could acquire in the one-room segregated school near her home in Lillington, North Carolina. After finishing the sixth grade, though, Fasse remained determined to go to high school and finally convinced him to allow her to live with families in Durham where she exchanged childcare and domestic work for board. She proudly graduated from Hillside Park High School in 1931.

Fasse soon learned, however, that a high school diploma did not open doors that segregation had closed. After short stints working in a tobacco factory and delivering flowers in a hospital, she moved to Fayetteville to attend the State Colored Normal School. Still poor, she worked in the campus laundry and cleaned the dining room to pay her expenses. After earning a teaching certificate, she got her first job in a one-room school heated by a small potbelly stove very similar to the one she had attended as a child. By the time the United States entered World War II, she was teaching and directing the glee club at Robeson County Training School. For extra money, she and the other teachers

waited tables at the nearby Laurinburg-Maxton Army Air Base officers' club in the evenings. In the late summer of 1944, a Red Cross representative from Washington, DC, came to her college alma mater to
recruit African American women for overseas service. Fasse knew that
the military was recruiting women but had not been interested. She
was, however, very interested in overseas service and applied, hoping
that she might work in Europe.

But even as Fasse prepared to do her part for the war effort, segregation framed her work and experiences. Because the Red Cross insisted on interviewing all African American candidates in person at
the national headquarters, she borrowed her roommate's coat and traveled to Washington, DC, for an interview about a month after completing an application. When she received the good news that she had
been accepted into the club program, she informed her school's prin-
cipal that she would be leaving. Proud of her decision to serve in the
war, he accompanied her to the superintendent's house to deliver the
news. As custom, if not the law, dictated, the pair called at his back
door.

Segregation followed Fasse as she sailed across the Pacific. She had
not received the European assignment she wanted but instead was assigned to the China-Burma-India theater where Red Cross officials
hoped she could make GIs' wartime experiences more tolerable. Her
own experiences proved quite intolerable at times. Although all of the
Red Cross women bunked together in the same room aboard ship, the
fifteen white Red Cross women refused to socialize with her and
the four other black women. The white women even complained so
much about the smell of the women's heated hair combs that they had
to stop using them. In another affront, none of the African American
women was invited to the Captain's Dinner, a highlight of the thirty-
one-day voyage. The slight "made us sad," Fasse noted, "because we
all were going overseas to do the same thing."[1] Their work might have
been the same, but when the women arrived in India, race again divided them. Fasse and the other African American women all went to
the Cosmos Club in Calcutta. They were among the two hundred
African American personnel working for the Red Cross in early
1945.[2] Six months later, the Red Cross sent Fasse to serve coffee and

sandwiches for soldiers building the treacherous Ledo Road, an Allied supply route between India and China. It was a very remote location, with primitive facilities surrounded by a jungle of wild animals that occasionally made their way into her living quarters.

After two years of wartime service, Fasse had grown to appreciate many parts of Indian culture but still longed to see Europe. When she learned that the Red Cross was turning over its remaining clubs in Europe to the Army's Special Services, she signed on. Before going to Europe, though, she returned home for a brief visit. The war against fascism had been won, but the one against racism, she quickly learned, had not. After sailing back to the United States, then enduring a long overnight train ride from New York to Raleigh in the "dingy coach reserved for blacks," she was "just beat down."[3] Hoping her Red Cross uniform would win her some sympathy if not respect, she asked for a cup of coffee at the only refreshment stand open. "I thought," she later wrote, "since I had worked in India and in the jungle of Burma where I could have been eaten by snakes and other animals that this would make a difference." Bolstering her courage, Fasse walked into the white dining room and asked for a cup of coffee. "Although I had done my part in helping to win the war," she recalled, she had not won the right to the most basic of requests.[4] "I'm sorry," the attendant replied, "we don't serve Coloreds here."[5]

Like Fasse, African American women who worked for the Red Cross and the USO navigated the varying practices of segregation in organizations that officially espoused but did not enforce racial equality along with a military that insisted on racial separation, especially in matters of sexuality. As the military deployed to non-Western theaters, American ideas of cultural supremacy fanned the already incendiary issue of race and sexuality. Officials attributed greater importance to the Red Cross and USO women stationed in these remote outposts than it did to those in Western environs. Although assigning women to such faraway posts initially met some resistance among civilian and military officials, even these cautious men ultimately concluded that women were essential to preserving a sense of decorum in what they considered an otherwise uncivilized and barbaric environment devoid of proper women. In all theaters, military officials attributed great significance to women's capacity to undo the negative effects of military life and wartime stresses. The fun, the dancing, and even the dresses women wore all played a part in helping to preserve a sense of normality in a decidedly not normal setting.

### THE FEMININE TOUCH

On Thanksgiving Day 1944, Red Cross Clubmobile women drove their two-and-a-half-ton trucks to "within three miles of the Siegfried Line." The women had moved from England to Europe after the Allied invasion and had been following behind the advancing troops for months. For the holiday, they brought their food and fun to "a division that had been in the line for two weeks and had suffered heavy casualties." The men were "soaking wet, tired, haggard and bearded," but as soon as they heard music playing on the Clubmobile's speakers, one of the women reported, their "faces lit up." The women served coffee and doughnuts, struck up conversation, and undoubtedly danced a few rounds with the war-weary men. When it was time for the women to drive back to their camp, the men announced that they could "go back and fight all the harder" after their brief break from the war.[6]

Military and civilian officials insisted that men needed these breaks from the war to sustain morale, relieve stress, rest their worn bodies, and briefly escape their militarized, all-male world. "I hardly ever get a chance to talk to a girl," General Omar Bradley lamented to one Red Cross club worker, because he was constantly surrounded by men and had "to talk nothing but the war with all of them."[7] The Red Cross and USO worked hard to ensure that all men, from generals to privates, enjoyed opportunities to socialize with American women through "regular daily programs of dancing, social parties, and entertainment," and they deemed these interactions vital to counterbalancing the effects of long-term enlistments, deployments, and militarization, especially for servicemen under great stress and those in remote posts.[8] The women's "feminine touch" provided soldiers with what Army Special Services commander Frederick Osborne called a "balance for his energies when he is not engaged in military duties."[9]

The feminine touch began with women's appearance—widely believed by military and civilian officials as well as the women themselves—to offer a refreshing change from the otherwise masculine, khaki, military environment. But, for organizations deeply concerned with respectability and for young women determined to maintain their individuality, striking the right balance of femininity, professional appropriateness, and youthful attractiveness proved to be an ongoing negotiation. In an effort to legitimize the women's unconventional work and their conventional femininity, Red Cross officials directed club women to wear a two-piece suit uniform with a skirt and jacket (over girdles to ensure "proper fit") and Clubmobile women to wear a uniform of slacks and a bomber-style jacket. Only when relaxing in their private living quarters or exercising, or if the military commanding officer in their area permitted it, could they wear civilian attire.[10] Uniformity did not preclude femininity, however, and related directives outlined ways for the women to appear feminine but not showy. Manicures were "important for appearance," for example, but "brilliant nail polish is not approved nor is excessive use of cosmetics."[11] A feminine appearance outweighed other considerations, such as practicality and the women's health. It would have made more sense for women working on runways to wear pants instead of dresses, for example, but officials insisted that women's utility suffered if they did not appear feminine. "The crews are sick of khaki," one reasoned, "and the value of meeting the mission is greatly reduced if the girls are not in fresh uniform dresses."[12] Officials even prohibited women from wearing slacks in Calcutta, despite the threat of malaria, because, as Hazel Bowman supposed, officials believed Red Cross "gals are prettier in dresses at their parties."[13]

Although Red Cross officials designed the women's uniform to be professionally feminine, women often felt that it symbolized the militarization of their own lives, not an alternative to it, and in the words of one woman, devised ways not "to lose all femininity."[14] Stationed at a club near Honeybourne, England, Nancy Jobson Foster wrote her family not long after arriving that she was glad she had brought some "civilian" clothes to wear off duty and on dates. "Let me tell you," she confided, "it's a treat to get out of a uniform and enjoy yourself for a change. Sure glad I brought a few accessories along."[15] It was not just Foster who enjoyed the more feminine attire. Not long afterward,

Foster asked her parents to send her red crepe dress so she could wear it during the Christmas holidays. "The boys like colors, especially red," she explained.[16] Halfway around the world in India, Hazel Bowman knew that looking attractive was part of her work as a "social butterfly" and asked her parents to send her dresses because "the boys get so sick of seeing us in uniforms that we get out as much as possible."[17]

A bit of youthful rebellion also inspired some women to defy strict uniform regulations. Rosalie Campbell Jordan spent her days serving coffee and doughnuts on a Clubmobile in England, then entertained soldiers at dances in the evenings. Because "the men really like to see us in feminine attire," she wore civilian dresses to the dances. One evening, though, she and the other women received a "strict reprimand from headquarters" and an order to wear their uniforms to such events. Although Jordan complied, she suspected that "one of the older dames up here got jealous of the attention showed us."[18] This youthful rebellious spirit extended to Jordan's choice of nail polish. Despite the prohibition against "brilliant nail polish," she thought bright red was "'high style.'" It was also, she admitted, "a color which made your mother throw up her hands in horror! We were told in no uncertain terms that only ladies of doubtful virtue used THIS color." Testing the line between respectability and allure, as many young women did, Jordan noted that opposition to the flashy color was enough of a reason to wear it and the women "all used it!"[19]

Hairstyles also constituted a regular point of contention between the organization and the women. Although prohibited from wearing bangs and directed to wear their hair above the collar in line with military regulations, some women—to the consternation of the Red Cross—adopted the popular Veronica Lake style of long, wavy locks. Judging the style too seductive, Red Cross Vice Chairman Richard F. Allen complained that the style gave the "wrong impression of the fine looking lot of women" working in the clubs. Perhaps wisely, Allen did not "intend to step into this question of the way the girls should fix their hair," but he did expect the women on staff to enforce regulations.[20]

Debates about appeal, style, and respectability were more contentious and public for the USO, whose Camp Shows performances by definition were to be eye catching and even glitzy. Camp Shows issued performers military-style skirt and jacket uniforms for travel but forbid them from wearing them during shows or when interacting with the men. "A G.I. doesn't want to see you in slacks and he's not interested in your uniform," instructions advised. "He wants to see you look like the girls back home on an important Saturday night date." To achieve this look, the USO recommended that the women wear artificial flowers in their hair, which could then be given to GIs as souvenirs, and that they pack nylon stockings. "They'll never be more appreciated," guidelines explained, "and not only by you."[21] At the same time, the organization warned that too much sex appeal was neither appropriate nor desired. "The soldiers and sailors you will entertain are definitely not sissies," it declared, as if necessary, "but they do not want off-color material or double-entendre jokes or business." The USO explained, "Call it sentimental, but when the doughboy thinks of girls from home, he thinks of his mom, his sister, or his best girl. He's seen enough of the other girls. Girls from home have to be nice." GIs preferred a woman "prim in an organdie dress" to one suggestively dressed, it insisted.[22]

Still, Camp Shows officials were no prudes. In 1942, a local reporter in Carmel, California, responded to recent coverage of actress Ann Sheridan's tour of Army camps. One article had described Sheridan as "the strawberry blonde with the oomph" who wore "skin-tight dresses," including one that "fits like a 1942 bathing suit." The black-and-white checked dress in question featured sequins, "those shiny things," the author helpfully explained, that give the dress a "a wet, sexy look." The reporter objected to her attire, but even more to the government's presumed endorsement of such sex appeal. Contrasting the War Department's banning of vice districts and prostitution across the country with its sponsorship of tantalizing USO performances, the author reasoned that shows like Sheridan's heightened soldiers' sexual appetites and left them unfilled. "Ann Sheridan might just as well walk naked into a camp of soldiers," the author speculated, "then thumb her nose at them and be jerked safely into the air and whisked away on the wings of a virtuous morning." Even more, the author warned that men's unsatisfied sexual urges could result in "domestic tragedies" for "young girls in towns adjacent to Army camps" and that their mothers should demand the War Department stop performances of women "who premeditatedly and literally display every mark of their sex."[23]

Camp Shows Vice President Lawrence Phillips responded by defending Sheridan's wardrobe choices as reasonable ways to provide men with reminders of women from home. He began by citing other newspaper articles that described Sheridan's wardrobe as "simple," "modestly-cut," and "conservative," and even enclosed photographs as evidence. More importantly, however, for men living under "the rigors of Army life and the stern necessity of war-time discipline," Phillips insisted, "a touch of femininity serves as a link between the realities of the present and the hopes of the future," not a dangerous awakening of their sexual desires.[24]

Even the simplest of tasks women performed served to contrast and counteract the effects of militarization. A Red Cross club manual directed women to conscientiously "try to get away from regular Army procedures that are trite to our men." While serving food, for example, the manual urged women to "serve in as attractive a manner as possible."[25] Food was not the real treat, women quickly learned. Marcia Ward Behr, who distributed coffee and sandwiches each morning to plane crews in Oro Bay, New Guinea, initially suspected the men only wanted the refreshments and feared that "women shouldn't have been in this man's world." Gradually, though, she learned that the Army "did not serve chow daintily" and that "a woman's touch" made even the most ordinary of dishes something special. "A young Red Cross woman would seem to be dishing out strawberry shortcake for dessert instead of canned peaches," she reasoned. Even in her military-style "khakis and G.I. shoes," Behr understood that she "symbolized a rare dish in that rough setting."[26]

This kind of symbolic work was not easy for women who needed to provide the proper balance of friendly banter and impersonal service at just the right moments. One Clubmobile worker in Italy explained that serving infantry troops fresh from battle proved most difficult. Although these men expressed "the greatest demand for doughnuts and for extra supplies, for entertainment and for someone to talk to," if the troops had lost many men, they were "apt to be preoccupied, depressed, surely, and it is a very delicate balance that you must achieve here." If the women were too cheery in their conversations, the men resented their seemingly uncaring attitude. Yet, if the women were too sympathetic, the men "feel more sorry for themselves." By contrast, troops fresh from victory who had not suffered too many losses proved a much simpler audience. The men "will be on the crest of the wave," she explained, "and everything runs easily and smoothly."[27]

The Red Cross and the USO's efforts to counter militarization took on added significance for the military when dealing with pilots.[28] In these instances, the military expected women to ease the men's mental stress and to equip them for reentry into the civilian world by maintaining a semblance of domestic gender relations. At airbases in England, Brazil, Italy, and North Africa, Aero Clubs featured snack bars, libraries, game rooms, and "most important of all—at least two American girls." The Red Cross intended its clubs to provide a cozy "home away from home" where "tired and tense" men could rest, relax, and, as Red Cross worker Helen Page remarked, "return to their normal selves."[29] Women symbolized comfort and safety for the pilots, a Red Cross woman at a US airbase near Natal, Brazil, explained, and helped the men feel connected to home. Pilots anticipating their first missions wanted "to have a last link with America," while those returning from extended tours "want a touch of the US again, by talking with an American girl."[30]

Military commanders attributed tactical significance to the women's calming presence and found that if women greeted pilots immediately upon their return from missions, the men were "more relaxed for interrogation and consequently have given fuller and more valuable reports." Army officers at one base in Libya believed the Red Cross women so vital that they insisted the women meet every returning mission. It was not the coffee and doughnuts that helped the men relax, one officer candidly noted, but the girls who served them.[31] As one Red Cross worker explained it, Red Cross women "helped give him back his sense of security."[32] Pilots agreed and even indicated that they liked to have the same woman meet them when they returned from missions "so they could feel they were returning to a

girl they knew." Women worked hard to develop a sense of camaraderie with the pilots by wearing perfume and makeup or presenting
them with gifts after they had completed their fiftieth mission.[33] Pilots were unwilling to sacrifice these relationships. Elizabeth Williams and her coworkers served coffee to pilots returning to base in
Manduria, Italy, in early 1945. When rumors circulated that the military planned to provide pilots with a stiff drink to ease their nerves
instead of sending women to the runways, the men protested. They
explained to commanders that they appreciated seeing the Red Cross
symbol on top of the Clubmobile as they approached the base,
because they knew that it meant the women were waiting. "There's
no way," one pilot assured Williams, "we're going to let them trade
you for an ounce of whiskey."[34]

The military also asked the Red Cross to assist in operating rest
homes, retreat-like places where aviators could recuperate after a given
number of combat missions or upon a physician's order that they be
temporarily relieved from flying. For seven to fourteen days, they con-
valesced in "an atmosphere of home life" that included civilian
clothing, good food, recreation, and American women.[35] As one
news story about a rest home at Capri described, these were places
were men can be "humored and pampered just as 'Mom' or wife did
at home."[36] To create this homelike atmosphere, women donned
"the prettiest dresses they can find"—not their uniforms—and spent
their time "bicycling, playing tennis and going fishing" with the men
in an effort to "tone down the military atmosphere ... and add hospitality."[37] Some women even served cocoa at night because they believed it helped the men rest well.[38] The Red Cross designed these
activities to help the men ease back into normal social relations with
American women. Specifically, Red Cross Chairman Norman H.
Davis explained, women provided the men with an opportunity to
"tell their story," to talk about their concerns with a sympathetic
woman. This environment, he concluded, was better for the men than
sending them to psychiatrists.[39] According to a postwar military report, the personal attention provided by the Red Cross hostesses was
"a material factor in the success of the program."[40] Lucille Brown,
who worked at a rest home in Tunisia, explained that the men in rest
homes took a bit of time to regain their confidence in interacting

with women but that "parties with women" allowed the men to "try himself out" with an American woman.[41]

While the military and Red Cross deemed women's work with pilots to be essential both for their effectiveness and their mental health, the work exhausted the women emotionally. Williams might have felt appreciated when the pilots insisted they wanted women to greet them after missions, but she quickly learned that she could not be as attached to the men as they were to her. Initially, she learned each pilot's name and inquired about him after his missions. When she began receiving reports that pilots had been killed, she decided to stop learning their names as a way to protect herself from the loss.[42] Williams was not the only woman who learned this hard lesson. One Red Cross official described the work at aero clubs as "a terrible emotional strain" on women who were tasked with maintaining soldiers' spirits even as they endured their own emotional turmoil.[43] After one woman experienced a breakdown, a Red Cross regional club supervisor warned that the organization needed to "take particular care of girls operating under trying conditions, particularly those associating with flyers." The women's physical labor was demanding, he noted, and the mental strain of forming friendships with pilots who did not return from missions exacted a high cost. Given the nature of their work, he recommended that the women take periodic leaves.[44]

## AMERICAN WOMEN IN FARAWAY OUTPOSTS

A break from military life also proved particularly important in remote and non-Western theaters, where contemporary notions of sexuality, race, and nation complicated women's symbolic representation of home, domesticity, and femininity. Military officials in these theaters attached much greater significance to American women than did their counterparts in theaters where (white) soldiers could meet and even marry local women, often through hospitality programs organized by local families. In non-Western theaters, by contrast, the military frequently restricted soldiers from socializing with native, non-white women, and erected numerous obstacles to marriages.[45] Such differences in policy help to explain the military's sense of urgency about women in these theaters. In 1942, for example, US Army Special Services Director General Frederick Osborne requested that the USO

USO performers high kick for attentive sailors on a beach in Guam. Military leaders deemed American women especially important in non-Western theaters, where they feared men would devolve into uncivilized and unwholesome behaviors without reminders of "good girls" from home.

send women to remote stations such as Alaska, instead of to England, where the men enjoyed more opportunities for recreation. "We have all fallen down in getting attractive women to Alaska," he complained. And, "now that winter is coming on," when the men would have even fewer recreational opportunities, "the need is terribly and increasingly acute."[46] Officials at other remote posts similarly complained that there were never enough USO shows, which they needed to keep their men from "bush alcohol and whores."[47] Like women working with pilots, women assigned to non-Western theaters labored in a heightened sexual climate, as military policies limited men's interactions with local women but dangled American women before them as appealing but off-limits reminders of all they missed.

To provide GIs with wholesome diversions from tempting foreign women, the USO and Red Cross both selected distinctly "American" women. Clubs in all theaters relied on local women workers to help prepare the food, clean the facilities, and perform a variety of essential tasks so that American women were free to interact with soldiers.[48] The organization intentionally refused to employ foreign women as the centerpiece of recreation programs, even though the policy occasionally meant that clubs were short-staffed. In early 1942, for example, the Red Cross refused the offer of the British Women's Voluntary Service to help staff clubs. Even at the cost of delaying its work, the Red Cross preferred to wait until it could train and transport American women.[49] As one Clubmobile official later explained about work in the China-Burma-India theater, personnel provided a reminder of "the American way of life which our American boys have been accustomed to."[50]

More than just being American, recreation women needed to embody a particular kind of middle-American wholesomeness that distinguished them from foreign women, and even white British women. Clubmobile programs, for example, sometimes used one English woman on the staff of three women because of personnel shortages. But, according to Red Cross officials, though these women performed their tasks satisfactorily, they could never remind the men of women from home. One official in Britain noted that "the soldiers do not hesitate to express a preference for the American girl."[51] A report from the China-Burma-India theater similarly clarified, "soldiers were interested in talking to their own kind." The Red Cross had employed a British woman to assist on the Clubmobile runs, but the report specified that the soldiers "wanted that type of an individual who would understand their language, be sympathetic to their problems and flash those smiles that they were so familiar with and which they had not seen for many many months."[52] Indeed, Red Cross recruiters sought out women who would seem familiar to GIs, who would be "easily recognized as Americans" and "be considered by service men as typically American."[53] Although the organization never specified the exact characteristics that identified women as appropriately American, it did note that unless a foreign language was required for the job, applicants should not have a "foreign language accent, nor any other un-American characteristics."[54]

The Red Cross and the USO insisted that GIs preferred white, demure American girls to exotic, sexualized native women, even if the reality of the situation was much more complicated. Despite the organizations' best attempts to hire American women, there were never enough women from home to staff the very popular dances held in Red Cross and USO clubs in all theaters. Thus, on occasion, the organizations invited local Allied women to serve as additional dance partners and symbols of the local population's appreciation of the American forces. The women were always carefully selected and supervised, and, though there were cases that might have challenged home-front racial customs, for the most part the women upheld white America's standards for racially appropriate partners for GIs. Dance partners for white GIs would have been considered racially white by most Americans, while local women brought to dances for African American soldiers would have been considered racially black.

In England, as well as in British colonies and parts of the Commonwealth, military and Red Cross officials enforced few restrictions on local white women who attended dances. Soon after the Red Cross began work in Britain, for example, the Washington Club in London held two to three dances per week, staffed "with the pick of nice girls chosen from the women's British service units." Although "matronly American ladies living in London sit around the sidelines for the sake of propriety," the Red Cross demonstrated little concern about strict supervision. "No wet-blanket chaperoning system is in force," a New York Times article confirmed.[55] Almost a year later, the Red Cross continued to rely on British women to fill the dance floors but relaxed its vetting process. To that point, dance volunteers had to submit recommendations and a photograph. The application process and three-week waiting period annoyed applicants and proved cumbersome for Red Cross staff who screened them for their "poise, affability and general attractiveness." In its place, the organization implemented a more efficient interview system, in which one staff member screened potential partners, sometimes even on the day of the dance.[56]

British women served as suitable dance partners in other areas of the Commonwealth as well. In Australia, a committee approved local white women for dances and parties at white Red Cross clubs, while a few Red Cross women spent considerable amounts of time seeking out and screening the daughters of British tea planters in India.[57] The Army provided transportation for the women, and on at least one occasion, a US Army Engineers' band provided jazz tunes that made the "Tea Planters' wives and daughters do the jitters." Most dances were British tea dances, held at Red Cross clubs or private Planters' clubs, and had a "professional air with jazz bands and pretty ladies in formal gowns."[58]

In other locations, American attitudes about interracial coupling determined which local women were deemed acceptable. At Red Cross clubs in Brazil, for example, the organization promised that GIs associated with the right kind of women by using only "carefully selected" and "the more desirable local girls" who had been recommended by the Brazilian Red Cross.[59] Local custom also demanded that the Red Cross "do a careful job of chaperoning" the women, but after GIs complained about the women bringing their entire families to dances, the Red Cross began inviting only mothers and daughters.[60] Conversely, in the West Indies, Canal Zone, St. Thomas, and Jamaica, officials explained that because the local women were "almost entirely Negro, there is no opportunity for normal and healthy feminine society."[61] Officials in New Caledonia, a French colony in the Pacific that hosted several Allied bases, also exported racial segregation to dances held at clubs on the island. While clubs permitted French women to dance with white soldiers, native Kanakas were brought in for dances with African American GIs.[62] The indigenous women were certainly not African American like her, club worker Jean M. Bright observed, but military and civilian officials considered them "black" and thus suitable dance partners for the men.[63] North African women were similarly off-limits for white GIs. One club in the theater scheduled several dances per week but found it difficult to staff them. "There were plenty of doubtful characters available," a Red Cross woman explained, "but few proper European girls."[64]

It was not always possible to find local women who neatly fit American binary views of race. Hundreds of thousands of soldiers and sailors were assigned to, or passed through, Hawaii during the war, and they competed for the attentions of a proportionately tiny number of women while there. Reflective of the racial diversity of Hawaii and the small number of white women, USO clubs on the islands enlisted the dancing services of local women from a wide range of Asian and European backgrounds. The women were carefully screened to ensure their respectability and inspired some men to expand their opinions about dating (if not marrying) women from backgrounds different than their own.[65] However much GIs might have enjoyed the company of local women, the Red Cross and USO presented a more familiar and comfortable image to the American public. In one press release, the USO declared that GIs in Hawaii were "bored with hula-hula costumes," but instead cheered "American girls daintily clad in checked pinafores with white blouses," à la Judy Garland in the 1939 film *The Wizard of Oz*.[66] Undoubtedly these assertions were at least partly designed to reassure a worried public that their boys remained loyal to the girls they had left behind. They also reflect *Time* magazine's finding that soldiers preferred wholesome images of white women to overtly sexualized images of exotic women. As the magazine described it, the men preferred the "peach-cheeked, pearl blonde" Betty Grable to other pinups such as the dark-haired, vaguely ethnic Rita Hayworth "in direct ratio to their remoteness from civilization."[67]

Although military and civilian officials insisted that they needed American women in remote locations, they worried that rough living conditions and desperate GIs would endanger the women and initially resisted assigning them to the posts. Several military officials, who were responsible for the safety of women assigned to their commands, expressed "real doubts" about sending women to forward areas where they feared the women would be more of a "liability" than an "asset."[68] Others worried that sending women to work in remote locations along the Ledo Road, for example, placed "undue strain" on women who would have to live and work "where there were no other women at all."[69] One Red Cross administrator in the Pacific warned that it was "unthinkable a few women should be . . . surrounded by thousands of men."[70] Officials in Europe and North Africa expressed similar concerns about the women's safety only when Clubmobile women were sent close to the front lines and even then, were reluctant to assign a soldier for protection because the men thought that guards reflected poorly on their "chivalry."[71]

Ultimately, these cautious men decided that the benefits of having women in remote theaters outweighed the risks. They remained concerned, nonetheless, not about the dangers of war but about American GIs, the "thousands of womenless men in the jungles" whom the women were sent to serve.[72] Officials feared that American men in all theaters would resort to rape to satisfy their sexual desires, but they expressed particular fears about those in remote stations. Moreover, Red Cross officials had devoted considerable effort to crafting the public image of the women who operated its clubs and canteens and sending them to work in coarse, homosocial environments raised a few eyebrows. As one Red Cross field director stationed on an isolated Pacific island described, men on the post had adjusted to living "in a man's world" and relished in the "freedom from conventions imposed upon them by a society in which women participated."[73] More specifically, one general described, men in such locations "run around almost nude and swim without costumes of any kind."[74] Even some otherwise adventuresome Red Cross women were turned off by the prospect of being surrounded by so many men. Before she was assigned to New Guinea, Marcia Ward Behr confessed her doubts that "a handful of girls up there amongst millions of men" could "hardly scratch the surface" in such an "abnormal place."[75]

Much of this concern derived from fears that the men's isolation from normal, heterosexual relationships would dispose them to sexual violence. The Red Cross described assignments in these theaters as "hazardous" because of the "lonely young men" who competed for the attention of so few women.[76] Even military commanders at times felt powerless to control the men. When Irma C. Bradford Bantjes and her fellow Red Cross workers arrived in the Philippines, a brigadier general escorted them to their club. Before they got in a jeep to drive across the island, he gave them all jackets and told them to tuck their hair under hats. Bantjes was initially a bit confused, but as they passed several groups of naked men walking to a swimming hole, she began to understand. The general confessed that there were 165,000 men on the island "and that he could just not be responsible if they realized there were women there."[77] There were, of course, women in the Philippines before the Red Cross women's arrival. What the general meant was

USO women on Guam in 1945 had to be billeted behind barbed wire and armed guard to protect them from the GIs on the island. Military commanders feared for American women's safety when they visited, but believed the risk necessary.

that he couldn't protect *American* women from his troops. The introduction of American women presented a new set of problems for commanders charged with their protection in what many considered an uncivilized and barbaric environment devoid of proper women.[78]

Fears about the women's safety grew so dire that in several locations in the Pacific women lived in tents surrounded by steel or wire fences and were under constant guard "to protect them from the men in the vicinity."[79] Women were required to be in their quarters by 11:00 p.m., not to travel unless with another woman and two armed officer or military police escorts, never to attend unapproved social functions, and not to stop between destinations while traveling.[80] Commanders in other locations enacted additional rules to fit local circumstances. In Guam, women were restricted to a 10:00 p.m. curfew and to travel during daylight hours, while women in Brisbane, Australia were warned that because of "various camps in the vicinity . . . it is unwise for women to go out unescorted" and that they could only leave the post unescorted if traveling by bus or private transportation.[81] An officer at Hazel Bowman's post in India ordered perhaps the most unusual directive when he told the women that if they traveled beyond their post, they were to arm themselves with hat pins, even though "there are Army and Marine guards everywhere."[82]

Women responded differently to these restrictions. "Romance with a gun in a holster dividing you was not most conducive to successful love life," joked Mary Ferebee Howard, "but as always, love found a way." Stationed on Guadalcanal where the women had to sign in and out of their living quarters, she noted that if the women really wanted to go out, rules "could be broken and no one was the wiser."[83] By contrast, Jacqueline Haring, who worked at a Red Cross club in New Guinea, described her wire-surrounded living quarters as a "prison camp." In a letter to her mother, she noted that military officials were "very strict here about the protection of women," and that the presence of military police was "really very reassuring." Perhaps knowing that her mother would likely find little comfort in the security, she assured her that though "unfortunate things" had happened, they had not occurred at her particular station.[84]

Despite well-intentioned restrictions and security, women in remote theaters frequently felt uneasy about GIs and sometimes faced harrowing experiences. Janet MacCubbin spent her war on the Hawaiian islands and could never quite decide how she felt about the Marines and soldiers. She insisted that she "never was afraid of the soldiers really," though she pointed out that a guard was stationed outside the women's living quarters. After the war, when asked to transfer to a club in Okinawa, her unease about the men led her to decline. Sending a few women to a camp of 50,000 men "creates problems," she explained.[85] Her fears were not unfounded. At the Naval Operating Base on Buckner Bay, Okinawa, a prowler tried to break into the women's billet before being deterred by a guard, while halfway around the world in Capri and North Africa, Margaret Chase could barely sleep at night because of the men banging on her bedroom door.[86] Even the military police were overwhelmed by crowds of men at a Red Cross dance in New Guinea. After forcing the men out of the dance hall, the police directed them to their barracks and then stood with bayonets drawn "waiting for the crowd to attempt to break down the fence that protected [the women] so scantily from all these hordes of men."[87] Threatening behavior continued even on the voyage home. While sailing across the Pacific, a ship captain moved a dozen women from a room on the lower deck to a high, open gun turret guarded by an armed soldier to "protect" them. Although most of the soldiers treated the women well, some felt the women unjustly took space on the ship from soldiers awaiting transport, while other men were "delirious from the successful end of the war" and "wanted to celebrate—especially with women."[88]

Some women even compared their fear of GIs to their fear of enemy soldiers. During alerts at the Chakulia Air Base in Bengali, India, Katherine Harris van Hogendorp took shelter in a trench. "The daytime alerts weren't as scary as the night ones," she explained, because she could see the men in the trench with her. Still, "when I was the only female in the trench," she noted, she "wondered who were more frightening—the Japs or the GIs."[89] At a club not far away, Libby Chitwood Appel acquired a Colt .45 for protection when the Japanese began pushing toward the Burma-India border. Although she never had to use the pistol for protection against an enemy soldier, it did prove useful one evening when a hitchhiking GI she had picked up became "unruly." The drunk and aggressive soldier asked her to stop the jeep so they could "pitch a little woo." Frightened, Appel thought about the gun she was carrying but was relieved to see another soldier whom she picked up in a successful attempt to defuse the situation.[90]

Despite these concerns and dangerous experiences—and in many ways *because* of them—the Red Cross and the military ultimately agreed that women were essential in remote locations. While admitting that the Red Cross had to take precautions to minimize the dangers of assigning women to forward locations, Vice Chairman Richard F. Allen argued that "the advantages of having women in these outposts far outweighed the disadvantages."[91] Army Air Force General Howard C. Davidson went so far as to suggest that even if women were killed in the course of their work, they were "expendable just as were the men and that the sacrifices were warranted."[92]

Davidson and many others came to such a harsh pragmatic conclusion because they believed that women "are exceedingly important to the war in maintaining the morale of the men."[93] Some commanders even insisted that the men "deserve" women and complained that more women were needed.[94] "Our boys have been overseas for 18 months," a Red Cross field director reported, "and even the sight of an American girl makes them go ga-ga."[95] In part, officials believed that women imparted a sense of normality to the otherwise entirely male domain and elicited more acceptable behavior. As Davidson explained in regard to the situation in Burma, "the presence of women in these far-away outposts made the difference for the servicemen between savagery and civilization."[96] He saw similar effects on men in the Southwest Pacific. Before the Red Cross women arrived, the men's morale had "reached a very low ebb which was virtually in a savage state." The men kept themselves "presentable" after the women arrived, however.[97] "The right sort" of "well-behaved" American women reminded the men, he explained, that "there were millions of such women back home."[98] Women reestablished some measure of domestic gender relations in isolated theaters, officials believed, while boosting the men's heterosexual desires. The women were, of course, off-limits to the GIs, and many military officials expressed concern that sex-deprived men would resort to rape. And yet, even concerns about sexual dangers could not dissuade the military from sending the women. The alternative was simply unacceptable.

## SEGREGATING AMUSEMENTS

While military and civilian officials enlisted women to help abate the war's deleterious effects on soldiers, they did so in ways that expanded Jim Crow's reach into Americans' war experiences. Both the Red Cross and USO professed integrationist ideals for their clubs and entertainment programs, but neither stood by its idealism. At the same time, neither the Red Cross nor the USO accepted the blame for its segregation but instead attributed it to military officials, soldiers, or the American public at large.[99] There was certainly enough blame to go around, and, like the larger history of racial segregation in the United States, the practice of segregation in military entertainment stemmed from whites' fears of the racial mixing of black men and white women. Still, the National Association for the Advancement of

Colored People (NAACP) and the African American women who entertained GIs in World War II upheld their work as the respectable, patriotic service of citizens and linked their personal experiences to a larger, organized struggle for freedom and civil rights.[100]

In 1942, the Red Cross adopted a policy it described as integrationist in which its clubs would be open to all soldiers, but those serving a predominately African American population would be designed specifically for those patrons.[101] This contradictory policy allowed administrators to assign staff by race, as in the China-Burma-India theater when one official requested two units of African American Clubmobile women because, he argued, the black men preferred "the cute little girl who can talk their language and who is apt in the 'jitterbug' as are they themselves."[102] In some locations, GIs preferred to attend clubs staffed by members of their race, while in others military commanders segregated clubs by deeming particular clubs out of bounds for white or black soldiers. In such situations, the Red Cross acquiesced to segregation for fear of running afoul of military officials upon whose cooperation they depended.[103] Other practices, such as locating clubs serving a predominantly black soldier population in red light districts or naming clubs after African American leaders such as Booker T. Washington or George Washington Carver also effectively segregated clubs.[104] Despite concentrated efforts to recruit more workers, these practices and the Red Cross's troubled record on racial discrimination hampered its efforts to recruit overseas workers.[105] Although the organization insisted that its clubs were integrated and that all staff were of "equal standing," as one official candidly noted, the phrase "Negro Staffed" was a "polite circumlocution which deceives nobody."[106]

The USO similarly expressed ideals of racial equality and tolerance but practiced little in the way of either. Dependent on public funding, it ceded to local custom regarding segregation in domestic clubs and shows and to military preference overseas.[107] Camp Shows also excluded African American performers, hiring only an occasional black performer to play the stereotypical role of a maid or butler, until it faced protests from the Negro Actors' Guild. Even after the formation of the Negro Entertainment Division, the organization deployed no black shows overseas until June 1943, and it staged minstrel shows throughout the war.[108]

In spite of the Red Cross and the USO's general practice of segregation, entertainment work facilitated some white women's first interracial experiences, and while some of them embraced new relationships, others allowed their prejudices to impede their work with African American GIs. While training for overseas work at Camp Patrick Henry, Mary Metcalfe Rexford was "kept hopping" at nightly dances where, for the first time, she "danced with men of different races, religions, and colors."[109] Stationed in Lae, New Guinea, Jean Holdridge Reeves was similarly inexperienced in interracial social interactions and concluded that working with the black GIs at her club was one of few positive consequences of the war.[110] Others were less open-minded. When Angela Petesch's Clubmobile unit visited two "colored camps" for Christmas, she deplored the fact that the officers had done nothing to bring holiday cheer to the men. Her sympathy, however, did not outweigh her discomfort as she and the other women tried to entertain them. "Because it was a colored camp," she explained, "everybody was more than a little self-conscious. It was most painful." She and the other women had a better time at a different camp where she was fascinated by the unit's "good hot negro band," former Cotton Club dancer, and spirituals singing, but racial differences clouded her perception of the men. In the dimly lit room, she observed, the men's "dark skins and their khaki uniforms made them look the same color all over."[111]

Other women had good intentions but stumbled a bit as they worked toward integration. Alma Geist Cap and her coworker, Mary, decided that they would serve both white and black soldiers at their club in the Philippines. On the first day the black GIs came to the club, however, the women played a record by Stephen Foster, noted composer of many famous American minstrel songs. The two oblivious women were confused when the GIs walked out of the club in protest but apologized for their offensive musical choice after they learned its significance. Still, their attempt at integration failed when white soldiers refused to attend the club if black GIs were present. Thereafter, the races attended the club on alternate days.[112]

The crux of the issue for Red Cross, USO, and military officials was their fear that integrated clubs and entertainment would facilitate interracial attraction and coupling between white women and black men and that such contact would offend white GIs.[113] Even the hint of interracial romance proved too inflammatory, and the War Department censored photographs of black soldiers and white women dancing or mixing socially.[114] Controversies over interracial coupling began almost immediately in England, where many white British women attended dances at clubs run primarily for black GIs. The women's apparent colorblindness disturbed Red Cross Chairman Norman H. Davis, who reported that there had been "too many mulatto babies" and that his "conscience is not clear on that." He considered stopping dances at the clubs as a way to prevent interracial mingling but knew that he could not end dances only for black soldiers.[115]

The problem of interracial attraction was not only a wartime matter, as Davis's remarks suggested. As Red Cross women and soldiers understood, wartime habits had the potential to spark postwar changes. Rosemary Norwalk wondered how black soldiers dated across the race line "without provoking a riot," while Angela Petesch envisioned that interracial coupling would lead to "further trouble when they get home."[116] White soldiers were outraged, according to military opinion surveys. One private first class with the 3267th Ordnance Depot Company complained that "the niggers here seem to be getting their share of English gals which results in a lot of fights and killings."[117] Another white soldier forecast that "we'll have another war with them when we get back home. They will probably try the same thing back home."[118] A captain in the 103rd Replacement Battalion warned that "every man in Ga. is going to have to carry a gun to protect the women."[119]

Given the ferocity of white resistance, military and civilian officials went to great lengths to keep wartime entertainment from facilitating interracial romance, and the efforts began at the top. General Dwight D. Eisenhower and other military authorities proposed sending African American women soldiers to run clubs and provide companionship for black GIs, a prospect that horrified Women's Army Corps leaders and African Americans at a time when many Americans suspected female soldiers had been enlisted merely to satisfy soldiers' sexual needs.[120] Although Eisenhower's proposal was not enacted, in 1945 the USO deployed the integrated all-women's band, the International Sweethearts of Rhythm, to distract black soldiers from local German women.[121]

Red Cross administrators got creative in personnel assignments and policies to head off the possibility of interracial attraction. Officials at an integrated club in Algiers prohibited white and black soldiers from dancing at the same time with white partners, while others in Rome and the Pacific only permitted dances sponsored by individual units, which, of course, were segregated.[122] In similar fashion, "Dixie tradition won a smashing victory," headlined the *Chicago Defender*, when the military ordered the segregation of a swimming pool in India after learning that white women in the area would be swimming there.[123] Here and elsewhere, the men had socialized freely on an integrated basis, but the prospect of competition for white women's attention resulted in forced segregation.[124]

The reassignment of women at two clubs on the Ledo Road reveals how carefully the organization managed interracial contacts. At the remote Burma Basha club in Burma, white women served a majority black soldier population and, according to a Red Cross official in the area, had "a very difficult time." After describing the club as having a feeling of "overwhelming brownness," she lamented that "white girls in these installations are frequently propositioned by colored men." The "level headed girls" had handled the propositions, she said, but warned that the organization should not assign white women to stations "where they have to undergo this experience."[125] Conversely, the Margherita club in Assam was staffed entirely by African American personnel, served both white and black soldiers, and was hailed by the *Chicago Defender* as a club "where democracy really works."[126] Despite this demonstrated success, the Red Cross transferred the club's black staff to replace the white workers at the Burma Basha club, then announced that the Margherita club was changing to a "white club" because of a shift in Army personnel in the area.[127] Reflective of a long history of sex across the color line, mingling between white men and black women at the Margherita club had not been problematic

Red Cross women Jeannette C. Dorsey and Willie Lee Johnson provide good-natured amusement for GIs in Assam, India. In the face of segregation in Red Cross clubs and the military, African American women embraced the work as their contribution for a Double Victory over the enemy abroad and racism at home.

enough to warrant a response from the Red Cross, but even the hint of black men coupling with white women at the Burma Basha club resulted in swift action.

In this wartime context of intensified focus on interracial coupling, with recreation and entertainment work already treading so carefully a line between wholesome comradeship and tempting sensual appeal, and in an era when most white Americans believed African Americans to be inherently and even dangerously sexual, black women found their work in wartime clubs and entertainment venues to be especially precarious.[128] The women, the black press, and the NAACP countered this predicament by casting women's service as the patriotic, respectable support of black womanhood. Their discussions of women's work sought to create a wholesome image of African American women doing their bit for the war effort by minimizing discussions of sexuality and by portraying the men who fawned over them as innocent boys longing only for home.

Unlike coverage of white entertainment women, articles that appeared in black newspapers devoted very little attention to the women's attractive qualities and attempted to dismiss any hint of romantic appeal in their work. Entertainment women became, as women did on the cover of the NAACP's *Crisis,* symbols of patriotic, middle-class feminine respectability. The women might have been pretty and were most often light-skinned, but they were not cast as sex objects.[129] An October 1943 *Chicago Defender* article about a club in Australia, for example, reported that the women's positive influence on the men was not "a tribute to their personal charm or pulchritude" but merely the effect of their Americanness. Some Australian "colored women" worked in the clubs who had "all the beauty, and personal charm a man could desire," but the men wanted American women. Indeed, before a Red Cross opened in their area some men stationed in New Guinea had not seen an African American woman in two years, and according to women at the club, "just stand and look at us as if we're rare animals in some zoo." One of the women, Clara Wells, had even received "several hundred proposals," including one from a man who left her an envelope containing more than $3,000 and a note promising her the money if she would marry him. Even amid these intense circumstances, the article noted, the women "are familiar enough with life to realize that they are merely symbols of loved ones at home."[130]

Other articles similarly affirmed both the women's level-headedness and the men's wholesome desires for a connection to home. An article about Hazel Dixon Payne, the first African American woman sent to work with soldiers building the Alcan Highway from British Columbia, Canada, to Fairbanks, Alaska, explained that women played a significant role in motivating soldiers. "We feel as if this war is really worth fighting for now that you have come to us," the men told her. They hung pictures of women on the club's walls, and Payne asked her friends to send photographs to add to their collection. "The folk back home should have seen them stand for hours at a time, staring at the pictures," she noted, even as she minimized any sexual suggestion. The men's "eyes would brighten up with glee" each time she entered the room, she reported, but they "seemed very much like children" and even asked her to read books to them.[131] In a very different climate in New Guinea, "five-foot, 103-pound Leila T. Gardner" "performs miracles in morale building," the *Chicago Defender* boasted. Although the only woman assigned to her area, her positive effect on the men was widespread. Even "a hundredweight of femininity, like a pinch of yeast to a batch of dough, can be leaven for a regiment," the article explained. Only once, she reported, had "a soldier made an indecent proposal to her," but his buddies quickly chastised the offending GI and made him apologize.[132]

While lauding the efforts of the women workers, the black press criticized the Red Cross and USO for their failures to provide adequate recreation for black soldiers doing their part for victory. A *Pittsburgh Courier* article complained that black soldiers in the Pacific had to rely on their memories of pretty girls because the USO failed to send black women entertainers.[133] Other articles confirmed that entertainment programs were understaffed.[134] The only black woman assigned to the Club Paradise in Oro Bay, Kitty Cox was, in the estimation of a *Chicago Defender* reporter, the "hardest working Red Cross girl in New Guinea." But while the reporter praised her determination and fortitude, he explained that Cox was overworked trying to attend to the needs of more than 10,000 men. She was lonesome and derived no satisfaction from being the "sweetheart of thousands of men," knowing that her popularity was simply a result of being "the only woman around." Like other women featured in the black press, Cox was a model of level-headedness amidst all of the attention and knew she was "just the symbol of all the sweethearts and wives the men have left behind."[135]

Despite the challenges black Red Cross and USO women faced in understaffed, segregated clubs and in segregated entertainment tours, they viewed their service as part of African Americans' fight for a Double Victory. While the NAACP likened Jim Crow entertainment to "a Hitlerian . . . way of life" and an affront on the ideals African Americans were fighting for in the war, women's battles with segregation were often more personal and less public.[136] Former Chicago school teacher Geraldine F. Smith had joined the Red Cross "to do something to help colored boys overseas," but was so angered when the Red Cross ordered the swimming pool in India segregated that she resigned in protest.[137] Other women held out a bit of hope that their wartime service would reap rewards and, like Payne, were "grateful . . . for the chance to serve my country and the American Red Cross." Serving in the war, she noted, made her "believe that this democracy is worth fighting for."[138]

## LASTING MEANINGS

Although wartime service did not immediately bring the returns African American women had hoped for, it did prompt all women entertainers to consider themselves as crucial parts of the larger war effort and as symbols of women's expanding place in the nation. When assessing the immediate and lasting significances of their work, Red Cross and USO women emphasized their hard work and professionalism. They welcomed the opportunities for challenging work, new experiences, advancement, and recognition. Their wartime work changed them in many ways by expanding their horizons, introducing them to new people and experiences, and separating them from others who had not shared in their war.

Many women's daily work proved physically and emotionally demanding. Traveling to procure supplies, coordinating activities with military officials, and maintaining a rigorous club or performance schedule was difficult, even in the best of circumstances; the women's regular tasks of organizing recreation programs, tending to the needs of nervous GIs, preparing food and drinks, and putting on a cheery smile at all times proved strenuous. Women stationed in remote theaters faced even more challenges as they seldom received the supplies they needed and lived in more meager circumstances than did their counterparts in more established and secure locations.

Whether they were in England, North Africa, France, or Germany, Clubmobile women worked a physically demanding schedule as they prepared large amounts of coffee and doughnuts, drove daily to remote and forward locations, maintained the Clubmobiles' engines, changed large tires and oil, and performed general maintenance. Such tasks were not commonly performed by women at the time, and the women boasted about having mastered these unfeminine tasks, symbols for them that they had adapted to a life similar to that of soldiers.[139] "If anyone has a notion that this job is glamorous, their minds should be changed for them," Angela Petesch insisted. The women "get dirty, messy and tired" and they constantly "smell of donuts," she described.[140] Their "battledress" uniforms of slacks, boots, jackets, and helmets distinguished them from other Red Cross and USO women required to wear more traditionally feminine attire but made the women feel more connected and similar to GIs. Wearing the uniform "seems to make us one of them," Petesch felt. "We're really in the Army now."[141] Gretchen Schuyler agreed. "We look exactly like our soldiers," she reported, while assuring that she had "never in my life been more dirty, more tired," or "more happy."[142] She believed that this kind of rugged lifestyle partly attracted Clubmobile women to the work in the first place. "The Clubmobile gals are the least 'frilly' of them all," she surmised. When someone described the "Clubmobile type" as "a girl who back in the States could and did wear blue jeans whenever she could find an excuse to do so," Schuyler wholeheartedly agreed.[143]

However difficult or strenuous entertainment women found their work, they remained dedicated to their tasks and, simultaneously, to proving that their commitment to the war was as firm as that of soldiers. Red Cross women were not bound to serve any length of time but could resign their position and come home at will. Cognizant of this option, Hazel Bowman wrote her family that she missed them and admitted that she sometimes felt like returning home to Florida. Despite her homesickness, she reasoned that there were millions of similarly homesick soldiers who could not resign, and that because they were committed to the war, she should be as well.[144] That sense of camaraderie guided Rosemary Norwalk's thinking a couple of months after the war's end. She continued to feel her work was useful for the men and wrote in her journal that she could not request to be sent home until more GIs had gone before her.[145]

Although many women viewed their work as a wartime obligation, they thrived in the newfound independence it brought them. Even traveling cross-country from California to Washington, DC, for Red Cross training was a liberating experience for Rosemary Norwalk, who happily remarked in her journal that her journey was "a fresh start in every sense of the word."[146] Living in a foreign country proved even more transformative. Jane Weir Phillips Scott boasted to her parents about how much she had grown since coming to England. Although only a year earlier she "didn't even know how to catch a train by myself," Clubmobile work had introduced her to a range of new experiences and perspectives. In a letter home, she wrote that she wished her parents could see her "nonchalantly dashing around this country, catching cabs, working and riding trains by myself talking to Englishmen, Czech, Polish, French, New Zealanders, and all the rest, as though I'd done it all my life!" She also boasted that she had been selected to join a Clubmobile unit that would follow the Allied invasion of France. The assignment would prove more difficult and dangerous than the work she had been doing in England, but she welcomed the challenge. "We never dreamed we'd be so lucky as to be in the first group of Red Cross girls to go," she wrote.[147]

As Red Cross women advanced to supervisory positions, they embraced the challenges of their new roles as a symbol of women's increasing—and much deserved—power. Expanding small canteens to full-functioning clubs, supervising hired laborers, inspecting the kitchen, keeping the club's financial records, and ordering supplies amounted to a "big job" for Libby Chitwood Appel, but one she gladly accepted.[148] Gretchen Schuyler's promotion to Clubmobile convoy supervisor during the French invasion was a similarly proud moment. She initially managed twelve women, two soldiers, seven vehicles, and four trailers, a tally that soon increased to thirty-one people and eighteen vehicles. Schuyler had long aspired to work her way up to this kind of position, and though it had been "a hard uphill fight," she told her father, she was proud to "show you I was winning my own battle for recognition."[149] She felt torn, however, about the Red Cross's decision to assign a man as her supervisor. At times, she confessed that she was glad to have someone share the burden and to have a man ultimately be in charge of the convoy's operation, yet she also complained that "it sure is hard to have a man boss take over." Accustomed to planning the daily schedule on her own, Schuyler found it frustrating to work with a supervisor to whom she had to teach basic Clubmobile operation.[150] Willie C. Powe, who helped organize a recreation club at Milne Bay, New Guinea, was less ambiguous about her feelings on male supervisors. When the Red Cross planned to name a man the club's director, she and the other women objected. "We want to prove that girls can do at least as good a job as a man," she told the *Chicago Defender*. "I personally think we can do a better job. We've made a good start and we've got to keep going."[151]

Red Cross woman Jane Anne Jack exemplifies both the personal transformation and the new attitudes that many women developed because of their wartime work. A newlywed, Jack traveled to England with her husband in the spring of 1942 and volunteered for Red Cross work. Although the two managed to see each other as often as they could, Jack frequently felt torn between her desire to play the role of a conventional wife and her commitment to her work. She often pined for her husband but confessed in a March 1943 letter that her efforts to arrange for a visit were distracting her from her work. Even as she broached the topic of quitting, getting an office job, and having "a little home for you," she insisted that this selfish concern "is wrong." "You know I love you so much," she assured him before insisting that though many couples were going on with their lives normally, they were "the other kind" of people who put war demands above personal desires.[152] Still, even as Jack maintained that she and her husband needed to stay the course, she continued to reassure him that she often wished for a "less military job where I could be more of a comfort to you."[153] As the war continued, Jack became more resolute in her determination and less preoccupied with domestic life. In July 1944, she informed her husband that she had been selected to join a Clubmobile group that would follow the American troops into Europe. Her husband would remain in England, and she anticipated his displeasure. "Please be with me in this," she implored, "it's something I want to do."[154] Even after the two visited each other and Jack witnessed her husband's frustration firsthand, she was no less resolved. "I hate making you unhappy," she confessed, but "I would not be happy staying in England. . . . I have to do this."[155]

Intertwined with recreation women's sense of pride about their accomplishments and commitments was their insistence that the work they performed was both respectable and professional. In letters home and in newspaper articles they penned, women ardently endorsed recreation as vital to the war effort and defended themselves against public suspicion that they had volunteered for the war out of anything other than purely altruistic motives. Red Cross club worker Elizabeth Phenix Wiesner admitted that she initially felt superior to the Clubmobile "glamour girls" and wondered if they could not better be utilized in club work. After assisting the women on an outing, however, she witnessed the men's enthusiasm for the women and doughnuts firsthand. "It was not the doughnuts that mattered to the men, or the coffee," she wrote in an article for her hometown newspaper. Insisting that the men behaved themselves with the utmost respect, she explained that "it was partly the urge for companionship, for something far removed from foxholes and canned food, that made them pass along the line two or even four times."[156] Nathalie Fallon Chadwick tackled the matter of respectability even more forthrightly. After receiving a letter from home that hinted at the women's romantic entanglements with GIs, she furiously rebutted the accusation in her diary. "To tell the truth," she scoffed, "we are sick of the sight of men and as for sex, there just isn't any." Although she admitted that "there isn't a girl in our unit who hasn't fallen hard for some guy" and that enterprising women might manage a tryst, she insisted that the women's lack of privacy hampered most attempts.[157]

Life magazine's story about Clubmobile worker Margaret (Peggy) Maslin's marriage to a war correspondent in Holland prompted similar outrage from several women who felt the article unjustly portrayed them and their work. The article featured a two-page photograph collage of the groom's friends all wrapping their arms around the bride while kissing her squarely on the mouth. Captions indicated that the men were "deliberate" and "soulful," that one man "gets one for the army," and another "does a thorough GI job." The kissing "got monotonous," one caption allowed, "but Peggy went bravely on." The article explained that the men were merely making good on a "wedding guest's inalienable right to kiss the bride" and that "men at war seldom get a chance to indulge in these pleasant customs of home."[158] Fellow Red Cross women vehemently disagreed, not necessarily with the men kissing their colleague, but with the magazine's sole focus on that aspect of the wedding. When Angela Petesch's family sent her a copy of the story, she angrily responded that it was a "darn shame the editors didn't show a little better judgment." Instead of featuring one of the "many episodes of the event that would've been interesting," she complained that the magazine "made the whole thing look like a brawl and I think did Peggy a dirty trick."[159] Clubmobiler Gretchen Schulyer assessed the article in similar fashion. "It stank!" she complained, and poorly conveyed the work of the Red Cross "in a combat zone."[160]

USO performers felt this tension between appeal and professionalism on a personal level and frequently emphasized that they were not lewd entertainers but, instead, wholesome symbols of women from home. Louise Buckley, who performed on a USO tour in New Guinea, insisted that American GIs were a discriminating audience. "Don't try to fool a G.I. with a Hollywood face and very little talent," she warned. And, "above all, don't underestimate him by thinking all he wants is a leg show and dirty cracks." Soldiers disliked one unnamed Hollywood star, Buckley noted, because the star "thought drunkenness and bawdy humor" was what they wanted. Instead, the men wanted exactly the opposite. "Every woman back home wears a halo now," Buckley clarified, "and those who represent her had better keep theirs on too."[161] Ballet dancer Jeanne Devereaux Perkins agreed. Having studied with famous Russian dancers, performed for the king and queen of England, and toured with the future Rockettes before joining USO Camp-Shows, she insisted that she engaged in pure art and that the GIs understood her performances in that way. "An art is an art," she asserted; "it has nothing to do with sex."[162]

Despite USO women's insistence that their work was asexual, even some Red Cross women needed convincing that the entertainers' work was reputable. Elizabeth Williams, for example, felt that because Red Cross workers like herself had to have an education they were quite different from the "showgirls" the USO brought over for entertainment.[163] Hazel Bowman also judged USO performers harshly. Broadway and Hollywood actress Paulette Goddard drew an audience of 20,000 in Burma, but Bowman felt that the GIs thought of her as "cheap, sexy, and generally foul." Actress and model Eugenia Lincoln

"Jinx" Falkenburg garnered no better praise. She "looked pretty for the boys and threw out the sex appeal," Bowman rued, "but she can't do anything except display her tummy."[164] Clubmobile women were even suspicious of the wildly popular singer Dinah Shore, who toured Europe with the USO. When Shore arrived to perform near Campeaux, France, Eliza King and her coworkers were "prepared to resist her glamour," but after Shore "washed her clothes with us out on the lawn, rolled up her hair . . . and cooked eggs on a Clubmobile, we accepted her as just another American girl who was doing what she could to make war a little more bearable for American soldiers." Shore's embracing of the rugged living conditions convinced the Red Cross women of her genuine motives and even made the women wish that they "could sing, too, instead of just being able to make doughnuts."[165]

Sharing wartime hardship might have bridged differences between Red Cross and USO women, but experiencing the war firsthand erected a wall of separation between them and women at home. Many women looked forward to peace and to returning to friends and family, but they also feared a difficult transition to domestic life. "Speaking of coming home," Gretchen Schuyler admitted, "the very thought of it has me a bit worried." After receiving a flyer that "reminded us what is done in polite society, and what not to carry over from our Army training when we do return," she and the other women had a good laugh. Soon, though, Schuyler began to fret about how her wartime habits might seem very unusual for a woman at home. "I can just see myself," she worried, "spilling glasses of water at beautifully set-up dinner tables . . . reaching for the butter, or asking for the grease . . . crossing my legs as though still in trousers . . . barging into furniture . . . slipping on rugs and polished floors . . . throwing butts and ashes on the floor, or 'field-stripping' the cigarettes in polite society." Even more, she continued, she would have to get used to walking in regular shoes after spending so long in boots.[166] These fears materialized for Elma Ernst Fay, who returned home to a job with the Red Cross in Chicago. More comfortable with the freedom her Clubmobile work had allowed, she struggled to adapt to an indoor desk job and "found myself getting fannyitis." She would much have preferred to continue her wartime habit of wearing "battle slacks and jump boots, and prop[ping] my feet upon the desk."[167]

Adjusting to postwar living and working conditions proved difficult for many women in part because they felt so disconnected from people who had not served overseas. As the end of the war approached in the fall of 1944, Anne Ferguson Boy decided to prepare her family for how the war had altered her. Suspecting that "it is perhaps normal that one's ideas should change over here," she cautioned them about her new perspectives. Although she clarified that the women were "by no means comparable to the boys in the front line of the fighting," she did believe that she and her coworkers shared a unique wartime perspective with them.[168] Her connection with GIs proved so strong for Elizabeth Phenix Wiesner that she sent her civilian fiancé a "Dear John" letter explaining that his lack of military service had "created a gap in our relationship that would be difficult if not impossible to bridge after the war."[169] Enduring the harsh conditions of India similarly united soldiers and women in Hazel Bowman's mind. Her wartime experiences would "set me apart from most Americans for the rest of my life," she anticipated, and would help her to appreciate "the good things of life" more than those who remained at home.[170] Only those who had served in war, Gretchen Schuyler expected, such as her World War I veteran father, would truly comprehend her "feelings and attitudes about this bloody business." Like two war buddies, she hoped that "after it is all over" they could "sit out in your cabin and rehash it all while the old fire blazes peacefully on."[171] This sense of shared experience and perspective made it difficult for some women to connect to their former friends. Elizabeth Williams, for example, felt disconnected from the women she addressed at Red Cross clubs whom, she felt, were only interested in their babies and husbands, certainly not her very different wartime experiences.[172]

In the end, women derived great personal meaning from their wartime work and from the ways it provided them with unique experiences and perspectives. Mary Metcalfe Rexford knew that the specific tasks she performed, such as "driving a truck and doing heavy hauling," would not translate directly to her postwar work, but the pay she saved during the war did fund a course in shorthand and typing. Besides the practical benefits, though, she believed that "few women have had a more meaningful or gratifying wartime experience."[173] Future professor Margaret Greene concurred. After the war, she taught education at the University of North Carolina–Greensboro, work that she found deeply fulfilling. And yet, even in her thirty-three years of work in education, she was never able to replicate the satisfaction she felt as a Red Cross club worker.[174] Fellow recreation worker Jean Holdridge Reeves likewise enjoyed her time in Red Cross clubs and believed that women's increased work and responsibilities during the war paved the way for even broader changes in women's lives. Women of her generation had proven their capabilities, she argued; feminists of the 1960s simply demanded recognition for what women like her had done long before.[175]

Another generation of women would add to the list of capabilities Reeves and her colleagues began, and their work started almost immediately. Although the war ended in August 1945, demobilization took longer than Americans had anticipated, and the military called on recreation women to help ease soldiers' frustrations and occupy their free time. Almost simultaneously, political divisions formalized into a Cold War that revived national conscription and deployed military forces to faraway places. Once again, the military and civilian organizations turned to Red Cross and USO women to domesticate the military and to remind GIs of why they fought and of the life to which they would return.

# 4

≡

## Dancing for Democracy

ENTERTAINING CITIZEN-SOLDIERS
IN THE EARLY COLD WAR

Helen Stevenson Meyner was only fourteen years old when her mother and father left home to serve with the Red Cross during World War II. Her parents, Eleanor and William Stevenson, established Red Cross services first in England, then in North Africa and Italy. Meyner missed them terribly, "so much that no one will ever understand," she confided to her diary. Her parents wrote frequently and as they described the importance of their work, Meyner adopted a mature, stalwart attitude that carried her through the war. She came to see her lonesomeness, though "too heavy a burden for a girl of my years," as her personal contribution to the "war effort." She was, in fact, carrying on a family tradition. Meyner's mother had spent World War I waiting for her own parents to return from service in London, where her father served as the scientific attaché to the American embassy. Women's wartime service was nothing unusual in the Stevenson family. When the United States embarked on a war in Korea only a few years later, Helen continued the family tradition.[1]

In October 1950, Helen's father sent her a telegram about an opportunity with the Red Cross. The organization was planning to open its first service club for soldiers in South Korea, and he and Eleanor believed their daughter was up to the task. They knew well the opportunities and the challenges she would face. Drawing on his and Eleanor's wartime experiences, William wrote encitingly that she "would see a lot of the world, meet all sorts of people." And though he warned that she would encounter "assorted wolves" and that "some girls wouldn't be able to handle" the work, he was convinced that she would be grateful for the opportunity.[2] Only a few weeks later, after completing training for club work in Washington, DC, Meyner recorded her anticipation about her upcoming adventure in another wartime diary. Feeling "very mature" as she set off, she excitedly wrote that she was "off with new people to a strange, dangerous war-stricken country."[3]

Meyner arrived at Red Cross headquarters in Tokyo eager to continue on to Korea, but much to her dismay, the rapidly moving military front prevented the Red Cross from sending women to the war zone. Thus, she and a few other women waited for several months in Japan, organizing recreation programs for recovering GIs at the Fifth Station Hospital at Johnson Air Force base.[4] Helen felt bad for the patients who, once they had recovered, were sent back to the front, but believed that she and the men shared a camaraderie based on their service. "It comforts them to know that I am going to go also," she surmised.[5] When not on duty at the hospital, she attended dances hosted by the local Special Services club, where she danced with "countless numbers of G.I.'s" and "held many sweating paws in my right hand."[6] She enjoyed getting to know the men and honed her nascent skills in organizing recreation programs, but she longed to get to Korea where she felt she could really be useful.[7]

In mid-April 1951, she finally got her chance. Working at what was then the only Red Cross club in the country, Meyner had her work cut out for her. Because the club was located near Pusan, through which military personnel were processed, it was constantly full. Her first day on the job was a "slow day" she noted sardonically, "because we only had 4,566 men in the Club."[8] Although the work was exhausting and the living conditions rugged—she teased her parents that they had a "sissy war" compared to hers—she loved her job.[9] She especially loved Clubmobile runs to visit troops in the field. Like the Clubmobiles of World War II, hers was a converted military truck—though ironically, not an American one but a captured Soviet truck. American GIs had confiscated it in North Korea and brought it south to Pusan, where they equipped it with doughnut trays and installed a window on the side from which the women could serve war-weary troops eager for their company.[10] After visiting the First Marine Division, Meyner noted that the men had no other available recreation and "could hardly believe their eyes when they saw a white woman." The men took "a million pictures of me and made such a fuss over me that you might have thought I was Lana Turner."[11]

While many elements of Meyner's experiences with the Red Cross echoed those of the women who had preceded her, her work was colored by the early Cold War and Korean War eras. Meyner's war was, in fact, different from her mother and father's in ways that changed the nature of military recreation and entertainment. In the first place, Meyner's "war" was not a war at all but one of several conflicts that peppered a very long standoff between the United States and the Soviet Union. Born just as World War II ended, the Cold War quickly moved the nation from demobilization to a standing drafted force that could be summoned to defend against attack at any moment. The nation's first peacetime draft proved quite controversial, and recreation programs formed one part of the military's effort to make a standing force acceptable to the public. Promising to mold the young men summoned to service into model democratic citizens, military officials enlisted Special Services women, Red Cross club workers, and USO entertainers as emblems of the domestic life the men had been called to defend.

Cold War domesticity was a complicated mix of concerns about family and sexuality that often embodied national fears of political and social turmoil. For many Americans, the white, middle-class nuclear family served as the ultimate safeguard against the dangers and evils of communism, and entertainment agencies deployed that family ideal to conflict zones in Europe and Asia. Women were to remind a young drafted force of the comforts of home and family for which they fought and to symbolize the promise that their own domestic bliss awaited them at the end of their service. As the USO boasted, its efforts would help "return these millions of young men . . . to their homes better citizens, better Americans."[12] But if entertainment promised to make American soldiers better soldiers and democratic citizens, the military's racial integration highlighted the lingering fault lines of American democracy. Recreation programs integrated and pledged to provide services without regard to race, but the sexualized underpinnings of entertainment made true integration difficult. Recreation women muddled their way through the changes, caught between their own ideas about race and foreign occupation zones that introduced another layer of racial complexity.

## A RECREATION TO OUR EYES

As World War II neared its close, a Red Cross official asked Army Air Forces General George E. Stratemeyer how the organization could be more helpful in the event of future wars. Setting aside any number of important services the Red Cross had provided during the war, including its blood donor program and emergency communication between military personnel and their families, the general answered simply: "more girls."[13] Stratemeyer was not alone in his desire for more American women in war zones. Surveys of enlisted soldiers in all theaters revealed that GIs enjoyed having Red Cross and USO women around and that they wanted even more.[14] Other military commanders likewise insisted at the end of the war that American women entertainers and recreation workers had been indispensable. As they contemplated soldier recreation going forward, they agreed that civilian women would remain a fundamental component of soldier life and the American military.

The war's end precipitated requests for USO shows and Red Cross clubs from commanders who feared the consequences of an idle force of frustrated men waiting to demobilize.[15] Although commanders deemed entertainment of any kind essential to combating boredom—within six months after V-E Day, Special Services had stocked 350,000 decks of cards and 21,000 basketballs—they particularly valued the continued services of American women.[16] When the Red Cross began closing hospitals and offices in military camps and recommended that the military assume responsibility for its off-post recreation clubs, commanders protested. They could do without much of the Red Cross's services, they explained, but "earnestly desired the American Red Cross to continue the operation of the club program." The organization had pledged to remain with soldiers until they were home, commanders had charged, and owed it to soldiers to keep the clubs open.[17]

The soldiers agreed, though they were more concerned with keeping the Red Cross women than they were with any fund-raising promises the organization had made. Soldiers feared a military takeover of recreation would mean even greater militarization and regimentation of their lives. And for them, Red Cross women symbolized the civilian life that finally seemed so close. As one man explained, the military could not provide a "woman's touch."[18] Red Cross women visually contrasted the military environment. "A woman sorta dresses up the place," one described, "like lights on a Christmas tree." Another insisted that he and his fellow soldiers needed Red Cross women because of their "kindness and decorative purposes" and because they provided "a recreation to our eyes." One GI echoed the organization's intent that women impart a sense of domestic normality in remote theaters when he insisted that women prevented the men's "social character and behavior from becoming stale."[19] Even soldiers who recommended the Army assume control of recreation suggested that Red Cross women remain a part of the program as a necessary feminine element.[20] The GIs' appreciation of morale-boosting and domesticating femininity shaped the ways the military and civilian organizations prepared for recreation as the military demobilized and then reorganized in anticipation of a much longer, new kind of war.

Despite the desires of commanders and GIs that the Red Cross and USO continue to provide American women entertainers, without a war to prompt financial donations from the American public, the organizations were simply unable to maintain their expansive entertainment network. The Red Cross negotiated with the War Department to have it assume some of its clubs' operational costs, then in 1946 slowly began transferring individual clubs to the Army and the Navy. By 1948, the Army's Special Services was operating all former Red Cross clubs.[21] USO-Camp Shows similarly retracted, despite military leaders' pleas for even more entertainment to pacify frustrated troops anxious to return home. The curtain fell for the last time on a Camp Shows performance in Europe in January 1947, while tours continued in the Pacific for the remainder of the year. In the two years following the end of the war, Camp Shows sent nearly 2,000 entertainers overseas.[22] In a January 1948 ceremony at the White House, President Harry S. Truman issued the USO an "honorable discharge," though he cautioned its former directors that he expected them to be "on call in case an emergency develops."[23]

To fill the void, the Army expanded its Special Services program and began deploying hostesses overseas. The Army first employed civilian women to staff on-post recreation clubs in 1919, and Congress authorized the creation of a formal hostess position in 1923. Until after World War II, however, few women served abroad. Only thirteen "carefully selected" hostesses had been assigned to Europe before V-E Day, where they worked in clubs and leave centers in Paris and Brussels. After the cessation of hostilities, and as the Red Cross retracted from club work, the Army increased its use of hostesses at Special Services clubs in France and Germany.[24] The Army deemed hostesses so vital to morale, in fact, that it prioritized their transportation to Europe. Demand outpaced supply, however, so the Army recruited among the women who had served in the war and were about to depart for home.[25] Jean Moore Fasse and Etta Barnett, for example, both transferred from Red Cross work to club work as Special Services hostesses in Europe.[26] Grace Hewell followed her wartime service in Germany as a second lieutenant in the Women's Army Corps with five years as a club director in Europe.[27]

Still unable to meet the continuing need for civilian women to work in entertainment, in September 1945 the Army began hiring Civilian Actress Technicians (CATs), twenty-one- to twenty-five-year-old women recruited from Hollywood, Broadway, colleges, and drama schools, to assist with soldier-produced entertainment. The program was conceived of by two former Special Services officers with theater experience who knew that a long occupation would require extensive entertainment and believed women could provide the necessary "glamour." The women taught GIs directing, casting, scenery, and acting, and they occasionally played female roles, "a duty," the *New York Times* reported, "roundly welcomed by top brass and buck private."[28] But if the men welcomed the women's arrival, some military and Red Cross women were less impressed. Since the war's end, they had been working hard to stage plays for the GIs' entertainment, one female soldier noted, but they were not earning "fat contracts," nor enjoying "luxurious" accommodations like the CATs. More problematic, it seems, was the women's perception that the CATs were fresh faces who had been brought to Europe simply for their good looks. They were "nothing but jobless Broadway hoofers nobody has heard of," alleged one soldier, who asked if she and the other women were disqualified from "the highly paid 'freshness, youth and unspoiled sweetness' class" simply because they were soldiers.[29] Perhaps they were, because Special Services continued to employ CATs through the 1950s, assigning them to Germany as well as Japan, Guam, the Philippines, and Okinawa.[30]

Although Special Services expanded its use of women in recreation, its monopoly on military entertainment did not last long. As civilian and military officials debated the functions of recreation and entertainment in the postwar military, the USO and Red Cross jockeyed for position. In 1948, the Department of Defense solicited the recommendations of several civilian committees on the future of military recreation. Comprised largely of former USO officials, the committees perhaps unsurprisingly recommended that a revived USO assume control of soldiers' off-post welfare both domestically and abroad. Initially left out of the conversation, the Red Cross protested that it was congressionally charged with military welfare and pressed for a continued role.[31] Without a war to provide clear rationale for its work with the military, however, the Red Cross was unable to revive its former position. The two organizations squabbled without resolving anything until the passing of the 1948 Selective Service Act refocused military attention on recreation and brought another restructuring of the relationship between the armed forces and civilian entertainment organizations. The USO reactivated in wake of the draft, but absent a war to mobilize the public, struggled to raise money and discontinued its work in January 1950. Several member agencies tried to keep work going under the auspices of the Associated Services for the Armed Forces, though their efforts were scattered and focused on services within the domestic United States.[32] Only a few months later, when North Korean forces crossed the thirty-eighth parallel into South Korea, recreation and entertainment agencies had the "war" that would revive their efforts.

## CIVILIANS IN UNIFORM

Demobilization previewed many of the concerns that guided the revival of military entertainment in the wake of the 1948 Selective Service Act. As Americans grappled with what a standing peacetime military would mean, military commanders and civilian officials turned to entertainment, and women in particular, to help make the draft palatable to a skeptical public. As one part of a broader effort to rethink the relationship between civil society and the military early in the Cold War, entertainment allowed civilian organizations to nurture middle-class American values among a younger and expanding armed forces. In many ways, this focus resurrected a World War I–era understanding of women entertainers as essential for steering men toward a wholesome lifestyle that, in the nuclear age, modeled Cold War preoccupations with the home, family, and sexuality. Recreation work thus operated with two related goals. The first goal, as it had been since World War I, was to keep soldiers "out of trouble."[33] At the same time, military and civilian leaders believed recreation could play a key part in developing democratic character among young citizen soldiers.

The revival of selective service in 1948, which happened only a few years after the United States had helped defeat the fascist powers, illuminated public fears that a standing, peacetime military marked the militarization of American society. To mitigate these concerns, President Harry S. Truman invoked the ideal of the citizen-soldier and insisted that a conscripted military was "a real democratic army, a real citizen army" that would benefit society as a whole.[34] Like President Franklin D. Roosevelt before him, Truman believed that civilians needed a hand in shaping citizen-soldiers, and he enlisted civilian organizations to provide religious, moral, educational, and recreational services for military personnel. While the commander in chief declared the work vital for "national security" and "military preparedness," the civilian officials charged with the task promised to mold citizen-soldiers into the "active citizens and leaders of tomorrow."[35]

Essential to producing these good citizens were military and civilian officials' efforts to maintain service members' connections to home and family. Some military members were able to take their families with them on extended deployments, a symbol of the American way of life in occupied lands and the growing importance of domesticity in the Cold War. With a large occupying force in Germany and Japan in the early Cold War, the military initially deployed married servicemen's families as a way to maintain morale, stem immoral behavior, and ward off potential relationships between American men and German and Japanese women.[36] Most service members could not take their families abroad or did not yet have families of their own, however, and civilian organizations attempted to fill the void. For all those without families, but especially the young men who comprised the majority of the force, recreation clubs' "friendly, homelike atmosphere" sought to provide a surrogate family that would prepare them for future domestic life.[37] As Truman envisioned it, the USO served as "a strong and steady link with the homes from which they came and to which they will be returning."[38]

Military and civilian officials attributed great significance to recreation's domestic influences in part because the average age of enlisted personnel dropped significantly under the 1948 draft. More than half of enlisted personnel were twenty-one years old or younger late that year—"newly inducted teen-agers," as the *Saturday Evening Post* dubbed them—and 80 percent were under twenty-five only a few months later.[39] Service members often found military life "strange," noted the Selective Service director in 1950, but an organization like the USO could "soften the hardships of GI life by providing them with a 'home away from home' . . . designed to keep them in touch with normal, wholesome civilian life."[40] In particular, military officials promised parents that their children would not be exposed to the seemingly standard issue "loose morals and evil companions" that many feared would inhibit young people's chances for a normal family life.[41] Invoking Woodrow Wilson's World War I pledge that the military would return the nation's young men with no dishonorable wounds, civilian organizations provided "wholesome surrounds" intended to help "men to improve their minds, their bodies, their personalities, and their attitudes."[42]

The intertwined goals of preventing trouble and building character were most visible in recreation officials' revived moralistic approach to sexuality. Certainly, the military remained concerned with the prevention of venereal disease in the early Cold War era, but with penicillin's growing availability, medical officers focused less on the dangers and consequences of venereal diseases and more on the ways extramarital sexuality threatened soldiers' character development and potential for a healthy family life.[43] These concerns were also paramount for civilian officials, who feared that the "extreme youth of the average serviceman" combined with the "availability of money and women" was bound to lead to "some trouble."[44] To ward it off, military officials implemented a venereal disease program that focused on "moral education rather than mechanical prevention." Medical officers and chaplains emphasized that "self-control and moral responsibility" would "insure personal happiness, the sanctity of marriage, and the security of the home."[45] Additionally, the military restricted infected soldiers, recommended that repeated offenders not be promoted or receive leave, and even suggested that commanders consider discharging those with "undesirable habits and traits of character including the repeated incurrence of venereal disease."[46]

This focus on sexual behavior mirrored a wider public and governmental association between nonmarital sexuality and Cold War insecurities about communism, changing gender roles, and the American family.[47] The military's campaign for sexual morality created a new image of the American soldier as an upstanding future father and community leader and enlisted recreation women in the effort to prepare him for these roles. Intentionally reversing the World War II connection between sexuality and martial aggression, the new venereal disease program more closely resembled that of World War I and sought to counter the "erroneous notions" among many young men that "sexual promiscuity is a token of personal prowess, to be boasted of as an indication of lusty manhood."[48] Instead of demonstrating their presumed manhood through sexual relations, the military exhorted, the young men should conduct themselves honorably so that "some day a healthy little youngster will be glad to call you father."[49] One naval psychiatrist saw USO clubs as key to shepherding young men to proper postservice family life by providing a place for the men to "meet girls, and through them, their parents." He even suggested that the men would attend church with the women. Without these services, he warned, the Navy "would be faced with many more problems of homesickness, wayward behavior, frank delinquency, [and] probably venereal disease."[50]

While punishing offenders and emphasizing the future rewards of good conduct, the military also utilized American women as alternatives to relations with disreputable local women.[51] As Lieutenant General Clarence R. Huebner, commanding general of the European Command, reported, recreation assisted "in the struggle against the moral gravity that inevitably pulls at the heels of an occupation army."[52] One Army report on West Germany warned of a "vast reservoir of infected women" who had been schooled in "Nazi doctrines, particularly in matters of moral laxity" and who would prey upon "some young, immature soldier" in an immigration ploy.[53] In fact, from September 1944 until October 1945, the military imposed a fraternization ban that restricted GIs from "friendly, familiar, or intimate" contact with any German national, and it forbade marriages between American soldiers and German women until December 1946.[54] The ban was never as effective as the military hoped, and some enlisted men suspected it served only to preserve for "the brass the first crack at all the good looking women."[55] Nonetheless, commanders struggled to enforce the bans because they feared sexual or romantic relationships would undermine good relations with the German people, and they employed recreation women as distracting lures.[56]

American Red Cross women worked hard, but the fraternization ban made their work much more difficult than it had been during the war. As occupying forces, the soldiers had free time, but with a fraternization ban in place, they could not blow off steam in local bars or meet area women as they might in other locations.[57] Under these circumstances, the men drank more than usual, and the women felt discouraged. "The guys don't care about donuts or us anymore," complained Bettie Gearhart Brodie, who had served on a Clubmobile during the war. Instead, they were focused on "German girls and 'sweating out' going home."[58] Fellow Clubmobiler Gretchen Schuyler likewise felt disheartened. Although Red Cross leadership expected the women to work "harder than usual to combat all the new tendencies," she believed that the program was no longer effective and should be discontinued.[59]

The organizations were not giving up so easily, however. The USO insisted that under a fraternization ban, it was "more important than ever that sufficient entertainment and recreation be provided." More to the point, officials believed that soldiers needed "to talk to an American girl" and initiated a focused recruitment campaign to get one hundred women abroad.[60] The Red Cross similarly described its clubs as an alternative space for soldiers away from German women. Since the war's end, the number of enlisted men's and officers' clubs had increased, but Red Cross officials argued that the clubs merely offered men a place to get a drink and perhaps shoot pool, as well as "a place to entertain a type of native girl not admitted to American Red Cross clubs."[61] Keeping the wrong kind of women out was one thing; Special Service clubs also helped cultivate moral behavior by enlisting "carefully selected women recreational directors of mature judgment and responsibility" to provide guidance for the men on questions of love and life.[62] At the same time, the American press emphasized that women from home modeled the best of femininity for the nation's new allies. "Thousands of charming women," boasted the *Chicago Defender,* were "carrying democratic ideals and the culture of the United States, to say nothing of their beauty," to occupied countries around the world.[63]

As the American presence in Germany extended into the Cold War and the bans on contact with German women were lifted, good relations between American soldiers and German women came to signify positive relations between the two countries.[64] Still, the military was particular about the kind of woman it believed acceptable for soldiers. Special Services hostesses interviewed and screened German women before they gained admittance to the clubs and worked with chaplains and officers to counsel the men on dating matters.[65] One Army report described acceptable women as "high-type girls obtained by the co-operation of churches, societies or clubs from nearby towns and cities."[66] Still, the ten German women who worked at the Bremerhaven American Red Cross Army-Navy Club were tested regularly for vene-real disease.[67]

By April 1949, the Army had opened more than one hundred ser-vice clubs in occupied and liberated countries, operated by 400 civilian women employees.[68] In spite of the women's essential role not only in boosting the morale of American forces but also in managing rela-tions between the United States and its Cold War allies, civilian offi-cials complained that the highest echelons of the military lacked sufficient commitment to entertainment. Although there were excep-tions in the Pentagon, civilian leaders grumbled that many consid-ered Special Services a "side show" and a "luxury."[69] Indeed, some Department of Defense officials felt that civilian organizations had pressured the military into adopting "significant social reforms" as a way of gaining public support for the standing military.[70] Whatever their intent or rationale had been, by the late 1940s the armed forces were a standing force that was also coming to terms with another profound change—racial integration—and with all of these changes as it committed to a "police action" in Asia.

## DANCING AROUND INTEGRATION

As the military, the Red Cross, and the USO organized recreation and entertainment programs in a standing, drafted force, it was, as Special Services worker Jean Moore Fasse noted, "still segregated time," though not for long. Having completed her work with the Red Cross in World War II, Fasse decided to continue working with soldiers and, after a brief vacation at home in North Carolina, became a Special Services hostess and traveled to Germany. For the next five years, she worked at a Special Services club in Mannheim, before transferring to others in Höchberg, Munich, and then France. Getting the Mannheim club up and running proved difficult, made all the more so when the col-onel in charge of her club failed to complete work assignments that were intended to make the club functional. White women did not face the same kinds of problems, Fasse discovered, but "had nice service clubs." Undaunted, she made an appointment with the commanding general in the area, who promptly rectified the matter. Soon, Fasse had an impressive club ready to entertain the many African American GIs in the region.[71] Until 1963, she continued her work establishing clubs for soldiers and enjoyed the fringe benefits of living and traveling throughout Europe, touring even behind the Iron Curtain to Czechoslovakia and Moscow.[72]

Military recreation provided African American women like Fasse with opportunities that many women of their generation did not enjoy. Even women who served only a one- or two-year tour in Germany, Japan, or Korea during the late 1940s and 1950s lived and worked in conditions that contrasted sharply with the ones they left behind in the United States. A 1947 article in *Ebony*, for example, featured Red Cross worker Myrtle Gross's "luxurious and leisurely" living conditions as a premier job benefit. Stationed in Giessen, Germany, she worked twelve-hour days but insisted her task was "more fun than work." She supervised four other Red Cross employees and thirty German workers and lived in a comfortable home tended by a cook, maid, and domestic servant—a notable perk in an era when many African American women worked those jobs themselves.[73] Other recreation women lived in similarly apportioned billets and, especially in Japan where many women had maids, found the experience a welcome, if initially unsettling, change.[74]

Ethyl Payne embraced change. As a child, she had it better than many African Americans in Chicago. The daughter of a Pullman porter who owned a home in the West Englewood neighborhood, Payne grew up in relative comfort, even as racism shaded all corners of her world. Her brother's experiences in a segregated force during World War II tempered her wartime fervor—"we weren't flaming patriots," she remembered—but she nonetheless did her part for the war effort by working as a hostess at Camp Robert Smalls in North Chicago. Nearly three years after the war ended, she signed up for similar work among occupation forces in Japan. She knew the military was still segregated, but an advertisement for Special Services hostesses intrigued her. Her work in Japan began a lifetime of international travel and launched a career in journalism that made her a fixture among Washington politicians.[75]

But while recreation work afforded many African American women the opportunity to live and work under relatively liberating circumstances, racial prejudice clouded their experiences, even after the military began to integrate in 1948. Red Cross worker Helen Stevenson Meyner's father William Stevenson had served on Truman's Committee on Equality of Treatment and Opportunity in the Armed Services (more commonly known as the Fahy Committee) that advised the military on implementing the integration order, and she assured him that the GIs "get along beautifully" and that she had not noticed any prejudice among them.[76] As a white woman, she did not experience racial prejudices, but she did witness the Red Cross's lingering discrimination and the ways that integration affected recreation programs. As she documented, racial prejudices and stereotypes themselves sometimes functioned as entertainment. On one occasion, a group of officers' wives "put on an oldfashioned minstrel show" for patients, complete with actors in black face who performed as stereotypical characters. Although Meyner described the show as "goodnatured fun" and "cute," she couldn't help but notice several African American patients who walked out of the show in protest. The men's opposition belied her own insistence that it was just "good fun" and left Meyner wondering if the men had been "overly sensitive" or had a legitimate complaint.[77] Other men also protested instances of racial discrimination in entertainment. In May 1946, a soldier stationed in Korea wrote to the *Baltimore Afro-American* that the area was "one of the worst theaters for soldiers because of the prejudiced white officers." The men had not seen a USO unit "with colored entertainers," a deficiency he attributed to the commanding general. "How about seeing what you can do," he asked the paper's readers, "to make it hot for him?"[78]

Racial integration proceeded in haphazard fashion following Truman's Executive Order to integrate in July 1948, and by the Korean War the military was still working to comply.[79] Entertainment and recreation agencies followed suit and pledged to serve GIs without racial differentiation. In 1951, when the USO began sending shows to Korea,

Red Cross club women Penny McCaskill and Shirley Hines play an audience-participation game with men from the Fifty-Fifth Military Police Company at Camp Red Cloud in South Korea. The racial integration of the military raised new questions about women's work with soldiers, even as work with the Red Cross offered African American women like Hines unparalleled opportunities.

it announced the shows would be cast on an integrated basis.[80] The Red Cross similarly pledged to integrate its staff when it announced plans to initiate services for the troops in South Korea in July 1950.[81] Indeed, among the initial recreation workers sent to Korea was Blanche Coombs, an African American woman who had recently graduated from Atlanta University and who worked in the first Red Cross club established in the country.[82]

Despite the organization's stated intent to be racially blind, it allowed racial prejudices to dictate some personnel assignments and programs and thus, like the forces it served, failed to truly integrate. In early 1951, for example, conditions in Korea forced the Red Cross to evacuate its club staff, including Coombs, to Japan where they joined other Red Cross staff who, like Meyner, had been prohibited from going on to Korea.[83] White club women delayed in Japan were assigned to work in hospitals, but the Red Cross assigned Coombs and two other African American women to perform clerical work at the organization's headquarters, where they grew increasingly frustrated. After visiting with them, Meyner wrote that the women felt "utterly useless" and wanted to work with GIs. Learning that the source of the problem was white Red Cross women who did not want black women assigned with them, Meyner charged that the prejudiced white women had no business working for the Red Cross. "Boy it burns me up," she wrote to her parents, that the organization's practice contradicted its professed notions of racial equality.[84] A couple of weeks later, she met with the recreational supervisor for hospitals and reported that she "gave [her] quite a talking to about the three negro girls." Countering the supervisor's insistence that assigning African American women to hospitals "would not work out," Meyner cited the presence of several African American staff at the hospital, including two nurses, a Special Service club worker, and many officers, in addition to about one-third of the patients, as evidence that the women would be well received.[85] Despite her efforts, it seems that the Red Cross never assigned the women to hospital work in Japan.[86]

The Red Cross's refusal to assign African American women to hospitals highlights the continued problem of racially integrated housing, however nice the housing might have been. Shortly after World War II, in fact, a Red Cross area director refused to send African American women to Guam because the women would have to be housed in the same area as white women. The *Atlanta Daily World* criticized the decision as having delivered the organization "a disfiguring black eye."[87] The Army's Special Services fared little better in the mind of one club woman who ultimately lost her position amid controversy over segregated housing. A former Red Cross employee, Margaret V. Scott transferred to Special Services in Inchon, Korea, in September 1947. All Special Services women lived together, in integrated fashion, for a few months before they were transferred to new, segregated, living quarters. According to Scott, the segregated quarters upset even the white staff who said they wanted "to live as well as work with their fellow staff members." When Scott inquired about the move, her supervisor told her that General Robert O. Shoe, Commanding General of Korea Base Command, ordered the segregation to prevent "any guests"—presumably, white guests—

from being "subjected to off-duty contact with the Negro girls and their guests should they object to such contact." Scott then received notice that she was being transferred to Pusan against her will for having gone outside the chain of command in inquiring about the segregation. Scott refused the assignment, which meant that she was in violation of her contract and had to pay for her own transportation home.[88]

If basic assignments and housing constituted a stumbling block for the Red Cross, dances proved a more challenging obstacle. Some clubs and programs continued to struggle with the question of integrated entertainment and dances in the months after the end of World War II, even as others offered examples of successful integration. In one instance, white Red Cross Clubmobile women visited African American units but only when accompanied by two white non-commissioned officers. African American soldiers took offense at the officers' presence, which they believed was designed to "protect the innocent missionaries from the wicked cannibals." The women "feign friendship" with the GIs, a reporter allowed, but "seem to have little real love for their work with tan Yanks." The fault line was dances. When black soldiers asked the white women to dance, the women reportedly claimed that they "have a headache, sprained foot or just aren't 'feeling well.'"[89] Conversely, integrated Red Cross clubs in Italy "created a new democracy" among "Negro, [Japanese-American] and white GIs," according to the *Chicago Defender*.[90] Although an incomplete model of integration that still prevented dancing between white women and black men, one club avoided controversy over what was once a "great headache—dances" by providing Italian women hostesses with whom African American servicemen could dance, while African American Red Cross women danced with white servicemen.[91]

Even with somewhat successful models, dances continued to crystalize racial conflicts that lingered just below the surface of an integrated military. Some women, including Meyner, seemed to have no qualms about the matter. She happily reported to her parents that at Service Club dances, "the white gals (local teenager army kids) dance with the negroes just like they would with any white soldier."[92] But

while "it doesn't bother me a bit" to dance with African American soldiers, she noted of her colleagues that the prospect of "whether or
not they should dance with negroes seems to get the gals down."[93] Apparently, the matter did more than make the women uncomfortable,
for one month later, Meyner reported that the Service Club dances
had been ended because the white Special Services women did not
like to dance with African American men.[94]

But even as she expressed distaste at racial prejudice, Meyner har-
bored racial ideologies that revealed the complex ways that integrated
recreation collided with a long history of white fears of interracial attraction. Meyner explained in a November 1951 letter home that African American soldiers frequented her canteen and that white GIs
"resent" their presence and romantic interest in the white women. The
African American men "proposition us," she reported, and had tried
to get into their barracks. Although Meyner insisted she was not prejudiced, this violation of historic prohibitions against relations between
black men and white women was too much even for a self-described
"broadminded" American woman.[95] Two weeks later, she explained
in another letter that she had "studied the matter carefully and like
most things in this world I discovered a reason behind it all." The men,
she had learned, faced discrimination at all levels of their military experience, from their work assignments to their (nonexistent) leave
policies and recreation options. Attributing the men's behavior to these
conditions, she explained that the "canteen is their only form of recreation and 'tis small wonder at times that they do get hopped up from
whiskey or dope and give us a hard time."[96] Meyer forecast, "We have
a long way to go before we wipe out racial prejudice completely."[97]

Race and sex became even more complicated in places such as
Japan and Korea, where American GIs socialized not only with black
and white American women, but also with local women. Reflecting a
long history of sexualized characterizations of Asian women, military
commanders deemed Asian women more tempting and more threatening than European women. An admiral stationed in the Philippines
explained that the USO was more important in "the Orient" than in
Europe or the United States because "there is more opportunity to
get into immoral activities." In that dangerous environment, he be-

lieved, the USO "maintains the American standards [and] provides opportunities for wholesome recreation." More to the point, he noted, it "keeps men out of dives."[98] USO officials agreed and concluded that Seoul, with its "complete absence of any wholesome recreational resources," demanded "the greatest and most urgent need" for entertainment.[99]

US soldiers similarly distinguished the two groups of women in ways that would echo in the Vietnam War by calling American women "round eyes" and Asian women "slant-eyes."[100] Although the men differentiated American and Asian women, Special Services worker Ethyl Payne reported that African American men found Japanese women to be attractive and willing partners. Despite military prohibitions against marriage and discrimination against racially mixed children, many African American men formed relationships with Japanese women and lived with them off-base. GIs had significantly more money than many Japanese men and were thus quite attractive to women in search of financial comfort. In turn, Payne noted that African American men were attracted to Japanese women's relative submissiveness and conventionally gendered family roles.[101] Neither the military nor civilian recreation organizations had solved the problems of integration when President Truman ordered troops to Korea in 1950. There, the problems of race and sexuality within the US military were compounded by matters of race and sexuality outside it.

### BESIEGED, SURROUNDED, AND OVERWHELMED IN THE KOREAN WAR

As the Korean War raged around him, the Forty-Fifth Division "Thunderbirds" chaplain took a moment to write to the Red Cross. Eight Red Cross women had recently attended his Christmas service, where they served coffee "from a 15 gallon stock pot . . . and doughnuts from cardboard 'C' ration cartons." The serviceware might not have been anything fancy, he admitted, but "nobody noticed." The women's presence so lifted the mood of the service, that they "might as well have had fine china instead of canteen cups." The women's interaction with the men "was a beautiful sight to watch," he noted, and as they moved through the crowd, "a gentle warmth was kindled." The Thunderbirds were not able to go home for the holiday, but in the chaplain's estimation, "home had come to them." A simple touch on a man's arm "fills him with all the tender memories of home." The chaplain confessed, "I know," because "it does the same to me." As a religious man, he admitted that he had not been "so enthusiastic" about the women before their arrival. With 17,000 men around, he feared "some serious problems" might result. However, the women's "highest moral quality and . . . perfect sense of personal behavior" struck the right balance of professionalism and friendliness and averted any problems. This blending of home comforts, model femininity, and domesticity converted the chaplain on the matter of women. The full effect of their "wholesome feminine contacts," he surmised, "no one can measure."[102]

It might have been impossible to quantify the effects of "wholesome" recreation, but the military, the Red Cross, and the USO all believed it essential in the Korean War. A "sampling" of "American home life," recreation and entertainment women brought a familial air to a young garrison force and made holiday dinners—like those with the Forty-Fifth Division—"as similar as possible to those the men enjoy at home with their wives, mothers and sweethearts."[103] But recreation involved more than holiday dinners, and the servicemen stationed in South Korea were often interested in something other than wholesome family life. While Special Services, Red Cross, and USO officials worked to provide the character-building recreation they believed was essential to the Cold War military, their efforts frequently collided with the more carnal concerns of soldiers. Military officials struggled to balance these desires in a war-torn country that witnessed the growth of a visible prostitution industry that made recreation all the more important and more difficult. In an era of heightened concerns about family, sexuality, and citizenship, women entertainers walked a fine line between wholesome morale and dangerous temptation.

Special Services and the Red Cross followed American troops into Korea and quickly set up clubs that provided a range of recreational options. General Douglas MacArthur had requested Red Cross services in July 1950, on the eve of American involvement, to alleviate some pressure from the military in trying to establish a recreation program so quickly. His request opened the door for the Red Cross to revive its club program, which had been assumed by Special Services after World War II. Similar to the arrangement between the Red Cross and the military in that war, the military provided facilities, equipment, billets, and transportation while the Red Cross provided female staff, comfort items, and recreation equipment. The first club opened at Pusan in November and three others soon followed in the same area, even as North Korean and Chinese forces pushed the Allied troops back toward the city.[104]

By spring 1951, with Allied troops again on the move northward, the Red Cross began plans to expand its recreation services through a revived Clubmobile program and launched a recruiting campaign to enlist sixty women for the work. Forty women quickly signed up, but before the Red Cross could begin the program, General James A. Van Fleet, commander of US and United Nations forces in Korea, specifically forbade any women other than hospital staff from serving under his command. Citing the fluid nature of the front, difficult transportation, and a lack of proper billets, in addition to fears that North Korean troops would not recognize the noncombatant status of Red Cross personnel if captured, the military halted the expansion of the Red Cross Clubmobile program. Instead, the Red Cross sent the forty women it had recruited to establish canteens at four airfields, where they served Air Force personnel and Army and Navy soldiers in transit. Van Fleet's decision limited the amount of recreation available, and soldiers in the field found the restriction of entertainment to bases frustrating.[105] Only after the cease-fire was the Red Cross free to launch its Clubmobile recreation program, renamed the Supplemental Recreational Activities Overseas program (SRAO).[106] The Red Cross announced the program in September 1953 and noted its "immediate objective" to recruit and train 125 women.[107] By the end of the year, eighty women were running ten Clubmobiles across South Korea.[108] The number of women assigned to Korea waxed and waned for the next twenty years, over which time nearly 900 women served doughnuts and smiles to GIs keeping the peace.[109]

USO-Camp Shows tried to augment the efforts of the Red Cross with live entertainment but was unable to provide as much as it would have liked. The organization reorganized in early 1951 at the urging of Secretary of Defense George C. Marshall, who asked agency leaders to revive their efforts in the face of "critical times" and the attendant expansion of the armed forces.[110] The USO began sending shows to Korea and other Pacific locations in May 1951, again relying on the work of little-known paid performers whose shows were eclipsed in the press by more well-known acts.[111] The military repeatedly emphasized the "special importance" of entertainment to alleviate the "monotony of occupation duty," but with requests for shows increasing and with limited funds at its disposal, the USO was never able to meet the military's demands.[112]

The US military's protracted presence in South Korea contrasted sharply with its concurrent occupation of Europe, and the differences fundamentally shaped the nature of entertainment provided to the forces. While many soldiers assigned to West Germany deployed for multiple years with their families, for example, the vast majority of those sent to Korea were young single men on one-year deployments.[113] Additionally, while military officials in West Germany eventually lifted the fraternization and marriage bans, they actively discouraged soldiers from socializing with Korean women, in large part due to the racial and cultural differences between them. As Major General George B. Peploe, Deputy Chief of Staff for the Army Forces Far East, wrote in 1957, Koreans' "faces appear strange and so do their customs." Racial differences and the discouragement of contact with local women made American women from home all the more important. As Peploe noted, "the only pretty American faces to be seen are those of the girls you send with Camp Shows, an occasional Red Cross representative, Special Services employees, or Department of Defense civilian women employed in Seoul and Pusan."[114] Yet, neither differences nor prohibitions precluded sexual relations between soldiers and Korean women, especially as the war contributed to the growth of a vast prostitution industry.

The US military had a tenuous relationship with prostitution in Korea from the onset of its presence at the end of World War II.[115] American military officials initially regulated prostitution in an effort to control venereal disease before officially distancing themselves from the practice. Both the US and South Korean governments vacillated between official endorsement and tacit approval (though always public condemnation) of prostitution throughout the 1950s and 1960s, but camp towns of sex workers nonetheless grew at "explosive" rates "in a symbiotic relationship with U.S. military bases." Crushing wartime poverty pushed many Korean women into some form of labor—often prostitution—for the US military. Racial differences also facilitated the growth of prostitution. Steeped in the legacy of Korean "comfort women," who were forced by the Japanese into sexual slavery during World War II, and a long history of Americans viewing Asian women as exotic sexual partners, many American military personnel viewed Korean women as unsuitable marriage partners but acceptable partners in sexual commerce.[116] In 1956, the South Korean Ministry of Health and Social Affairs estimated that 262,000 prostitutes catered to US military personnel.[117]

American military commanders and recreation officials explained entertainment as a way to keep GIs from the camp towns and thereby ensure they could return home to be productive citizens and family men. Without the USO, the chief of staff of the UN command in Korea feared GIs would "go to bars and . . . meet some undesirable women."[118] Admiral Felix B. Stump, commander of the Pacific Fleet, stated the matter more bluntly. Most of the men he commanded were "very young," and stationed in areas "where women are cheap, where dope is cheap and available." He, like the president, wanted "our young Americans to return home healthier and not less wholesome and good than when they left" and thus called upon the USO to act as the men's link to home, as a reminder "that their friends back in Main Street, USA, are thinking of them."[119] A captain in the Army Medical Command similarly held up American women as necessary alternatives to prostitution. In a session for new SRAO arrivals, he explained that some soldiers escaped the tensions of war by drinking or "associat[ing] with the local women." As symbols of "ladies back home," SRAO women's "very presence," he suggested, "may serve as a reminder of why he should observe high standards in all respects."[120]

At times, though, recreation and prostitution abutted in strange ways. Helen Stevenson Meyner's Red Cross club was located next door to a "house of prostitution." One day, while she was playing volleyball with a group of soldiers, several of "The Girls" called to the men from across the barbed wire fence that separated the two buildings, distracting the "boys that I was trying to engage in a nice out-door healthy sport." She wryly noted about the incident, "Never a dull moment."[121] Meyner's interrupted volleyball match was not an isolated occurrence. Military officials reported that Special Services clubs served as meeting places for soldiers and prostitutes, and one hostess even recalled military officials bringing in prostitutes for checkups, all despite official prohibitions.[122]

In this challenging hypersexualized environment, devoid of a family friendly military culture, colored by racial differences between American soldiers and Asian locals, and framed by a growing and institutionalized prostitution industry, the USO insisted on a "standard of decency" in its programs. Officials carefully auditioned and monitored every act, Vice President Lawrence Phillips declared in 1953, and even worked with the Armed Forces Chaplains Board to ensure shows upheld that standard.[123] Performers were forbidden from using crude language and making "disparaging jokes" about government officials, American history, US allies, servicewomen, the Red Cross, or the USO. Also forbidden were references to sexual situations, including prostitution and men and women "about to enter into a seduction."[124] In an effort to uphold a sense of morality, the organization even resisted a Department of Defense request that it stage shows exclusively for officers and allow alcohol to be served. Since its founding in World War II, the USO had forbidden alcohol at performances, and though its shows were intended primarily for the benefit of enlisted men, all military personnel were welcome. The Department of Defense's request thus raised warning bells for USO officials who feared that the combination of entertainment, alcohol, and—interestingly—officers could "deteriorate into 'night club shows' unless proper precautions were taken."[125] With or without alcohol, sexuality was a fundamental part of military entertainment. Press coverage of two USO tours to Korea highlighted the troops' desires for sexualized performances and sparked a public debate about the role of sexualized entertainment in the Cold War's new military, dedicated as it was—at least publicly—to the fostering of sexual morality.

For her Christmas 1953 tour, film actress Terry Moore designed a "cute, but controversial" costume that, in her words, made her "look like a little Santa Claus."[126] The ensemble consisted of a strapless white ermine suit, with a pixie bonnet, fur-lined white boots, and gloves. An actor in several 1940s and early 1950s popular films, Moore had been billed "Hollywood's sexy tomboy" on the cover of *Life* magazine only five months earlier.[127] GIs anticipated her visit, and, according to some, had been promised she would wear the festive costume featured in her publicity photographs. Thus, when she walked onto stage wearing a cape on Christmas Eve, the soldiers in attendance shouted for her to remove it, and she obliged. American newspapers reported the next day that Moore had been ordered to return to the United States, both because of her "strip tease" and costume, though it remained unclear who had dismissed her.[128] The USO's Hollywood Committee chair, George Murphy, claimed that he had told Moore not to wear the costume and that she had assured him three times that she would not. He insisted that he only dismissed Moore because the Army asked him to do so, but the Eighth Army and Tenth Corps headquarters both denied having any problem with Moore's "little Santa Claus" rendition. One Army representative, in fact, declared that the Army felt the suit was "just fine for the boys in Korea."[129] Moore also insisted that the soldiers liked her show, while radio personality Johnny Grant, who accompanied her on the tour, reported that even the chaplain in attendance "complimented us on having a good clean show." Regardless, someone in authority insisted that Moore not wear the costume again, and she continued her tour wearing more modest slacks and a sweater.[130]

Two months later, Marilyn Monroe unleased an even bigger firestorm when she sashayed onto stage in a revealing sequined dress and implored in her trademark sultry lyrics for GIs to "come and get it." Interrupting her honeymoon with Joe DiMaggio, Monroe spent four days on a USO tour entertaining 100,000 soldiers, sailors, airmen, and Marines who clambered over each other, climbed telephone poles, and

America's leading sex symbol, Marilyn Monroe, braved South Korea's freezing temperatures to sing suggestive lyrics for the thousands of GIs who flocked to see her. On several occasions during her tour, they nearly rioted to get a closer look.

peered through telescopes to catch a better glimpse of the blonde bombshell. At the Forty-Fifth Division, 6,000 soldiers booed and threw rocks at the opening act, then rushed the stage so violently during Monroe's performance that one GI was trampled and had to be evacuated by ambulance. (No word on whether he was awarded a Purple Heart for his wounds.) The soldiers of the Fortieth Infantry Division made their colleagues' behavior seem downright respectable. American newspapers reported that the men nearly rioted and almost broke through a line of military police (MPs) attempting to protect the performers. The pleas of the regimental commander did little to calm the crowd of 10,000 men, who continued to press forward during Monroe's brief performance. In fact, security proved to be a concern throughout her tour. While servicemen shoved and scrambled to see her wherever she went, the MPs charged with her protection often spent more time snapping photographs than maintaining order.[131]

The men might not have received as much entertainment as their commanders had hoped, but it was more than simple boredom that led to the GIs' raucous and threatening actions. The men "stampeded" to see the nation's leading sex symbol.[132] When Monroe toured South Korea in February 1954, she was at the cusp of her career. She had played bit parts in several films in the late 1940s and early 1950s, but Monroe insisted that her career really took off because of servicemen in Korea. The Army newspaper *Stars and Stripes* named her "Miss Cheesecake" in 1951, and according to *Life* magazine, her pinup photographs were a "standard military item" among GIs.[133] It seems another ubiquitous item was her "Golden Dreams" nude photograph that adorned a widely reproduced 1952 calendar, the same photograph Hugh Hefner selected for *Playboy* magazine's first centerfold the following year. According to Monroe, soon after the calendar's publication, thousands of GIs began sending fan mail to 20th Century Fox, impressing the studio with her star power.[134] At least one group of officers had decorated their club with the nude photograph, though the Associated Press reported that the men removed it prior to Monroe's visit so that she would not be embarrassed.[135] The officers need not have worried. Every aspect of Monroe's tour was sexually charged.

From her arrival in Korea, "wearing an army shirt and GI trousers which failed to obscure much," to her performances in a "low-cut, skin-tight purple dress," her clothing featured prominently in press coverage.[136] Monroe encouraged the attention, telling reporters that she had to wear the dress because it was the only thing she brought besides "a lace brassiere and some borrowed Army woolens." She needed the woolens, it seemed, because the cold Korean weather had forced her to "break her habit of sleeping in the nude."[137] Her characteristically sultry singing further enhanced the sexual allure of Monroe's performances, and according to her, ran afoul of the Army. In her autobiography, she notes that after performing "Do It Again" at a hospital, the officer in charge of her tour told her she needed to sing a "classy song" instead. She countered that she had not performed the song with "suggestive meaning" but "as a straight, wistful love song" and pointed out that it was a respectable George Gershwin song on any account. Although she says she changed the lyrics to "kiss me again," video recordings of her stage performances in Korea record her crooning, "I may say no, no, no, but do it again," much to the delight of the GIs in attendance.[138] Monroe also claimed innocence after her goodbye to the Forty-Fifth Division incited another near riot. While "waving and blowing kisses" to the men, she claimed to have meant to say the Japanese word for goodbye—"sayonara"—but instead "heard myself yelling 'Eleewah!'" a Korean word she "picked up along the way" that translates as "come to me." Immediately, the "jeep was stampeded by men, men and more men," she wrote. "We were besieged, surrounded, overwhelmed by them."[139] The men understood the word and its suggestive connotation, which in the context of Monroe's tour and in a war zone with a booming prostitution industry, highlights the underlying connections between entertainment and sex, even if Monroe was as innocent as she claimed.

*Life* magazine covered her tour with a two-page spread of photographs that illustrated for readers at home how the popular pinup figure had "wriggled off barracks walls and took shape in the shimmying flesh."[140] Three weeks later, Mrs. J. Broadus Haynes of Seattle noted her disapproval of the publication's coverage of Monroe "in a too-tight dress posturing before GIs" and wondered if any of them "resent[ed] the strong aroma of the act enough to decide they'd rather play checkers or go for a walk—in another direction?" The attendance counts from Monroe's shows suggest few did. According to Lieutenant James F. Orlay of the Second Infantry Division, who also wrote to the magazine that week, the men approved of "The Blonde" (his capitalization) "who looked so fresh, healthy and American," and whose visit was like "the World Series, the Fourth of July and the Mardi Gras rolled into one." Mrs. Haynes might have objected to Monroe's sexual display but it was essential for Orlay. Morale had "ebbed" since the end of hostilities, he explained, and Monroe's visit made him and his fellow soldiers "feel like men again."[141]

Other commentators criticized the sexual nature of USO shows, and indeed all entertainment provided by women, as an indication that the Cold War military had lost its backbone. *New York Times* military affairs editor Hanson W. Baldwin wrote a scathing editorial that heralded Monroe's and Miller's USO tours as evidence of "low service morale and impaired military discipline." Describing the GIs as having "behaved like bobby-soxers in Times Square, not like soldiers proud of their uniform," Baldwin suggested that their "poor discipline" was a sign of "degradation and decline in the United States" and a reflection of "some of the softness on the 'home front.'" While commentators from another era might have understood the GIs' enthusiasm as a sign of their virility, Baldwin argued that unbridled masculine sexuality was a detriment to good order and discipline and to national defense. "Sweater girls and young ladies scantily clad in ermine-trimmed bathing suits have nothing to do with military morale," he argued.[142] The *Army Combat Forces Journal* agreed, noting that while troops in Korea might be "jubilant" about entertainment, the men's wives and mothers were "somewhat less elated." USO shows and Red Cross women "are all well and good," the author allowed, but warned that "dependency upon glossy gadgets" can't replace "old-fashioned leadership."[143] The standing Army of the atomic age might have embraced civilian values, but these critics insisted that those values need not go too far. Servicemen should be stoic and composed, not in need of, and certainly not vulnerable to, the teasing performances of scantily clad women.

Not all servicemen agreed. For Lieutenant Orlay and many others, Monroe's performances intertwined Americanness, civilian values, masculinity, and sexuality in acceptable ways. When the *Pittsburgh Post-Gazette* described Monroe's performance as a "kootch show" and recommended that the Army remember "it is not in the burlesque business," three men from Company B of the Twenty-Third Infantry Regiment vehemently defended "Mrs. DiMaggio." Their version of respectable entertainment allowed for a measure of sexual allure, which they insisted was "beyond reproach." They also took offense to allegations that the soldiers had behaved poorly or, as Baldwin charged, like hysterical teenage girls swooning for their favorite star and countered that critics should remember "just what we are doing in Korea and what few diversions we have." They explained, "though temporarily soldiers, we are and always will be men," affirming both their adult and heterosexual status in the face of critics'—and the military's—efforts to constrain both. As men, they were entitled to and in need of such entertainment.[144]

### WARMTH, FRIENDLINESS, AND A READY SMILE

Marilyn Monroe was the most famous USO performer to visit South Korea, and her tour provoked the most controversy. While women in other kinds of entertainment did not elicit the same kind of vitriolic resistance nor the same kind of unrestrained enthusiasm that Monroe did, they faced the same tensions between providing service personnel with the kind of wholesome, character-building entertainment authorities believed would make them good citizens and giving GIs the kind of sexually charged entertainment they desired. This tension had shaped military entertainment from World War I on, but as the Cold War politicized sexuality and deemed its "containment" crucial to national defense, the effort to balance the military and GIs' conflicting expectations proved particularly frustrating. Tasked with creating a "home away from home" for a young force, Red Cross, Special Services, and USO women found themselves balancing conflicting ideals of entertainment, laced with competing generational divides about sexuality in a Cold War that infused it with national significance.

Official directives and policies betrayed the difficulty. A 1953 Army pamphlet, *Introduction to the Army Service Club Program,* written to familiarize new recreation workers with their job, captures the Army's frustrated attempt to emphasize the "serious, professional objective" of recreation without discounting the value of women's "warmth, friendliness, and a ready smile."[145] In forty pages, the pamphlet described the history of recreation work and outlined the Army's expectations for the women selected to continue that tradition. Throughout, the author attempted to distance women's work in Service Clubs from domestic labor yet proved unable to sever the tie completely. The pamphlet boasted that the title "Army Hostess" had been obsolete for a couple of years but explained that the recreational assistants and the recreational director planned parties, organized entertainment, offered a sympathetic ear, and made each guest feel welcome—tasks the pamphlet likened to "giving a party in your own home." This characterization of the service club as a "home away from home" both echoed the domestication of recreation in earlier wars and highlighted the importance of women's domestic work at a time when domestic comforts symbolized the American way of life around the world.[146]

Red Cross officials faced a similar conundrum in trying to name its recreation program. GIs called the women in clubs and on Club-mobiles' "Donut Dollies," and although SRAO National Director Mary Louise Dowling admitted that the men used it affectionately, she deplored the term as a "misnomer" that could impede recruitment by detracting from the professional nature of the women's work. Much to her dismay, the Red Cross never developed a better alternative.[147]

If women's domestic work remained important, it also required great dexterity. Cold War domesticity centered on a happy, sexually fulfilled couple, and as recreation clubs symbolized American domes-ticity in war zones around the globe, they held up the women who staffed them as symbols of the family life awaiting GIs after their ser-vice.[148] Officials wanted clubs to represent the potential of domestic life, not the reality. Thus, although recreation organizations had uti-lized married women during World Wars I and II, and though they could have turned to underemployed servicemen's wives stationed in Europe to fill personnel shortages, the Red Cross, USO, and Special Services now required all women to be single.[149] The requirement al-lowed for the possibility that men would develop attachments to the unattached women, and while the Army deemed such feelings "per-fectly natural," it charged the women with the responsibility of pre-venting personal connections from becoming inappropriate. To that end, the Army recommended a "Friendly but Impersonal" approach that would allow women to "be cordial without being forward."[150] Women should encourage men to participate in the club's activities but not spend their time participating in those activities alongside them. There were simply too many men for the women to spend their time dancing with one or chatting with a few.[151] And yet, the goal of recreation was, in the words of the chief Army hostess for the Far East command, to make each soldier "feel like an individual, not just one of a herd."[152] Devoting the right amount of personal attention to GIs was difficult, but it was essential to safeguarding the women's reputation, tied as it was to their sexuality. They were free to associate with or date whomever they wished, but they needed to exercise discretion so that their romantic and work lives did not interfere. "Like Caesar's wife," the Army expected them to "be above reproach."[153]

Nonetheless, with a population of young people both staffing and visiting clubs and in an era of record-setting numbers of young marriages, romantic entanglements developed. Women joined recreation programs for a variety of reasons, but for some, work with soldiers seemed a good opportunity to find a husband. "Girls" joined the CAT program to pursue an acting career, to travel, and to fulfill a patriotic duty, a newspaper article explained in the late 1940s. Some joined for a good time, and a "few" candidly admitted they hoped the work would facilitate their finding a husband. Their hopes were not in vain; several CATs married soldiers overseas or returned home to marry men they had met abroad. The "marital record is, in fact, quite satisfactory," the article noted.[154] However satisfactory, marriage proved a considerable problem for Special Services officials who had to replace 40 percent of women workers annually, as most of those who left the program had married servicemen.[155] Jean Moore Fasse, for example, had worked as a Special Services hostess in Germany since 1946, but had to leave her post when she married in 1963.[156] Turnover in the Red Cross was not so dire, but even there, 15 percent of Clubmobile workers married servicemen they met during their assignment in the mid-1950s.[157]

However troublesome the turnover was for the programs, as Cold War society attributed geopolitical importance to the nuclear family, entertainment organizations and the military were reluctant to completely dissuade the women from marriage. They even suggested that marriage could be a perk of the position. An article in the Army's area headquarters newspaper at Heidelberg, Germany, for example, described the Special Services "girl" as adventurous and ventured that "she likes her men in US Army uniform."[158] The *Pittsburgh Courier* was more circumspect when it announced the engagement of Special Services worker Gloria B. Hedrick to a sergeant she had met in Germany. Careful to convey an aura of middle-class respectability that was especially crucial for African American women, the article noted that her engagement was announced at a Valentine's Day party hosted by the local chaplain and his wife.[159] Yet, even in an era of marriage frenzy, recreation work allowed some women to escape a life of domesticity. A nice young man had proposed to Ethel Payne before she left to work at a Special Services club in Yokohama, Japan. She expected she might marry him after she returned but decided that she preferred adventure to marriage. "I wanted to have an exciting life, [a] challenging life," she explained. "I just didn't want to be caught in the humdrum routine . . . I wanted to do something."[160]

But if recreation work sometimes served as a matchmaker, the organizations did not want to attract women whose sole purpose was to snag a husband or who would use the military as their personal dating service. The USO, for example, warned that "the date crazy girl" frequently got into trouble and had to be sent home. Lamenting that "this date business has gotten a great many girls into a great deal of trouble," the USO warned women that private rendezvous, especially when combined with alcohol, could result in sullied reputations or, worse, physical danger. To prevent both, USO officials recommended that women conduct their social activities in groups, where they would have "just as much fun" and "no trouble." Even more, the organization directed that performers limit the amount of time they spent in recreation and mess halls and that all members of the unit remain together during the visit.[161]

Selection criteria, however, exacerbated the problems by ensuring that recreation women were attractive potential partners. Army officials had suggested at the end of World War II that the minimum age requirement of twenty-five was too high and that younger hostesses would be more appropriate.[162] Sixty percent of enlisted men, the chief of the Recreation Branch of the Special Services Division explained, were under twenty-two, which meant that recreation programs needed a "younger approach."[163] It was not just common experiences that made younger women seem more appealing to recreation administrators. As the President's Committee warned rather bluntly, soldiers "don't want to dance with old ladies of 21."[164] Still, it took several years for the Army and Red Cross to lower the age requirement, and when they did, they did so only slightly, to twenty-three.[165] Red Cross and military officials had increased the educational requirements to a four-year degree in an effort to professionalize the work, and this requirement made it difficult to lower the age requirement dramatically.[166]

Even with a slightly lowered age requirement, women employed by Special Services or the Red Cross were notably older than the average GI.[167] The age difference stifled potential romance, at least on the part of one Special Service hostess, though it did not prevent the GIs from holding out hope. Stationed in Europe in the mid-1950s, Grace Swank Alexander noted that she and the other women were "enough" older than the soldiers that they were not interested in them romantically. Even unrequited, some of the soldiers, she noted, sometimes "fasten themselves on you."[168] Ethyl Payne similarly thought her age would stymie romance but discovered that African American women were "a rare object" in Japan, and so neither age nor looks deterred men with romantic intentions.[169]

If the Army vacillated on how young recreation women should be, it insisted that they have a pleasing personality and attractive physical appearance. A 1956 Army report noted that women hired to work in service clubs should have "perfect physical and mental health," along with a "well-groomed appearance."[170] Physical attractiveness outweighed other qualifications for one USO performer who, because she had a sore throat and was unable to sing, performed a pantomime act. She "is much too pretty for the boys not to see," the group's manager concluded.[171] Similarly, Service Club worker and professional concert singer Thelma Campbell's "smooth pleasant personality, and well-groomed looks" were enough to entice soldiers "who ordinarily go in for bop and re-bop" to attend her performances of "high brow classics."[172] The phrase "well-groomed" regularly appeared in news articles about the program, though at times it was replaced or augmented by the more specific descriptor: "trim."[173] As a *Chicago Daily Tribune* article explained, "the army is looking for trim, well groomed, attractive girl college graduates to don French-blue uniforms and help entertain soldiers." Although the article reiterated that the "girls" should have an "attractive appearance," it clarified that "glamor is not a requisite."[174] It probably would not have hurt, for as the Army newspaper at Headquarters Area Command in Heidelberg, Germany, described her, the average Special Services "girl in the pert blue uniform" was five foot, five inches tall and 120 pounds, a frame that "balance[d] the scales with the best Hollywood can offer." Unfortunately, the paper lamented, "no circumferencial measurements" were available.[175]

Whatever their measurements, recreational assistants all wore a standard uniform that accentuated and harnessed the women's good looks. Though military-esque, it was stylish. The armed forces hired couturier designers to revamp women's uniforms in the 1950s in part to create a more flattering public image of servicewomen, and the Special Services uniform was part of the overhaul.[176] Produced by the D'Armigene company, which also designed several airline stewardesses' uniforms, the club uniform consisted of a respectable blue two-piece suit, a service cap, heels, white gloves, and, because "good grooming and established custom" required them, nylon stockings. Additional guidelines echoed military regulations that required above-the-collar hair styles and minimal jewelry.[177] Instructions warned women not to adorn the uniform in any way, both because soldiers were forbidden from altering their uniforms and because any embellishment would make the women "foolishly conspicuous." Properly maintained, the uniform was "attractively feminine" on its own merits, and the women were free to express their individuality through their off-duty civilian clothing.[178] Failure to wear the uniform properly and a careless attitude about personal appearance were not treated lightly, but were, in fact, read as an indication of one Special Services woman's "lack of personal discipline" and a sign of her unsuitability for the work.[179]

Intended to visually associate the civilian club women with the military, the uniform was also meant to protect the women from scrutiny. The "uniform made us official," the director of service clubs told Sandra Lockney Davis when she arrived in Korea. "It protected us."[180] In turn, the military expected that the women embody the feminine respectability the uniform conferred. "You have a *responsibility*, a big responsibility," the Army emphasized, "to make sure that the uniform

In the October 1957 issue of *Mademoiselle,* Army Special Services advertised working in clubs with GIs as a unique opportunity for young women to combine international travel and work. Wearing her couture blue uniform, this respectable Special Services woman appeared en route to an exciting adventure that might end in marriage to an eligible American serviceman.

always typifies the best of American womanhood. Any questionable act of yours reflects discredit on everyone in the same uniform."[181] The USO similarly used uniforms to deem women's work officially respectable. Breaking from their World War II insistence that women don feminine attire in their off-duty hours, in the early postwar era, USO administrators instructed women to wear a Camp Shows uniform at all times when not performing.[182]

Attractive uniforms, however, only did so much. With turnover rates remaining high throughout the 1950s, and with women enjoying expanding professional opportunities for recreation-related work in civilian communities, Special Services faced an uphill battle in procurement.[183] Officials recruited at colleges and universities, stationed recruiters in large cities, placed advertisements in professional recreation journals, ran spot announcements on television, and arranged for human-interest stories about recreation women in hometown newspapers.[184] In the mid-1950s, the Army implemented a uniform allowance to subsidize the $250 uniform cost in an attempt to make the service more appealing.[185] Few of these efforts proved as effective as the Army hoped. Advertisements in *Glamour* and *Mademoiselle* returned the greatest amount of interest, but the number of applications resulting from those ads proved small, only eight and thirty-nine, respectively.[186]

Though less productive than Special Services hoped, recruitment materials advertised recreation work as a unique opportunity to earn a good salary and travel internationally. Invoking the classic tag line to "join the Army and see the world," one Special Services representative described working in a service club as a chance for a civilian to "travel to far away places," while also performing patriotic service.[187] With positions available in Germany, France, Italy, Japan, Korea, Okinawa, Panama, Alaska, and Hawaii, Special Services indeed provided women with many opportunities for adventure.[188] In any of these locations, the *Mademoiselle* advertisement boasted, work and leisure blurred, allowing women to experience "the exciting thrill of international travel as well as living in enchanting Germany or France."[189] A 1948 society piece on Special Services worker Grace Hewell in the *Atlanta Daily World* described her eleven-day tour of Italy where she met Pope Pius XII. For an African American readership still restricted by Jim Crow, this kind of freedom to travel must have seemed all the more alluring.[190]

Competitive salaries facilitated international travel. In 1955, Red Cross Clubmobile women assigned to Japan, Korea, and the Philippines started out earning between $2,760 and $3,252 annually, with free housing, compared to $2,100 earned on average by women working full time.[191] By 1959, the average woman working a year-round, full-time job earned $3,200 annually. Special Services women, by contrast, received a $4,040 annual salary that stretched even further since the Army provided the women with free living quarters.[192] Adding to the excitement of living abroad, Special Services women also enjoyed the perks of free or inexpensive travel services and access to the PX's vast stocks of cheap consumer items, which allowed them to stretch their dollars and "cash in on those European vacations."[193]

Not all recreation women enjoyed European vacations, of course, but recruitment tactics captured the contradictions of early Cold War entertainment and recreation work. The Red Cross, Special Services, and the USO all attempted to professionalize the domestic work women performed. Providing a "home away from home" for the nation's cold warriors proved complicated, however, in that sexuality formed a significant part of Cold War domesticity and culture. Whatever aims the military held for entertainment women, they all came to the work for their own reasons and managed its complications the best they could.

## MANAGING AFFECTIONS

Recreation work attracted adventurous, independently minded women with a travel bug. Soon after the Korean War broke, Grace Swank Alexander left her teaching position for a direct commission in the Navy. She described joining the Navy and working at the Pentagon as an "adventure," one she extended by joining Special Services after a two-year stint. Assigned to Germany, she and her coworkers took advantage of the travel opportunities their positions offered by visiting cities such as Venice, Rome, Florence, and Paris, as well as Spain and Holland. "The world was right there," she explained, noting that she and the other women had been partly motivated by the chance to travel.[194] The opportunity for travel lured Ethel Payne to work for Special Services, though travel also meant an opportunity to "get away" from her stifling library work at the Chicago Public Library.[195] It was a good job, better than working in domestic service like so many other black women in Chicago, but she found the work "boring" and jumped at the chance for an adventure.[196] A decade later, the same itch for travel prompted Sandra Lockney Davis to consider a career in Special Services. She had contemplated work with the US Foreign Service, but after meeting a Special Services recruiter who lured her with promises of international travel, a good salary, and an assurance that she would be the center of attention for thousands of soldiers, she signed up for work in Korea.[197]

A similar desire for travel combined with an independent spirit for Special Services worker Shirley Horning. The University of Alabama alumna loved living in Europe, where her wages, though not extravagant, provided her with the means to travel during her free time. "I'm traveling every minute I can," she wrote to her family in 1953, "because I'm eager to see everything I can."[198] Her salary and travel also bolstered Horning's sense of self-reliance, while distinguishing her from many other women of her generation. Her sister Gloria also worked in Europe with Special Services, and Shirley frequently chastised their parents for repeatedly loaning Gloria money. She and her sister were capable of providing for themselves, she insisted, and generous monetary gifts were "unwittingly destroying our independence and self-respect." Shirley had traveled across Europe, purchased what she wanted, and still saved money, she reminded her parents, before asking them "how much money have you sent me?"[199]

But while Horning prized her self-reliance, she admitted that it made finding a spouse difficult. When her father suggested she was too restless to settle down to family life, Horning countered that she would indeed marry and have children "should the right opportunity come along." However, she was "better off" at the moment. "I'm learning more . . . seeing more . . . doing more than those poor little creatures with husbands who are bored by their day in and day out routine." Moreover, she explained, her vast experiences made it difficult to find someone with a similar background. Even among soldiers "who have led the interesting life that I have," she had not yet found someone who could relate to her worldly experiences.[200] A few years later, while still working in Europe, she again noted that her travels separated her from most people. "I've gone far beyond the narrow life that is lived in [her hometown of] Mobile," she reasoned, before closing her letter with a note that she was looking forward to upcoming travels to Ireland, Scotland, and perhaps Copenhagen.[201]

For the moment, though, Horning had her choice of men who flocked to her and tried to make a good impression. As Valentine's Day approached in 1953, Horning received "undying protestations of affection from three frustrated men." They each gave her gifts, and though she enjoyed the attention, she seemed surprised by it. "I've never before in my life felt so much like a femme fatale," she confessed. "I look in the mirror and see this somewhat flabby face . . . and wonder what in the world they can get so excited about." For their part, the men seemed in need of a supportive woman. One of them was getting a divorce and another struck Horning as unhappy in his marriage. Reluctant to dissuade the men who took her on dates and bought her gifts, she harnessed her resolve "to keep a straight face" and keep the men from learning of the others' intentions.[202] Six months later, at least one of them was still around, though she had weaned him "down to one date a week."[203]

Juggling three men proved stressful, but manageable. Groups of men were more troublesome and problematic. After returning from leave feeling reenergized, Horning went to her service club and "was mobbed by the boys asking me where I had been and if I had a good time and did I miss them." She noted, "for the most part," the men were "as good as gold" and reminded her of puppies clamoring for attention. One of her "pets" had heard her say that she liked moustaches and decided to surprise her by growing one while she was gone. Not all of the men were "puppies," however. Some were "little monsters."[204] When she took a group of twenty men bowling, they razzed her about her skills, then followed her back to the club where they continued to annoy her. "In one of their frisky moods," the men's attentions turned physical. They tickled, pinched, and squeezed her, and patted and pulled her hair. Horning neither welcomed nor enjoyed what would in later years be termed sexual harassment, but in an era when such physical interactions were routine in the workforce, she dismissed them as simply part of the job. "Such affection," she ruefully noted.[205]

Helen Stevenson Meyner similarly struggled to keep the men at bay. GIs often became envious of other men who were seen socially with American women, and it was the women's responsibility to prevent any such jealousy from getting out of hand. Meyner even noted that the men's jealousy made it difficult for the women to go on dates, and she avoided walking in sight of the GIs when she was with an officer to avoid offending them.[206] The Red Cross had warned the women not to become "brass happy," but many women were nonetheless taken with officers who were, by virtue of the organization's age requirements, closer to their own age. Whatever their commonalties, the GIs did not appreciate the officers commandeering the women's time and affections. All the attention was flattering, she admitted, with the exception of that of "an old leech" colonel who was "hot on my trail."[207]

Managing the affections of lonely men was one thing; managing one's own emotions proved particularly difficult for women who were also far from home, eager for personal connections, and past the average marrying age for the time.[208] Whether they wanted friendship or romance, associating mainly with officers presented the women with "a new problem," as Meyner called it. "Most of the attractive officers" she met were married, she confided to her parents, and though many of her coworkers disapproved of "having anything to do with a married man," she believed their attitude "silly." Citing her father's belief that married men were lonelier than single men during war because they missed their wives, she explained that she went out with married men but ensured that the "relationship stays strictly on a 'pal' basis."[209] Having worked in the Red Cross during World War II, her parents no doubt understood the difficult predicament in which their daughter found herself. They also understood that "dating" in that context most often involved groups of people or couples who gathered socially, and that even when a single couple ventured out, they did not necessarily have romantic intentions. Yet, when the family circulated Meyner's letters to other family members, they deleted portions that referred to her dates with married men.[210] Whatever unusual arrangements might have been acceptable during war, family and friends were unlikely to understand or condone them.

One married man, Lieutenant Tom Moore, proved especially challenging to Meyner's "pal" rule. Only a couple of weeks after arriving in Japan, she wrote that she had been "dating" an attractive but married navigator whose wife had given birth to a daughter three months earlier. Although she insisted that the two were "just friends," she confessed that their relationship was one that only made sense in the war. "Somehow over here," she reasoned, his marriage "seems to make little difference." Still, as one colleague warned her, "you just gotta watch it."[211] Indeed, though Meyer maintained that she "never loved him," her reflections reveal both a depth of feeling that exceeded simple friendship and the struggles of a young woman to make sense of her unusual circumstances.[212] In one letter, she noted that his marriage was unfortunate, and she admitted to her diary "almost resenting his wife."[213] Shortly before Moore left for home, they celebrated the New Year with dinner, dancing, and a kiss.[214] Reflecting on their relationship after he had returned to the United States, she concluded that while he was happily married, "in a strange sort of way he loved me," even as she continued to insist that she had not also fallen in love.[215]

Whatever her true feelings, the experience shaped her subsequent outlook on wartime romance. Although she continued to date married and unmarried officers, she assured her parents that she did not want to marry any of them.[216] She enjoyed the social life women in her position inherited simply by virtue of being so outnumbered by men. "Social life here is of course excellent," she wrote, "(as would it be for almost anything that wears skirts)."[217] Even with the attention, she had no plans for serious romance. "I have plenty of time yet," she noted, and a "job to do over here."[218] Besides, she reported to her parents, "it is an actual fact that the attractive men over here are all married." The one exception was an Ethiopian captain who wrote her love letters in broken English and who "is black as coal but just as cute as pie." But the scarcity of single men could not overcome the deep chasm of race even for a Red Cross worker who saw herself and her family as racially progressive. In a postscript to the letter, she teased, "The Ethiopian is single—should I nab him-?? (he, he, he.)."[219]

This kind of focused attention was not anything new in wartime entertainment, and recreation officials anticipated it. Hinting at the fortitude that such work would require, Special Services cautioned that women should be "emotionally mature" to work in a club with 500 to 700 enlisted men.[220] Warnings didn't prepare Sandra Lockney Davis. After signing up for the Red Cross's SRAO program in 1964, she received an assignment to South Korea. From the minute she boarded the plane, she "was treated as if I were knock-down gorgeous." As a child, she had been overweight, and though she had matured into a healthy young woman who was considered "cute by some and pretty by others," Davis could never accustom herself to the attention.[221] Living on base exacerbated it because she was essentially always on duty, regardless of whether she was in the club, at the mess, the PX, or the post office.[222]

Davis adamantly insisted she and the other women were "objects of their affection, rather than sex objects" but even honorable attention grew tiresome.[223] At times, it bordered on dangerous. When Davis noticed a man staring at her two days in a row, she reported him to her supervisor, who concluded that he must be new in country and shy. Davis accepted this rationale, but when, a few days later, she went to the PX and found the man following her, she became very concerned. "His look was frighteningly intense," she wrote later. "My gut tightened and I felt more like flight than fight."[224] When her supervisor learned that he was a sergeant in the military police unit at the camp, Davis's fear intensified as she then felt she could not turn to the police for protection. Her supervisor was not much help either and suggested that if she just ignored the man he would lose interest. He did not. He continued to stalk Davis, and she finally became so scared that she alerted the Criminal Investigation Division at a nearby Army camp. Unfortunately, the investigator told Davis that unless her stalker "does something" he could not intervene. "There was nothing to be done," she noted, "except go to work as usual and try to pretend everything was all right." But again, everything was not all right, and even after the man showed up drunk at a service club, the investigator told her he could do nothing.[225] Feeling "vulnerable and totally unprotected," Davis concluded that she "wasn't safe anywhere" and that "the authorities were no help."[226] One of her friends decided to take matters into his own hands and went to the sergeant's living quarters and punched him. The next day, both she and her

friend were transferred to other locations.[227] Davis's experiences typ-
ified women's predicament when faced with what would later be
called sexual harassment, and though she ultimately managed to
avoid a physical attack, the underlying problem remained unre-
solved and followed her to her next assignment in Vietnam.

Despite the many challenges and difficulties, entertainment
women were proud of their work and believed they performed a necessary service. She was "sold on this type of work," Helen Stevenson
Meyner informed her parents near the end of her tour in Korea and
predicted that she would "join up again quick as a wink if U.S. troops
went to war elsewhere." She had thoroughly enjoyed her work, had
"never been happier and wouldn't have missed it for anything!"[228]
Meyner did not continue her work with the Red Cross after she returned home, and by the time US troops again went to war she was
well beyond the organization's age limit for recreation workers, but she
did go on to a long career of public service. After working as a guide
at the United Nations in New York City, a stint as a consumer advisor
for Trans World Airlines, and a season on the campaign trail for Adlai
Stevenson, Meyner married New Jersey governor Robert Baumle
Meyner. As first lady of New Jersey, she extended the kind of work she
had performed in Korea to the governor's mansion, entertaining political guests, participating in civic affairs, and writing a newspaper
column. In 1974 she was elected to the US House of Representatives,
a position she held until 1978.[229]

Ethyl Payne's acclaimed career in journalism began while she was
working with Special Services in Japan. When a *Chicago Defender* reporter published her accounts of African American GIs' romantic
entanglements with Japanese women, military leaders were not
pleased, but the newspaper editor knew he had found a gifted writer
and offered her a job. After gaining some experience writing feature
stories, she became the paper's local reporter in Washington, DC,
where she covered political events and world politics. In 1967, she
traveled to Vietnam to report on the experiences of African American GIs.[230]

If wartime recreation work helped to launch the careers of some
women, it marked a less tangible but nonetheless profound experience

for Grace Swank Alexander. Modest about her work, she explained that she had not attempted to move beyond the conventions of her time even though she was proud of her accomplishments. She acknowledged the limitations on women's careers, especially in the military, but she insisted that she "wasn't fighting the discrimination battle then." She explained, "I just accepted what was there and worked with the challenges that were there." Still, in reflecting on her experiences in the Navy and in Special Services, Swank noted that she and women like her were the forerunners of the women's movement that began a decade later. "I think . . . any young woman who wants to do something different probably looks to another time or another woman . . . and says to herself, 'If that person could do it, so can I.'"[231]

Like Alexander, recreation and entertainment women worked within the conventions of their time to foster a familial image of the Cold War military that bolstered national preoccupations with domesticity and contained sexuality. Yet, in subtle ways, they also pushed against the boundaries that confined them. Some lobbied for meaningful integration as they resisted discriminatory practices, others embraced the independence that working abroad provided, and some pressed against conservative ideologies of sexuality that guided their performances. If these were only the sparks of change in the early Cold War, they soon engulfed the women who continued the work in its second hot conflict.

# 5

≡

# Look, but Don't Touch

SEXUALITY AND ENTERTAINMENT
IN THE VIETNAM WAR

Debby Alexander lived during—but was not wholly a part of—the 1960s. She spent her childhood in Stockton, California, an agricultural city ninety miles east of that era's cultural center of San Francisco. Her midwestern parents had moved there during World War II when her father was sent to the Army Air Corps' Advanced Flying School, and they decided to put down roots after the war. Both her parents became teachers, and together they created a conventional middle-class existence for their four daughters. Although the city's agricultural industries attracted a diverse population, de facto segregation divided the city ethnically and racially so that the Alexander girls lived in a fairly homogenous neighborhood and attended a mostly white high school. Alexander later compared her childhood to a bubble, noting that her typical Republican parents taught her that "all policemen are good and all firemen are good . . . the military keeps us all safe." These idealistic notions eventually began to crumble for Alexander as the political, social, and cultural events of the 1960s betrayed their shallow footing.[1]

When this "really young, very, very nice girl from Stockton" enrolled at San Francisco State College in the fall of 1964, her eyes were opened to the events that defined her generation. As Alexander moved into the freshman dorm and acclimated to college life, students across the bay at the University of California at Berkeley returned from a summer of civil rights organizing, ready to continue the revolution at home. That semester, in response to crackdowns on political organizing on campus, they launched the Free Speech Movement. Alexander's first semester was no less revolutionary, though she participated in no overt political demonstrations. Her revolutions were more personal. Among the most memorable of her experiences that first semester was her budding friendship with a woman in her sociology class. Only midway through the semester did she learn that her new friend was, in fact, not a woman, but a man who regularly donned women's clothing. As Alexander came to know him, she awakened to the sexual revolutions that defined her generation.

San Francisco had long attracted people like Alexander's new friend. Over the course of the four years she spent there, the city became a home for artists, bohemians, and countercultural hippies who rejected the prevailing social and cultural norms that framed the lives of women like Alexander. Although she loved meeting new people and enjoyed the music of the era, she and her friends were content to sing "folk songs and pretend like we were hippie types." They had no interest in becoming the real thing. They visited Haight-Ashbury district but always in a group and never at night. The epicenter of the countercultural movement, the district was flooded with hippies hoping to tune in, turn on, and drop out. It was "kind of creepy," she described, and she and her friends feared that someone might try to give them LSD surreptitiously. Alexander's closest brush with drugs came when she inadvertently poisoned herself by swallowing a diet pill and a caffeine pill with a cup of coffee in an attempt to stay awake to study for exams. The clinic at the school called her parents and told them she had had a drug overdose. But Alexander was not the kind of girl to overdose on drugs, at least not the drugs of "sex, drugs, and rock and roll" fame. She and her roommate could not even bring themselves to smoke cigarettes and were so naïve, Alexander confessed, that they dared themselves to say "fuck" and then did so only under their breath. Not too long after that hushed profanity, Alexander found herself in Vietnam, where, she said, "you just heard it all the time."

The US military began sending combat troops to Vietnam in the spring of Alexander's freshman year, and the war, the draft, and the relationship between universities and the military quickly came to dominate campus discussions and politics. Although college protected most of the men at SFSC from the draft, in the spring of 1967 students attempted to persuade the university president to refuse to turn over student records to the Selective Service Board. They did not succeed, but protests against the presence of military and government recruiters on campus proved convincing and galvanizing. The campus attracted national attention in the fall and winter of 1968 when a collective of student groups known as the Third World Liberation Front staged the longest student strike in the nation's history, resulting in the establishment of the nation's first ethnic studies program.[2] Again, Debby Alexander watched, but did not participate.

Although surrounded by wartime political discussion and activism, Alexander admitted she knew little about the war in Vietnam. She knew enough, though, to know that her decision to go to Vietnam would not be popular on campus, especially not with a close friend who deeply opposed the war, and so she told no one other than her roommates that she had interviewed for a job with the Army's Special Services. She had majored in sociology and expected that she would eventually become a teacher like her parents, but she longed to travel. As a child, she had been fascinated by her aunt's stories of missionary life in India, and she feared that if she began a teaching career immediately, she would not have another chance to travel. She considered becoming an airline stewardess but after a campus career counselor explained the benefits and career potential of a government job, she decided to interview with Special Services. Moreover, as the daughter of a World War II pilot, she felt guilty that in a family of four daughters, no one was serving in the war of her generation. As luck would have it, Alexander interviewed at just the right moment. Like other entertainment organizations, Special Services had trouble finding enough women to go to Vietnam and lowered the age requirement to twenty-one. When Alexander boarded a plane in June 1968, she was the youngest woman in the service.

Alexander joined several hundred other Special Services, Red Cross, and USO women who entertained American GIs in Vietnam. While continuing what was by then a well-established tradition of American women going to war zones to bring a bit of home to GIs, the Vietnam War facilitated the development of an expansive smorgasbord of entertainment programs that provided American GIs with many ways to spend their free time. The Red Cross, USO, and Army Special Services provided recreation clubs and entertainment shows—and, of course, girls from home—similar to those soldiers had found in war zones since World War I. The war also witnessed an explosion of private, yet officially sanctioned, entertainment that offered American troops a different version of womanhood, one less reflective of conventional middle American values but more indicative of the ways sexuality infused the war itself. This mix blurred the lines that had formerly distinguished the "wholesome" entertainment the public and military envisioned as beneficial for the health of troops and other, unapproved entertainments troops could find just outside their bases and camps. While American women entertainers in earlier wars had found their work shaped and challenged by prostitution, the tenuous relationship between the military and an expansive prostitution industry in Vietnam made the work of Donut Dollies, USO performers, and Special Services women even more fraught than it had been in the past.

From the time that the first American combat troops set foot on Vietnamese soil in 1965 until the US withdrawal in 1973, American society and culture underwent dramatic changes. While the United States waged war in Vietnam, it also waged a war of sorts on the home front, where Americans fought for civil rights and black freedom in places like Selma, Alabama, and Chicago, Illinois. Gay women and men launched a cultural war to end discrimination that crystallized at the Stonewall Inn in Greenwich Village, New York City. College women on campuses as far removed as Lawrence, Kansas, and Fort Worth, Texas, fought for the end of in loco parentis restrictions and the same kinds of sexual freedoms men enjoyed. And women in offices, factories, and homes from Washington, DC, to Detroit, Michigan, challenged, in both subtle and direct ways, the conventions of gender and domesticity that restricted their personal and professional lives.

With American military personnel arriving in South Vietnam on a daily basis, the transformative changes occurring on the home front found their way to the Mekong Delta and the Central Highlands in short order. American GIs were well versed in the social and cultural changes happening back home, and American women brought the era's changing mores, assumptions, and even fashions with them to recreation centers and clubs on bases that spanned the country. These changes frustrated the efforts of military and civilian officials to uphold conventional images of women as idealized supporters of the nation's soldiers. While feminism's challenge to traditional gender roles proved one obvious obstacle, the growing antiwar movement, the civil rights and black power movements, and the sexual revolution also undermined attempts to project the same kind of traditional images of women offered in earlier wars.

### THE HEART OF HOMETOWN AMERICA

In the mid-1950s and early 1960s, the US military sent Special Forces "advisers," mostly officers, to provide political, military, and economic guidance to South Vietnamese anticommunist officials. As this advisory period gave way to a combative engagement in early 1965, and as the number of American personnel stationed in Vietnam ballooned to half a million by 1968, the military relied less on career officers and more on conscripted soldiers to wage war. On one-year tours and unaccompanied by families, the personnel assigned to Vietnam were, for the most part, young, single men.[3] As in prior wars, this kind of force presented particular challenges for commanders concerned with morale and relations with local populations. The nature of the war complicated matters further. With personnel called upon more to win hearts and minds than to accomplish conventional aims such as direct engagements or holding territory, the old adage that war is mostly boredom punctuated by moments of terror rang especially true in Vietnam. Support personnel vastly outnumbered combat troops and frequently had time to kill on the mushrooming American bases and installations that housed them. Even combat troops periodically made it to the bases; when they could not, Red Cross and USO women took a brief reprieve from the war to them. Whether on large posts or at remote fire support bases, military leaders used recreation programs to fill the GIs' off-duty hours and thereby keep them out of trouble, just as they had for the men's fathers and grandfathers in earlier wars. As the war dragged on into the late 1960s and early 1970s, and as antiwar sentiment, racial strife, and drug abuse increased, many commanders complained of plummeting morale and relied even more on entertainment for an antidotal symbol of a supportive home front.[4]

The USO, the Red Cross, and Special Services were all providing recreation and entertainment programs in Korea and Europe when the United States committed itself to a ground war in Vietnam. Thus, military and civilian leaders had only to request an expansion of those services as they planned entertainment for what was currently the hottest conflict of the Cold War. The USO responded quickly and opened its first club in Saigon in September 1963 before expanding to a total of eighteen clubs across South Vietnam at the request of the Pentagon. Women on two-year tours staffed the clubs, which featured—in addition to books, magazines, musical instruments, and tape recorders—snack bars and canteens that served "stateside-tasting hamburgers, cheeseburgers, ice cream, [and] milk shakes."[5] USO Shows also worked with the Hollywood Overseas Committee, the American Educational Theatre Association, and the National Music Council to recruit 569 tour groups that staged more than 5,600 performances in Vietnam and the surrounding region. Its largest production—the annual Bob Hope Christmas Special—traveled to Vietnam every year from 1964 to 1972, but more common were smaller variety units of aspiring performers eager for experience and an audience. At venues large and small, GIs could find a USO show that fit their style, whether it was a folk-singing trio, a rhythm and blues (R&B) soul group, a country and western ensemble, a vaudeville-type variety show, or a fully staged play. Although male performers outnumbered women, women frequently upstaged even the most famous men. Ann-Margaret and Raquel Welch (not to mention their miniskirts and go-go boots) added alluring visuals and bore the brunt of Bob Hope's vaguely sexual humor, while young women trying to break into the modeling business provided a bit of feminine flair on celebrity "handshake tours" that helicoptered in to visit small groups of troops in the field.[6]

As the Red Cross expanded its Supplemental Recreational Activities Overseas (SRAO) program to Vietnam, it continued its efforts to bring a bit of home and American womanhood to the troops. Expecting not only that American forces would be in Vietnam for a

American GIs had many options for entertainment in Vietnam but especially enjoyed seeing women from home, including actress and sex symbol Raquel Welch. In her stylish miniskirt and go-go boots, Welch embodied the more open sexuality of the Vietnam era for the lucky marines called on stage to dance with her.

"long duration" but also that it would be difficult to maintain high morale among combat-ready troops likely to experience long periods of boredom, the Department of Defense requested that the Red Cross establish its Clubmobile program in Da Nang in May 1965, only two months after a couple thousand Marines arrived.[7] Young women whom the troops called Donut Dollies ran the Clubmobile program and, because of the difficult terrain and sporadic nature of the war, relied on the military to provide transportation via helicopter and jeep, instead of driving vehicles as their predecessors had done. At landing zones and fire support bases, they engaged the men in audience participation games often modeled on popular television trivia shows. By the time the Donut Dollies made their last visit to a firebase near Bien Hoa in 1972, 627 women had served Kool-Aid and smiles to American GIs.[8]

Meanwhile, the Army's Special Services ballooned. Charged with coordinating recreation and entertainment for all military personnel, Special Services managed everything from athletic equipment to libraries, PXs, an arts and crafts program, the rest and recuperation (R&R) program, and dozens of Special Services clubs operated by young women charged with being friendly to the thousands of GIs who came in search of amusement.[9] Special Services also supervised all live entertainment, including soldier-provided and commercial entertainment, in addition to USO-sponsored shows. GIs with musical or theatrical talent could audition for and be temporarily assigned to Command Military Touring Shows, which took musical entertainment to insecure outposts unable to host civilian groups, or they could perform in musical and theatrical groups organized on bases and in smaller areas.[10]

In addition to these official, government-provided entertainment options, independent booking agents contracted performances with servicemen's clubs and messes. These entertainers had no government sponsorship or affiliation, as did USO performers, but had to audition before a Special Services board that evaluated their talent and assigned them a corresponding fee they could charge for their performances. Although some units included Americans hoping to launch their musical careers, many more featured Vietnamese, Korean, Filipino, or Australian entertainers who developed a reputation for performing in various degrees of undress.[11] Special Services regulations stipulated that "only wholesome entertainment will be approved" and forbid any "vulgarity, or lewd connotations," but one chief of Special Services in Vietnam clarified that "'partial strips' are permitted if they are an integral part of the show."[12] Another Special Services officer explained that Korean and Filipino women "were mostly for show—a show of plenty of female flesh and feminine pulchritude." Some of the women were talented singers, but "the troops didn't seem to mind at all whether the girls could sing or not."[13]

The introduction of this kind of non-government-sponsored yet approved entertainment was possible because of the unusual nature of the Vietnam War itself. Unlike in earlier wars in which the US government tightly regulated travel, it could not restrict travel to South Vietnam, an independent country that was not, officially at least, a war zone. Thus, performers, talent agents, and entrepreneurs were free to apply for visas, which the South Vietnamese government was free to grant. This fluid situation allowed for the growth of an entertainment industry that operated outside, but with the sanction of, official military channels. While the Red Cross, the USO, and Special Services carefully regulated the ways American women were presented, independent contractors introduced their own brand of entertainment—one that offered a less controlled picture of American women. International theatrical agent Richard L. Bast, for example, announced in March 1967 that he was seeking ten to twenty "American girls 'of high caliber'" to "contribute to the war effort" by dancing in the topless go-go club he planned to open in Saigon. Wanting to provide GIs with "nice, wholesome American girls," Bast required applicants to be between twenty-two and twenty-six, to sign a contract that they would remain single for six months, and to pass a lie-detector test that Bast promised would weed out any communists. Although it is not clear whether Bast opened the club, the unorthodox wartime relationship between the United States and South Vietnam made such a situation possible.[14]

With commercial entertainers offering GIs a more flagrantly sexual form of entertainment, USO, Red Cross, and Special Services officials waged a constant war to distinguish their workers and performers. "Help us, will you?" implored an Army Entertainment Branch official in 1970. Hoping to offset the widespread assumption among soldiers that all shows were sponsored by the USO, the official asked Special Services officers to "stop the rumors going 'round that the Korean skin show at the NCO club last night was the best USO show we ever had."[15] One SRAO assistant director in An Khe even refused to comply with a general's decision to house Donut Dollies and Asian performers in the same billet to avoid associating the two groups of women.[16]

American soldiers in Vietnam enjoyed a vast network of recreational amenities that, while not altogether different from those available in earlier wars, did expand to a staggering scope. In his 1976

Surrounded by sandbags and a 105mm howitzer, Red Cross Donut Dollies Nickie Roska and Loretta Clause offer men of the First Infantry Division a brief reprieve from the war. The Red Cross sent more than 600 women to Vietnam as symbols of a supportive home front that in reality was increasingly divided over the war.

retrospective on the war, General William Westmoreland, who commanded US forces from 1964 to 1968, explained the proliferation of these "creature comforts" as "good for morale."[17] To that end, the military made sure that soldiers had access to the latest consumer goods, as well as to every conceivable recreational outlet, from golf courses to bowling alleys, swimming pools, and beaches.[18] Although the post–World War II economic boom rippled unevenly across the United States, and although conscription's economic inequalities drafted a force of soldiers disproportionately from the working class, military officials believed that typical soldiers expected these amenities. GIs were "accustomed to the greatest variety of recreational opportunities in the history of mankind," one Special Services officer explained, and would not go quietly if deprived of all forms of entertainment.[19] But while GIs enjoyed plenty of options for amusement, officials believed that entertainment from home was "essential" in offering a "live representation of the American way of life to service personnel stationed at isolated and remote sites overseas."[20]

It took more than consumer goods and entertainment shows to represent the "American way of life." As in earlier wars, women proved essential to creating a sense of home. Foremost, women's perceived feminine qualities offered a contrast to the war zone. Red Cross Donut Dollies—"pert American girls," according to program leaders—"in their fresh, light blue uniforms" offered the men "a refreshing break in the military routine."[21] Even more than a reprieve, officials characterized the women as altering the military environment in positive ways. "Civilization hit the 25th Infantry Division base camp at Cu Chi this week," one press release read, "with the arrival of three Red Cross girls."[22] Another noted more specifically that the women added "a bit of warmth and grace to the landscape of war."[23]

Recreation clubs and American women allowed GIs to escape the war and think of home for a time. At Red Cross, Special Services, and USO clubs, GIs could play pool, watch television, and attend parties, but the main attraction was the women who staffed them and who, more than anything else, symbolized home.[24] Quizzing the men on sports, music, movies, and even recent *Playboy* Playmates of the Month "took them back to a time before there was killing and dying," one Donut Dolly explained. "For a few minutes they could be home."[25] Special Services explained the connection between women and home more directly. Its clubs provided GIs with ways to occupy their time, stimulate their minds, and busy their idle hands, but "there is no substitute for the conversation or the sympathetic interest of a girl from the States. It's as close to home as you can get in Vietnam."[26]

Although most commanders recognized that Donut Dollies, Special Services women, or USO women could boost morale for the moment, they did not all agree that the women had a lasting positive effect.[27] For company commander John P. Otjen, the women's effect was "very ephemeral." Others ascribed more lasting, though ultimately negative, consequences. Instead of taking the men's minds off the war, John C. Truesdell believed that the women reminded his men "of exactly where they were and what world they were in." His morale, as well as everyone else's in the unit, declined after their visits.[28] Richard F. Timmons agreed that the visits ultimately did more harm than good. Precisely because "those girls looked so good, and were so friendly and nice," he found it difficult to refocus the men's attention on the war after their visits. "It was terrible," he explained, "to go into a stop motion, and then pick up a little piece of civility and light, and then have them wisked [*sic*] away."[29]

Still, most officials held out hope that entertainment could affirm the American public's commitment to the soldiers. An early request for professional entertainment justified live shows as "concrete evidence to servicemen that their devotion to duty and personal sacrifices . . . are recognized by the U.S. public."[30] As entertainment programs mushroomed, a 1969 official military history boasted that "the USO was as familiar to the serviceman as [Military Payment Certificates] and the malaria pill." Individual performers mattered, but even more, the ubiquitous nature of the shows provided "a constant reminder that the servicemen and women in [South Vietnam] had not been forgotten."[31] As public support for the war dwindled, entertainment programs attempted to clarify their work as support for American military personnel, irrespective of political ideologies about the war. In 1971, for example, the USO characterized its activities as a reflection of "the heart of hometown America" and its concern for "our servicemen and women as people." It emphasized, "Regardless of our feelings about the military and military policy, WE CARE about our sons and daughters in uniform."[32]

Westmoreland also used entertainment as a lure to "keep American soldiers and their dollars on their bases and out of the towns and cities." Fearing that "thousands of free-spending Americans" would unleash havoc on the "tremulous economy" of South Vietnam, he knew that a troublesome economic relationship could be utilized as propaganda against the American presence.[33] In particular, Westmoreland knew that GIs could get into all manner of trouble and cause irreparable harm to the fragile US–South Vietnamese relationship by visiting hot spots off base. Only a few months after the United States committed combat troops to Vietnam, the *New York Times* reported that military officials were developing entertainment programs to offset the temptation for GIs to visit "the tawdry night spots of Saigon."[34] More than two years later, they were still fighting to keep American GIs away from the brothels and bars by moving the men onto American bases and increasing recreation programs.[35] When the USO opened clubs in Da Nang and Cam Ranh Bay in 1966, for example, it located the clubs on base specifically to "limit the military presence in the towns adjacent to the large military installations."[36]

Keeping GIs on base seemed especially important as the prostitution industry mushroomed in a symbiotic relationship with the war. As the war destroyed villages and rendered thousands homeless, it pushed women to seek employment in cities and in the booming areas outside of American bases. Many women found work cleaning billets, washing laundry, and staffing PXs. Others had few options besides prostitution. In cities, small villages, and camp towns, GIs purchased sex in brothels, restaurants, bars, and just about anywhere.[37] Military authorities discouraged GIs from soliciting prostitutes, at least officially, though their concern stopped short of World War I and early Cold War–era moralistic concerns.[38] Nor were they overly concerned with preventing venereal disease, which could be easily treated with antibiotics and did not result in significant amounts of lost manpower hours.[39] One physician in the Office of the Army's Surgeon General complained sarcastically in early 1972 that military authorities "cannot even tell [soldiers] how to cut their hair anymore, let alone change their sex habits." Efforts to reduce high incidences of venereal disease through education, prophylaxis devices, and the "shipment of volleyballs and ping-pong tables" all failed, in his estimation, to have a notable effect.[40] One Donut Dolly came to a similar conclusion. Her charge to "keep a lot of guys on the straight and narrow for their sweethearts back home" was "a noble thought," but probably impossible.[41]

Vietnam-era military directives about sex were rooted in concerns about how sexual encounters between GIs and Vietnamese women could negatively affect the relationship between the US military and its South Vietnamese allies. Prostitution became a point of contention between South Vietnamese and US military officials, who claimed publicly that they were devoted to quashing the practice even as they condoned and openly sanctioned it.[42] The sex trade, in fact, was legal in Vietnam at various times. And, on occasion, US military officials created regulated systems of prostitution for their soldiers. An official

Army history of infectious diseases in the war notes that regulation "was attempted on occasion by a number of units in Vietnam but never received overt support and was carried out almost surreptitiously."[43] Captain Jesse H. Denton commanded a company in the 199th Infantry Brigade in late 1967 that lived in a small hamlet alongside about 340 Vietnamese. When the "young hard-chargers" he commanded began "making overtures" toward the Vietnamese women, Denton created a system of "legalized prostitution." In cooperation with the local chief and police, he issued identification cards to women who, after mandatory weekly medical exams and penicillin shots, were allowed to charge regulated prices that were not exorbitant for GIs. Four other company commanders in Denton's battalion created similar systems, which he believed was "the most efficient way of satisfying one problem without creating another"—a polite way of saying that prostitution prevented rape—and had the added benefit of preventing the men from acquiring venereal disease. It was simply a pragmatic decision, and Denton could not understand "why good people crucified one of our finer junior officers" who had installed his own system of regulated prostitution.[44]

Beyond instances in which military officials were directly complicit in prostitution, several practices suggest that they were happy to facilitate men's access to sex, or at least to ignore something that they knew happened on a massive scale. A lieutenant colonel from the First Cavalry Division cooperated with South Vietnamese authorities in An Khe to plan the opening of a center that would house forty-eight bars with eight women each, "many" of them prostitutes who would be examined by South Vietnamese and American medical personnel. Although American military personnel knew that "acceptance of quasi-official prostitution here will not be popular" back home, they, like Denton, considered it a pragmatic measure.[45] Numerous accounts suggest that US military personnel were widely involved in providing medical examinations for prostitutes and monitoring camp towns to ensure that GIs were safe while visiting brothels.[46] Additionally, Special Services' R&R program sponsored one-week trips to Pacific countries, where GIs could put into practice the official and unofficial advice they had received on how to find disease-free prostitutes.[47] And, a congressional investigation into a large massage parlor and steam bath that operated on Long Binh Post suggests the webs of corruption that entangled American and South Vietnamese officials who alternately ignored and condemned the growth of prostitution on military bases.[48]

As the separation between the military and prostitution blurred, and as the distinction between approved and unsanctioned entertainment became less stable, entertainment officials wanted Donut Dollies, USO performers, and Special Services women to symbolize the "all-American girl," an upstanding, wholesome, supportive woman from home who contrasted the sexual labor of Vietnamese women and the sexualized performances of women in commercial shows. In many ways, GIs did see American and Vietnamese women as different—they referred to all American women with the racialized term "round eyes." As Donut Dolly Jeanne Christie explained, "As silly as this may sound, we personified the American women to the men. We were their homes, their sisters, their mothers, their wives, their girlfriends."[49] But, it was not so easy for officials to disentangle the various threads of sexuality that ran through the war. Entertainment organizations struggled to employ American women as symbols of a home in an era in which they were no longer bound so tightly to it. Likewise, as the war divided the home front, and as the image of a female hippie came to symbolize the antiwar movement, it proved difficult for organizations to mobilize an uncontested image of supportive femininity.[50] Perhaps most significant, American culture was flooded with competing notions of what it meant to be an all-American girl.

### THE GIRLS NEXT DOOR

The men of Company B had had a rough few weeks. The Bravo Bulls, as they called themselves, were part of the 173rd Airborne Brigade, one of the first combat units assigned to Vietnam in early 1965. They were doing their best to defend an airstrip at Bien Hoa, a few miles northeast of Saigon, but their new M16 rifles kept jamming, making that job more difficult than it was already. When the men weren't in firefights, they waged a war of attrition against the leeches and spiders that crept into their uniforms. Although the men's newly arrived, young Lieutenant Jack Price could not do much to stop the insects, he did manage to get the cleaning rods they needed to keep their rifles firing by calling in a favor from a college buddy. Price's resourcefulness earned the men's appreciation and convinced them that he could deliver another item that they believed would make their war more endurable.

On a whim, the men told Price that what they really needed was a personal visit from one of *Playboy* magazine's Playmates. A few years earlier, the magazine had launched a promotion that anyone who bought a lifetime subscription would have the first issue personally delivered by a Playmate. It seemed a long shot, but Price sent a formal request to Hugh Hefner, "from the depths of the hearts of 180 officers and men." Price mused that "loneliness in a man's heart is a terrible thing" and would be particularly acute during the upcoming holidays. Although "the beauty of Vietnamese women is unquestionable," he admitted, what the men needed was "a real, living, breathing American girl." After careful consideration, they had "unanimously decided" that the girl they most wanted to see was Jo Collins, the 1965 Playmate of the Year, though Price promised that any Playmate of the Month would "be received with open arms." He enclosed the $150 subscription fee and closed by saying that if the men's request could not be met, Hefner should "please just forget about us, return our money order and we will fade back into the jungle."[51] Collins did not make it in time for Christmas or for New Year's, but she did fulfill the men's dreams when she made a personal visit early the next year. After delivering the first issue to Price, who was then hospitalized with a devastating arm wound, she greeted the Bravo Bulls as they returned from patrol. One confident grunt locked her in a long kiss on behalf of his cheering—and probably very jealous—comrades. They renamed their unit "Playboy Company" in her honor.[52]

Collins's visit captures many of the intentions and contradictions of Vietnam War recreation programs, even if the leaders of the Red Cross, the USO, and Special Services would have vehemently denied that a Playmate had anything in common with the women they employed. In attempting to provide GIs with the "living, breathing American girls" the men in Bravo / Playboy Company desired, recreation organizations all aimed for a model of womanhood that increasingly diverged from the realities of women's lives in the 1960s and early 1970s. For many recreation and military officials, girls next door were college coeds—young, single, "good" girls biding their time until they found the right man and settled down. And yet, that image was a complicated one in the 1960s and early 1970s, in part because it was the same image embraced by *Playboy* magazine. Wholesomeness and sexuality were not incompatible but the intertwined defining qualities of *Playboy* women Hefner described as "provocative" as well as "innocent." A Playmate, he insisted, "is never sophisticated, a girl you cannot really have. She is a healthy, simple girl—the girl next door."[53] Hefner's Playmates were not, of course, attainable for most GIs who instead resigned themselves to carrying the women's centerfolds in their pockets. They were far more likely to see Donut Dollies, USO women, and Special Services women. Although these women were expressly forbidden from the kind of free sexuality *Playboy* magazine advertised, their work placed them somewhere in the middle of these competing images of the girl next door.

In crafting an image of the girl next door, recreation programs characterized women as icons of demure femininity and middle-class America. In December 1970, for example, a group of sorority sisters from Colorado State University, known as The Colorado Kappa Pickers, spent their holiday on a USO tour performing for nearly 11,000 servicemen.[54] Promotional materials characterized the "five lovely young ladies" as average American coeds whose accolades included being named prom queen, singing in the church choir, being a Pom Pom girl, and serving on Student Council.[55] Evaluations of their performances suggest that military audiences "were more than overjoyed" by the women's "attributes of youth, charm, talent and especially being typical all American college girls."[56] One especially revealing review explained that even though the group "lacked the professional touch," the women's "personality and enthusiasm" more than compensated for the GIs, who "indicated that wherever an American Girl is on stage she is more than welcome." It concluded by commending the women for giving up their holiday and "bringing a little of home to the men in Vietnam."[57]

Embodying middle-class American womanhood was not an asexual task, but one that aimed to remind men of a romantic or familial sexuality that contrasted the commercialized sexuality of Asian women. "We wore perfume because we wanted them to smell that smell from home," Donut Dolly Sherry Taylor explained, "and we wore ribbons in our hair because we wanted them to know that we were soft, that we were just like the girls next door, you know, like those girlfriends back home and those wives back home."[58] Reminders of demure femininity knew no age limit. When former pop singer Jeanne Ewing toured Vietnam, she was much older than GIs, but the age difference did not impede her effectiveness. The GIs "love seeing pearls on a woman," she explained, because it reminded them of going on dates with girls from home.[59] Other women found that the most mundane activity could transport a man home in his mind. Donut Dolly Margaret Mary Kelly did not intend for a GI to see her in her hair curlers, but he told her that the sight had made his day. He could see beautiful women singing in clubs whenever he wanted, he said, but her hair curlers reminded him of "home."[60] Even the symbol of American womanhood herself, Miss America, had to adhere to this vision. Miss America 1970 Pamela Anne Eldred was proud "to represent all the girls back home," but when she appeared on stage in "oriental costume," the GIs booed. Her costume choice was "singularly inept," a Special Services employee explained, "since the men in Southeast Asia are surrounded by Asiatic / Oriental culture 24 hours per day."[61]

Even as recreation organizations characterized American women as wholesome all-American girls, the Red Cross and Special Services fashioned the women as potential romantic and sexual symbols by lowering the age requirements and requiring them to be single.[62] Red Cross leaders initially considered an age range of twenty-three to forty but ultimately decided that because "the servicemen for the most part will be young," Donut Dollies should be between twenty-one and twenty-four years old.[63] Special Services women had to be twenty-three until staffing needs led the Army to lower the requirement to twenty-one.[64] Although both organizations' requirement that the women be college graduates created a significant cultural chasm between them and enlisted men, age and marital status requirements meant that Donut Dollies and Special Services

Two American GIs get chummy with Donut Dolly Barbara Barrett while relaxing on bombs in Da Nang, Vietnam. With her braided pigtails and happy smile, Barrett perfectly symbolized the girl next door of the Vietnam War era.

women were, as a group, younger than their predecessors and closer in age to soldiers who were also younger on average than those of earlier wars.[65]

Neither the Red Cross nor Special Services actually wanted their women to form romantic attachments with individual soldiers but instead enforced policies designed to preserve the women's image as wholesome symbols of desire for all GIs. Although the organizations might have liked to prohibit the women from dating, they only expressly forbid relationships with married men. The Red Cross warned Donut Dollies that they would probably feel more comfortable around married men and to watch out for "geographical bachelors" who would neglect to mention that they had wives waiting at home. Still, any relationship was a cause for concern for the organization, which found that it lost more women to marriage than anything else. Thus, program directors rotated women several times during their tour to prevent them from becoming too close to men in their area.[66] Red Cross protocol held that the women were to be available "for all the men," Donut Dolly Leah O'Leary explained, and discouraged all "special relationships."[67]

Additional regulations attempted to protect the women's—and the organizations'—reputations by imposing a curfew, forbidding women from inviting men to their bedrooms, and, in the case of the USO, forbidding sexual relationships between women and their military escort officers.[68] As the women knew all too well, even baseless rumors spread quickly, and the organizations sought to prevent and squash rumors to ensure that a woman's reputation was not irreparably harmed. When GIs began spreading tales of one Donut Dolly's "'extracurricular' activities," for example, the Red Cross transferred her, even though the rumors were unfounded.[69]

Some women overtly resisted the rules intended to prevent them from becoming too close to men. On one of the many USO tours Hollywood personality Johnny Grant made to Vietnam, three women billed as his Armed Forces Radio and Television Service "Girl Friends" accompanied him. A veteran of such tours, Grant attempted to prevent too much fraternization between the attractive young women and the GIs by enforcing strict rules and curfews that the women found too restrictive. One evening, one of the women attempted to go out dancing and complained that "it just wasn't fair for Johnny to keep us pinned up like animals." Even with a curfew, however, soldiers found their way to the women. The tour's escort officer repeatedly had to fend off interested men—officer and enlisted alike—who hung out near the women's hotel rooms, invited themselves to private meals, and tried to accompany the women on their tour.[70] Silky Nolan, the lead vocalist in the USO's R&B group Silk and Soul, made it clear to her Special Services escort that she "was 24-years old, single, and looking for a husband." She seemed to enjoy being "swarmed by onlookers" after performances, who, in the escort officer's mind, were not attracted by her "mediocre" talent but by her "other obvious characteristics."[71] Women who successfully violated the rules—as did one USO performer who stayed all out night with a GI—were kicked out of their program and sent home.[72]

As entertainment programs struggled to craft an aura of virginal femininity around the women, their efforts to recruit attractive women further underscored the difficulty of constructing the girl next door image. The Red Cross wanted young women who were conventionally attractive—not overly suggestive or modern in appearance. When Jan Morehead applied to the Red Cross in late 1965, she included her graduation photograph in the application. She wore the traditional black velvet drape and was astonished when an administrator suggested that perhaps the drape was too low-cut and revealing.[73] In later years, administrators seemed more concerned that women not appear too casual or too similar to the increasingly popular look of the counterculture. When the organization updated its recruitment brochure "For the Best Year of Your Life" in 1969, for example, SRAO director Mary Louise Dowling issued careful guidelines on how to depict women in the program. Although two Donut Dollies took "very good photos," she instructed the photographer to feature other women who "are attractive and clean-cut looking."[74] Peace Corps veteran Michele Marganski impressed one Red Cross official with her forthright manner, sincerity, and outgoing personality, but her appearance and clothing style caused some concern. A training evaluation described her as "average height, a little stocky." The evaluator affirmed that Marganski knew she needed to watch her weight but also noted that she dressed "a little 'mod' . . . in the current pantsuit, overblouse, boots, etc." and warned that "she may have a tendency to be a little careless about her personal appearance."[75]

The Red Cross used strict uniform regulations to help craft what its leaders saw as a respectably attractive image—one that was youthful, feminine, and professional. It was also an image that evolved, ever so slightly, across the war, in response both to practical demands and the changing sense of style among the women. Early in the war, Donut Dollies wore a light blue knee-length dress that buttoned in front, with black loafers and a hat. Climbing onto and out of helicopters, however, quickly revealed the dress's fatal flaw: it flew up in the wind, revealing all that it was intended to hide. In 1966 the Red Cross agreed to change the dress to culottes, which looked like a skirt but had the security of a center seam.[76] Still, the young women who came from college campuses where women's fashions rapidly transformed complained that it was dowdy and often surreptitiously hemmed it well above the knee.[77] Special Services women, who were required to wear a skirt uniform, similarly complained and either shortened the skirt by hemming it, rolling it at the waist, or replicating the Donut Dollies' culottes.[78]

Special Services and the Red Cross seemed to realize they had an unwinnable war on their hands. Special Services officials generally ignored the uniform adjustments as long as the women wore regulation attire when they visited headquarters.[79] In 1971, the Red Cross formally allowed Donut Dollies to hem their uniforms two to two and a half inches above the knee in part to "appear more current and attractive in style," though officials continued to insist that "mini-skirt length is not 'conservative.'"[80] Hair styles similarly evolved. Initially, regulations dictated that, in line with military protocol, women wear their hair above the collar, but as long hair became more fashionable, the women persuaded Dowling that wearing long hair tied in the back looked professional. The move highlighted Dowling's attempts to balance professionalism with GIs' sense of attractiveness. In justifying the change, she noted that the style would be similar to that worn by "the young ladies the serviceman has known at home."[81]

In similar fashion, organizations instructed women to dress in ways that GIs would find attractive. One set of USO guidelines recommended that women wear a moderate amount of makeup because "the guys appreciate a natural look most of all."[82] Women were not to appear anywhere in public with their hair in rollers and were prohibited from wearing pants in military dining facilities.[83] "Remember the troops like to see girls in skirts!" instructions for performers admonished.[84] Although performers received fatigues and boots to wear when traveling, all entertainment directors agreed that military uniforms detracted from the women's appearances and recommended that they wear culottes or "pant dresses" instead.[85] The Red Cross even expected Donut Dollies to be appealing to men when off duty, as long as they left the "short short mini and the décolletage dresses at home."[86] The SRAO director in Vietnam recommended the women bring clothing that would be easy to launder but cautioned that even in difficult circumstances, "practicality shouldn't be carried to the extent that femininity is lost."[87]

The USO was freer than either the Red Cross or Special Services to permit fashion-forward styles and embraced them as supportive of its overall mission to remind the GIs of home. Three women on "The Going Thing" tour in August 1970, for example, staged fashion shows and modeled "very mod outfits that typify 'back in the world' clothes."[88] The fashion shows were the "USO at its best," one review concluded. "No Bob Hope jokes. No television routines. Just the commercials for American womanhood and the styles in which they would like a guy to keep them accustomed."[89] On many tours, women's bodies themselves were the performance and the attraction. Promotional materials regularly featured the women's measurements and included publicity photographs of the women in bathing suits for admiring GIs.[90] The USO advertised three "Armed Forces Radio and Television Girl Friends and Hollywood Pinups" as beauty contest winners and models and included their "vital statistics," or their bust, waist, and hip measurements, for the GIs' information.[91]

Recreation programs further refined the all-American girl image in recruitment materials that characterized her as a careful mix of primness and spunk, of feminine graces and an adventurous spirit. Gena Kay Tanner fit the bill perfectly, both in appearance and personality. A Red Cross interviewer described her as "generally attractive," with a "pretty complexion." The interviewer went on, "a southern girl in mannerisms," she seemed "gentle, but firm with a lot of 'spunk' and confidence."[92] Eager for adventure, the ideal Donut Dolly was "Sugar 'n' spice and everything nice," according to the Red Cross, but also required "a dash of mud, a sprinkle of monsoon, a spray of dust, and a coating of sweat from a searing tropical sun."[93] Braving danger in her efforts to support the troops, she embraced the challenge of working "out in the boondocks" and in taking "audience participation programs to the combat and combat-support troops, getting as near the front lines as security permits."[94]

Careful to avoid making women's work sound too risky, the Red Cross minimized the danger involved in the work and instead emphasized its conservative regulations and safety. A *Washington Post* article about the SRAO program quoted a Donut Dolly who complained that the 7:00 p.m. curfew would be "hard on [her] bridge game" and surmised that she would "have to learn to knit all over again."[95] An April 1969 brochure designed to recruit women "For the Best Year of Your Life" emphasized the challenges they would face but guaranteed a year of "personal growth and development of leadership potential."[96] The SRAO director also continued to try, unsuccessfully, to change the term "Donut Dolly"—a term she believed suggested that the women were engaged in unprofessional food service.[97] A Special Services recruitment video similarly characterized club women as seizing the opportunity to serve their country while having new experiences and pushing themselves to adapt to new situations. Working in a war zone would prove challenging, but the video insisted that they would not be in danger. Instead, they would have fun shopping, sightseeing, and traveling to exotic places during their free time.[98]

The Red Cross instilled its delicate balance between professionalism and gentility in ten-day training sessions designed to give Donut Dollies practice designing audience participation games and planning club activities. But even with lessons in Red Cross history and military structure, many women felt that the sessions focused more on the organization's desired image of womanhood than the realities of their work or the war. Jan Morehead complained that the training "was terribly sexist and bordered more on how we were supposed to dress and act, and not do, as opposed to the job itself."[99] Others concurred that the training emphasized a vision of womanhood steeped in class and race. As Jeanne Christie recalled, training focused on learning "What good, proper young ladies should do," something Leah O'Leary described as having "a genteel quality." Officials referred to her and her colleagues as "ladies" and lectured them on maintaining proper sexual boundaries.[100] Leaders instructed the women to be "nonsexual symbols of purity and goodness . . . be sister, mother, girl next door, but don't have affairs; that's a no-no." The lectures left out a critical part, however, according to Penni Evans. "What they didn't tell us was what to do about the rumors, the comments, the come-ons."[101] As Evans suggested, being the girl next door was not as uncomplicated a task as the Red Cross might have imagined.

For recreation officials, the girl next door was a symbol of wholesome American girls who supported their boys at the front. But

American women held a variety of ideas about what constituted American womanhood, not to mention the war itself. Even women who became Donut Dollies, who worked in Special Services, and who toured Vietnam with the USO often felt that the image they upheld was outdated. "I couldn't believe we were really being trained to go to a war zone and play games with soldiers," noted O'Leary. Although she overstated it when she said that "half of American womanhood was burning their bras and finding their feminist voices, the other half were out on the picket lines and marching in anti-war demonstrations," she felt that her own experiences of "going off to play games and 'skits' with G.I.s in Vietnam" seemed regressive by comparison.[102] Some women would have agreed, but not all. Donut Dollies, Special Services women, and USO performers all came to the work for a variety of reasons that suggest the complicated nature of American womanhood during the Vietnam War era.

### BRIGHT, BUBBLY PEOPLE

Sherry Taylor knew many women who followed the traditional route for middle-class white women of marriage and motherhood, but she felt drawn to a different path. Even as a child, her mother saw "something in me that would take me places," but when she entered Oklahoma State University in the mid-1960s, Taylor felt limited to three career options: nurse, teacher, or secretary. She was drawn to architecture and had scored high in mechanics on an aptitude test but discovered that a ten o'clock curfew for women precluded her from pursuing the field, as she could not participate in nighttime charrettes with the other students. Instead, she settled for teaching and became the first college graduate in her family. Her career might have been conventional, but in an attempt to embrace "the adventure that life offers to us," she decided during her senior year to move to an interesting place and accepted a teaching job in Colorado. An article about Donut Dollies in *Cosmopolitan* changed everything. Having grown up as an Air Force brat, she felt compelled to support the men her age who were being sent to Vietnam, and she'd been captivated by stories her pilot friends had told her about the Far East. Plus, serving in a war zone offered her a way to "grab the world by [the] tail" and "go in a different direction" with her life. One month after graduation, she was at training in Washington, DC.[103]

Like Taylor, many women who served in recreation programs during the Vietnam War had been military children and had grown up all over the country, moving from place to place with their father's assignments.[104] Some, like Nancy Smoyer, had traveled on their own, often studying abroad for a time during college. Smoyer traveled as far as England, France, Israel, and Australia. When she got lonely in France, she hung out at the USO club where she felt comforted by being around other Americans. Later, she decided to go to Vietnam because she wanted to provide that same feeling of comfort to GIs far from home. After looking into work with the USO and Special Services, she joined the Red Cross because it sent women closer to the war's action than the other services.[105]

A "yen to travel" often coalesced with a desire to escape the trappings of conventionality.[106] Jennifer Young had no interest in settling down with a husband immediately after college. "Who in their right mind would want to tie themselves down," she wondered.[107] Like Taylor, Jeanne Christie had a teaching job lined up before she graduated from college, but she wasn't too excited by the prospect of becoming a "typical destined-to-be-old maid schoolteacher." She wanted something different for herself and "decided that if I was going to do anything, I had to do it now."[108] The timing was right for Susan Conklin as well. She had grown up reading *Brenda Starr, Reporter* comics about a glamorous redheaded journalist and longed for similar adventures. Conklin had no plans for the domestic life that many of her friends were set upon. "That was good for everybody else, but not for me," she explained. "I had no desire to get married. I just wanted to see the world, travel, and do something." After a friend told her about a Red Cross ad in the *Denver Post,* Conklin applied. The Red Cross was looking for "bright, bubbly people," and Conklin fit the bill. Working as a Donut Dolly in Vietnam was her chance to "see the world and let somebody else pay for it."[109]

Although much of recreation women's work modeled conservative gender ideals, working in a war zone was anything but conventional. Women had, of course, served in these roles in earlier wars, but without the kind of national mobilization that had accompanied the world wars, the American government did not promote or celebrate women's service in Vietnam as a model of patriotic duty. Moreover, as the women's liberation movement grew and expanded, and as the war increasingly divided the American public, women who worked in Vietnam did so without the kind of public support and understanding that women before them had taken for granted. Some even defied family wishes to go. The Red Cross insisted that women state in writing that their parents concurred with their assignment to Vietnam, but not all women had their parents' unfettered support.[110] Holley Watts's parents, like many others, were not pleased with their daughter's decision to go to Vietnam, but she remained determined nonetheless. She was a legal adult, after all, she said, and her parents could not prevent her from going.[111] A woman's decision to go to war often signified more than a rejection of family concerns. Going to Vietnam was "the first time in my life I ever bucked society," Donut Dolly Susan Bradshaw McLean remarked. Having grown up in the South and been "raised a lady," she always did what her parents wished. They had been relieved when her brother was not sent to Vietnam and never expected that their daughter would want to go. They worried for her safety, of course, but also what people in their community would think. Undeterred, McLean "decided that I really needed to do this" and headed off to war.[112]

The war in Vietnam was *the* event of their generation for many women, and they were determined to play their part. Coming of age in an era of economic prosperity and motivated by President John F. Kennedy's call to service, women like Linda K. Morgan Maini wanted to be part of something bigger than themselves. Without concrete postgraduation plans, Maini considered voluntary services in Vietnam and the Peace Corps before she was drawn to the Red Cross as a way to serve her country and other Americans.[113] Maureen Nerli wanted "to be part of this war," and working in the USO lounge at the San Francisco airport did not get her close enough. After seeing a lot of returning soldiers, she decided to go to Vietnam where she could "show the men that I saw every day coming in and out of the USO that somebody really cared."[114]

Many women felt compelled to wartime service out of a sense of duty, especially as they watched their male friends face the possibility of being drafted. Gloria Glover Gates did not want to join the military but felt that, just as her father and grandfather had served in wars, she too owed some kind of service.[115] Other women even considered it unfair that women were not subject to the draft.[116] The only women Margaret Mary Kelly knew of who went to Vietnam were nurses, and so she had to do some research to find a way for a woman like herself to go to Vietnam. After interviewing with the Red Cross and Special Services, she joined the Red Cross.[117]

Donut Dolly Leah O'Leary felt similarly drawn to service, especially after working in Honduras the summer between her freshman and sophomore years of college. When she returned to campus she "felt like all the action was going on somewhere else."[118] Even more, she considered draftees to be "victims" and felt a need to support them.[119] As she approached her senior year, she began to search for ways to go to Vietnam and found that only the Red Cross would guarantee her an assignment. "Part of me thought the whole idea of 'recreational activities'—board games, quiz competitions, etc.—was crazy," she admitted, "but hey, if this was the only way to get there, I'd go play games."[120] Although she did not support the war effort, she felt no incongruity with her work in it. Playing games with soldiers would not "make a difference in the execution of the war effort," she determined, but it "was compassionate."[121]

As O'Leary suggests, women often struggled to reconcile their opinion about the war with their service in it. Indeed, entertainment organizations faced great difficulties in recruiting women for work in Vietnam from the earliest days of the conflict. SRAO Director Dowling complained in 1965 that the absence of a "high degree of patriotic fervor" like that of the World War II and Korean War eras explained young people's unwillingness to devote themselves to wartime service.[122] College campuses seemed especially adverse recruiting grounds, and Dowling warned recruiters to expect a hostile response. Any mention of the war in Red Cross materials might "arouse the political activists who seem to be on the lookout for something to be against," she cautioned, and so recruiters should "make clear the completely non-political character of our services to military personnel as individuals."[123] Efforts to characterize the Red Cross as apolitical do not appear to have been as effective as Dowling hoped. Although she nearly met recruitment quotas for the first couple years of the program, by 1968 she warned of "an extremely critical staffing situation in Vietnam," even as military requests for the women increased.[124]

Antiwar sentiment hampered USO recruitment as well, particularly among "younger and not so well established" performers who worried that appearing to support the war would harm their "box-office appeal."[125] Bob Hope's Christmas tour and Martha Raye's regular visits to Vietnam inspired some performers, but the military wanted more than were volunteering.[126] When former Special Services worker Ethyl Payne interviewed African American GIs for the *Chicago Daily Defender,* she reported that the men were upset to learn that opposition to the war was to blame for the paucity of shows. "It's a long, lonely war," she admonished, before asking the State Department to "get some more warm bodies, preferably feminine, over here to relieve the monotony."[127] Even General Westmoreland tried. He specifically requested "more stars" in early 1967, but to no avail. As the war grew more and more unpopular, "big names bowed out" and the USO relied more on "obscure acts" or the "faithful stars."[128]

Even as antiwar sentiment challenged recreation organizations' recruitment, women like O'Leary did not let their opposition to the war effort stop them from serving. Donut Dollies Emily Strange and Cherie Rankin had both protested the war while in college but joined the Red Cross in part to learn about the war for themselves. "It was very easy in my naiveté to believe that the war was wrong," Strange explained, and she decided after hearing a general speak about the war that she should experience it for herself. Protesting was "easy" among friends, but she "wanted to know the reality."[129] Rankin also felt there was more she should know. Her brother had enlisted in the Marine Corps and been sent to Vietnam, and she could not help thinking— despite her opposition to the war—"that there were guys over there like my brother—guys who grew up with apple pie and country, guys who did what they were told and didn't question it." Although she

It was too hot in Vietnam for coffee, so Donut Dollies like Virginia Yerly took cups of Kool-Aid to soldiers instead. Many Donut Dollies sought out wartime service as a way to support GIs, even if they did not support the war itself.

"didn't want to support the war," she did want "to support those guys." After deciding that service with the Red Cross would not "be a statement in favor of the war," she volunteered to go to Vietnam.[130]

The ability to separate the war and its soldiers proved an invaluable asset for recreation women once they arrived in Vietnam. As Donut Dolly Sharon Vander Ven Cummings described it, her job was to "smile and be bubbly—no matter what the situation."[131] In this way, American women felt that they were apolitical symbols of comfort and support for GIs. If the men "could still relate to a soft, feminine person, and they could still laugh," Donut Dolly Sherry Taylor explained, they could believe that "things might be normal again." She noted, "We kept them grounded, so that they knew they could go home."[132] This emotional and symbolic work was not easy and, according to Special Services worker Judy Jenkins, demanded that the women ignore their own fears and concerns because they had to "take [the men's] minds off the war and listen to their problems." She "was there to make things better for the guys," she said, "to be mother, sister, the girl next door."[133]

However apolitical the work might have been in some ways, military officials utilized women to bolster the war effort by assuring the men that women from home supported them and their actions. Donut Dollies learned quickly, especially when working with troops engaged in combat, to keep any negative opinions about the war or the men's behaviors to themselves so that the men would not feel as though their efforts or losses were in vain.[134] Even when GIs showed their collections of Vietnamese body parts to Jeanne Christie, she refrained from judgment because she feared the men would be devastated if she did not empathize with their situation.[135] Her colleague Emily Strange described this work as putting on her "Eleanor Rigby" face. Like the woman in the 1966 Beatles song, she put on her makeup and a smile every morning, regardless of what she encountered. On days when she worked with troops preparing for missions, that face became especially critical, both for her and the men. If Donut Dollies visited the GIs beforehand, she explained, they believed that they would be safe.[136]

Donut Dollies' visits, of course, did not protect the men, and commanders frequently enlisted American women as symbols of support when their units had "suffered heavy losses."[137] Recreation women received no training in counseling, and they found the work especially difficult.[138] When Marines near Khe Sanh came into the Red Cross center after a particularly rough mission, they were "filthy, wretched, dirty," Jeanne Christie remembered. They appeared to be "in a total fog and daze," and Christie felt that all she could do to help was to "just be as normal as I possibly could be around them to let them decelerate."[139] Jill York sometimes felt as though she was "intruding on people's grief." She and her coworkers were called once to have chow with a unit after several of the men had died in battle. Though she struggled to help, she believed that a woman's presence was critical for grieving men who might find comfort in being with and talking with a woman in a way that they could not with fellow soldiers. "We were mothers, sisters, daughters, whatever they needed on a particular night," she explained.[140] As another Donut Dolly put it, they offered the men "a small, much needed, female reaffirmation of their self-image."[141]

As women negotiated their roles as morale boosters and symbols of a supportive femininity, they also learned to anticipate men's needs in various situations. This task was made all the more complicated because, much like notions of femininity, notions of manhood were in flux and contested during the Vietnam era. The war, the draft, and the antiwar movement all led many young men to question the prevailing models of martial masculinity.[142] The civil rights movement and black power movement added an additional layer of complexity to notions of manhood and shaped the ways men and women understood the purposes of recreation and entertainment.

### SOUL SISTERS FROM HOME

In July 1966, two GIs wrote to *Ebony* magazine. Henry J. Thomas noted that the Red Cross had recently opened a recreation center in An Khe "to give us fighting men that 'home away from home' feeling." He and the other men of the First Cavalry Division appreciated the center, especially the "three lovely young ladies" who staffed it. The problem was that while "a white soldier coming to the center can look forward to sitting and engaging in pleasant conversation and warm friendship with these workers," black soldiers like himself could not expect the same hospitality. "No matter how dedicated and impartial" the women were, he explained, "the prejudices among white GIs prevent them from displaying the same wholesome friendly attitude toward Negroes." Thomas felt slighted in his access to the women, but a sense of racial solidarity and pride also underscored his plea for black Donut Dollies. "We would like someone we can identify with, who will remind us of the girl we left behind. To be perfectly honest," he explained, "'Miss Ann' doesn't remind me of the soul sister I left back home in Birmingham."[143] Thomas had most likely never met sailor Ed Madison, but the two men concurred about the state of entertainment in Vietnam. "Why?" Madison asked, had there not been but two black entertainers to have performed in Vietnam. "There are a lot of us here. I am sure that we would rather see some of our own people entertaining the troops here once in a while."[144]

The publication of these two letters launched a flurry of activity in the Red Cross both to publicize its efforts to address racial disparities and to recruit African American women. Officials were well aware of the problem; at the time of the letters' publication, only one of the sixty-two Donut Dollies in Vietnam was African American.[145] The organization had tried repeatedly to get articles published in *Ebony* and other African American publications, had distributed recruitment materials to the African American women's sorority Delta Sigma Theta and to historically black colleges and universities, had sent representatives to a career conference sponsored by the Urban League, and had set quotas intended to procure black women. Despite these efforts, in August 1968, only one of the 113 Donut Dollies in Vietnam was black and by January 1971, the organization was facing the possibility of having no African American women in the program at all.[146] The USO had greater success in recruiting African American performers, though it, too, struggled to fulfill troops' desires for a diverse slate of entertainers. In early 1972, Special Services estimated that 25 percent of American performers had been black, and that half of the music performed was of a style "popularly credited to Black origins."[147]

Recreation and entertainment organizations had failed to provide a group of women who mirrored the racial makeup of the military they served in each of the wars of the twentieth century. The Vietnam War, however, highlighted the problem in acute ways, occurring as it did against the backdrop of the civil rights movement and the black power movement's celebration of black culture and beauty.[148] Racial tensions simmered in Vietnam as well, as the draft disproportionately selected black troops for combat service and as many black soldiers resisted their part in what they saw as a white colonial war and a racist military hierarchy. In this environment, expressions of culture were matters of pride and politics, and entertainment was but one venue through which racial tensions played out in country. Military and entertainment officials struggled to meet GIs' desire for appealing entertainment and women to whom they could relate, but they were ultimately unsure of how to handle larger questions of racial equality and racial pride.

Military and entertainment officials understood that black troops felt a stronger connection to black women than they did to white women, even if white women exhibited no obvious racial prejudices. The commander of the Fourth Infantry Division went out of his way to facilitate the connection for some of his soldiers by asking the Red Cross to assign African American women to the Clubmobile unit that visited his area. He and his men appreciated the Donut Dollies' visits, and though white women did not display "any bias or prejudice," he observed that "the colored soldiers seem reticent and hesitant to participate" in activities. Assigning "a colored Red Cross girl would alleviate this condition," he reasoned, "and encourage greater participation on the part of the soldiers."[149] Red Cross officials seemed sympathetic but had no African American women to assign.[150] The assistant director of the China Beach USO club similarly implored readers of *Ebony* magazine, especially "gals between the ages of 18 and 23," to send letters and photos that could be posted on the club's bulletin board. "We get almost no letters from sisters for the black GIs, or from black families," she explained, and it was disheartening for the men not to see letters from their "own people."[151]

Black soldiers were drawn to black women out of familiarity and racial pride. Ethel Payne, who had worked with Special Services in Korea before writing for the *Chicago Daily Defender,* reported from Vietnam that black soldiers were desperate to see black women from home. The men could find plenty of Vietnamese women and "darker-skinned Cambodian girls who remind the fellows of 'soul sisters'" in the bars they frequented in a section of Saigon known as "Soulsville." But nothing compared to the sight and touch of black women from home. One GI, she reported, spotted a black woman sunbathing at her billet and—despite a warning shot fired by the guard on duty—ran up to her, grabbed her hand, and told her that he just had to shake the hand of the "first soul sister I've seen in 11 months."[152]

Recreation work fostered close—even romantic—connections between American women and GIs of all races. In some cases, white women were unsure how to respond to these connections. Donut

Dolly Kathy Ormond visited a group of GIs and played a game with them that one of her colleagues had developed, where the women predicted each man's love life based on prewritten scenarios. In one case, the prediction suggested that because the man had a roving eye, he should wait to marry but vowed that the wait would be worth it, as his future wife would be "tall and blonde and beautiful." When she read the fortune to a black GI, however, it struck Ormond as nonsensical. "What negro boy wants a blonde?!" she asked. She determined to write more generic predictions because the "boys want to have things apply to themselves and it's up to us to be really sensitive to this."[153] Although at that moment interracial love seemed an impossibility, over the course of her tour, Ormond realized that romance developed across the color line. In two gushing letters written on subsequent days, GI Oscar Colbert professed his love to Ormond, though he had only met her briefly when she made a Clubmobile visit to his unit. Colbert acknowledged that the odds were stacked against him as he was "a negro young man trying to win a beautiful white young ladies [sic] love."[154] Ormond revealed nothing about her thoughts on the matter in existing letters to family and friends, but her collection of letters from GIs suggests that race was the only distinguishing factor to Colbert's feelings.

Other white women dealt with interracial romance more directly.[155] Nancy Smoyer and Jennifer Young were both friends with African American men whose feelings grew beyond the bounds of friendship. Young confessed that though she should have seen it coming, "given the way our conversations have gone," she was still surprised when her friend asked her to join him at a party. She knew that the only reason to turn him down would have been because he was African American and she would have been ashamed of herself if she did. Although she found out later that "a lot of people" disapproved of their pairing, she went with him and had a good time. Smoyer also felt that her relationship with a black lieutenant was "a little bit unusual," but didn't recall anyone having a problem with it. Even as they tread carefully in their relationships, both women discounted them as having little significance in the unusual circumstances of the war. "How can you date in an environment like that?" Young asked.[156]

African American women felt all the pressures that other women did of being conspicuous in the war zone, in addition to the added weight of being so sought out by black GIs. It wasn't that white GIs were not also drawn to black women. As Shirley Hines insisted, all men in Vietnam were lonesome and "it doesn't matter if he's from one of the southern states and you're as black as soot." All she had to do was walk into a room and introduce herself, and "that guy lights up." But black GIs seldom saw African American women from home, and she "had to be careful" not to date just one man or show one man too much attention lest the others feel left out. She encouraged other black women to sign up for the work to convince the men that not everyone from home had forgotten them.[157] Donut Dolly Barbara Lynn knew she would be the only "soul sister" in Vietnam and expected to be popular among the "brothers," but she was unprepared for the extent of her popularity. She "never dreamed that my being there would mean so much to them," she admitted, but the men told her that "seeing a 'sister' when you came back from the rice paddies was something else."[158] Her colleague Carolyn "Tee" Johnson was similarly surprised. When she and her coworkers passed black GIs, the men did a double take. "She can bring so much more of home to these men than we can," a white Donut Dolly explained.[159] Other non-white women felt similar connections to non-white GIs. A Lumbee Indian from North Carolina, Paulette Sweeney described herself as looking like a "native girl." Although a few GIs guessed that she was Native American, others suspected she might be Italian, or Hawaiian, or Greek. Essentially, she reflected what the soldiers wanted to see. "Whatever olive skin culture GI was looking at me," she explained, "I was a touchstone for them."[160]

Race complicated black women's experiences in other ways. Basic matters such as hair care were difficult for black women like Johnson, who solved the problem by wearing her hair short.[161] Hines became so lonely during her tour that the Red Cross sent another African American staff member to her area for a month.[162] Larger political concerns framed the women's experiences as well. Sharon Wesley's decision to join the Red Cross and go to Vietnam did not come easily. Her colleague Reese Eisler recalled that she "had real political doubts about her role there and the neutral position required for our jobs," on top of concerns about racial policies in the United States and the military. Once she decided to go to Vietnam, however, she embraced her mission and went out of her way to reach out to black troops.[163]

These personal connections indicated entertainment and recreation's significance as a conduit for broader matters of racial diversity. In the wake of racial violence following the assassination of Martin Luther King Jr., for example, the army mandated each company-level unit to have a Human Relations Council to advise them on race relations, as well as relations between enlisted men, officers, and noncommissioned officers (NCOs). One such council in the Qui Nhon area recommended that, in light of "the current push to bridge cultural and ethnic gaps," army commanders use their influence to secure "a more equitable appropriation of shows." The men reasoned that a more diverse slate of entertainment would appeal to black troops, as well as to "other minority groups e.g. Spanish, Mexican and Indian" and "would be an excellent vehicle to effect better cultural understanding."[164] Army headquarters responded that the USO was still actively seeking diverse groups and noted that three "ethnic-oriented shows" were scheduled for tours in the next two months. Although officials did not discount the soldiers' request, they did express concern that troupes not be so specialized as to limit their appeal to "one ethnic group."[165]

Black women entertainers and recreation workers found that striking the right balance of cultural pride and universal appeal was a difficult proposition. The tours of Miss Black America illustrate competing understandings of black cultural pride and, in particular, the appeal of black women. The Miss Black America pageant began in 1968 both as a protest against the discrimination of the Miss America pageant and an affirmation of black women's beauty amid the broader growth of black cultural nationalism. When the pageant began touring Vietnam in 1970, USO promotional materials emphasized its universal appeal, not its revolutionary challenge to notions of femininity. The purpose of the Miss Black America pageant, one press release noted, was to "acclaim and applaud Black Beauty and parade the women of color as a universal symbol of pride." The pageant's owner echoed this notion of universal appeal by assuring that "both black and white will appreciate the true beauty of the black woman."[166] *Ebony* magazine confirmed that GIs in Vietnam did. In its coverage of the pageant tour, the magazine noted that black GIs were "especially excited" to see her since few black women performed with the USO, but it also emphasized in text and images that white GIs welcomed the "chance to shake hands with a beautiful girl."[167] Military personnel reviewed the tour in glowing terms that made no mention of race but commended the variety of songs performed.

When the pageant reprised its annual Vietnam tour in early 1971, however, the tour evoked the ire of several military officials who concluded that the performances were "directed mainly to and for black military personnel" and recommended a "broader spectrum of entertainment."[168] Advance publicity for the show repeated verbatim statements made the prior year about the universal appeal of black women's beauty, and local military personnel made no mention of race in their reviews, but accounts of the show's performances highlighted the ways that the show became a venue for expressions of black pride. At several performances, audience members came on stage, gave the black power salute, and solicited funds for the defense of black political activist Angela Davis.[169] The *Seventh Air Force News* reported that "The soul brothers were turned on" and that their black power salute was intended for the "soul sisters who sang their songs, danced their dances and talked to them in their language."[170] Military officials were unsure how to respond, with one major ruling the displays of black power symbols "not excessively militant . . . not overdone" and a colonel describing all but one of the troupe's members as having "displayed a constant posture of arrogance to and disdain for all white personnel with whom they came into contact."[171]

Identifying too much with black GIs could also lead to trouble for recreation women. Millie Majette, a club worker at the Cam Ranh Bay USO, associated with GIs in Black Brothers United (BBU), a civil rights group that actively protested instances of discrimination against black soldiers. Military and USO officials asked for her removal, charging that she used USO facilities and equipment to aid the BBU, repeatedly violated curfew, demonstrated an impertinent attitude, and focused too much attention on the black soldiers. At the same time, the USO and military feared her removal would cause as many problems as it would solve. "Almost all black soldiers at Cam Ranh Bay respect her and are drawn to her as a female with whom they can identify," the acting commander at Cam Ranh Bay noted, and her removal could "subject the command to charges of racial discrimination."[172] The Inspector General recommended "a quiet, low key" transfer, but with no other black women in the USO or the Red Cross available to transfer to the area, Majette remained at her post.[173]

Although recreation and military officials sought to facilitate and seemed pleased when black women made personal connections with black GIs, as Majette discovered, those connections were to be rooted in notions of familiarity and home, not the racial politics that underscored both. When the racial undertones of recreation work bubbled too close to the surface, trouble erupted. Keeping the sexual roots of entertainment under control proved similarly difficult.

### WHERE THE BOYS ARE

A January 1966 *Washington Post* article began with the tantalizing lead "Girls, do you want to go where the boys are?" It followed with a description of Donut Dollies riding helicopters across Vietnam to visit troops "out in the boondocks, where the boys are," painting a tantalizing picture of working with GIs in hope of attracting women to the program.[174] The reference to "where the boys are" was a nod to the popular 1960 novel and film of the same name, which followed four midwestern college girls as they spent a rollicking spring break chasing—and being chased by—boys on the beaches of Fort Lauderdale, Florida. The film featured several well-known actors, including pop artist Connie Francis, who performed the title song and in 1967 toured Vietnam with the USO.[175]

In likening recreation work in Vietnam to a spring break vacation, the article suggested that women would spend the year surrounded by romance and fun. Yet, *Where the Boys Are* was not just a tale of four college coeds innocently flirting their way through a week of fun and sun. It was also a film that warned of the consequences of unbridled female sexuality. One of the four coeds is especially determined to find love on the trip and has sex with the first two men who pay her any attention. Desperate for reassurance afterward, she plans to meet one of the men at their usual rendezvous and is surprised when his friend arrives and rapes her. Although the article's author surely did not intend to suggest Donut Dollies would meet the same fate, the assault scene in fact made the reference all the more apropos. However much recreation and entertainment organizations couched women's work in a language of all-American wholesomeness, sex appeal remained the underpinning of programs that utilized women as symbols of men's desires. And that appeal, all too often, placed Donut Dollies, Special Services women, and USO performers in very real danger as they faced untoward propositions and outright attacks from soldiers who assumed that the women were theirs for the taking.

As in earlier wars, entertainment women had to carefully balance the sexual nature of their work. Some suggestions of romantic love and desire were deemed appropriate and even useful, while too much flaunting of sexual appeal or lust was not. The Vietnam War era added an additional layer to this complicated task, as the sexual revolution and feminist movement brought sexuality into public discussion and challenged the sexual double standard that had long separated what most Americans considered appropriate behavior for men and women. Legal precedents changed as well. At beginning of combat operations, for example, the birth control pill was not universally available to single women, but by the time American forces withdrew from Vietnam, the Supreme Court had ruled in favor of a woman's right to contraception and abortion. All of these changes shaped the ways entertainment organizations framed women's work, as well as the ways women and men understood women's purpose in the war.

Women often insisted that their interactions with GIs were more like those between siblings than anything sexual, even as they acknowledged the difficulty in keeping their relationships platonic. There were too many men and too few women, not to mention too little privacy, to have romantic relationships, explained Donut Dolly Susan Conklin. Women and men socialized and engaged in "all kinds of friendly teasing and kidding," but she and her colleagues had to "keep yourself kind of neutral" so that all soldiers would feel comfortable with them.[176] Linda K. Morgan Maini agreed. Being so outnumbered by men meant that the women were "always on duty." She wanted to have a sisterly or friendly relationship with the soldiers, "not a sexual kind of thing . . . not a flirtatious kind of thing," but she admitted that this goal "was a little bit hard to do sometimes."[177] In the concentrated wartime environment and in an era of freer sexual expression, women's efforts to police the boundary between friendship and sexual attraction proved quite difficult. "We were all young, active humans and there were attractions," Donut Dolly Paulette Sweeney confessed. "The hormones were raging."[178]

Young twenty-something recreation women sometimes found themselves attracted to the American men who surrounded them, and in those instances worked hard to guard theirs and their employer's reputation. Donut Dolly Penni Evans "fell in love about three times" during her year in Vietnam but was determined "to protect the image of the Red Cross," so she refrained from sex. Despite her restraint, rumors spread that she was "having mad, passionate affairs," and Evans concluded somewhat jovially that she "totally blew the opportunity of a lifetime!"[179] Relationships were hard, according to Sandra Lockney Davis, complicated by "fear, stress, isolation, short assignments, long working hours, and other obstacles." Even more, officers monopolized the women's free time, geographical bachelors abounded, and rumors "ran rampant." Although she and her friends had fun, most were "more concerned with surviving and escaping reality than looking for a lifetime partner."[180]

The war itself complicated connections between hormones and entertainment even further. Many of the men recreation women knew lived and worked under stressful circumstances that influenced the ways they viewed the women.[181] "You were constantly being put in situations with men who were horny as hell," Donut Dolly Cherie Rankin explained. "Men who were angry, who had had all sorts of miserable things happen to them, who were disoriented for all kinds of reasons. So there were many, many times when you were physically, emotionally, and psychologically threatened, just in the course of doing your job."[182] When Liz Malleson Longstreet rejected the advances of a soldier who said he was in love with her, another GI

On a USO tour with the group "The Going Thing," aspiring actress Gabrielle Herrera walks a gauntlet of GIs to model the latest American fashions. Women's work with the troops often put their bodies on display in ways they found uncomfortable and even threatening.

charged that she had no right to reject him and attempted to knife her. Another soldier intervened, but the officer in charge dismissed the attack as the consequences of wartime stress. No charges were filed.[183] Indeed, for some GIs, American women only made the war worse. "All you are doing is teasing us," a soldier in Quang Tri told Penni Evans. "'Look but don't touch.' You are a bunch of cock-teasers, and you shouldn't be here."[184]

Women did not necessarily see themselves as a tease, but they did function as sexual symbols, and the meaning of those symbols varied with each circumstance. For example, Donut Dollies, Special Services, and USO women frequently staged fashion shows for GIs' entertainment. Women modeled clothing they brought from home or bought on R&R trips to Australia and Asia, and, according to a Red Cross press release, also "showed what the female figure could do to such mundane garb as combat fatigues, flight suits, and bell-bottom trousers."[185] After word spread at Cam Ranh that Donut Dollies had staged a small fashion show at the Steppin' Groove Red Cross Center, the generals decided that the women should repeat the show for thousands of men in the area. They arranged for a walkway, band, and stadium lights, and the women modeled their "little hot pants and miniskirts" for "three thousand horny guys," as Cherie Rankin described them. The women concluded the show by calling a few GIs on stage to dance but only the drunk and stoned were willing, and they grabbed the women, making them all feel very "nervous." Rankin and the other women had felt comfortable in their center with GIs they knew, but this much larger show felt "out of control" and put them on display in ways they did not appreciate.[186]

Women's work also called on them to actively frame themselves as sexual objects. Donut Dolly Marcy Stennes went on a date with a soldier she chose in her club's reproduction of the popular television show *The Dating Game,* even though she felt uncomfortable in the situation.[187] In the USO tour "Daniel and Friends," the show's namesake (a "famous French hair stylist") traveled with three "pretty girl models" whose fashion shows were "extremely well received by the male audience."[188] When they visited the naval hospital ship USS *Sanctuary,* 450 sailors appreciated the group's humor, which the ship's Special Services officer approvingly described as "bordering on, and frequently treading upon, the risqué."[189] The USO women who traveled with Skip Young (best known for playing Wally on *The Adventures of Ozzie and Harriet*) similarly intimated sexual encounters. At one fire support base, the women crawled inside tents and bunkers to wake the sleeping men who were astonished to find a woman "in bed" with them.[190] Armed Forces Radio and Television Service weathergirl Bobbi Keith made innuendo her trademark, as she danced and signed off the news with an admonition for GIs to "have a pleasant evening, weather-wise and you know, of course, otherwise." Eventually, producers put a stop to her sign-off, deeming it too suggestive; her revealing pinup photographs seem to have elicited no such response.[191]

Some military personnel expressed concern that this kind of entertainment could have serious consequences. In her brief introduction to Special Services work, Debby Alexander learned a very important rule: never touch the men. Inexperienced in sexual matters, Alexander thought that this instruction was a euphemism for sexual relationships, but she soon discovered that military officials meant it literally. One day at her club, a black GI told her a funny story and as she laughed, she innocently reached out and touched his forearm. Immediately, a white sergeant pulled her aside and chastised her. The men would "think there's more that they could expect from you," he cautioned, though Alexander suspected he was also unnerved by the fact that she had touched a black man in a friendly way. Echoing the instructions of a Special Services manual from the 1950s, she noted that her role was to be "friendly but impersonal."[192] Other officials feared that women's presence inflamed GIs' sexual longings to the point that they sought sexual release through prostitutes.[193]

In this tense environment, military officials knew that the women's work and small numbers placed them at risk and took precautionary steps to protect them. USO performers traveled with armed military escort officers; military police and security guards provided additional protection at hotels.[194] Donut Dollies and Special Services women lived in military-provided billets guarded by American soldiers, military police, or Vietnamese guards. Some billets were even fenced in to provide an additional level of protection, and as Donut Dolly Leah O'Leary clarified in a letter to her parents, the cause for concern was American men.[195] These protections did not prevent all intrusions. Men attempted to break into the Red Cross billets all the time, Jeanne Christie noted, but the women "learned to live with it."[196] They also learned to protect themselves. When Jenny Young and her fellow Donut Dollies got stranded overnight after a Clubmobile run, the women chose their sleeping quarters intentionally so that they could bar all the entrances themselves.[197]

Although military personnel seem to have taken the women's safety very seriously, they dismissed inappropriate male behavior as inevitable and expected women not only to anticipate but also to ward off the men. "Boys will be boys" seemed sufficiently self-explanatory for many military officials. In August 1971 a group of helicopter pilots in Nha Trang raided two USO performers' billets, took their bras and panties, and wore them at a party they had invited the women to attend. The pilots eventually returned the items, and their captain dismissed the men's actions as a harmless way to blow off steam. "War is hell," he explained simply. This rationale did little to assure the women's escort officer who found the base commander's insistence that the men "were gentlemen" ironic in light of their panty raid. The officer slept in the women's living room during their visit because the doors had no locks.[198]

As the escort officer understood, the distinction between harmless pranks and physical danger was murky at best. The escort officer assigned to the Skip Young show, for example, condoned the response of an "over-anxious soldier" who "grabbed" one of the women on the tour and "planted a big kiss on her mouth." Although the escort officer "quickly broke up the mad embrace," he deemed the kiss an innocent symbol of the men's appreciation. "Everyone had a good laugh and no harm was done," he insisted. His lack of concern in this situation is curious, especially since he removed the women from a visit to another location after some of the men made "a few obscene remarks directed toward the ladies."[199] Obscenities turned to threats at a Harrison-Tyler Show USO performance at the Cam Ranh Air Base. Several GIs shouted sexual innuendoes and made obscene gestures toward the female performers before someone yelled, "Get off the stage bitches or we'll shoot you off." Air Force officers present during the show did nothing to stop the men and indicated to the group's escort officer that they had no intentions of punishing the offenders.[200] Instead, the area entertainment director for Special Services noted that the "the girls must understand that 5 Amer[ican] girls on review are going to generate much enthusiasm and remarks."[201] Facing a threat of physical and sexual violence, military officials responded that the women should have seen it coming.

Indeed, women learned very quickly that they had to manage the expectations of men who, as Rankin put it, "thought we were theirs."[202] Officers proved particularly troublesome. Several "dirty old men colonels" offered to let the Donut Dollies at Phan Rang use their bathtubs—an almost unheard-of luxury in Vietnam—but after Jeanne Christie learned that the men had peepholes in the walls, she refused to allow the women in her unit to accept the offer.[203] Most of the time, women had no such protection from men's inappropriate behavior. When a colonel came to a meeting with former Mouseketeer Sherry Alberoni's USO troupe wearing only a towel and "showed the girls how to sit Vietnamese style," the women had little recourse but to "quickly [turn] their heads in shocked disbelief."[204]

Officers exerted considerable influence over women whose clubs and centers existed only at the pleasure of the officers in charge and sometimes used their power for untoward intentions. Not long after she arrived at her first duty station in Soc Trang, a colonel sent a driver to bring Debby Alexander to a party. When she arrived, he told her that the area was under red alert, meaning that an enemy attack was imminent, and that she would have to stay overnight. Alexander was suspicious but also knew that the colonel could have her transferred from the area for not following orders and so she stayed in his billet that night. Rumors spread quickly that the two had spent the night together, and Alexander was "mortified" that her reputation had been besmirched. When she reported the officer's actions to Special Services leaders in Saigon, they told her that there was little they could do. Jenny Young felt similar pressure from a wing commander at the Cam Ranh Air Base who invited the seven Donut Dollies at the local Red Cross center to attend a party and ordered special dresses for them to wear. When the dresses arrived, the women discovered they were very short, and Jenny Young, being very tall, described hers as a "'super' miniskirt." Although she felt uncomfortable in the dress, she needed to "pay my respects" to colonel, so she let the hem out, "got up my courage," and made an appearance. The commander, expecting to see more of Young than he did, remarked that her dress was "too long."[205]

Recreation work placed women in untenable situations that sometimes turned to real danger. Cherie Rankin volunteered at a Vietnamese orphanage during her free time and had to walk a "long deserted road" to get there. When two GIs in a truck offered her a ride one day, she declined. She had "always been very perceptive" about men and felt that something was odd. The men waited at the orphanage, then offered her a ride home. "My instincts told me not to get in the truck," Rankin later recalled, but she felt torn between her instinct and her job. "You're supposed to be nice to the guys," she explained. "You never know if you're the first American woman they've seen, so you always tried to be friendly." Immediately, one of the men began to "molest" her. "His hands were everywhere—up my dress, in my panties. I was biting him and yelling at him." After she began screaming and told the men that she could be their sister, the driver stopped the truck and let her out. Even afterward, Rankin rationalized the men's behavior as understandable given their stressful wartime environment. Although she considered reporting the incident, in part to protect other women, Rankin ultimately upheld the expectations of her job to put the men's needs ahead of her own and decided not to "do anything to screw up what was already a bad experience for them."[206]

Commercial entertainers reported flagrant behavior from club managers and other military personnel who pressured them to engage in sex to secure contracts. In early May 1969, two women in the group "The All-Stars" reported that they were accosted by the custodian in charge of the Fourth Infantry Division's NCO Open Mess club at Pleiku. In sworn statements corroborated by their manager and members of other groups, the women stated that after refusing the man's advances, he canceled the group's remaining scheduled performances at a loss of $3,500 to the group. The Army's Criminal Investigative Division found no reason to discount the women but uncovered "no further investigative leads" and in June referred the incident to the Fourth Infantry Division's Provost Marshal.[207] By the end of September, the group had received no additional information.[208] The investigative trail also ran cold for the group "Shades of Holly," which also had a contract canceled after two women resisted the sexual fondling of a club manager.[209]

Not all situations were so flagrant, but American women found that nearly every aspect of their day-to-day work with soldiers was sexualized, and they struggled to adapt. Donut Dolly Leah O'Leary explained that in working with "sex-starved G.I.s, a lot of experiences were sexualized." When serving food, the women even learned to avoid offering the men chicken breast or leg "to avert the inevitable wise crack." Sophomoric humor might not have been so bad, but as O'Leary described, working with soldiers often felt as though she was "being sexually harassed in one form or another every day and sometimes several times a day." GIs interpreted everything she said as having "a sexual subtext," and so she learned to adjust her interactions. She stopped asking soldiers how they were doing, for example, because the men inevitably responded with "a loud, resounding 'WITHOUT!'" She and the other women knew "what they meant," she explained. "We were standing up there as a reminder of what they were without."[210] Women had to learn to manage these situations on their own and to differentiate between inappropriate and threatening behavior.

In this sexualized context, many GIs assumed that all American women in Vietnam—and especially civilian entertainers and recreation workers—moonlighted as prostitutes.[211] The rumor was very specific—a man expected to pay the equivalent of a month's combat pay, or $65, for an American woman's services—and rooted in hundreds of years of thinking that war zones were no place for respectable women. Some soldiers believed that Red Cross, Special Services, and USO women worked as prostitutes for the officers and were offended that the women were not available for them as well. Other men took matters into their own hands and propositioned the women directly. "I only got propositioned once," Jenny Young recalled, as though she expected more. The man approached her matter-of-factly, honestly believing that "that was the business I was in."[212] An eighteen- or nineteen-year-old "kid from farm country in Idaho or Iowa or one of those farm states" was a bit more subtle when he approached Leah O'Leary, but the intent was the same. After about twenty minutes of conversation, O'Leary realized what he was asking and then "gently clarified" the situation. Embarrassed, he asked for her forgiveness.[213]

Not all men bothered to proposition the women. Donut Dolly Jeanne Christie stopped a couple of men attempting to break into the women's living quarters at Phan Rang, but afterward, she dismissed them as being "quite harmless and seeking trophies to prove they had been in our quarters." Even in the face of danger, she and her coworkers tried not to worry about their own safety. If they had, they "never would have been able to go to work. We had to trust the men until they proved they were untrustworthy," Christie insisted.[214] Unfortunately, some men did just that. One day, an airman offered to walk her back to the women's billets, then followed her into her room and raped her. Though stunned and upset, she did not report the incident because she feared the Donut Dollies would have been removed from the location and that the man would have lost his Air Force commission.[215] Moreover, Christie had no faith in the military to prosecute. "If you got raped you really had no recourse," she explained. "The military was very nasty about it, and naturally it was always the woman's fault."[216] This culture kept many women silent about their experiences of sexual assault.[217] In fact, by the time Christie was preparing to leave Vietnam, she was so tired of warding off men that when an officer grabbed her breasts, she indignantly pushed him away but did not even consider reporting the assault.[218]

Sandra Lockney Davis did report an incident to the Criminal Investigation Division but found the response lacking. One night she awoke to find a man standing above her. She told him to leave and he did, but he promised to return in a few days. The following morning, Davis reported the break-in, but the only assurance the police gave her was that if she saw the man again she should call them immediately. Living in fenced, but unguarded billets with only a latched screen door, she "felt alone, vulnerable" and debated "which was worse, the incident or the response by the CID." A few weeks later he returned and the police arrested him. The next day, a police officer came to tell her that the man had been confined in his company area, but just at that moment, she looked up to see the man walking toward her. The officer grabbed the man and took him away, but Davis knew that her problems were not solved. Restraining him to his company area did not solve anything; his company area was adjacent to her living quarters, and he worked at the mess hall where she ate. Determined, Davis complained to the commanding general who did not seem "sympathetic to my situation" and told her she was being "unreasonable." Two days later, the man returned to her club and told her he was being transferred to another location where he expected "to be killed" in combat operations.[219] Instead of confronting the underlying problems of a lack of security for the women, or addressing ways to better protect women whose work positioned them as sexual objects, the military simply transferred offenders.

### THIS CRAZY IDEA OF PLAYING GAMES

As their tours in Vietnam came to a close, women tried to come to terms with what their experiences had meant. Some, like Davis or Christie who had faced horrific assaults on their bodies, undoubtedly struggled a great deal to reconcile all they had given to the GIs with the treatment they had received in response. Others simply grew tired. Echoing the sentiments of women from earlier wars, Donut Dolly Emily Strange noted that she struggled to find time when she could be alone. Not even meals provided a respite. Though she could have eaten in the officers' mess, she usually ate alone in her hooch. "I didn't want to have to smile at anybody," she explained. "I didn't want to have to talk to anybody. I didn't want to have to listen to anybody. I just wanted to eat dinner."[220] Kathy Ormond expressed a similar resignation about the social life that had initially seemed so exciting. Both enlisted men and officers liked to visit the house she and the three other women shared, but after spending her days "seeing men and smiling at them," she wrote to her mother, "I'm really not up for seeing 'em at night."[221]

The war also took its toll on the women who adopted various ways to deal with the emotions they felt. As friends and acquaintances were killed, women learned to keep their distance. After Susan Conklin asked the GIs at a Clubmobile stop about a particular soldier she had met on a prior visit, she learned not to repeat the same mistake. The man had been killed, and her asking for him had only upset the other men.[222] This kind of situation repeated itself in clubs and centers across Vietnam as women like Sharon Vander Ven Cummings found it difficult to remain enthusiastic about her work with men she knew might be killed.[223] Women coped by building an emotional wall around themselves. Especially when visiting hospitals, Jeanne Christie explained, she and the other women learned to contain their own emotions so that they "could literally look at somebody dying and smile like Miss America or whatever we personified to them."[224]

Although the work was physically and emotionally tiring, it was also fulfilling for women who then struggled to adjust to life once their tour ended. Some, like Donut Dolly Jeanne Christie and Special

Services worker Judy Jenkins, took their time getting home. Jenkins spent six months traveling alone in Asia before deciding to return to Vietnam with Special Services, while Christie traveled for a month in the United States before she made her way to her home in Wisconsin.[225] Still unsettled, she entered a graduate program in art education at Miami University in Ohio. Confident and now with a streak of anti-authoritarianism, she barely graduated after getting into trouble for using profanity in an exhibit.[226] Adapting to conventional life "like all the other girls at home" proved even more difficult. After enjoying "responsibility, power, ability" in Vietnam, back "at home I felt I was a totally inept boob."[227] Sharon Vander Ven Cummings noted a similar disconnect. As a Donut Dolly, she had felt valuable, creative, imaginative, and resourceful, but her experiences in recreation did not easily translate to a fulfilling job in the United States. Instead, she felt pressured to marry, have a family, and become a housewife.[228]

Many women made their way back to working with military personnel but were never able to replicate the fulfillment and accomplishment they had felt in Vietnam. After two months at home, USO club worker Maureen Nerli decided to return to recreation and went to work at a USO club in Thailand. Absent a wartime environment, this assignment paled in comparison to her work in Vietnam, so she joined Special Services and went to South Korea for an eighteen-month assignment.[229] Christie also returned to an overseas assignment, this time with the USO in Guam, and though she found her work there less exciting than her work in Vietnam, it allowed her to live abroad in a way that her parents found acceptable.[230] Linda K. Morgan Maini returned to Vietnam with the Red Cross and provided emergency services in military hospitals but found the sedentary work unexciting compared to her prior work as a Donut Dolly.[231]

Others made recreation work with soldiers a career. Donut Dolly Susan Conklin came home from Vietnam and taught second grade for over a year before joining Special Services and going to Germany where she worked with GIs and their families. She followed this work with stints in the USO and the Navy's Morale Welfare and Recreation programs. In the early 1990s, she regretfully declined an offer to go to the Persian Gulf in Operation Desert Storm because she had two young children at home.[232] Former Donut Dollies Linda Johnson Jones and Shirley Hines found their way back to war with the Red Cross. Jones went to Desert Storm and later to Bosnia, providing emergency communication for soldiers.[233] Hines served as deputy director of operations at the US Central Command during the First Gulf War.[234]

As they settled into postwar life, women interpreted their work in the context of the broad changes that framed women's lives during the era. While much of the actual and symbolic work they performed drew on conventional notions of womanhood, much of their lives and their wartime experiences failed to conform to tradition. Debby Alexander's youthful naïveté and conventionality had made her an ideal candidate for Special Services before she went to Vietnam, but she came home a much different, more mature woman. Organized feminist groups did not necessarily see recreation and entertainment work as instilling the kind of changes that women needed. Perhaps most famously, the New York Radical Women decried the Miss America USO show as a "cheerleader-tour . . . to pep-talk our husbands, fathers, sons and boyfriends into dying and killing with a better spirit" and charged that the tour paraded the women as "Mascots for Murder."[235] Few, if any, USO, Special Services, or Red Cross women would have agreed. "We were not obviously in a role that sounded like part of the feminist movement, in one sense," Jill York explained. Yet, she and her colleagues were also "doing something that other women weren't doing."[236] Jeanne Christie even described Donut Dollies as "tacit women libbers" and progressive models for women.[237]

Feminists or not, all women tried to reconcile their work with the larger war effort and their own feelings about it. Many came home skeptical, if not outright opposed to, the US effort in Vietnam. Having come to see the Americans as invaders in Vietnam, Donut Dolly Jeanne Christie wrote to President Richard M. Nixon in 1970 to oppose his expansion of the war into Cambodia and told her brothers that if they were drafted, she would take them to Canada.[238] The Cambodian invasion proved a watershed moment for her colleague Jennifer Young who, like many Americans afterward, came to believe that the government was lying about the war's progress.[239] As the American public came to disagree with the war effort, Cherie Rankin feared that others would think she supported the war and simply did not talk about her role in it. Still, she remained proud. "What I did over there was valuable," she insisted.[240]

Other women had trouble deciding if what they had done was valuable. After she returned home, Leah O'Leary met with the head of the Red Cross's International Division, a former mentor who had introduced her to the SRAO program. She was surprised and offended, then, when he suggested that perhaps a thousand "camp followers" might have accomplished the same goals. Although she acknowledged that she had a hard time finding meaning for "this crazy idea of playing games with soldiers in a war zone," she insisted that the work had been valuable. It did not matter that it seemed silly; O'Leary believed that Donut Dollies like herself "helped remind [the GIs] of who they were at their best in a situation that was structured to allow the worst."[241] Other women grappled with the same question. "Does a smile and a game really take away the tragedy of fighting a war?" Mary Blanchard Bowe asked herself.[242] Jennifer Young didn't think that smiles and games affected the "grand scheme of things," but remained optimistic about the women's effect on soldiers. If she and her colleagues "made a difference in his outlook for that day or made him feel better about something, then okay," she concluded. "I'll take that."[243]

This kind of deeply personal satisfaction had made the hardships of war work bearable for women since the beginning of the century, and it would continue to motivate recreation and entertainment workers through the century's end. After the Vietnam War, however, changes in the makeup and structure of the military mandated significant alterations to the nature and meanings of entertainment programs. As Donut Dollies, Special Services women, and USO club women left South Vietnam, they closed the door on recreation programs intended primarily as enticing diversions for young single soldiers. The women who continued the work in later eras found it expanded in its goals, audience, and method. The end of the Vietnam War did not mean the end of entertainment focused on women, though it would shift focus and adapt to new realities as the military reorganized and deployed to new corners of the world.

# 6

===

# No Beer, No Booze, No Babes

## ENTERTAINING THE ALL-VOLUNTEER MILITARY

Gina Cardi Lee describes herself as an ordinary "suburbanite kid who grew up in a nuclear family," but her career in Army recreation gave her anything but an ordinary life. Raised in a working-class Italian family in Brook Park, Ohio, on the outskirts of Cleveland, her parents worked hard in factories so that Gina and her brother could go to college. At Bowling Green State University, only a couple hours away, Lee gravitated toward studies in recreation administration. After graduating in 1981, she immediately entered a master's program in recreation management and earned her graduate degree the following year. She returned home to Brook Park, where, though overqualified, she worked twenty hours a week at the town's large community recreation center. Her family wanted her to stay in the area and teach physical education in a local school, but Lee had no interest in teaching or staying home. She wanted to use her education, make money, and experience the world outside of small-town Ohio. When she saw an advertisement for a one-year, overseas position in the back of a parks and recreation journal, she jumped at the chance.

The ad did not provide much detail about the job, not even where it was located, but it did mention full benefits and a $20,000 annual salary, both "unheard of" in recreation work at the time. Not long after Lee mailed in the application, she was offered a position as a recreation specialist at an Army base in South Korea. She had two days to decide whether to accept. Although she didn't consider herself "brave or an adventure seeker," and though she knew nothing about the military, she decided that she could do anything for a year and accepted the offer. She received no training for her work before she left, only a few days of in-processing once she arrived, and soon found herself planning activities at a recreation club at Camp Casey, just a few miles south of the demilitarized zone.

Although the military of the 1980s was becoming a more diverse force than it had ever been, the forces Lee worked with did not reflect recent changes. Camp Casey housed several thousand soldiers of the Second Infantry Division, which, at the time, included no women. Many of the soldiers were young, and all were on unaccompanied tours, which meant that even if they were married and had children, their families remained at home. Thus, Lee's work mirrored the work of women who had operated recreation clubs in years past, and she found herself trying to "act like the mom or the big sister" to "kids, 18, 19 years old" who were not that much younger than herself. American forces had been in South Korea for three decades by the time Lee arrived, and the camp towns of prostitutes that had grown alongside the American presence continued to motivate recreation work. "Right outside the gate were opportunities you won't want to go home and tell mom about," Lee explained, and even something as simple as a card tournament was intended to provide the men with alternative ways to spend their free time.

Although Lee loved the work and took great satisfaction in knowing that she helped to make a lonely tour more bearable for the soldiers, the job was a difficult adjustment for her. Something of a tomboy, Lee was "very socially awkward" when she arrived in South Korea. She had not had a serious boyfriend before but discovered almost immediately that nearly every man at the camp was interested in dating her. "It took a lot of learning and a couple of times a broken heart," she admitted, before she learned how to keep the soldiers' hopeful expectations at bay while also demonstrating genuine concern for their well-being. She tried to manage the men's expectations by making it clear that even if they shared a meal or went somewhere together, she intended nothing more than a professional friendship. When necessary, she adopted a "tough love" approach and told soldiers directly that she was not interested in a romantic relationship. Still, she felt it imperative to maintain a professional demeanor at all times and so she went outside of the camp when she needed time to herself or wanted to relax with a drink at an officers' club. Eventually, she "got to be a pretty tough gal" and earned the respect of the commanders in the region who could see the sincerity of her concern for their men and the value of her efforts.

In 1986, Lee transferred to West Germany, where her work changed dramatically. By this time, the Army had formalized a shift in recreation programming from a primary focus on single soldiers to families. The change was part of a broader concern for families that had been developing since the mid-1970s and had recently been mandated from the highest echelons of the Army. Recreation clubs that had long focused on providing a wholesome environment for young, single soldiers morphed into community centers with programs targeting soldiers, their spouses, and their children. In addition to planning activities for young single soldiers, Lee also developed morale programs for spouses, arranged family outings to chop down Christmas trees, planned Halloween parties, and organized communitywide chili cook-offs that attracted Army families from all over Europe. The expanded focus also changed Lee's relationship with soldiers and, in her mind, legitimized her as a professional recreation worker, not simply the "rec center lady." Whereas most soldiers in Korea had wanted a personal relationship with her, in Germany, they saw her as a professional worker who cared for the needs of the entire Army community. Commanders, too, ascribed great significance to her work. While military leaders had attributed importance to recreation in all eras, in the mid-1980s the morale of the soldiers and their families became a category of evaluation. Installation commanders, Lee felt, depended on recreation providers to do their job effectively and relied on workers like herself to ensure that everyone's needs were met.

After a few years in Germany, Lee fell in love with an Army officer and the pair returned to the United States where they married and began a family. By the 1980s, marriage and children no longer disqualified women from working in Army recreation, but frequent moves and childcare demands made a full-time career difficult. Over the course of several years, she and her husband moved their five children to assignments in Hawaii, Arizona, and Virginia. Although she no longer worked in formally organized recreation programs, as her husband advanced in rank, she found that the Army expected her to perform informal, unpaid morale-boosting services for the units he commanded, especially when they deployed. The Army had long expected, and indeed relied on, the volunteer work of wives to sustain essential community services, and their efforts had played both overt and subtle roles in their officer husbands' evaluations for many years. When Lee's husband came up for evaluations, his commander told him that the portions regarding his unit's morale were the "parts about Gina." Having spent many years working with the military, she fully understood these expectations when she married and welcomed the work. Increasing numbers of Army wives resisted these expectations, but Lee happily baked cookies, welcomed families to stay at her home when necessary, and stocked the apartments of returning soldiers with supplies. It was a long way from her first days in the recreation club at Camp Casey, but Lee embraced the unwritten expectations as her own personal morale program, similar to the work she had done in Korea and Germany.[1]

Lee's work in recreation and morale services mirrored the broader changes occurring in military recreation during the last decades of the twentieth century. The Red Cross ended its Supplemental Recreational Activities Overseas program when it closed the last clubs in Korea and Vietnam and refocused its efforts on emergency communication and social support services. Its days of sending women to serve doughnuts and chat with young soldiers had come to an end.[2] The military's Special Services programs branched out into more broadly conceived morale programs designed to support the entire military community, not just single and unaccompanied male soldiers deployed far from home. After a close brush with the possibility of shuttering its operations, the USO similarly adapted. While retaining its historical ties to show business by providing celebrity entertainment, the organization expanded the work of facilities intended to serve the many evolving needs of military personnel and their families.

This broadening of focus reflected significant changes in the makeup of the US military after the Vietnam War, most of which resulted from the military's switch from a conscripted to a volunteer force in 1973. Facing a new requirement to attract sufficient numbers of personnel, recruiters touted the benefits of service and relied on increasing enlistments of racial minorities and women to meet personnel demands. What had, for most of its history, been a martial force comprised of mostly white, single men, became in the last years of the twentieth century a more racially and ethnically diverse force whose families also endured the stresses of frequent moves and deployments. Although the United States has not declared war since World War II, military personnel deployed to war zones and conflicts across the world with increasing regularity in the late twentieth century.[3] In each of these situations, as they had done for decades, military and civilian officials saw to it that soldiers, sailors, airmen, and Marines had all they needed to keep their minds occupied and their bodies out of trouble.

But while the ultimate goal of morale programs remained similar to the goals held in earlier years, women's work changed in significant ways. The military's increasing reliance on servicewomen and families led to a reconsideration of the ways women and women's bodies had been used in and as entertainment, and women like Lee who worked in morale programs found their jobs broaden considerably. All of these changes came to a head in the First Gulf War, where American military officials attempted to balance rapidly evolving American notions of entertainment and Saudi cultural autonomy.

## IN THE INTEREST OF THE NATION

In March 1976, amid national bicentennial celebrations, the USO convened its annual meeting at a Philadelphia hotel. Held only a few years after American troops had withdrawn from Vietnam, the gathering of the organization's leaders, military representatives, congressmen, and civilian volunteers operated as a kind of retreat for military personnel embroiled in the transition to the All-Volunteer Force (AVF) and public skepticism about the controversy-laden military. Gone were the "carping critics" who "will harp on Mylai [*sic*] or ask embarrassing questions about dope-smoking in the barracks." Those who gathered to discuss the USO's future counted themselves among the military's fiercest supporters. As one journalist described, it was "not really a convention. It [was] a meeting of a mutual admiration society." In panels and sessions, attendees lamented the decline of military budgets and unequivocal support for the military, with their discussion focusing on how the recent shift to a volunteer force was changing the work of the USO. The increase in women personnel seemed especially irksome. "If we have a dance," asked one veteran USO official, "are we supposed to invite good-looking young men to dance with the servicewomen?"[4]

The question reflected the reality that the military's move from a conscripted to a volunteer system in 1973 brought significant demographic changes to an institution that for its entire history had been populated primarily by young, single men. Before the AVF, women were restricted to sex-segregated corps and to particular specializations in the medical and support fields. When forced to recruit and not draft members, the service branches began to recruit increasing numbers of women who integrated service academies, aviation training, ships, and most specializations. By the end of the decade, women had grown from 1.3 to 7.6 percent of the military. Indeed, Army commanders attributed the success of the volunteer system to increasing numbers of women.[5] Many of these women brought or began families. Growing numbers of their male comrades did so as well.

While the old axiom "if the military wanted you to have a wife, it would have issued you one" seemed to guide family policy through World War II, the beginnings of peacetime conscription in the late 1940s initiated a growth in military families, especially among the enlisted ranks. That growth ballooned even more once the volunteer force began. Whereas at the end of the Vietnam War, 40 percent of enlisted personnel were married, by 1985, 58 percent were married, and 73 percent of them had children. Another 10 percent were single parents. Although military families in many ways mirrored broader social trends of increasing marriage ages and dual-income partners, they still married younger and had more children than civilian families. In some cases, both parents served on active duty, and in most instances, spouses and children accompanied the service member to overseas assignments.[6]

These demographic changes demanded more significant changes in military recreation and entertainment than the question about dance partners suggested. The USO had to reconsider the relationship between civilian society and a standing volunteer military. When President Richard M. Nixon mandated the AVF, he did so on the recommendation of free market economists who believed that competition on the job market would force the services to make themselves more appealing to the American public through increased pay and benefits. No longer required to serve by notions of citizenship or obligation, volunteers would join, they argued, because the military offered recruits the most attractive benefits.[7] This reasoning, however, challenged the relationship between the military and civilian organizations that had developed since World War I. As the military based itself on an occupational model that emphasized benefits as a compensation for work, civilian and military officials at the USO convention feared that the public would find no reason to fund entertainment and services that the military should provide itself.[8]

Their fears were grounded in recent events. Less than a year after the military conscripted its last soldier, the United Way, which channeled most of the public's contributions to the USO, recommended that, in the wake of the switch to a volunteer force, USO programs, "especially the overseas ones," should be funded by the military instead of private donations. Citing military-provided service clubs and other recreational amenities, as well as the increased salaries of service members, the United Way reframed responsibility for military welfare as belonging to the military itself.[9]

Already faced with a decline in contributions after the end of the Vietnam War, a loss of United Way funding "would have meant the death of U.S.O.," warned National Chairman Dr. Elvis J. Stahr Jr.[10] In response, the USO asked the United Way and the Department of Defense to create a Blue Ribbon Study commission to evaluate the need for civilian-provided morale services. USO leaders began a public relations campaign to justify the organization's existence and began working to secure a Congressional charter that would secure a permanent role for the organization in times of both war and peace.[11] In many ways, their arguments extended early Cold War concerns about the need to maintain civilian influences on a conscripted peacetime military. As the Cold War continued to frame the US military's considerable worldwide presence, the USO carved out an expanded role for itself as a guardian of democracy among a volunteer force of professionals. Previously, military and civilian officials had insisted that a civilian-military connection was critical to reminding young soldiers of the moralizing influences of home and family, to exerting democratic values on soldiers who would return to civilian life at the end of their enlistment. Military officials echoed some of these rationales as justification for the USO's continued work with soldiers. In particular, with an extensive military presence in Okinawa, South Korea, and Thailand, military officials referred to the presence of "camp followers who developed villages around the military bases" that specialized in "unsavory and unwholesome activities." In this environment laced with "disease and violence," the USO provided a space where American personnel and local peoples could gather "on a better footing and in a more sympathetic way than can be found in the bars and clubs where the worst kind of abrasive and basically contemptuous relations develop."[12] Stahr concurred, describing USO clubs as often "the only wholesome outlet available to these young people, these fellow citizens of ours who are away from home temporarily."[13] At the same time, however, USO officials wanted to refashion the organization's image into one more responsive to a new kind of military. The "USO's image as a home away from home, as a staunch institution, as a substitute for mom, and as a surrogate [Young Men's Christian Association] or social club," its public relations committee warned, "is no longer enough to encourage support."[14]

Branching out from its conventional wartime work in entertainment programs and homey clubs for wartime soldiers, the USO staked out a new, permanent role for itself as providing essential civilian support for the volunteer military. The Blue Ribbon Study found that, despite the military's expansion of the number and kinds of services it provided its personnel, these efforts were insufficient to meet evolving needs. Moreover, even if the military could meet the demand, the study determined that some services needed to be provided "in a non-military setting, by non-military personnel." Importantly, it concluded that if the USO could not offer these essential civilian services, another organization like it would have to be created.[15] USO officials could not have agreed more. The ending of conscription did not remove the need for civilian interaction with military personnel, they insisted, but in fact reaffirmed the need for a "vital humanitarian, personal link between those back home and those sent off to protect them."[16]

Moreover, as the United States moved to a volunteer military with no ostensible connection to a cross-section of Americans, USO officials insisted that their organization was essential to preventing the creation of "a force of 'mercenaries.'"[17] Executive Director Michael Menster warned that the military could "become culturally isolated from the civilian society, but only when the public acquiesces in this isolation." Apathetic civilians with no direct military connection could easily forget about "strangers who are overseas or stashed away in some God-forsaken military post," and thus, he argued, "the American people need USO just as much, if not more, than the serviceman."[18] Military leaders agreed, seeing in the USO an opportunity to keep the military at the forefront of Americans' minds, especially during peacetime, when "armies tend to become invisible."[19] Ultimately, though, the Blue Ribbon Study attached the most significant meaning to the USO, one "concerning a fundamental premise of this nation since its founding." Arguing that civilian control of the military was essential to "the continuation of a democratic form of government," the study concluded that retaining the USO's civilian connection to the military was, therefore, "in the interest of this nation."[20]

With its purpose secured, the USO set to rethinking how it could best serve the needs of a volunteer force. Military and USO officials had anticipated that family concerns would become a pressing concern in the post–Vietnam War era, and the USO began adapting its work even before the AVF formally began. In 1972, USO clubs in Okinawa, Manila, Guam, and Taiwan that had catered primarily to single men became community centers that offered programs for wives and children, including a summer day camp for dependents in Guam.[21] One USO representative called on the organization to expand this type of work further by helping to address the already problematic housing and day-care shortages that were sure to be exacerbated by the families of volunteer soldiers.[22] Indeed, the organization adopted service to families as one of four new programmatic goals in 1973 and immediately began incorporating those services into its public relations material.[23] One 1976 brochure, *Reaching out to Today's Armed Forces*, illustrated this new priority by featuring a cover image of a young couple with a baby and noted that the USO was responding to the "military baby boom" by helping to establish childcare facilities near military installations.[24]

Despite these efforts and the growing presence of uniformed women, USO officials recognized in 1976 that most programs in USO centers still catered primarily to men.[25] As they had during World War II, USO clubs relied on female junior volunteers in their late teens and early twenties to dance with visiting servicemen. Encouraged to adorn themselves in respectable, yet "becoming" attire, the young women were to display a "welcoming smile" for the men and not allow their attractions to any one man to overshadow their attentions to the others. Although servicewomen had been welcome to visit USO centers for decades, even in the early 1970s they sometimes found themselves serving as dance partners for their male colleagues.[26] National USO officials knew they needed a better way of working with servicewomen and directed in June 1976 that women should "retain their identity as military personnel" when they entered clubs, instead of being used as de facto civilian volunteers. In an unfortunate turn of phrase, they directed that the "USO should get women out of the 'escort business.'"[27]

USO Shows remained in the entertainment business, though its focus gradually shifted to exclusively celebrity entertainment. After the Vietnam War, it continued to enlist little known talent and college theater groups who performed on a voluntary basis. Officials insisted that the "wholesome contact" between them and military personnel transported "some of the warmth and companionship of hometown America" to bases around the world.[28] Dire financial troubles in the mid-1970s threatened this focus, however, and officials warned that the outlook for the program was "less than encouraging." What had been a bicoastal effort of seven staff based in New York and Hollywood consolidated in 1975 to one office of three people in New York. And, despite increasing calls from overseas commanders for more entertainment, the number of shows declined precipitously, from ninety-five shows in 1974 to forty the following year.[29]

In response, the military began to augment the dwindling number of USO shows through its DOD Showcase (also called DOD Overseas Shows), a program run by the Armed Forces Professional Entertainment Office (AFPEO) that recruited and funded noncelebrity entertainment.[30] USO Shows, meanwhile, increasingly solicited corporate sponsors for its big-name tours, such as the Miss America Pageant, Miss Black America Pageant, and handshake tours of professional athletes.[31] In 1982, the USO and AFPEO formalized this division of labor between amateur and celebrity entertainment, though AFPEO coordinated all entertainment tours, a role it would continue into the twenty-first century.[32] While both offices maintain that their work is essential to maintaining morale among the armed forces, the USO's shift in focus to exclusively celebrity tours ended its historical efforts to put average civilians into contact with military personnel through entertainment. The average citizens whom it insisted were vital for the volunteer military could volunteer their time and connections through the increasing number of USO centers, airport lounges, fleet centers, and information desks across the country and near military installations around the world.[33]

## MILITARY WOMEN AND FAMILIES

About a year before the volunteer force began, a female soldier stationed in Greece wrote to the official US Army magazine *Soldiers* and called for an end to the "old and hoary practice of including cheesecake pictures." Her objection to the suggestive, full-page photographs of women in bathing suits and negligees prompted an informal polling of readers, who responded 48 to 37 percent in favor of removing the images, though an additional 15 percent of respondents requested that the magazine include an occasional male pinup. If readers were divided on the images, *Soldiers* editor Colonel Lane Carlson insisted that, as a woman, she saw no problem with them, and explained that the "the prettiest, sweetest girls we can find" were a "plus for the magazine." She even doubted the readers' objections, noting that the images of aspiring models, actresses, and Playboy models she endorsed were no different than the Betty Grable pinups of World War II. Whether the images of pinups in the 1940s and the 1970s were similar or different was beside the point for the soldier who instigated the debate. Adopting the language of feminists who critiqued the connections between sexual images of women, patriarchal culture, and institutional limitations on women's lives and careers, the soldier alleged that revealing photographs of women "reinforce the woman-as-an-object mentality and are an insult to the many professional military women who are included in your readership." Women like her had enough problems being accepted in the military, she argued, "without our own publications continually undermining their fight for recognition as equals."[34]

Revealing images of women in military publications were only the tip of the iceberg as the volunteer military reconsidered the ways it used women in recreation and entertainment and, indeed, reconsidered the very purpose of recreation itself.[35] With the Red Cross having ended its Donut Dolly program and the USO shifting the focus of its centers to family programming, the military's Special Services recreation clubs remained the last vestige of the World War I–era intention to send wholesome young women to socialize with young, single, enlisted male soldiers. But even this ideal was quickly fading in the 1970s as personnel policies changed, illustrating major shifts in military leaders' thinking about the nature of recreation and the place of women in that effort. However, only Navy leaders seem to have given much thought to how morale programs might meet servicewomen's particular needs, and then not until the mid- to late 1990s, when they considered how recreation aboard ships might help facilitate gender integration. Recreation specialists suggested that morale program leaders concertedly plan programs that would appeal to both women and men and facilitate respectful—not competitive—relationships among them. Building this kind of meaningful working relationship, however, also required some changes, and recreational specialists "strongly recommended that events that emphasize sexuality be eliminated, such as the shipboard version of The Dating Game and dances aboard ship."[36]

Despite a lack of more dedicated thinking about women's morale needs, as the military increasingly integrated women into all aspects of military life, and as family needs gradually subsumed the military's focus on single men, Special Services women saw their roles broaden considerably. From the origin of Special Services recreation clubs, the women who staffed them had been required to be single—a policy that helped to heighten the women's appeal for young soldiers. Around 1969, however, the Army dropped the requirement and a number of women working in recreation clubs married.[37] In 1971, Harriet Rice married a helicopter pilot she met while working at Hunter Liggett military reservation, while Kim Mills fell for a man who frequented the music room at her club at Johnson Barracks, near Nuremberg, Germany. After she transferred to another location, he continued to visit before finally mustering the courage to propose. The pair married in 1975.[38] Although military leaders still "expected" resignations from women who became pregnant, some continued to work. Debby Alexander Moore, who had married a lieutenant at the end of her two tours in Vietnam and had two young children, returned to Special Services clubs while she and the children accompanied her husband to his post in Korea.[39]

Perhaps even more disruptive to the traditional mission of using women as morale boosters, Special Services began hiring men to fill positions in recreation clubs. Men had worked in Special Services from its beginnings, but until the mid-1970s they worked in administration, not as recreation club staff.[40] While working as a recreation center director in Bad Kissingen, Germany, in 1979 and 1980, Joan Capella supervised one of the first men to work with soldiers and their families in a recreation center. The men who visited the club liked the male worker, she thought, but were never drawn to the center by him as soldiers had been drawn to centers by women workers in the past.[41]

By 1973, the Special Services blue uniform had also become a relic of the past. Harriet Rice began her career in 1966 wearing the uniform that women of earlier generations had deemed so critical. A supervisor even reprimanded her once for exiting a tour bus without her hat, but she was one of the last women to receive such criticism.[42] Kay Johnson worked in the Special Services entertainment office in Vietnam from 1969 to 1970 and formally challenged the uniform policy. She hated the "horribly out of style" uniform, which she found impractical as she traveled via helicopters while escorting USO shows around the country. Not long after she arrived she simply stopped wearing it and instead wore a camouflage pants outfit she had tailor made. Her male colleagues did not have to wear a uniform, yet she and her colleagues had to pay a portion of the cost for their required skirt, blouse, hat, gloves, heels, stockings, and handbag. These requirements constituted sexual discrimination, in Johnson's mind, and she filed a formal grievance with the Army's newly formed Equal Employment Opportunity office. The Judge Advocate General had already determined the policy to be discriminatory, independent of Johnson's complaint, though it took until 1972 for women's uniform requirements to be lifted.[43] The Army never ruled on Johnson's grievance and informed her that her case was being dropped because she was by then no longer an Army employee.[44]

As the terms of recreation employment evolved, women found that the nature of their work changed as well in the late 1970s and 1980s, much like Gina Lee had while working in clubs in South Korea and Germany. Programmatic changes in clubs developed over time and varied greatly, reflecting the needs of the personnel at various installations. Joan Capella began her long career in recreation at Camp Howard in southern South Korea in 1974. On unaccompanied tours, the soldiers she worked with were either single or temporarily separated from their families, and so Capella found her work very similar to that of women in earlier eras. And, as it had for women who had grown up similarly "sheltered," working at a camp of 400 unaccompanied men proved quite an eye-opening experience. Posted signs at the camp's gates noted the venereal disease rate at various clubs in the surrounding villages, and Capella knew full well that she and other women like her "were a wholesome alternative" to the clubs.[45]

Other women knew this intent, but introduced new approaches to keep the men away from the villages. Judy Max joined Special Services in 1972. For the next six years she worked in recreation centers in Okinawa and South Korea that catered primarily to young, unaccompanied soldiers who needed a "distraction" from the stress of their work and who, in their commanders' minds, needed to be kept out of trouble. But while she arranged the same kinds of card games and pool tournaments that recreation women had done for many years, she suggested new activities as well. Not having been formally trained in recreation, Max was not invested in the "more structured, sweet kind of recreation program" that "the old Special Services girls" valued. They were quite astounded, then, when Max and her coworker began offering shoulder massages in the club. "It was really very innocent," and there was "nothing sexual" about the massages, she insisted. The men simply enjoyed the personalized attention and the chance to talk with American women. Still, Max knew that offering massages directly competed with the "massages" that the men could have paid for in Korean towns, and she felt that the more she reminded the men of home, the less likely they were to "go get their urges met downtown."[46]

As the massages suggested, women who came to Special Services in the 1970s brought with them the era's changing mores about sexuality. The "ancient" directors who determined policy "had an image of rec center girls and didn't want that image tarnished," Capella believed. She was "the representative of home" to men in her club, and her supervisor expected her to preserve that image. Soldiers who "had an idealized notion" of American women were therefore shocked and even embarrassed when they saw her in clubs in the village. Her presence seemed incongruous to the men, who also "didn't want me to see them and what they were up to." These idealistic expectations led Capella to leave the camp when she had time off or went on a date. Like Gina Lee, she felt it better to avoid the awkwardness that resulted when the men saw her in social settings outside of the club.[47]

In an era of sexual revolution and free love, young women in their twenties often held very different notions of sexual respectability than did their supervisors who, Max noted, "probably thought you should be pretty virginal." Max thought nothing of accompanying military officers who distributed condoms to GIs in the village bars near her installation, for example, and thought it hilarious when the commander gave her a VD card indicating she was free of disease. Her supervisors were not so amused. And, though Max was careful not to "flaunt" her relationships with soldiers in front of the GIs who had few opportunities to date American women, she thought very little about her partners' marital status. It "didn't mean a thing to me," she explained, if a soldier was married because she had no interest in a long-term relationship and knew that she "wasn't taking him away from his family."[48] Before Kim Mills went to work in Germany, the supervisor at her orientation echoed the warnings issued by prior women and cautioned her and the other women to watch for the geographical bachelors—who would conveniently forget to tell the women about their wives waiting at home—that they would encounter. Although they were free to date as they pleased, Mills knew that it would be frowned upon if she "got a reputation." Still, for a mid-twenties young woman, being surrounded by so many men was "like being a kid in a candy store," she laughed.[49]

Freer notions of sexuality did not mean that women were free of the sexual harassment that women before them had confronted. While working in the recreation center at Fort Ord in the mid- to late-1970s, Harriet Reed experienced varying degrees of harassment, though in all instances she explained, "you just have to learn to ignore it." When a group of men began lounging in the center's lobby and making improper comments toward Reed and her colleagues, one of them removed all of the furniture in an attempt to deter the annoying loiterers. The tactic did not last long, however, as the supervisors instructed the women to return the furniture to the lounge. Other men were more direct in their presumptions. After Reed invited one soldier to her apartment for dinner, he "thought he was going to get dessert" but left when she rebuked his advances. Another was less cooperative. Women's work, as it had for decades, required them to be friendly with all men, including one who "mistook my being pleasant for something else." Inferring more from Reed's demeanor than she had intended, the soldier found out where she lived and came to her door. "My instincts told me not to let this guy in," she noted, and fortunately her stalker left.[50] In cases like these, Judy Max explained, women were "left to our own defenses."[51]

While recreation women resisted unwanted advances, the military struggled to rid entertainment of women's bodies. Scandals about the management and funding of officers' and noncommissioned officers' (NCO) clubs during the Vietnam War had led to some oversight, but clubs continued to present problems. The military attempted to curtail strip shows throughout the 1980s, for example, but club managers continued to exercise discretion over the performers hired, and female strippers and dancers remained a considerable draw. The Army, Air Force, and Navy had all banned topless dancers by March 1980, with the Navy specifying that dancers must "'appear in attire which covers, in a tasteful manner, those portions of the body which are normally kept covered in public.'"[52] It is unclear whether, or to what degree, these prohibitions were enforced. The manager of a group known as the "Hollywood A Go-Go Dancers" received letters of endorsement in 1983 from an Army official who described the dancers as beneficial for morale.[53] And, in 1988, the Navy found it necessary to issue another prohibition against topless and bottomless dancers.[54] The military's increased reliance on servicewomen helps explain the new restrictions on strippers after many years of outright condoning the practice or turning a blind eye. Servicewomen complained, and a Navy advisory panel echoed some feminists' argument that nude dancers contributed to "an environment in which all females are regarded with less or no respect, and abusive behavior toward all women is not only passively accepted and condoned but encouraged."[55]

Oddly, at the same time that the services were attempting to end the hiring of strippers in military clubs, some clubs began to hold Ladies' Nights that offered women the same kind of sexualized entertainment that they had offered men for many years. The Army's Commercial Entertainment Office, which auditioned and oversaw all club entertainment in Europe, forbid topless and bottomless dancers and insisted that "principles of decency and good taste" apply to all performances. These guidelines framed the Mainz Pathfinder Community Club's first Ladies' Night in April 1984. The officers' and enlisted men's wives who attended—with the permission of their husbands, one article confirmed—seemed to enjoy the two male dancers who stripped down to the barest of underwear, though it was the only chance they had.[56] The show prompted the area commanders to review their policies on dancers, after which they forbid "entertainers whose dress or performance is designed to be sexually stimulating." Morale programs should "provide wholesome and diversified activities that meet the needs and interests of the greatest number of our soldiers and their families," one commander explained, and thus "only clean, healthy, and wholesome entertainment, capable of withstanding critical external scrutiny" would be permitted.[57] While female strippers had been common practice in the club system, once male strippers performed, officials reviewed and promptly put an end to the practice. By the mid-1990s, the Department of Defense had forbid any "programs that may offend the audience, including topless or nude entertainers or participants" and directed that all entertainment "adhere to standards of good taste and . . . be able to withstand objective scrutiny."[58]

The gradual elimination of strippers in military clubs illustrates the degree to which entertainment came to focus less on single men and more on families. Before the mid-1970s, military recreation and entertainment programs welcomed but did not cater to military families. Since their advent in World War I, the rationale and focus of programs had been the single male soldier. Even as more and more soldiers married in the early 1960s, an Army memorandum noted that although families were essential to soldier morale and were welcome in recreation facilities, problems arose when dependents visited the facilities too much. The number of military personnel determined the funding for the programs, which meant that participating families stretched budgets and resources. Moreover, officials worried that increased use by dependents would deter enlisted men from the clubs and push them toward "undesirable temptations" available in other places.[59] A 1968 regulation even stipulated that programs specifically designed for children should not "interfere with or curtail" Special Services programs intended to serve single soldiers.[60]

By the mid-1980s, however, recreation programs had shifted focus. After Army wives drew attention to the pressing morale needs of families at several Army Family Symposiums, military leaders recognized that family problems were readiness problems.[61] In 1983, Army Chief of Staff General John A. Wickham Jr. issued his white paper "The Army Family," which argued that soldiers' commitment to the military required a reciprocal "moral obligation to support their families." But it was not only an obligation, Wickham insisted. Supporting Army families would help the Army, as increased family stability would lead to greater individual effectiveness and thus, overall success.[62] As one Army historian explains, "quality of life" issues became more important to Army leadership than ever before, as they recognized that improving family life was essential to the success of the AVF.[63] Studies of Army families even revealed that spouses' attitudes toward military life could be more determinant of a soldier's reenlistment than his or her own morale, and morale programs thus paid significant attention to the needs of spouses.[64]

Women recreation workers attributed most of the changes they saw in recreation clubs to this increasing focus on families. When she began her career at installations comprised primarily of unaccompanied men, Kim Mills believed that her purpose was to combat homesickness by providing a sense of home. After General Wickham prioritized families, however, Mills felt that she and her coworkers no longer symbolized the girl next door or even a vague sense of home. Home now traveled with the forces to their overseas assignments. Instead, she and her colleagues worked to make deployments more enjoyable for soldiers and their families and to help them experience the local culture. She offered classes in English for foreign-born spouses and even once prepared Thanksgiving dinner for families moving into the area who did not yet have permanent housing.[65]

Family programming constituted quite a change for Marcy Stennes, whose first experiences in Special Services had been in Vietnam. Although few families at Bindlach Post in Germany came in an official sponsored status, some soldiers brought their wives and children and lived in the surrounding community. Living off post made it difficult for the families to get to know each other, especially when the husbands deployed to the German-Czechoslovakian border for patrol duty, so Stennes organized programs for wives and children at the recreation center. In addition to bingo games and trick-or-treat parties for kids, she took families to participate in local activities to integrate them into the Bavarian community. These were all healthy and positive activities, Stennes knew, but she did not feel they served the purpose of keeping soldiers out of trouble as had her work in Vietnam.[66] In part, the presence of families served as a check on soldiers' behaviors. As Judy Max put it, families provided "stabilizing elements" to a military installation.[67]

Structural changes to recreation programming reflected this growing focus on family concerns. What had since World War II been called Special Services; then Recreation Services; Morale Support Activities; and, finally, Morale, Welfare, and Recreation (MWR) centralized under the US Army Community and Family Support Center in 1984.[68] The name change highlighted the expanding focus of morale efforts that increasingly incorporated everything from community centers (the former Special Services clubs staffed by civilian women), libraries, arts and crafts programs, theater, and sports facilities, to military-only resorts, talent shows, day-care facilities, and spousal hiring programs.[69] With the focus of recreation programming varying so widely, certain professional and educational standards required of Special Services women in the past fell by the wayside. As Gina Cardi Lee put it, "everybody became a recreator."[70]

Funding for these programs also changed dramatically. Throughout the 1970s, 1980s, and into the 1990s, the military branches adapted as Congress made considerable cuts to the appropriated funds earmarked for morale services. By the early 1990s, most recreation programs needed to be self-funded, with the exception of those deemed "mission sustaining," such as the AFPEO, physical fitness facilities, libraries, and recreation centers, which received a total of $1.3 billion in appropriated funding in fiscal year 1988. "Basic Community Support Activities" such as child development centers, music and theater, youth activities, and the publication *Stars and Stripes* were considered important but less essential and thus operated through a mix of appropriated and nonappropriated funds.[71] By the early 2000s, many MWR workers observed a significant decline in funding that further emphasized a move away from programs focused entirely on single soldiers to those intended for families—primarily childcare facilities.[72]

Military officials did not stop caring about the particular needs of single soldiers. In 1989, partly "to counterbalance the emphasis on family programs," the Army created the Better Opportunities for Single Soldiers program, which coordinates recreation activities designed specifically for young, single, or unaccompanied soldiers; provides a venue for them to voice quality-of-life concerns to senior leaders; seeks to integrate them into local communities through volunteer work; and offers activities designed to help them enjoy the local culture and community without going to bars.[73] The Navy followed in 1995 with its Single Sailor Program, which, as one naval official testified, provided "healthy recreational opportunities for our young Sailors."[74] Even for programs focused on healthy activities for young, single soldiers, however, military officials no longer enlisted women as suitable, wholesome dance partners or attractive alternatives to prostitution. The military's morale efforts had expanded widely to include everyone in the military "family."

## A RECREATIONAL DESERT

Eight weeks after American forces deployed to Saudi Arabia in the military's first major engagement since the end of the Vietnam War, a *Los Angeles Times* reporter noticed handwritten signs posted on barracks and tents declaring "No Beer, No Boose [*sic*], No Babes."[75] The discontented signs advertised the major changes in recreation and entertainment that accompanied military personnel to the Persian Gulf. Gone were the days of beer and liquor rations, cute young girls from home serving coffee and doughnuts, and tantalizing dancers wearing just enough. The military that deployed in the summer of 1990 was a different force than the ones that had preceded it. The average soldier was twenty-seven years old; 20 percent were reservists who were often in their thirties or forties, 10 percent were women, and 60 percent left behind families.[76] Moreover, and in some ways even more importantly, those forces deployed to a staunchly Muslim country where cultural and religious concerns shaped the ways Americans could and could not relieve their boredom and their stress. As the *New York Times* put it, Saudi Arabia was "a recreational desert for the thousands of soldiers, marines and airmen stationed here."[77]

As commander of the American forces, General Norman H. Schwarzkopf understood, as had Generals Westmoreland, MacArthur, Eisenhower, and Pershing before him, that soldiers needed recreation. And he, like they, understood that how soldiers spent their free time could present diplomatic challenges if not managed carefully. When American forces landed in Saudi Arabia on August 2, 1990, they did so at the invitation of a Saudi government that forbid alcohol, enforced strict laws requiring the separation of the sexes, and required Saudi women to cover themselves fully. As one veteran described it, "Saudi Arabia is not a place where a young GI can get away with whistling at girls. This is not Vietnam or Panama or even Beirut."[78] Operation Desert Shield, and then Desert Storm, was not a conflict in which commanders had to manage their soldiers' interactions with foreign women. There were no bars, no brothels, and no strip clubs with which to compete.

But even entertainment among American forces posed problems. Not wanting to appear as though they were allowing the Americans to unleash debauchery on the country, Saudi government and military officials insisted on a few limitations to the kinds of entertainment Americans brought with them. Schwarzkopf had tried to forestall any problems from the outset and, in General Order No. 1, prohibited alcohol and pornography, which he defined as "girlie magazines as well as X-rated stuff."[79] To be certain that GIs weren't sneaking in the items, Saudi customs agents searched the mail. Chairman of the Joint Chiefs of Staff Colin Powell informed the Senate Armed Services Committee that if officials found anything offensive, "such as a scantily clad lady smoking a Salem cigarette," they "obliterated [it] with magic markers."[80] No actual scantily clad women were making it into the country, either. Schwarzkopf promised Khalid bin Sultan, commander of the joint

Arab forces, that no "female entertainers" would be brought into the kingdom.[81] American efforts to appease the Saudis went so far, a *Philadelphia Inquirer* reporter asserted, that military censors deleted references to pilots aboard the USS *John F. Kennedy* watching porn before bombing missions because it "would be too embarrassing to report."[82] Schwarzkopf explained, "Nothing would have ruined our welcome sooner than for us to let it all hang out the way some Americans had in Vietnam."[83]

Schwarzkopf's efforts nearly derailed in mid-September when American and British employees of the Saudi oil company Aramco staged a performance for the Eighty-Second Airborne, portions of which were broadcast on network and cable news. The women in the show wore what the *New York Times* described as "teddies," and though one soldier dismissed their dance routine as "nothing big" by US standards, Khalid was outraged and Schwarzkopf scrambled to cancel additional performances.[84]

Recreation-starved American personnel did not give up so easily, however, and some called for more entertainment like the Aramco show. "You need these kinds of shows for men here," one GI explained. "It's a morale booster. It makes you want to carry on with the mission."[85] One commander took up the cause and argued that his troops had a constitutional right to pornography. Schwarzkopf reminded him that the US Constitution did not apply in Saudi Arabia.[86] A group of Marines simply accepted what they could get and were happy to adopt Provo, Utah, narcotics investigator Jacqueline Phillips Guibord as their favorite pinup. Her Wrangler advertisement apparently raised no concerns for Saudi censors, who let slip through the image of Guibord wearing jeans, a red long-sleeved shirt, boots, and her police officer's badge. No conventional sex symbol, this wife of a former Marine and mother of an eighteen-month-old toddler sent several signed posters to her adoring fans.[87] The men's commander, Marine Corps Commandant General Al Gray tried simply to forbid "morale problems" and "boredom" and even insisted it was "ludicrous" to send USO shows because entertainment "detracts from the mission at hand."[88] His orders seem to have fallen on deaf ears, however, as the USO began sending shows that continued through the holiday season.

These were not the USO shows of the Vietnam War, with miniskirt-clad beauty queens, or even the comparatively demure performances of swing dancers in World War II. In part, the USO's newfound approach to entertainment reflected the changes in the military itself. "Our whole focus is family entertainment," Director of Marketing and Communications Kevin McCarthy explained. Local customs also played their part. "We're still the USO," he maintained, "but you won't see any dancing girls in Saudi Arabia."[89] Instead, comedian and actor Steve Martin inaugurated "USO entertainment, Desert Shield-style" in October, but even he was restricted by Saudi prohibitions against public entertainment to signing autographs and shaking hands with the 500 soldiers who had waited for hours to see him.[90] Despite Schwarzkopf's assurances, some women made it into Saudi Arabia, such as Martin's wife Victoria Tennant and Bob Hope's wife Delores, but when the USO suggested model and actor Brooke Shields for a solo handshake tour, the Saudi Embassy asked the US government to deny her visa application.[91] Bob Hope returned to the stage for a Christmas tour, but did so without the customary accompanying beauties. "How am I going to go without the girls," he complained, in typical Hope-style humor. "I'd hate to think I was the only pretty face there."[92]

Pretty faces did sneak in, albeit in limited ways. *Playboy* magazine founder Hugh Hefner revived his wartime support for the troops by launching "Operation Playmate," a campaign to dispatch letters and signed photographs of the magazine's Playmates to soldiers in the Gulf. The photographs had to conform to Saudi cultural standards, which meant that centerfolds were replaced by head shots. "That's never going to take the place of Miss December romping starkers through a creek bed," a *Los Angeles Times* reporter cracked, "but hey, man, this is war, or at least near-war, and everyone's going to have to make sacrifices."[93] General Schwarzkopf declared the women "true patriots" for their efforts.[94]

However much the Playmates might have been appreciated, even the Playboy organization knew that its target audience was a shrinking portion of the forces. Ten percent of the forces in the Gulf were women, who were even more restricted by Saudi cultural norms than were their male colleagues.[95] Playboy made a half-hearted effort to boost their morale by asking male readers to write to women soldiers, though it was unclear if those readers were to send head shots of themselves.[96] An op-ed writer for the *St. Louis Post-Dispatch* sardonically pointed out the possibility that female soldiers with gender-neutral names might accidentally receive one of the Playmates' photographs.[97] Army MWR officials also recognized the larger problem. "Merely providing battle fatigued soldiers access to alcohol, slot machines, shopping, and go-go dancers is perhaps real in terms of what some of the young single adults might want," one administrator explained, but a significant portion of the troops were older, married, and had different concerns.[98]

With the exception of the USO tours, however, the military's efforts to provide any kind of morale-boosting activity proved slow.[99] Every unit that deployed had been authorized to take a recreation kit with paperback books and basic sports equipment but, in part because the military was unsure how long the deployment would last, it took a little more than five months to send more extensive recreation programming and staff. Ultimately the Army's Community and Family Support Center deployed a total of sixty-three civilian employees to staff recreation centers that offered a range of sporting, arts and crafts, and leisure options.[100]

Unlike the Navy and the Air Force, the Army deployed only civilian recreation workers because MWR officials insisted that only civilians could serve as "a link to 'home' that soldiers can readily relate to."[101] The women and men who staffed recreation centers echoed the sentiment. Shirley Booker, who worked in recreation and commercial entertainment at Fort Hood, Texas, before deploying, explained that she felt she should demonstrate her support for the military and the country by volunteering to go and hoped to be a "sounding board for those who wanted to talk about their concerns." Kathy Brown and Greta Plough, who volunteered from their posts at Camp Zama, Japan, and Fort Monmouth, New Jersey, respectively, both understood their work as a way to demonstrate concern for the troops. Their colleague Skip Walker, a former soldier who worked in community recreation in Germany, echoed one of the oldest and most consistent justifications for wartime recreation when he explained that he "wanted to provide a touch of home" for soldiers in the Gulf.[102]

Following a week of training that covered security, terrorism, cultural awareness, and chemical warfare, the Army's MWR workers established Soldier Activity Centers with physical fitness equipment, movies, reading and writing areas, and a room for soldiers to make videos they could send home to their families. The Navy provided shipboard recreation programs on more than one hundred ships deployed to the region in support of the war. Marines took basic recreational equipment with them, as had Army soldiers, but this was "not enough to provide the thousands of modern day warriors with the kind of rest and relaxation needed for a recharge of energy and morale in the desert of Saudi Arabia." Eventually, the First Marine Expeditionary Force leased "Club Saudi" from the Saudi government, a recreation complex with two swimming pools, a snack bar, movie theaters, a gift shop, and telephones.[103]

Club Saudi was but one of several efforts to provide American personnel with the kind of recreation their predecessors had enjoyed. In October 1990, the US military received permission from the Saudi government to use a local facility as an in-country recreation center. Five hundred troops visited daily and made use of the cinema, outdoor pool, bowling alley, tennis and basketball courts, and water skiing amenities. Male and female troops visited together, though Saudi prohibitions against alcohol remained in place.[104] A couple of months later, the troops had something even better. For $31 million, the Army chartered the Cunard *Princess,* a luxury liner that could accommodate up to 900 passengers at a time. Docked off the coast of Bahrain and dubbed the "Love Boat," the ship functioned as a rest and recuperation (R&R) facility for personnel who enjoyed four days and three nights aboard. With no military hierarchy, regulations, antifraternization rules, or even minimum drinking age enforced, personnel were free to relax on their own terms and enjoy a cold brew. Although rooms were segregated by sex, no curfew was imposed and no rules about guests of the opposite sex seem to have been enforced.[105]

Despite these efforts, Army officials concluded that they could not afford such a slow response in the future and adapted the relevant regulations in the September 1994 Field Manual, a handbook for commanders that outlines wartime personnel policies. The manual declared morale services "mission-essential," which meant that they would be "funded by mission dollars." Within the first thirty days of an operation, commanders were directed to ensure that service personnel had access to athletic equipment, basic hygiene supplies, books, and games. Civilian recreation workers were to deploy "as early as the situation permits." Live entertainment, additional recreation workers, recreation clubs, USO shows, and R&R centers should follow within four months.[106] The new regulations affirmed recreation and entertainment as essential to the military's work in maintaining the morale of wartime, or at least deployed, soldiers.

Writing in December 1990, a *Washington Post* reporter suggested that the military's increased reliance on women, the absence of sexualized entertainment, and the Muslim culture of Saudi Arabia had combined to create a radically different military culture, one devoid of sexuality. It was ironic, he wrote, that "chastity, virtue, even celibacy" arrived at the very moment when women had become a critical component of the military, and when military couples were serving together in the war. In some ways, the reporter was correct. Married couples received no special concessions to be together. As Army Sergeant Christina Wall explained, because most male soldiers felt it unfair for married men to "have something they don't," she and her husband spent very little time together even though they deployed to the same area.[107] And, no conventional pinups or dancing beauties accompanied troops as they had in the past. But sexuality remained a fundamental part of military culture and entertainment, as the "Love Boat" suggested. It just lay hidden beneath the surface, ready to reappear in another setting.

## AMERICA'S SWEETHEARTS

In the summer of 1997, 7,000 American military personnel were stationed in Croatia, Bosnia, and Hungary on a NATO mission to enforce peace accords following the Yugoslavian civil war. It was the last major American military deployment of the twentieth century. Putting into practice the lessons learned from the First Gulf War, military

MWR specialists quickly opened facilities with fitness equipment, telephones, televisions, and videos not long after the troops deployed, and the USO began a regular circuit of tours featuring comedians Jay Leno and Sinbad, pop star Sheryl Crow, country singer Larry Gatlin, and handshake tours of National Football League and Major League Baseball players, all of whom volunteered their time.[108] The Dallas Cowboys Cheerleaders, who had made biannual USO tours to military stations since 1979, staged a holiday show in December 1996 and then returned to the war-torn region that summer, but something about their dance performance did not sit well with an Army wife in Germany and an American peacekeeper in Croatia.[109]

In separate letters to *Stars and Stripes,* Kristie Lovelace and Specialist Russell A. Cleveland noted several objections to the show. Although both appreciated the generosity of performers willing to give their time to entertain military personnel, they questioned whether the Dallas Cowboys Cheerleaders were appropriate entertainment. "How are the Cowboy cheerleaders entertaining our peacekeepers?" Lovelace asked. "By cheering? Or by letting it all hang out?"[110] Cleveland made the point much more directly. "I simply have better things to do than be teased and smiled at by women who have no interest in me or my fellow soldiers," he wrote.[111] Lovelace and Cleveland were not the first to object to the cheerleaders, who were used to defending their performances. In March 1980, while touring American installations in South Korea and Germany, one cheerleader insisted that though physical attraction was part of the women's appeal, they were not "sexpots." The group's vice president, Suzanne Mitchell, who accompanied the tour, argued that "there's nothing wrong with being sexy," and that the women and their "attractive costumes" should be afforded creative license as entertainers.[112]

That rationale appeased neither Cleveland nor Lovelace, who objected to the performance as a government and military-sponsored skin show. Cleveland explained that since he had deployed to Croatia, his wife had given birth to their son and was raising him alone. "The last thing she needs to hear," he ventured, "is how my government is sending us women to look at." Sixty-five percent of the men in his platoon were married, while others had girlfriends back at home, and he suggested that the government send them instead. His and the other men's morale "would be substantially higher after a visit," he affirmed.[113] Lovelace went so far as to call the performance "immoral entertainment." She conceded that it might have been understandable if the soldiers were all single but complained that it harmed the morale of families at home. Moreover, she ventured that if a group of male performers like the Chippendales were sent to boost the morale of wives at home, few soldiers "would be happy about it."[114]

By the mid-1990s, the cheerleaders had modulated their performances to be more family-friendly. Joan Capella escorted the group during one of their earliest tours to Germany and was less than impressed. Although "the guys loved them," she found the cheerleaders "very demanding" and "very amateurish." Their entire purpose, she believed, was to be pretty.[115] With time, however, being pretty must have seemed insufficient. James Sohre, chief of Army entertainment in Europe in the mid-1990s, noted that the group occasionally brought along Cowboys players and ran cheerleading camps for dependent children so that their tours were not just a "display of sex."[116] The group improved their act in other ways, according to MWR entertainment coordinator Kathleen Cole, who escorted them on their 1996 holiday tour of American bases in the Balkans. In her mind, the Dallas Cowboys Cheerleaders were more professional, "constrained and monitored" than any other cheerleading organization. They "yes ma'amed and no ma'amed me to death," she recalled, and their supervisor monitored their every move.[117] Indeed, the cheerleaders spent more of their time signing autographs and talking with soldiers than they did performing the dance routines that drew criticism.[118] Still, as Sohre put it, the cheerleaders were "attractive women" and "that's why they're there." This implicit rationale meant that the cheerleaders walked "a fine line" between being a "perk" for the men without offending the men's families or the women with whom they served.[119]

Servicewomen were at the forefront of many military members' minds in 1997. Allegations of sexual assault made against Navy and Marine Corps aviation officers at the annual Tailhook Association Symposium in 1991 focused national attention on a culture of misogyny in the military, while more recent news of assaults at Aberdeen Proving Grounds and Fort Leonard Wood had kept the problem in the news. In this context, the cheerleaders' tour seemed especially heinous to Lovelace and Cleveland, who each drew a connection between sexualized entertainment and sexual harassment. "Every day there are articles about sexual harassment, sexual assault, adultery, etc., committed by soldiers ranging from the lowest private to the sergeant major of the Army," Cleveland noted, "then you send me women to stare at and lust over. How many more sexual harassment and adultery charges do the U.S. armed forces need," he asked, "before they understand they are sending mixed messages?"[120]

Lovelace and Cleveland's objections to the Dallas Cowboys Cheerleaders highlighted the broad context in which military entertainment operated at the end of the twentieth century. In contrast to the largely conscripted forces of young, single men that had marched to two World Wars and two "cold" wars in Korea and Vietnam, the military of the late twentieth century was populated mostly by personnel with families and an ever-increasing number of women. These changes did not come easily or without struggle, and they ushered in significant changes to the ways that civilian and military officials thought about what it meant to entertain them far from home.

Military and civilian efforts to entertain service members had changed considerably since World War I but also retained some historical trappings. It's unlikely that anyone in the 1990s military thought that cheerleaders would keep service members out of trouble in the same ways that military and civilian leaders had hoped American women would do in earlier eras. Military and civilian officials no longer created programs with the specific intent of providing women whose friendly smiles would counter the negative consequences of mobilization and deployments. Indeed, the forces that deployed to the Persian Gulf and the Balkans in the 1990s were the first to deploy without American women specifically chosen to be surrogate mothers, sisters, wives, or sweethearts who would serve them coffee and doughnuts and dance with them in recreation centers. Nonetheless, even as morale programs broadened their focus in the years following the Vietnam War, and even as military officials made some efforts to desexualize entertainment, female MWR workers sometimes found that servicemen sought them out, seeking to connect with a woman from home.[121] And, even as the military relied on increasing numbers of family members and servicewomen, and as officials confronted embarrassing scandals about sexual harassment, women continued to dance across stages for the amusement—and the derision—of men and women in uniform. The inherent contradictions that underscored military entertainment in the early twentieth century remained integral to it at the century's end.

# Epilogue

During a December 2003 USO tour, two Washington Redskins cheer-leaders dressed in burkas carried their pom-poms onto a stage at a US airbase in Kandahar. Former *Saturday Night Live* comedian and future US senator Al Franken introduced the women as the Taliban Cheerleaders and asked them to perform for the American troops. One of the women nervously whispered something in Franken's ear, to which he replied, "You're not allowed to dance? . . . Or even listen to music?" Franken protested incredulously that "we liberated Afghan-istan from the Taliban" and implored the women to dance. On cue, C+C Music Factory's hit song urged, "Everybody dance now." The women began what Franken described as a "bump-and-grind" routine while still wearing the burkas before ripping them off and continuing the dance in their cheerleader uniforms "as the guys [went] nuts." While musing that the routine "worked like a charm every time" and that "no USO Tour is complete without NFL cheer-leaders," Franken made clear exactly what made them appealing. He had only been away from home for a week and confessed that he didn't know how the soldiers managed a nine-month deployment. "The first thing I'm going to do when I get home," he admitted to the crowd of male and female soldiers, "is have sex with my wife—while thinking about the cheerleaders. Not so different from you guys, ex-cept I won't be alone."[1]

Franken performed in several USO tours over the next few years, none of which made many headlines. However, in late 2017 fellow performer Leann Tweeden accused Franken of sexually harassing her during their tour and provided a photograph of him smiling for the camera while placing his hands over her breasts as she slept. In the face of such damning evidence and at a time of intense public outcry about sexual harassment, Franken resigned from the US Senate.[2] His behavior was egregious by most standards but is only one example of how early twenty-first-century military entertainment has catered to the basest of sexual innuendo and risqué humor.

Sexual longing and desire have underscored the work of all women who have entertained American troops since World War I, but in recent years the sexual appeal has become more blatant than ever before. Franken's USO tours, for example, included a skit in which his character offered to give his female coperformer a breast exam and then joked that she had given him an erection, while the women he toured with called male soldiers on stage and kissed them as part of the routine. Many entertainment shows have featured barely clothed, gyrating dancers, including teams of professional cheerleaders, a popular group known as the "Purrfect Angelz," and Hooters restaurant waitresses wearing tank tops that advertised "Weapons of Mass Destruction."[3] The sexual innuendo embedded in these performances is barely camouflaged, covered by the tiniest of costumes or signaled by thinly veiled references to women's bodies.

This hypersexualized entertainment seems especially remarkable, as the military relies on increasing numbers of servicewomen who serve in all specializations, including combat, and as it faces an astounding epidemic of sexual harassment and assault. Performances that present women's bodies as sexualized entertainment starkly contrast the image of the professional female soldier that the forces also uphold and thus suggest a deeper problem within the military about the place of women. Moreover, hypersexualized entertainment occurs with the sanction of military officials who approve the performances and through the support of congressionally appropriated monies.[4]

Not all women in military entertainment perform sexually suggestive dance moves or are the butt of jokes about masturbation, of

Two Dallas Cowboys Cheerleaders salute the troops in Baghdad, Iraq, on an annual USO tour in 2007. The US military that deployed in the War on Terror included more women and families than it ever had, but suggestively clad professional cheerleaders remained a staple of military entertainment nonetheless.

course. Traveling as representatives of the USO or under the auspices of the Armed Forces Professional Entertainment Office, female country music singers, pop stars, gospel artists, actors, athletes, politicians, comedians, and authors have made the trek to entertain the military personnel who have deployed to Iraq, Afghanistan, and other stations in the Middle East since 9/11. Other women have traveled to conflict zones to operate recreation facilities, manage fitness centers and communication hubs, and coordinate entertainment shows sponsored by the USO and the Department of Defense.[5]

This juxtaposition of scantily clad performers and morale workers might also seem odd but is, in fact, a modern iteration of the conflicting, yet intertwined, ways the military and civilian organizations have utilized women in recreation and entertainment programs throughout the past century. Enlisted as symbols of home and as surrogate mothers, sisters, wives, and sweethearts, YMCA girls, Salvation Army Lassies, Red Cross Donut Dollies, USO performers and club women, and Special Services hostesses were called on to embody a wholesome and sexual appeal that would domesticate the all-male military, keep GIs on post and away from local populations, socialize servicemen for their reentry into civilian society, and motivate men to fight. Thousands of women throughout the twentieth century gladly took on these tasks, and many of them embraced the conventions of their work. Others recognized the limitations but nonetheless derived great satisfaction from their efforts to comfort and cheer men who were called on to wage war in their name.

It is not a bad thing that these programs came to an end. In using women as symbols of the family for which men fought and to which they hoped to return, the military and civilian organizations associated women with home and the home front, even when they went to war. Programs employing women to serve hot chocolate and Kool-Aid to soldiers positioned them as servicemen's supporters, not their equals. Organizations that held up women as symbols of both wholesome and sexualized ideals placed them in untenable and often dangerous situations. And, recreation and entertainment programs that offered women as antidotes to the military suggested that they had no place in it.

But the military still needs, and the American public still wants, to send a bit of home to personnel stationed in conflict zones around the world. As women comprise an ever-increasing part of the American military, and as the military becomes a more diverse group of personnel, it is worth reconsidering women's role in military entertainment. To be sure, simply ending performances by scantily clad women will not solve the military's problem with sexual harassment. Nor will it remove all barriers to women's equality, though it is not a bad place to start. Perhaps, in the place of overtly sexual entertainment, we could turn to the examples of women like Emma Young Dickson, B. J. Olewiler, Jean Moore Fasse, Helen Stevenson Meyner, Debby Alexander, and Gina Cardi Lee, women who offered their time and talents to bring a brief reminder of home to wartime soldiers.

# Abbreviations

| | |
|---|---|
| AEF | RG 120 Records of the American Expeditionary Forces (World War I) |
| AGO | RG 407 Adjutant General's Office |
| Army Staff | RG 319 Records of the Army Staff |
| ASWWI | Armed Services World War I–Related Records |
| BNP | RG 24 Records of the Bureau of Naval Personnel |
| Bowman Collection | Hazel L. Bowman Collection 10.0050, WWII Institute |
| Camp Shows | Camp Shows Publicity Records T-Mss 1991-007, Billy Rose Theater Collection, New York Public Library for the Performing Arts, New York, NY |
| CBI | RG 493 Records of the US Army Forces in the China-Burma-India Theaters of Operations |
| Chaplains | RG 247 Records of the Office of the Chief of Chaplains |
| Christie Collection | Jeanne Christie Collection (2678), TVA |
| Christie Papers | Jeanne Bokina Christie Papers, 1966–1983, MS 267, Sophia Smith Collection, Smith College, Northampton, MA |
| Clubmobile Collection | MC 550 American Red Cross Clubmobile Service Collection, 1940–1998, Schlesinger |
| Deane Papers | Julia Coolidge Deane Papers, 1919–1962, Schlesinger |
| Dickson Papers | Emma Young Dickson Papers, YMCA |
| EBAAR | USARV Special Services Agency (Provisional) Entertainment Branch After Action Reports RE: USO Tours in Vietnam |

EBGA                    USARV Special Services Agency (Provisional) Entertainment Branch General Administrative Records

Fasse Papers            WV0390 M. Jean Moore Fasse Papers, WVHP

Fortune Collection      Janet Olson Fortune Collection (1100), TVA

Frizzell Collection     Sabrina Frizzell Collection (371), TVA

Horning Papers          Shirley J. Horning Papers

JANBC                   RG 225 Records of Joint Army and Navy Boards and Committees

JANCWR                  Joint Army Navy Committee on Welfare and Recreation

MacCubbin Papers        WV0463 Janet MacCubbin Papers, WVHP

Meyner Papers           Series II: Helen Stevenson Meyner (Personal), Robert B. and Helen Stevenson Meyner Papers, 1910–1998, Lafayette College Special Collections & College Archives

MHI                     Military History Institute, Army Heritage and Education Center, Carlisle, PA

NAACP                   Papers of the NAACP, microfilm edition

NARA                    National Archives and Records Administration, College Park, MD

NCCS                    National Catholic Community Service Records, American Catholic History Research Center and University Archives, Catholic University of America, Washington, DC

OMR                     RG 2 Office of the Messrs. Rockefeller, Rockefeller Family Archives

Ormond Papers           Kathy Ormond Papers, Iowa Women's Archives, The University of Iowa Libraries, Iowa City, IA

OSG                     RG 112 Records of the Office of the Surgeon General (Army)

Purviance Papers        RG 20.68 Purviance, Helen G., 1889-1984 Personal Papers and Manuscripts, SA

Red Cross 1935–1946     RG 200 Records of the American National Red Cross Central Decimal Files, 1935–1946

Red Cross 1947–1964     RG 200 Records of the American National Red Cross Central Decimal Files, 1947–1964

Red Cross 1965–1979     RG 200 Records of the American National Red Cross Central Decimal Files, 1965–1979

Red Cross Archives      Hazel Brown Red Cross Archives, Lorton, VA

Reeves Papers           WV0383 Jean Holdridge Reeves Papers, WVHP

Rice Papers             Harriet E. Rice Papers, MHI

| | |
|---|---|
| Rockefeller Archive | Rockefeller Archive Center, Sleepy Hollow, NY |
| SA | Salvation Army Archives and Research Center, Arlington, VA |
| Schlesinger | Schlesinger Library, Radcliffe Institute, Harvard University, Cambridge, MA |
| Schuyler Papers | 2006-M174 Gretchen Schuyler Papers, Schlesinger |
| TVA | The Vietnam Archive, Texas Tech University, Lubbock, TX |
| USFSEA | Record Group 472 Records of U.S. Forces in Southeast Asia, 1950–1975 |
| USO | USO Archive, USO World Headquarters, Arlington, VA |
| VHP | Veterans History Project, American Folklife Center, Library of Congress |
| Weil Papers | Frank L. Weil Papers, Jacob Rader Marcus Center of the American Jewish Archives, Cincinnati, OH |
| WVHP | Betty H. Carter Women Veterans Historical Project, University of North Carolina–Greensboro, Greensboro, NC |
| World War II Institute | Institute on World War II and the Human Experience, Florida State University, Tallahassee, FL |
| YMCA | Kautz Family YMCA Archives, University of Minnesota, Minneapolis, MN |
| Young Collection | Jennifer Young Collection (1645), TVA |

# Notes

## INTRODUCTION

1. Amy Argetsinger and Roxanne Roberts, "To Honor and Humor: USO's Surprise Guest," *Washington Post*, October 8, 2008. Simpson had posed in an American flag bikini, camouflage pants, and dog tags on the cover of GQ magazine in July 2005.

## 1. A NEW KIND OF WOMAN IS FOLLOWING THE ARMY

1. April 3, 1918 diary entry, Dickson Papers.
2. April 11, 1918 diary entry, Dickson Papers.
3. Howard Chandler Christy, "Gee!! I wish I were a man, I'd join the Navy," 1917 poster, available at the Library of Congress, http://www.loc.gov/pictures/item /2002712088, accessed July 4, 2013.
4. Speech at Hut Opening Valdelancourt, May 14, 1918, Dickson Papers.
5. June 30, 1918, diary entry, Dickson Papers.
6. May 31, 1918, diary entry, Dickson Papers.
7. July 7, 1918, diary entry, Dickson Papers.
8. Emma Young Dickson to mother, April 23, 1918, Dickson Papers.
9. June 2, 1918, diary entry, Dickson Papers.
10. Emma Young Dickson to mother, September 4, 1918, Dickson Papers.
11. Women had, of course, provided support for the US military since its beginnings, and their work often involved providing domestic comforts. The US Sanitary Commission, for example, loosely organized Union women during the Civil War to provide food and clothing for soldiers. World War I, however, marked the first time that women were sent to war to provide these services directly.
12. Anne M. Butler, *Daughters of Joy, Sisters of Misery: Prostitutes in the American West, 1860–1890* (Urbana: University of Illinois Press, 1985), 122–149; Thomas P. Lowry, *The Story the Soldiers Wouldn't Tell: Sex in the Civil War* (Mechanicsburg, PA: Stackpole

Books, 1994); Mary Renda, *Taking Haiti: Military Occupation and the Culture of U.S. Imperialism, 1915–1940* (Chapel Hill: University of North Carolina Press, 2001), 215–216; Weldon B. Durham, *Liberty Theatres of the United States Army, 1917–1919* (Jefferson, NC: McFarland, 2006), 23–28; Paul A. Kramer, "The Darkness that Enters the Home: The Politics of Prostitution during the Philippine-American War," in *Haunted by Empire: Geographies of Intimacy in North American History,* ed. Ann Laura Stoler (Durham, NC: Duke University Press, 2006), 366–404.

13. Allan M. Brandt, *No Magic Bullet: A Social History of Venereal Disease in the United States since 1880* (New York: Oxford University Press, 1985), 52–57; Edward M. Coffman, *The War to End All Wars: The American Military Experience in World War I* (New York: Oxford University Press, 1968), 76–81; Frederick Palmer, *Newton D. Baker: America at War,* vol. 1 (New York: Dodd, Mead, and Company, 1931), 296–297.

14. Brandt, *No Magic Bullet,* 53–54.

15. Raymond B. Fosdick, *Chronicle of a Generation: An Autobiography* (New York: Harper and Brothers, 1958), 137.

16. Palmer, *Newton D. Baker,* 1:298. Also Fosdick, *Chronicle of a Generation,* 135–141.

17. M. J. Exner, *Prostitution in Its Relation to the Army on the Mexican Border,* Publication No. 91 (New York: American Social Hygiene Association, 1917), 8, Social Hygiene Pamphlets, ASWWI, YMCA [reprinted from *Social Hygiene* 3, no. 2 (April 1917)].

18. Exner, *Prostitution in Its Relation to the Army on the Mexican Border,* 14.

19. Susan Zeiger, *Entangling Alliances: Foreign War Brides and American Soldiers in the Twentieth Century* (New York: New York University Press, 2010), chap. 1.

20. Brandt, *No Magic Bullet,* 70–77.

21. Palmer, *Newton D. Baker,* 1:298.

22. Bristow argues that the CTCA "envisioned the remaking of the soldiers' training environment as the first step in a more complete transformation of American culture." Nancy K. Bristow, *Making Men Moral: Social Engineering during the Great War* (New York: New York University Press, 1996), xvii.

23. William Howard Taft et al., eds., *Service with Fighting Men: An Account of the Work of the American Young Men's Christian Association in the World War,* vol. 1 (New York: Association Press, 1924), 118.

24. Quoted in Taft, *Service with Fighting Men,* 1:112.

25. Frank E. Vandiver, *Black Jack: The Life and Times of John J. Pershing,* vol. 2 (College Station: Texas A&M University Press, 1977), 662.

26. Georges Clemenceau offered to establish "special houses" for the sole use of the AEF. Pershing was incensed at the offer, as was Secretary Baker, who warned that if President Wilson heard of it he would "stop the war." See Hugh Young, *A Surgeon's Autobiography* (New York: Harcourt, Brace and Company, 1940), 329; Fosdick, *Chronicle of a Generation,* 171; Brandt, *No Magic Bullet,* 104–106.

27. George Walker, *Venereal Disease in the American Expeditionary Forces* (Baltimore: Medical Standard Book Co., 1922), 135. On French prostitution see Michelle Kathleen Rhoades, "'No Safe Women': Prostitution, Masculinity, and Disease in France during the Great War" (PhD diss., University of Iowa, 2001). On British poli-

cies toward prostitution see Clare Makepeace, "Punters and Their Prostitutes: British Soldiers, Masculinity, and *Maisons Tolérées* in the First World War," in *What Is Masculinity? Historical Dynamics from Antiquity to the Contemporary World,* ed. Sean Brady and John H. Arnold (Houndsmills, UK: Palgrave Macmillan, 2011), 413–430.

28. Brandt, *No Magic Bullet,* 98–102; Vandiver, *Black Jack,* 2:662. General Order No. 6 is found in Walker, *Venereal Disease in the AEF,* 58–59. Walker offers a comprehensive overview of the AEF's work in studying and regulating venereal disease. See also Donald Smythe, "Venereal Disease: The AEF's Experience," *Prologue* 9 (Summer 1977): 65–74; Fred D. Baldwin, "The Invisible Armor," *American Quarterly* 16, no. 3 (Autumn 1964): 432–444; Young, *A Surgeon's Autobiography,* 264–293, 301–312, 318–327.

29. Frank W. Weed, *The Medical Department of the United States Army in the World War,* vol. 6, *Sanitation in the American Expeditionary Forces* (Washington, DC: Government Printing Office, 1926), 906–909; Brandt, *No Magic Bullet,* 103–106.

30. Brandt, *No Magic Bullet,* 23–31.

31. Edward L. Munson, *The Management of Men: A Handbook on the Systematic Development of Morale and the Control of Human Behavior* (New York: Henry Holt and Company, 1921), 197.

32. M. J. Exner, *A Square Deal* (New York: Association Press, 1919), 12–13, Social Hygiene Pamphlets, ASWWI, YMCA.

33. John Dickinson, *The Building of an Army: A Detailed Account of Legislation, Administration and Opinion in the United States, 1915–1920* (New York: The Century Company, 1922), 203.

34. *Handbook of American Y.M.C.A., A.E.F.* (Paris: YMCA, 1918), 22.

35. *Keeping Fit to Fight* was the title of a pamphlet prepared by the American Social Hygiene Association and distributed widely among AEF forces. The pamphlet, and the film later based on it, both warned doughboys of the dangers of sexual activity. The pamphlet is available at the University of Minnesota's online archive, http://purl.umn.edu/111740, accessed June 13, 2013.

36. On British canteen and recreation services in the war, see Michael Snape, *God and the British Soldier: Religion and the British Army in the First and Second World Wars* (London: Routledge, 2005), 205–240; J. G. Fuller, *Troop Morale and Popular Culture in the British and Dominion Armies, 1914–1918* (Oxford: Clarendon Press, 1990), chaps. 7 and 8. Sarah Cozzi examines Canadian social clubs in Britain in her article, "'When You're a Long, Long Way from Home': The Establishment of Canadian-Only Social Clubs for CEF Soldiers in London, 1915–1919," *Canadian Military History* 20, no. 1 (Winter 2011): 45–60.

37. Always concerned with efficiency, the AEF dictated that these social organizations not duplicate each other's work. General Order 26 (issued on August 28, 1917) delineated the work of the YMCA and Red Cross as being concerned with recreation and relief, respectively. One Red Cross history suggests that the organization opened some canteens in 1918. See Bulletin No. 76, June 27, 1918, in *Handbook of American Y.M.C.A., A.E.F.,* 25–26; *Summary of World War Work of the*

*American YMCA* (International Committee of Young Men's Christian Association, 1920), 198; Foster Rhea Dulles, *The American Red Cross: A History* (New York: Harper and Brothers, 1950), 183–187. The Knights of Columbus decided against employing women as workers in its huts. The JWB eventually sent about one hundred women to Europe, but raging anti-Semitism in America meant that Jewish workers faced a series of obstacles in getting passports and visas that ultimately limited and delayed their efforts. Maurice Francis Egan and John B. Kennedy, *The Knights of Columbus in Peace and War,* vol. 1 (New Haven, CT: Knights of Columbus, 1920), 253–279, 297–339, 374–378; Susan Zeiger, *In Uncle Sam's Service: Women Workers with the American Expeditionary Force, 1917–1919* (Ithaca, NY: Cornell University Press, 1999), 29–30.

38. Quotes in Helen Ives Gilchrist, "AEF-YMCA Women's Work in the World War," 78, Women's Work in the World War, ASWWI, YMCA; also "American Expeditionary Forces Young Men's Christian Association, Statement of the Work Organised in the United Kingdom for the Men of the American Army, May 1917–February 1919," 14–16, AEF in Great Britain, both in ASWWI, YMCA; *Summary of World War Work of the American YMCA,* 23.

39. Quoted in Dickinson, *The Building of an Army,* 207.

40. "Her Share in War," *New York Times Magazine,* June 2, 1918.

41. *AEF Bulletin* 54, August 7, 1918, in Walker, *Venereal Disease in the AEF,* 66–67.

42. Taft et al., *Service with Fighting Men,* 1:118.

43. "The Present Work of the National War Work Council," April 13, 1920, 7, National War Work Council, minutes and documents, 1917–1921, ASWWI, YMCA; William Howard Taft et al., eds., *Service with Fighting Men: An Account of the Work of the American Young Men's Christian Association in the World War,* vol. 2 (New York: Association Press, 1924), chap. 42; Gilchrist, "AEF-YMCA Women's Work in the World War," chap. 12. On military concerns about sexuality in occupied Germany see Erika Kuhlman, "American Doughboys and German *Fräuleins:* Sexuality, Patriarchy, and Privilege in the American-Occupied Rhineland, 1918–1923," *Journal of Military History* 71, no. 4 (October 2007): 1077–1106. Susan Zeiger discusses the American military and public's perceptions of German women and marriages between German women and American soldiers in *Entangling Alliances: Foreign War Brides and American Soldiers in the Twentieth Century* (New York: New York University Press, 2010), chap. 1.

44. Edward Frank Allen with Raymond B. Fosdick, *Keeping Our Fighters Fit for War and After* (New York: The Century Co., 1918), 7; *Y.M.C.A. On Duty Wherever Our Boys Are in Khaki: Keeping the Home Ties from Breaking* (brochure), Fundraising Materials–National War Work Council 1917 Campaign, ASWWI, YMCA.

45. Luther H. Gulick, *Morals and Morale* (New York: Association Press, 1919), 3.

46. Gulick, *Morals and Morale,* 70–72.

47. Gilchrist, "AEF-YMCA Women's Work in the World War," 2–5, and "Y.M.C.A. Workers arriving France for A.E.F., since January 1st, 1918," AEF-YMCA Budget, ASWWI, YMCA.

48. Early in the war, the Y's War Work Council coordinated the selection of women, but in summer 1918 as the demand for women workers grew, the newly created Women's Division of the War Personnel Board assumed the task. Gilchrist, "AEF-YMCA Women's Work in the World War," 3, 41–42; *Summary of World War Work of the American YMCA,* 113.

49. Gilchrist, "AEF-YMCA Women's Work in the World War," 42; on passports, see *Summary of War Work,* 118.

50. Taft, *Service with Fighting Men,* 1:257–258; Gilchrist, "AEF-YMCA Women's Work in the World War," 41–42.

51. *Summary of World War Work of the American YMCA,* 112, 114; Gilchrist, "AEF-YMCA Women's Work in the World War," 44.

52. James W. Evans and Gardner L. Harding, *Entertaining the American Army: The American Stage and Lyceum in the World War* (New York: Association Press, 1921), 258.

53. W. A. McIntyre to Ensign Purviance, August 2, 1917, Purviance Papers.

54. Edward H. McKinley, *Marching to Glory: The History of the Salvation Army in the United States of America, 1880–1980* (San Francisco: Harper & Row, 1980), 121; "Salvation Army Workers in France," World War I Doughnut Girls, SA. Salvation Army women received no pay during their wartime service but received four dollars per week's work after their term expired to help them adapt to postwar life. See Evangeline Booth, "Mothering the Boy at the Front," *Forum* (September 1918): 304–305.

55. National War Work Council News Bulletin No. 258, May 26, 1918, 1, Press Releases National War Work Council, ASWWI, YMCA.

56. Elsie Cleveland Mead, "A Woman's War," 209, A Woman's War, ASWWI, YMCA.

57. Taft, *Service with Fighting Men,* 1:257–258; Gilchrist, "AEF-YMCA Women's Work in the World War," 41–42.

58. Mead, "A Woman's War," 209.

59. Taft, *Service with Fighting Men,* 1:258–259; *Summary of World War Work of the American YMCA,* 117; Gilchrist, "AEF-YMCA Women's Work in the World War," 49–50; "Women's Overseas Service General Information" (Chicago: War Personnel Board Women's Division, n.d.) and "Women's Overseas Section Preliminary Information" (New York: National War Work Council of the Young Men's Christian Associations, n.d.), both in Women Secretaries—Miscellaneous Publications, ASWWI, YMCA.

60. See "Report of the Investigation of the Y.M.C.A.," 2:229, Investigation of YMCA, Records of the General Staff Entry 445, AEF, NARA.

61. Zeiger, *In Uncle Sam's Service,* 33–41; *Summary of World War Work of the American YMCA,* 115–116; George Browne, *An American Soldier in World War I,* ed. David L. Snead (Lincoln: University of Nebraska Press, 2006), 18.

62. Gilchrist, "AEF-YMCA Women's Work in the World War," 45; National War Work Council News Bulletin No. 548, September 26, 1918, 2, Press Releases National War Work Council, and Committee on Public Information, "War Work of Women in Colleges," April 1918, 18, Women Secretaries—Miscellaneous Publications, both in

ASWWI, YMCA. In her analysis of YMCA personnel files, Susan Zeiger finds the following age distribution: 23 years old and younger: 3.2%; 24–27 years old: 22.1%; 28–31 years old: 28.9%; 32–35 years old: 18.6%; 36–39 years old: 11.8%; 40–43 years old: 6.4%; 44–47 years old: 5.1%; 48 years old and older: 3.9%. Her analysis suggests that nearly 85% of the Y women who worked with the AEF were under 40 years of age. Zeiger, *In Uncle Sam's Service*, 35, table 2. Y-produced histories of war work suggest that no women workers received home allowances, but a history of the canteen program notes that a "few" women sent abroad had dependents and that "several" of them received the same allowance that men with children received. See Burt C. Pond, "Brief Historical Statement Concerning the National War Work Council of the Young Men's Christian Associations of the United States," 1919, 113, Histories: Overseas Work by Bert Pond Folder 2, ASWWI, YMCA; Taft, *Service with Fighting Men*, 1:259; Gilchrist, "AEF-YMCA Women's Work in the World War," 50.

63. Gilchrist, "AEF-YMCA Women's Work in the World War," 45.

64. Gilchrist, "AEF-YMCA Women's Work in the World War," 45.

65. Mead, "A Woman's War," 102.

66. "More Girls Wanted for Overseas," *Boston Post*, November 7, 1918, news clipping in Biographical Files, YMCA.

67. "Women's Overseas Service General Information," 3–4.

68. Gilchrist, "AEF-YMCA Women's Work in the World War," 45.

69. "Her Share in War."

70. On the history of women camp followers, see John A. Lynn II, *Women, Armies, and Warfare in Early Modern Europe* (New York: Cambridge University Press, 2008); Thomas Cardoza, *Intrepid Women: Cantinières and Vivandières of the French Army* (Bloomington: Indiana University Press, 2010); Holly A. Mayer, *Belonging to the Army: Camp Follower and Community during the American Revolution* (Columbia: University of South Carolina Press, 1999).

71. Mead, "A Woman's War," 37. Mead discussed similar concerns about women who powdered their face and exhibited "flashy" behavior in correspondence with Caroline Slade, chair of the Women's Overseas Committee. See [Caroline Slade] to Mrs. Robert G. Mead, November 6, 1918 and Elsie Mead to Carole [Slade], September 25, [1918], Slade-Mead Correspondence, 1918–1919, ASWWI, YMCA. See also "How Overseas Canteen Workers are Selected," *The Index*, August 17, 1918, news clipping in Cornelia Cree collection, YMCA Women, World War I Veterans Survey Collection, MHI.

72. Munson, *The Management of Men*, 197.

73. On the policing and incarceration of women suspected of violating notions of feminine respectability in the vicinity of military men, see Jennifer L. Koslow, *Cultivating Health: Los Angeles Women and Public Health Reform* (New Brunswick: Rutgers University Press, 2009), chap. 5; Christopher Capozzola, "The Only Badge Needed Is Your Patriotic Fervor: Vigilance, Coercion, and the Law in World War I America," *Journal of American History* 88, no. 4 (2002): 1354–1382; Mark Thomas Connelly, *The Response to Prostitution in the Progressive Era* (Chapel Hill: University of

North Carolina Press, 1980), chap. 7; David J. Pivar, "Cleansing the Nation: The War on Prostitution, 1917–1921," *Prologue* 12 (Spring 1980): 29–41; Linda Sharon Janke, "Prisoners of War: Sexuality, Venereal Disease, and Women's Incarceration during World War" (PhD diss., State University of New York at Binghamton, 2006).

74. "How Overseas Canteen Workers are Selected."

75. Gilchrist, "AEF-YMCA Women's Work in the World War," 45.

76. Taft, *Service with Fighting Men*, 2:60.

77. "Why the Salvation Army is at the Front," *War Service Herald* 8, no. 1 (January 1918): 15.

78. E. C. Carter to William Sloane, August 27, 1917, AEF-YMCA Chief Secretary's Files Volume G, ASWWI, YMCA. Also Gilchrist, "AEF-YMCA Women's Work in the World War," 1–2; Taft, *Service with Fighting Men*, 2:57.

79. "Report of the Special Committee to the Executive Committee of the War Work Council of the Young Men's Christian Association," May 17, 1918, 7–8, Chief Secretary's File Volume D, ASWWI, YMCA.

80. Mead, "A Woman's War," 51, 65.

81. "Her Share in War."

82. "Relax Ban on Relatives," *New York Times*, July 31, 1918. It is unclear, however, whether Y policy forbid all canteen women from marriage. On July 19, 1918, the Y issued a press release celebrating the "happy culmination of a wartime romance" between a canteen woman and a sailor. See National War Work Council News Bulletin No. 415, July 19, 1918, Press Releases National War Work Council, ASWWI, YMCA.

83. National War Work Council News Bulletin No. 443, August 1, 1918, Press Releases National War Work Council, ASWWI, YMCA.

84. Mead, "A Woman's War," 48.

85. Mead, "A Woman's War," 65–66.

86. "Bishop Brent" in the letter is Bishop Charles Henry Brent, Senior Chaplain for the AEF. Raymond B. Fosdick to Mrs. R. G. Mead, February 27, 1919, Women Secretaries Correspondence, ASWWI, YMCA.

87. Katharine Grinnell Prest, *One of 9000* (Boston: Marshall Jones Company, 1934), 15–21. Prest writes the narrative in the third person, referring to herself as "Kasheen." Occasionally, the narrative refers to her as Mrs. G___ or Grinnell. I use her name during her time of service throughout the text. Other Y documents confirm that Mrs. Katharine Grinnell served in a canteen in the Le Mans region. See her service card at the YMCA and *Summary of Service in the Embarkation Center from December 1918 to July 1919* (Portland, OR: Arcady Press and Mail Advertising Company, 1920).

88. The YMCA managed the vast majority of canteens for the AEF but both the Y and the military agreed at the end of the war that the arrangement was not to their liking. Thereafter, the military established its own post exchange system. For a brief overview, see James J. Cooke, *Chewing Gum, Candy Bars, and Beer: The Army PX in World War II* (Columbia: University of Missouri Press, 2009), chap. 1. The YMCA

detailed its difficulties in operating canteens in "Report of the Investigation of the Y.M.C.A.," 2:229.

89. In many ways, the experiences of canteen workers parallel those of women office workers in the early twentieth century. Women were seen as dangerous because of their sexuality because they tempted men with ever-present and uncontrollable desires yet were expected to manage the men's attentions by being respectable and upholding middle-class values. See Julie Berebitsky, *Sex and the Office: A History of Gender, Power, and Desire* (New Haven, CT: Yale University Press, 2012), chap. 1.

90. James Albert Sprenger and Franklin Spencer Edmonds, *The Leave Areas of the American Expeditionary Forces, 1918–1919: Records and Memories* (Philadelphia: The John C. Winston Company, 1928), 107.

91. Bertha Laurie letter, December 6, 1917, Miscellaneous Reports—Women Secretaries, ASWWI, YMCA.

92. "Report of the Special Committee to the Executive Committee of the War Work Council of the Young Men's Christian Association," May 17, 1918, 8, Chief Secretary's File Volume D, ASWWI, YMCA.

93. "Report of the Women of the Paris Region," January 1, 1919, 21, Women's Work in the Paris Region Helen King, ASWWI, YMCA.

94. Gabrielle A. Raszewska, "Hut Equipment: Its Use in 'Wet' Canteens, Bulletin No. 2" (France: Equipment Department of the General Supply Division, March 1919), 7, AEF-YMCA Publications Miscellaneous, ASWWI, YMCA.

95. Gertrude Bray Diary, 38, Gertrude Bray, YMCA, World War I Veterans Survey Collection, MHI.

96. Sprenger and Edmonds, *The Leave Areas of the American Expeditionary Forces*, 107.

97. "Information for Candidates Y.M.C.A. Canteen Work Overseas," June 1918, Biographical Files, YMCA.

98. Diane Winston, *Red-Hot and Righteous: The Urban Religion of the Salvation Army* (Cambridge, MA: Harvard University Press, 1999), 153.

99. Marian Baldwin, *Canteening Overseas, 1917–1919* (New York: Macmillan, 1920), 38.

100. H. A. Herrick, "Special Report to Mr. C. V. Hibbard, Overseas Department Y.M.C.A., New York City," May 1, 1920, 9, Histories: American Forces in Germany Folder 1, ASWWI, YMCA.

101. Addie W. Hunton and Kathryn M. Johnson, *Two Colored Women with the American Expeditionary Forces* (New York: Brooklyn Eagle Press, 1920), 137.

102. Katharine Duncan Morse, *The Uncensored Letters of a Canteen Girl* (New York: Henry Holt and Company, 1920), 149.

103. Taft et al., *Service with Fighting Men*, 2:60–61.

104. Evangeline Booth, "Mothering the Boy at the Front," *Forum* (September 1918): 309. Diane Winston argues that the Salvation Army doughnut evoked memories of home and held religious significance. Made of bread and assuming a circular form, she suggests that the doughnut functioned as a symbol of shared religious community and ritual. Winston, *Red-Hot and Righteous*, 219.

105. Hunton and Johnson, *Two Colored Women with the American Expeditionary Forces,* 143.

106. See National War Work Council News Bulletin No. 226, May 13, 1918, and Bulletin No. 237, May 12, 1918, both in Press Releases National War Work Council, ASWWI, YMCA.

107. Evangeline Cory Booth, "Pies and Doughnuts in the Trenches: The Touch of Home the Salvation Army Gives Our Boys 'Over There,'" *Ladies' Home Journal* (September 1918): 21. See also McKinley, *Marching to Glory,* 122.

108. "The Motherly Salvationists," *Literary Digest,* May 11, 1918, 32.

109. "Report of the Women of the Paris Region," February 1, 1919, 33, Women's Work in the Paris Region Helen King, ASWWI, YMCA.

110. *Summary of World War Work of the American YMCA,* 40. See also National War Work Council News Bulletin No. 507, September 3, 1918, 2, and National War Work Council News Bulletin No. 639, September 29, 1918, 2, both in Press Releases National War Work Council, ASWWI, YMCA.

111. *With the First Division in France: Letters Written by a Y.M.C.A. Canteen Worker while on Active Service in France* (n.p., 1919), 40.

112. Mary L. Ryan, World War I Memories, July 1974, 2, RG 20.2 Mary Bishop 1893–1991 Personal Papers and Manuscripts, SA.

113. Elsie (Merrifield) Corliss, World War I Memories talk, Spring 1941, 5, RG 20.43 Elsie Merrifield Corliss Personal Papers and Manuscripts, SA.

114. Munson, *The Management of Men,* 198.

115. Franklin Spencer Edmonds, "The Army Leave Areas," n.d., 7, Leave Area Materials, ASWWI, YMCA.

116. *With the First Division in France,* 11, 8–11.

117. Hunton and Johnson, *Two Colored Women with the American Expeditionary Forces,* foreword, 142. Historian Nikki Brown argues that African American canteen women similarly saw themselves as surrogate relatives and believed they served as "the living embodiment of women who kept the home-fires burning." Nikki Brown, *Private Politics and Public Voices: Black Women's Activism from World War I to the New Deal* (Bloomington: Indiana University Press, 2006), 100.

118. Bray Diary, 31–32.

119. Bray Diary, 32–33.

120. Bray Diary, 45.

121. Gilchrist, "AEF-YMCA Women's Work in the World War," 79.

122. Edna Perrin, January 23 letter to Family, in Edna Perrin, "Edna Perrin Letters to Her Family: Supplemented by Selections from her Diary Her Year of Service with the YMCA, 1918–1919" (self-printed, 1994).

123. Edna Perrin, March 7 letter to Family, in Perrin, "Edna Perrin Letters to Her Family."

124. Edna Perrin, January 1919 letter to Hazel and February 18 letter to Folks, in Perrin, "Edna Perrin Letters to Her Family."

125. Gilchrist, "AEF-YMCA Women's Work in the World War," 80.

126. Gilchrist, "AEF-YMCA Women's Work in the World War," 80.

127. Gilchrist, "AEF-YMCA Women's Work in the World War," 77–78.

128. Gilchrist, "AEF-YMCA Women's Work in the World War," 82.

129. Gilchrist, "AEF-YMCA Women's Work in the World War," 82–83.

130. On the US military's use of women as motivation for doughboys, see Andrew J. Huebner, *Love and Death in the Great War* (New York: Oxford University Press, 2018); Kuhlman, "American Doughboys and German *Fräuleins,* esp. 1085.

131. Raymond B. Fosdick, "Reports on Conditions of Morale in the A.E.F. Submitted to Secretary Baker and General Pershing," 1919, 34, Report on Morale, ASWWI, YMCA.

132. *A Red Triangle Girl in France* (New York: George H. Doran, 1918), 104.

133. Baldwin, *Canteening Overseas,* 42–43.

134. Baldwin, *Canteening Overseas,* 75, 88.

135. Helen Purviance, "A Doughgirl on the Firing Line," *Forum,* n.d., 648, Purviance Papers.

136. Prest, *One of 9000,* 6.

137. *A Red Triangle Girl in France,* 145.

138. Purviance, "A Doughgirl on the Firing Line," 651. On women's memorializing war dead during and after the Civil War, see Caroline E. Janney, *Burying the Dead but Not the Past: Ladies' Memorial Associations and the Lost Cause* (Chapel Hill: University of North Carolina Press, 2008).

139. Baldwin, *Canteening Overseas,* 87. Eleanor Roosevelt noted in her account of her work establishing the Aix-les-Bains Leave Area that more than 4,000 men could enjoy the facilities. See "War Work of Roosevelt's Daughter-in-Law," *New York Times,* January 12, 1919.

140. Baldwin, *Canteening Overseas,* 87–88, 91–92.

141. On the prescriptions that guided middle-class women's social engagements, see Beth Bailey, *From Front Porch to Back Seat* (Baltimore: Johns Hopkins University Press, 1989). For a consideration of women's flaunting of those prescriptions, see Chad Heap, *Slumming: Sexual and Racial Encounters in American Nightlife, 1885–1940* (Chicago: University of Chicago Press, 2009).

142. Zeiger, *In Uncle Sam's Service,* 31–34; Jennifer D. Keene, *Doughboys, the Great War, and the Remaking of America* (Baltimore, MD: Johns Hopkins University Press), 18, 20; Jennifer D. Keene, *World War I* (Westport, CT: Greenwood Press, 2006), 37; Nancy Gentile Ford, *Americans All! Foreign-Born Soldiers in World War I* (College Station: Texas A&M University Press, 2001), 3; Durham, *Liberty Theatres of the United States Army,* 41.

143. Bray Diary, 38, 51.

144. *A Red Triangle Girl in France,* 154, 156–157.

145. Julia Coolidge Deane to mother, May 12, 1919 and to Popsie, May 26, 1919, Deane Papers.

146. Katherine Shortall, *A "Y" Girl in France: Letters of Katherine Shortall* (Boston: Richard G. Badger, 1919), 78–79.

147. Hunton and Johnson, *Two Colored Women with the American Expeditionary Forces,* 25, 33–34, 162. Twelve additional African American women served in France after the armistice. See Zeiger, *In Uncle Sam's Service,* 28. On the YMCA's segregated policies during the war, see Brown, *Private Politics and Public Voices,* chap. 4; Adriane Lentz-Smith, *Freedom Struggles: African Americans and World War I* (Cambridge, MA: Harvard University Press, 2009); Nina Mjagkij, *Light in the Darkness: African Americans and the YMCA, 1852–1946* (Lexington: University Press of Kentucky, 1994).

148. Hunton and Johnson, *Two Colored Women with the American Expeditionary Forces,* 38.

149. Julia Coolidge Deane to her sister, April 10, 1919, Deane Papers.

150. Julia Coolidge Deane to mother, May 12, 1919, Deane Papers.

151. Julia Coolidge Deane to mother, August 2, 1919, Deane Papers.

152. Bertha Laurie letter, November 25, 1917, Miscellaneous Reports—Women Secretaries, ASWWI, YMCA.

153. Elsie Cleveland Mead, "A Woman's War," 105, A Woman's War, ASWWI, YMCA.

154. Marian B. C. Watts letter, December 27, 1917, Miscellaneous Reports—Women Secretaries, ASWWI, YMCA.

155. "Young America: Letters of Mary Lee," *Atlantic Monthly* 124 (October 1919): 520. Lee also wrote a novel about her experiences, *It's a Great War!* Steven Trout discusses the controversy the book sparked when it won a literary prize sponsored by the American Legion and Houghton Mifflin publishing company. See *On the Battlefield of Memory: The First World War and American Remembrance, 1919–1941* (Tuscaloosa: University of Alabama Press, 2010), 100–105.

156. Shortall, *A "Y" Girl in France,* 30.

157. Diane Winston argues that the Salvation Army uniform identified Army officers as religious figures, bridged class differences, and, for women in particular, allowed them to work in disreputable locations by shielding their reputations as religious servants. See Winston, *Red-Hot and Righteous,* 85–94.

158. Sprenger and Edmonds, *The Leave Areas of the American Expeditionary Forces,* 107.

159. J. Campbell Brandon, interview by Mr. Morse, Mr. Handy, Dr. Miller, Meeting of the War Historical Bureau of the Young Men's Christian Association, December 18, 1919, 73, War Historical Bureau, interview with J. Campbell Brandon, ASWWI, YMCA.

160. Mead, "A Woman's War," 145.

161. Edna Perrin letter to Family, November 1919, in Perrin, "Edna Perrin Letters to Her Family."

162. Edna Perrin, January 23 letter to Family, in Perrin, "Edna Perrin Letters to Her Family."

163. *With the First Division in France,* 57.

164. Baldwin, *Canteening Overseas,* 42.

165. Morse, *The Uncensored Letters of a Canteen Girl,* 7, 262.

166. "Report of the Investigation of the Y.M.C.A.," 2:268.

167. "Report of the Investigation of the Y.M.C.A.," 2:270.

168. Brandon interview, 76.
169. "Report of the Investigation of the Y.M.C.A.," 2:268.
170. Mrs. Mead, Women's Bureau to Women Workers of the Y.M.C.A., January 13, 1919, Miscellaneous Reports—Women Secretaries, and E. C. Carter, Bulletin No. 40, February 18, 1918, AEF Chief Secretary's File-Official Bulletins, both in ASWWI, YMCA. See also Gilchrist, "AEF-YMCA Women's Work in the World War," 45–46. When, "in a few isolated cases," women were caught smoking in public, the YMCA investigated and enforced "disciplinary measures." H. F. Sheets to C. V. Hibbard, August 1, 1918, AEF-YMCA Chief Secretary's Files Volume G, ASWWI, YMCA.
171. Carter, Bulletin No. 40.
172. "General Federation of Women's Clubs Unit Confidential Report," October 14, 1919, 11, also 3, 15, Miscellaneous Reports—Women Secretaries, ASWWI, YMCA.
173. Mead to Women Workers of the Y.M.C.A., January 13, 1919. See also Gilchrist, "AEF-YMCA Women's Work in the World War," 45–46.
174. Mead to Women Workers of the Y.M.C.A., January 13, 1919. See also Gilchrist, "AEF-YMCA Women's Work in the World War," 45–46.
175. Julia Coolidge Deane to mother, May 12, 1919, Deane Papers.
176. Raszewska, "Hut Equipment," 7.
177. Edmonds, "The Army Leave Areas"; Sprenger and Edmonds, *The Leave Areas of the American Expeditionary Forces;* Taft, *Service with Fighting Men,* 2:142.
178. *Summary of World War Work of the American YMCA,* 28, 170.
179. "Report by William Sloane and Harold I. Pratt to the Executive Committee, War Work Council," August 22, 1918, 8, 7, Chief Secretary's File Volume D, ASWWI, YMCA. See also Franklin S. Edmonds, interview by Mr. Morse, Mr. Handy, Dr. Miller, Mr. Spencer, January 31, 1920, World War I Relations: American Red Cross Correspondence and Reports, ASWWI, YMCA.
180. *Summary of World War Work of the American YMCA,* 170–171. Also Taft, *Service with Fighting Men,* 2:62.
181. Taft, *Service with Fighting Men,* 1:131.
182. Taft, *Service with Fighting Men,* 2:161.
183. Gilchrist, "AEF-YMCA Women's Work in the World War," 94.
184. Gilchrist, "AEF-YMCA Women's Work in the World War," 44.
185. Baldwin, *Canteening Overseas,* 61, 61–62.
186. Katherine Mayo, *"That Damn Y": A Record of Overseas Service* (Boston: Houghton Mifflin, 1920), 190.
187. Mayo, *"That Damn Y,"* 191.
188. Mayo, *"That Damn Y,"* 191.
189. Mayo, *"That Damn Y,"* 192.
190. Taft, *Service with Fighting Men,* 2:155–156.
191. Edmonds interview, 71; "War Work of Roosevelt's Daughter-in-Law," *New York Times,* January 12, 1919; Taft, *Service with Fighting Men,* 2:155–156.
192. Baldwin, *Canteening Overseas,* 90–91.

193. Margaret Mayo, *Trouping for the Troops: Fun-Making at the Front* (New York: George H. Doran Company, 1919), 142–143.

194. Ada Alice Tuttle, *A "Y" Girl Overseas: Extracts from Letters Written to Her Parents from Europe* (Portland, OR, 1919), 89.

195. Tuttle, *A "Y" Girl Overseas*, 94.

196. Julia Coolidge Deane to mother, May 5, 1919, Deane Papers.

197. Tuttle, *A "Y" Girl Overseas*, 89–90.

198. Shortall, *A "Y" Girl in France*, 43–47.

199. Quotes in Mayo, *"That Damn Y,"* 302 and Taft, *Service with Fighting Men*, 2:63. Also Gilchrist, "AEF-YMCA Women's Work in the World War," 92.

200. Edna Perrin February 11 letter to Mother, in Perrin, "Edna Perrin Letters to Her Family."

201. James W. Evans and Gardner L. Harding, *Entertaining the American Army: The American Stage and Lyceum in the World War* (New York: Association Press, 1921), 134.

202. Zeiger, *In Uncle Sam's Service*, 93–93.

203. National War Work Council News Bulletin No. 233, May 13, 1918, 2, Press Releases National War Work Council, ASWWI, YMCA. See also "Miss Martin Saw Two Paris Air Raids," *New York Times*, March 17, 1918.

204. National War Work Council News Bulletin No. 130, March 17, 1918 and National War Work Council News Bulletin No. 233, May 13, 1918, both in Press Releases National War Work Council, ASWWI, YMCA.

205. National War Work Council News Bulletin No. 233, May 13, 1918, 2.

206. *Handbook of the American YMCA, AEF* (Paris. YMCA, 1918), 12, Handbook of American YMCA, ASWWI, YMCA.

207. Corliss, World War I Memories talk, 6.

208. *With the First Division in France*, 88.

209. *With the First Division in France*, 83.

210. Baldwin, *Canteening Overseas*, 44.

211. Baldwin, *Canteening Overseas*, 134.

212. Baldwin, *Canteening Overseas*, 142–159.

213. Baldwin, *Canteening Overseas*, 159–160.

214. *With the First Division in France*, 88.

215. Shortall, *A "Y" Girl in France*, 50.

216. Edna Perrin to Mother and Dale, June 9, in Perrin, "Edna Perrin Letters to Her Family."

217. Tuttle, *A "Y" Girl Overseas*, 68.

218. Morse, *The Uncensored Letters of a Canteen Girl*, 117–118.

219. Helga Ramsay, "War Service in France and Army Occupation in Germany," 8, RG 20.4 Ramsay, Helga 1891–1979 Personal Papers and Manuscripts, SA.

220. *With the First Division in France*, 33.

221. *With the First Division in France*, 37.

222. *With the First Division in France*, 33.

223. Julia Coolidge Deane to mother, June 28, 1919, Deane Papers.

224. Julia Coolidge Deane to mother, September 17, 1919, Deane Papers.
225. Julia Coolidge Deane to mother, September 17, 1919, Deane Papers.
226. Baldwin, *Canteening Overseas,* 120–121.
227. Frances J. Gulick to Family, April 6, 1918, Miscellaneous Reports—Women Secretaries, ASWWI, YMCA.
228. Morse, *The Uncensored Letters of a Canteen Girl,* 175.
229. Mead, "A Woman's War," 101.
230. Mead, "A Woman's War," 136D, 136B–136D.
231. Quoted in Mary Ross Hall and Helen Firman Sweet, *Women in the Y.M.C.A. Record* (New York: Association Press, 1947), 77.
232. Mead, "A Woman's War," 273D.
233. Mead, "A Woman's War," 103.
234. Morse, *The Uncensored Letters of a Canteen Girl,* 218.
235. *A Red Triangle Girl in France,* 137.
236. Quoted in Lentz-Smith, *Freedom Struggles,* 213, also 210–214.
237. "Address of the President of the United States," September 30, 1918, United States Senate, Woodrow Wilson Presidential Library eLibrary, http://wwl2.dataformat.com/Document.aspx?doc=30740, accessed June 18, 2013.
238. Brandon interview, 78.

### 2. TAKE YOUR PRETTIEST DRESSES AND GO

1. B. J. Olewiler, *A Woman in a Man's War: Reflections of a Red Cross Donut Girl of World War II* (Philadelphia: Xlibris, 2003).
2. Olewiler, *A Woman in a Man's War,* 15.
3. Olewiler, *A Woman in a Man's War,* 23.
4. Olewiler, *A Woman in a Man's War,* 64, 33.
5. Olewiler, *A Woman in a Man's War,* 62.
6. Olewiler, *A Woman in a Man's War,* 129.
7. The Red Cross cannot provide an exact number of women who worked in clubs and Clubmobiles overseas during the war. One Red Cross history notes that 6,683 individuals trained for overseas club work. I assume that most of these individuals were women. Men who worked in administrative positions in clubs or the Clubmobile program could be included in that number or could be accounted for separately; the information provided is not clear, though even if they are included in this number, the vast majority would still be women. I also assume that the vast majority of these individuals worked overseas. Some women could also have completed another kind of training, such as camp service training for domestic work, and then volunteered for overseas service. Red Cross data also notes that 7,961 women returned to the United States after working overseas. Although most of that number was club and Clubmobile women, it also includes women who worked in administrative and hospital positions. See American National Red Cross, *Red Cross Service Record: Accomplishments of Seven Years, July 1, 1939–June 30, 1946* (Washington, DC: American National Red Cross, 1946), 28, 30, 38.

A history of the Red Cross during the war provides a higher estimate. It notes that paid personnel reached 24,000 in 1945, about equally divided between domestic and overseas workers. It also notes that of those abroad (about 12,000), 75 percent were women working in clubs and Clubmobiles (9,000 women). A 1949 Red Cross statement confirms this number. See Foster Rhea Dulles, *The American Red Cross: A History* (New York: Harper and Brothers, 1950), 374; Summary of Statement, The American National Red Cross at the Meeting of the Joint Army–Navy–Air Force Committee on Welfare and Recreation, July 7, 1949, 10, 610.02 Joint Army–Navy–Air Force Committee on Welfare / Recreation, Red Cross 1935–1946, NARA.

For general descriptions of Red Cross recreation work, see "Meeting with Mr. Harvey Gibson, Commissioner from Great Britain," June 11, 1943, 900.11 ETO, Club and Clubmobile Departments, Red Cross 1935–1946, NARA; Robert Bremner, Minna Adams Hutcheson, and Lucille Stein Greenberg, *The History of the American National Red Cross*, vol. 13: *American Red Cross Services in the War against the European Axis, Pearl Harbor to 1947* (Washington, DC: The American National Red Cross, 1950), 51–64; General Board, United States Forces, European Theater, "American Red Cross Activities in the European Theater," Study No. 5 [1945–1946], MHI; Dulles, *The American Red Cross*, 368–370.

8. This number reflects the period from the first overseas tour in October 1941 through the end of 1945. "USO Camp Shows, Inc. (Stage, Radio, and Screen) Report on Year of 1945," January 1, 1945 December 31, 1945, 7, United Service Organizations, Camp Shows Reports, 1945, Weil Papers. By the end of 1947, the USO had sent 7,336 entertainers abroad. Of them, 7,031 received salaries. See "Operation USO: Report of the President," January 9, 1948, 33, USO–Printed Material–Press Releases, Series P Welfare-General, OMR, Rockefeller Archive.

9. Several women use this phrase to describe the constant attention they received from men while serving in the war. See Rosalie Campbell Jordan, "Let It Not Be Forgot," 135–136, Rosalie Campbell Jordan, box 10, folder 7, Clubmobile Collection; Hazel Bowman to parents, November 27, 1944, Bowman Collection; Ann D. Hill, "Recreation Report–October 1944," 900.6161 Brazil Office, Enlisted Men's Recreation Club–Val de Cans Field Belem, Brazil APO 603, Red Cross 1935–1946, NARA.

10. Although their names changed several times during the war, the Army's Special Services Division managed welfare work and the PX, while the Welfare and Recreation Section of the Training Division of the Bureau of Naval Personnel operated leisure activities on ships and naval stations. "Welfare and Recreation of Soldiers and Sailors," March 29, 1941, Chaplains folder, General Subject Files, JANCWR, JANBC, NARA; "Chronology of Special Service in World War II," April 1944, Special Services Division 1944, General Subject Files, JANCWR, JANBC, NARA; President's Committee on Religion and Welfare in the Armed Forces, "Free Time in the Armed Forces: A Study of the Armed Forces' Special Services and Recreation Programs" (Washington, DC: n.p., February 28, 1951), 73–74; Fowler Harper comments, Morale Officers' Conference, January 19–23, 1942, Morale Branch Conference, General

Subject Files, JANCWR, JANBC, NARA; Technical Manual No. 21-205, Special Service Officer (Washington, DC: War Department, May 12, 1942), 6–12; James J. Cooke, *American Girls, Beer, and Glenn Miller: GI Morale in World War II*, American Military Experience (Columbia: University of Missouri Press, 2012).

11. John D. Rockefeller Jr. to Chancellor Carmichael, April 10, 1942, John D. Rockefeller Jr. Correspondence (hereafter JDR Jr. Correspondence), Series P Welfare-General, OMR, Rockefeller Archive; Frank Coffey, *Always Home: 50 Years of the USO* (Washington, DC: Brassey's, 1991), 3; Richard C. Lancaster, *Serving the U.S. Armed Forces, 1861–1986: The Story of the YMCA's Ministry to Military Personnel for 125 Years* (Schamburg, IL: Armed Services YMCA of the USA, 1987), 126–130. An October 1941 summary of USO policy notes that General Frederick Osborne, head of Army Special Services, convinced Roosevelt to insist that civilian—not government—agencies would direct welfare work outside of military establishments. "USO Policy and Its Relation to the Citizens Committee and Local USO Committees," October 6, 1941, JDR Jr. Correspondence, Series P Welfare-General, OMR, Rockefeller Archive.

12. Lancaster, *Serving the U.S. Armed Forces*, 124–148; Coffey, *Always Home*, 3; Julia M. H. Carson, "The History of USO, Part I," 26–27, Lindsley F. Kimball papers, 1939–(1974–1979), Rockefeller Archive; Meghan K. Winchell, *Good Girls, Good Food, Good Fun: The Story of USO Hostesses during World War II* (Chapel Hill: University of North Carolina Press, 2008), 2. Although there was great internal debate about the degree to which cooperation or competition between the constituent agencies guided the USO's efforts on the home front, combining the six organizations' efforts aimed to avoid the competition and overlapping work that characterized recreation work during World War I. See JDR Jr. to Chancellor Carmichael, April 10, 1942, and Raymond B. Fosdick, Memorandum on the USO, April 23, 1942, both in JDR Jr. Correspondence, Series P Welfare-General, OMR, Rockefeller Archive.

13. Frederick H. Osborn interview transcript, chap. 5, 5–6, Frederick H. Osborn Papers, MHI.

14. Richard F. Allen to Mr. Bondy, Mr. Don Smith, Mr. Wesselius, March 3, 1944, 900.616 All Theaters, Recreation 1944–1945, Red Cross 1935–1946, NARA.

15. Richard F. Allen to Mark Tomas, June 3, 1943, decimal .080 1943–1945 ARC Policy, General Correspondence, Special Services Section, CBI, NARA; also see Allen to Bondy, Smith, Wesselius. The Army's Special Services assigned few women to overseas posts during World War II and did not begin staffing clubs exclusively with women until after the war. It assigned some women to the Caribbean and Hawaiian theaters in 1941. Thirteen Army hostesses worked in AEF clubs in Paris and Brussels beginning in December 1944. Eighty-eight women were on duty in October 1945. *An Introduction to the Army Service Club Program*, Department of the Army Pamphlet No. 21-59 (Washington, DC: Department of the Army, 1953), 12–13; General Board, United States Forces, European Theater, "Special Services Clubs," Study No. 121 [1945 or 1946], 5, MHI.

16. George Marshall to United Service Organizations, Chester I. Barnard, May 31, 1942, USO: Agreement with War Department 1942, Armed Services United Service Organizations—Related Records, YMCA.

17. Army Chief of Staff George C. Marshall explained to USO President Harper Silbey that the Red Cross had been selected to provide recreational services in theaters of operation because of its previous experiences in similar work and its international character. See George C. Marshall to Harper Silbey, March 6, 1942, USO-Overseas, Series P Welfare-General, OMR, Rockefeller Archive. Also Bremner, Hutcheson, and Greenberg, *The History of the American National Red Cross,* 13:3–13.

    The USO did open clubs in a few overseas locations: Bermuda, Newfoundland, Hawaii, Panama, the Caribbean, and Alaska. Several agreements dictated the terms of which agency, the Red Cross or the USO, operated in specific overseas theaters. See George Marshall to Harper Sibley, December 19, 1941, USO: Agreement with Red Cross, Armed Services United Service Organizations—Related Records, YMCA; "Service to the Armed Forces Joint Statement of the American Red Cross and the United Service Organizations, Inc.," March 2, 1943, USO: Agreement with Red Cross, Armed Services United Service Organizations—Related Records, YMCA; War Department Memorandum No. W850-9-43, "Welfare and Recreational Activities of the Red Cross and USO and United States Army Forces Overseas," March 15, 1943, American Red Cross General 1943, General Subject Files, JANCWR, JANBC, NARA; Associates of the Historical Division, *The History of the American National Red Cross,* vol. 6: *National Headquarters in World War II* (Washington, DC: The American National Red Cross, 1950), vii79–vii89, vii95–vii96, in 494.2 General—History of the ANRC (Monographs), Red Cross 1935—1946, NARA.

18. "Camp Shows, Inc. a/k/a USO-Camp Shows, Inc. Records, 1941–1957," 1:xii–xiii, Records of Camp Shows, Inc., 1941–1957, Special Services Division, AGO, NARA.

19. Quotes in Report of Activities, November 1–30, 1942, 1, 2, 900.118 CBI, Camp Service Monthly Narrative Reports 1942, Red Cross 1935–1946, NARA; also Mark A. Tomas, Operations Report, China-Burma-India Command, May 16, 1942 through December 31, 1943, 1–3, 19, 900.08 CBI, Special Operations Report May 16, 1942–December 31, 1943, Red Cross 1935–1946, NARA.

20. "Statement on Program" (Exhibit B), Agreement with Agencies, 1941–1942, Series P Welfare-General, OMR, Rockefeller Archive.

21. Carson, "The History of USO, Part I," 69, 67–68.

22. *To New York City Parents and Neighbors* (pamphlet), 4–5, JDR Jr. Address, July 8, 1941, Series P Welfare-General, OMR, Rockefeller Archive.

23. Lindsley F. Kimball interview by Joseph W. Ernst and J. William Hess, March 10 through April 9, 1980, transcript, 90–91, RG 13 Oral Histories, Rockefeller Foundation Archives, Rockefeller Archive. Four men served as USO presidents during the war: Walter Hoving (February–July 1941), Harper Silbey (July 1941–March 1942), Chester Barnard (March 1942–April 1945), Lindsley Kimball (April 1945–June 1952).

24. Coffey, *Always Home,* 4; Kimball, interview by Ernst and Hess, 90–91. Also "American Red Cross China-Burma-India Command Instructions Governing the Operation of On Post and Camp Clubs on Military Reservations," 900.494 All Theaters (CBI), Club Manual, Red Cross 1935–1946, NARA. The Red Cross supervisor of recreation, Grey Lusty, also noted that because the clubs were to exude an American atmosphere, American personnel needed to be directly involved in work with soldiers. The Red Cross hired thousands of local workers to assist in club operations, but Lusty insisted that American personnel had to do more than just organize programs. See Minutes, Club Directors Conference, Recreation Section, July 8, 1943, 900.04 FETO, Conference of Club Directors, Red Cross 1935–1946, NARA.

25. Eleanor (Bumpy) Stevenson with Pete Martin, "I Knew Your Soldier," *Saturday Evening Post,* October 28, 1944, 70.

26. Ann Elizabeth Pfau, *Miss Yourlovin: GIs, Gender, and Domesticity during World War II* (New York: Columbia University Press, 2008), chap. 1, www.gutenberg-e.org/pfau, accessed July 1, 2018.

27. "USO War Activities Conference," April 12, 1942, 3–4, USO War Activities Conference—April 1942, General Records of Recreation Services Section, BNP, NARA.

28. He also opposed the military's policy of nonfraternization with German women in the wake of the German invasion on the grounds that soldiers were "entitled to" what they had captured. Quoted in Fred Ayer Jr., *Before the Colours Fade: Portrait of a Soldier, George S. Patton, Jr.* (Boston: Houghton Mifflin Company, 1964), 208.

29. Joel T. Boone, "The Sexual Aspects of Military Personnel," *Journal of Social Hygiene* 27, no. 3 (March 1941): 114, 116–117, http://hearth.library.cornell.edu/cgi/t/text/text-idx?c=hearth;idno=4732756_873_003, accessed June 7, 2012. See also John Costello, *Virtue under Fire: How World War II Changed Our Social and Sexual Attitudes* (Boston: Little, Brown, and Company, 1985), 76–77, 91–92.

30. Mary Louise Roberts, *What Soldiers Do: Sex and the American GI in World War II France* (Chicago: University of Chicago Press, 2013), 174, 182; Marilyn E. Hegarty, *Victory Girls, Khaki-Wackies, and Patriotutes: The Regulation of Female Sexuality during World War II* (New York: New York University Press, 2008), 46–47, 85, 91–93, 98; Elizabeth Alice Clement, *Love for Sale: Courting, Treating, and Prostitution in New York City, 1900–1945* (Chapel Hill: University of North Carolina Press, 2006), 248; Beth Bailey and David Farber, *The First Strange Place: The Alchemy of Race and Sex in World War II Hawaii* (New York: Free Press, 1992), 99–100; Costello, *Virtue under Fire,* 52. When a soldier from the segregated Ninety-Fifth Regiment was arrested in 1943 for assaulting a nurse, a military policeman felt it prudent to note in his report of the incident that the soldier had "been in the bush for nine months and hadn't seen women in that time." Quoted in John Virtue, *The Black Soldiers Who Built the Alaska Highway: A History of Four U.S. Army Regiments in the North* (Jefferson, NC: McFarland and Company, 2013), 143.

31. Allan Bérubé, *Coming out under Fire: The History of Gay Men and Women in World War Two* (New York: Free Press, 1990), 45–51.

32. "Annex #1 to Sanitary Report, April 1943, 190th Station Hospital," May 5, 1943, 5, HD 730 Neuropsychiatry 1943 Morale and Psychiatry ASF Reports, World War II Administrative Records, ZI, OSG, NARA.

   As Mary Louise Roberts describes, Twenty-Ninth Infantry Division commander General Charles Gerhardt opened a brothel for his men in France because of similar concerns. The "men were 'preoccupied' with sex because they were 'removed from feminine contact'" and Gerhardt feared they would turn to each other for sex if forced to go without. Roberts, *What Soldiers Do*, 174, also chap. 6.

   The fear indicated in the report that the isolation of men would lead to homosexuality was not a universal one, however. The American Social Hygiene Association disavowed the notion that soldiers and sailors with no access to "normal sex relations" would "be driven into homosexual practices." See Dr. William F. Snow comments, Morale Officers' Conference, January 19–23, 1942, Morale Branch Conference, General Subject Files, JANCWR, JANBC, NARA.

33. Costello, *Virtue under Fire*, 149–153.

34. Charles S. Stevenson comments, [Morale Officers' Conference, January 19–23, 1942, Morale Branch Conference,] General Subject Files, JANCWR, JANBC, NARA.

35. Allan M. Brandt, *No Magic Bullet: A Social History of Venereal Disease in the United States since 1880* (New York: Oxford University Press, 1985), 161–163; Hegarty, *Victory Girls, Khaki-Wackies, and Patriotutes*, esp. chaps. 1 and 2; Elizabeth Alice Clement, *Love for Sale*, 240–258.

36. Boone, "The Sexual Aspects of Military Personnel," 114, 116 117; Stevenson comments; Brandt, *No Magic Bullet*, 164.

37. Clement, *Love for Sale*, 249–258; Christina S. Jarvis, *The Male Body at War: American Masculinity during World War II* (DeKalb: Northern Illinois University Press, 2010), 72–85.

38. Quoted in Brandt, *No Magic Bullet*, 164.

39. Brandt, *No Magic Bullet*, 161–169; John Boyd Coates Jr., ed., *Preventive Medicine in World War II*, vol. 5, *Communicable Diseases Transmitted through Contact or by Unknown Means* (Washington, DC: Office of the Surgeon General, Department of the Army, 1960), 143–146, http://babel.hathitrust.org/cgi/pt?id=mdp. 39015037507178#view =1up;seq=1, accessed July 24, 2013; Jerome H. Greenberg, "Venereal Disease in the Armed Forces," *Medical Aspects of Human Sexuality* (March 1972): 185.

40. Bailey and Farber, *The First Strange Place*, chap. 3; Coates, *Preventive Medicine in World War II*, 5:204–216, 271–278; Roberts, *What Soldiers Do*, chap. 6.

41. Kimball, interview by Ernst and Hess, 68.

42. Technical Manual No. 21-205, 75.

43. Joseph Earle Moore comments, [Morale Officers' Conference, January 19–23, 1942, Morale Branch Conference,] General Subject Files, JANCWR, JANBC, NARA. Marilyn Hegarty's discussion of Moore's comments implies that he advocated using these women as sexual companions for soldiers, but his recommendation was more nuanced. Moore warned that supervision of young men and women's social

activities was essential to productive recreation, and he implied that women would draw on their good sense to guide their behaviors. Hegarty, *Victory Girls*, 87–88.

44. Albert Meyers to Thomas M. Dinsmore, November 19, 1942, 900.616 Brazil Office, Recreation Activities, Red Cross 1935–1946, NARA.

45. Warren Stearns to Shannon Little, December 30, 1943, 900.616 Brazil Office, Recreation Activities, Red Cross 1935–1946, NARA. Military officers in the CBI similarly attributed a lowered VD rate to the presence of women in Red Cross clubs. See Arthur Mayer, "Report to the Chairman of the Red Cross in China-Burma-India," 13, 900.06 All Theaters, Visits and Inspection Trips, Red Cross 1935–1946, NARA.

46. "Report of Red Cross Activities at Adjacento Field, Fortaleza, Brasil," [May 1944], 900.6161 Brazil Office, Enlisted Men's Club Adjacento Field Fortalega, Ceara, Brazil APO 619, Red Cross 1935–1946, NARA. Similarly, a *New York Times* reporter concluded in October 1942 that a lack of "places that provide a normal evening's relations" in Britain "is driving the men to the pubs and to the companions one finds there." Frank L. Kluckholn, "A.E.F. Found Short of Recreation Aids," *New York Times*, October 13, 1942.

47. Frank L. Kluckholn, "A.E.F. Found Short of Recreation Aids," *New York Times*, October 13, 1942. Concerns about the dangers of "over paid, over sexed, and over here" American GIs were common in England, Australia, and Ireland. See David Reynolds, *Rich Relations: The American Occupation of Britain, 1942–1945* (New York: Random House, 1995); Juliet Gardiner, *"Overpaid, Oversexed, and Over Here": The American GI in World War II Britain* (New York: Canopy Books, 1992); Sonya O. Rose, "Sex, Citizenship, and the Nation in World War II Britain," *American Historical Review* 103, no. 4 (October 1998): 1147–1176; Marilyn Lake, "The Desire for a Yank: Sexual Relations between Australian Women and American Servicemen during World War II," *Journal of the History of Sexuality* 2, no. 4 (April 1992): 621–633; Michael Sturma, "Loving the Alien: The Underside of Relations between American Servicemen and Australian Women in Queensland, 1942–1945," *Journal of Australian Studies* 13, no. 24 (1989): 3–17; John Hammond Moore, *Over-Sexed, Over-Paid, and Over Here: Americans in Australia, 1941–1945* (St. Lucia: University of Queensland Press, 1981); Leanne McCormick, "'One Yank and They're Off': Interaction between U.S. Troops and Northern Irish Women, 1942–1945," *Journal of the History of Sexuality* 15, no. 2 (May 2006): 228–257.

48. Margaret Chase, *Never Too Late* (San Francisco: Ausonia Press, 1983), 55. A Red Cross history agreed with the general's assessment: "There was little opportunity in North African cities for the G.I.'s to amuse themselves other than by going to native dives. The incidence of venereal disease tended to be unusually high, and nowhere was a perennial Army problem more acute. The clubs provided a place where restless or homesick G.I.'s could go for normal, healthy recreation in an atmosphere that the Red Cross workers tried to make as homelike as possible. Wherever clubs were established, the rate of venereal disease declined." See Dulles, *The American Red Cross*, 437.

49. As Sherrie Tucker writes, such innocuous images of GIs and American girls helped create an "image of doughnut-chomping, mail-craving, homesick 'boys' that inspired a public, once fearful of military stranger, to become such enthusiasts of boys in uniform that they would pick them up hitchhiking and take them home to their families." See Sherrie Tucker, *Swing Shift: "All-Girl" Bands of the 1940s* (Durham, NC: Duke University Press, 2000), 268–269.

50. Melissa A. McEuen, *Making War, Making Femininity: Femininity and Duty on the American Home Front, 1941–1945* (Athens: University of Georgia Press, 2011). On pinups, see Robert Westbrook, "'I want a girl, just like the girl that married Harry James': American Women and the Problem of Political Obligation in World War II," *American Quarterly* 42, no. 4 (December 1990): 587–614; Maria Elena Buszek, *Pin-Up Grrrls: Feminism, Sexuality, Popular Culture* (Durham, NC: Duke University Press Books, 2006), esp. 209–210; Joanne Meyerowitz, "Women, Cheesecake, and Borderline Material: Responses to Girlie Pictures in the Mid-Twentieth-Century U.S.," *Journal of Women's History* 8, no. 3 (Fall 1996): esp. 15–18. On nose art, see Pfau, *Miss Yourlovin,* esp. chap. 4. On map reading, see McEuen, *Making War, Making Femininity,* 134.

51. Clement, *Love for Sale,* 242–243; Hegarty, *Victory Girls.* See also Brandt, *No Magic Bullet,* 167–168.

52. Vernon Pope, "GI Joe's Best Girl," *Los Angeles Times,* August 20, 1944.

53. Schuyler Dean Hoslett, "Personnel Administration in the American Red Cross during World War II" (PhD diss., Ohio State University, 1949), 75–87, 266–268.

54. Applicants to overseas Assistant Club Director positions continued to travel to Washington, DC, for final approval. "Red Cross Teaches Help for Military," *New York Times,* November 5, 1943; Hoslett, "Personnel Administration," 73, 89a–104.

55. The Red Cross hired women for many kinds of work in addition to work in recreation. It hired women with backgrounds in social work, for example, as personal service directors to provide counseling and loan services to military personnel. Women also worked as field directors and assistant field directors in military stations for the various women's military auxiliaries. And, they worked in several positions within the Red Cross's programs for military hospitals. Some women assigned to hospitals worked in recreation programs designed not only to entertain but also to rehabilitate injured men. Here, I focus on women whose primary task was to entertain what the Red Cross termed "able-bodied" men, those for whom large-scale recreation and entertainment programs were primarily designed.

56. "American Red Cross Employment Opportunities (Abridged)," March 1943, Virginia Storts Hall, box 2, folder 10, Clubmobile Collection.

57. Richard F. Allen to Helen Deming, Helene Deming, box 2, folder 3, Clubmobile Collection.

58. Bremner, Hutcheson, and Greenberg, *The History of the American National Red Cross,* 13:465.

59. ARC 831: General Guide for Selecting Assistant Club Directors, 494.1 ARC 831 General Guide for Selecting Assistant Club Directors; ARC 830a: General Guide for

Selecting Assistant Program Directors, 494.1 ARC 830a General Guide for Selecting Assistant Program Directors; ARC 828: General Guide for Selecting Staff Assistants, 494.1 ARC 828 General Guide for Selecting Staff Assistants for Overseas Club and Recreation Centers (June 1943 and August 1945 revisions); all in Red Cross 1935–1946, NARA. Staff assistants earned $150 per month initially. The Red Cross held a life insurance policy worth $2,000 on each woman and promised disability payment of $25 per week for one hundred weeks if she was disabled during her service. Allen to Deming.

60. Hoslett, "Personnel Administration," 252–253.

61. Chicago Speech by Mr. Lawrence Phillips, February 5, 1945, 10, USO Camp Shows—Speech by Lawrence Phillips—2/5/15, Series II—Reports and Office Files, Camp Shows.

62. Lynn O'Neal Heberling, "Soldiers in Greasepaint: USO-Camp Shows, Inc. during World War II" (PhD diss., Kent State University, 1989), 81–82.

63. Sam Weisbord Memorandum to Abe Lastfogel, December 30, 1942, in "Camp Shows, Inc. a/k/a USO-Camp Shows, Inc. Records, 1941–1957," vol. 3, 1219, Records of Camp Shows, Inc., 1941–1957, Special Services Division, AGO, NARA; Untitled Camp Shows history, May 1, 1942, United Service Organizations, April–May 1942, Weil Papers.

64. ARC 828: General Guide for Selecting Staff Assistants (August 1942, June 1943, and August 1945 revisions), 494.1 ARC 828 General Guide for Selecting Staff Assistants for Overseas Club and Recreation Centers, Red Cross 1935–1946, NARA. A woman who had several years of experience working in community recreation programs, for example, might be considered even if she did not hold a bachelor's degree in a recreation-related program. See J. Lloyd Baird to J. H. Whiting, February 25, 1944, 494.1 ARC 828 General Guide for Selecting Staff Assistants for Overseas Club and Recreation Centers, Red Cross 1935–1946, NARA.

65. Hoslett, "Personnel Administration," 93.

66. Ralph A. Brandt to Robert C. Lewis, "Monthly Report for May 1944," 900.118 CBI, Club and Recreation Service Monthly Narrative Summary, Red Cross 1935–1946, NARA.

67. Baird to Whiting.

68. "American Red Cross National Employment Service Recruiting Manual for Positions in S.A.F. Foreign and Domestic," June 1, 1943, 3, 494.2 Recruiting Manual (SAF), Red Cross 1935–1946, NARA.

69. "Girls in Gray-Blue," *Newsweek*, September 28, 1942, 33.

70. "Installations on Base B, New Guinea (APO 503)," 900.118 FETO, Club and Recreation Service Reports—July 1944," Red Cross 1935–1946, NARA.

71. Quoted in Hoslett, "Personnel Administration," 92.

72. Rita A. Feld to NAACP, June 23, 1944, American Red Cross, Walter White, 1943–1944 Reel 0342, Group II, Series A, General Office File, Part 15: Segregation and Discrimination, Complaints and Responses, 1940–1955, Series B: Administrative Files, NAACP.

73. Oscar Whitelaw Rexford, *Battlestars & Doughnuts: World War II Clubmobile Experiences of Mary Metcalfe Rexford* (St. Louis, MO: The Patrice Press, 1989), 3.

74. James MacDonald, "With the Red Cross in Action Overseas," *New York Times,* February 21, 1943. Also "Girls with Red Cross in Britain Learn One Duty Is Always to Look Their Best," *New York Times,* October 5, 1942; Ernest O. Hauser, "Darling of the Tigers," *The Saturday Evening Post* (December 4, 1943), 51.

75. Anne Hagner, "What Do You Pack When You Don't Know Where You're Going?," *Washington Post,* October 6, 1942.

76. Anne Hagner, "77 D.C. Area Women Serving Red Cross in Posts Overseas," *Washington Post,* July 11, 1943.

77. Warren Stearns to Shannon Little, December 30, 1943, 900.616 Brazil Office, Recreation Activities, Red Cross 1935–1946, NARA.

78. ARC 830a: General Guide for Selecting Assistant Program Directors; ARC 831: General Guide for Selecting Assistant Club Directors.

79. Bremner, Hutcheson, and Greenberg, *The History of the American National Red Cross,* 13:324–325; "Clubmobile Personnel," [January 1945], 900.341 All Theaters, General Rules and Regulations, Red Cross 1935–1946, NARA.

80. ARC 828: General Guide for Selecting Staff Assistants (August 1942 and June 1943 revisions); Robert E. Bondy to Area Administrators, January 11, 1943, 300.1 Staff Assistants (overseas clubs); ARC 828: General Guide for Selecting Staff Assistants (August 1945 revision), all in Red Cross 1935–1946, NARA.

81. American Red Cross Club Program Division European Theater, "Program Handbook," 3, 900.494 All Theaters (ETO), Program Handbook, ARC Club Program Division, Red Cross 1935–1946, NARA.

82. Mayer, "Report to the Chairman of the Red Cross in China-Burma-India," 14.

83. Rebecca Jo Plant, *Mom: The Transformation of Motherhood in Modern America* (Chicago: University of Chicago Press, 2010); Celia Malone Kingsbury, *For Home and Country: World War I Propaganda on the Home Front* (Lincoln: University of Nebraska Press, 2010); Pfau, *Miss Yourlovin,* chap. 1.

84. "American Red Cross National Employment Service Recruiting Manual for Positions in S.A.F. Foreign and Domestic," 3. Also "Clubmobile Personnel."

85. "Clubmobile Personnel"; "Installations on Base B, New Guinea (APO 503)."

86. "Excerpt from Arthur Mayer's 'Report on American Red Cross Operations in MTOUSA,'" 900.3 All Theaters, Female Personnel, Red Cross 1935–1946.

87. Mayer, "Report to the Chairman of the Red Cross in China-Burma-India," 6.

88. Winchell, *Good Girls, Good Food, Good Fun.*

89. James T. Nicholson to Douglass Poteat, September 11, 1945, 900.3 All Theaters, Female Personnel, Red Cross 1935–1946, NARA.

90. Clayton Hamilton, "Keep 'em Laughing! A Commentary on the Contribution of USO-Camp Shows, Inc. to the Winning of the War," September 15, 1945, 12, USO Camp Shows Typescript Outline "Keep 'em Laughing," Series I—History of the USO, Camp Shows.

91. Kimball, interview by Ernst and Hess, 87.

92. Frank D. Dennis to William R. Arnold, December 11, 1943, Office Management Division Decimal File 1920–1945, 250.1 Morals and Conduct, vol. 1 (Entertainment), Chaplains, NARA.

93. Lawrence Phillips to Chief of Chaplains, October 19, 1943, Office Management Division Decimal File 1920–1945, 250.1 Morals and Conduct, vol. 1 (Entertainment), Chaplains, NARA.

94. Pamela Bloom, "Jim Crow Entertainment: The Segregated USO during World War II" (MA thesis, Hunter College of the City University of New York, 2003), 63, 65.

95. Lawrence Phillips to Editor, *The Pilot* (Boston), November 30, 1944, in Annual Report, 1944, 87–90, USO Camp Shows—Annual Report 1944, Series II—Reports and Office Files, Camp Shows. A postwar report on chaplains' work in the war suggested that chaplains found shows staged by soldiers more problematic than USO-Camp Shows. The trouble stemmed primarily from the masters of ceremonies ad-libbing instead of sticking to the approved script. See General Board, US Forces, European theater, "The Army Chaplain in the European Theater," Study No. 68, File 322.01 / 4, 36, usacac.Army.mil/cac2/cgsc/carl/eto/eto-068.pdf, accessed March 14, 2016.

96. Jean Holdridge Reeves, interview by Kim Adkins, February 14, 2007, transcript, Reeves Papers.

97. Janet McCubbin, interview by Sharon Brown, May 14, 2009, transcript, MacCubbin Papers.

98. Todd Parnell, *Mom at War: A Story of Courage and Love Born of Loss* (Springfield, MO: PFLP Publishing, 2005), 12–13.

99. Foster, *Letters Home*, 12.

100. Rosemary Norwalk, *Dearest Ones: A True World War II Love Story* (New York: John Wiley & Sons, 1999), 6–7.

101. Elizabeth Phenix Wiesner, *Between the Lines: Overseas with the Red Cross and OSS in World War II* (Chevy Chase, MD: Posterity Press, 1998), 3–4.

102. Lillian Jones Dowling, *One of the Boys but Always a Lady: The Life of a Red Cross Recreation Worker in Combat Troop Camps in Australia during the War with Japan* (New York: Vantage Press, 1998), 2–8.

103. Rexford, *Battlestars & Doughnuts*, 2.

104. James H. Madison, *Slinging Doughnuts for the Boys: An American Woman in World War II* (Bloomington: Indiana University Press, 2007).

105. Mary Haynsworth Mathews, interview by Eric Elliott, November 9, 1999, transcript, WV0119 Mary Haynsworth Mathews Collection, 1944–1945, WVHP.

106. Minutes of Mass Meeting Held at the Beverly-Wilshire Hotel, November 11, 1943, in "Camp Shows, Inc. a / k / a USO-Camp Shows, Inc. Records, 1941–1957," 3:1300–1301.

107. Ruth White, interview by Eric Elliott, June 2, 1999, transcript, WV0089 Ruth White Papers, WVHP.

108. Mayer, "Report to the Chairman of the Red Cross in China-Burma-India," 2. See also Violet A. Kochendoerfer, *One Woman's World War II* (Lexington: University Press of Kentucky, 1994), 1–35.

109. Jean M. Bright, interview by Hermann Trojanowski, April 2, 2004, transcript, WV0295 Jean M. Bright Collection, 1944–1946, 2004–2005, WVHP.

110. Libby Chitwood Appel, *Dancing with GIs: A Red Cross Club Worker in India, World War II* (Cornelius, NC: Warren Publishing, 2004), 6–7.

111. Jordan, "Let It Not Be Forgot," quote on 3, also 2, 5.

112. The length of the training course varied as the war progressed. Hoslett, "Personnel Administration"; Pope, "GI Joe's Best Girl."

113. Mary Thomas Sargent, *Runway towards Orion: The True Adventures of a Red Cross Girl on a B-29 Air Base in World War II India* (Grand Rapids, MI: Triumph Press, 1984), 23.

114. American Red Cross Club Program Division European Theater, "Program Handbook," quotes on 3, also 4.

115. Sargent, *Runway towards Orion*, 23.

116. Ralph A. Brandt to Robert C. Lewis, "Monthly Report for March 1945," April 17, 1945, 900.118 CBI, Club and Recreation Service Monthly Narrative Summary, Red Cross 1935–1946, NARA.

117. Norwalk, *Dearest Ones*, 116.

118. The famous USO-run Stage Door Canteen barred servicewomen because they "len(t) further military appearance" to the club. See Gretchen Knapp, "Experimental Social Policymaking during World War II: The United Service Organizations (USO) and American War-Community Services (AWCS)," *Journal of Policy History* 12, no. 3 (2000): 336n39; Maryann Lovelace, "Facing Change in Wartime Philadelphia: The Story of the Philadelphia USO," *The Pennsylvania Magazine of History and Biography* 123, no. 3 (July 1999): 143–175.

119. Helen Walmsley, "Conference with Major Anna Wilson (WAC) Pentagon Building, 10 / 26 / 43," 900.61 All Theaters, Service to Servicewomen, Red Cross 1935–1946, NARA.

120. Bremner, Hutcheson, and Greenberg, *The History of the American National Red Cross*, 13:460–462. Several letters between Red Cross officials outline conflicting policies, including: Edwin J. Beinecke to Richard F. Allen, June 12, 1943, and Harvey D. Gibson memorandum to All Departments, August 4, 1943, both in 900.61 All Theaters, Service to Servicewomen, Red Cross 1935–1946, NARA.

121. Club Department Headquarters to All Club Directors, Club Division Circular No. 149, n.d., 900.031 ETO, Club Division Circulars, Red Cross 1935–1946, NARA.

122. James T. Nicholson to Robert C. Lewis, January 5, 1945, 900.61 All Theaters, Service to Servicewomen, Red Cross 1935–1946, NARA.

123. Quotes in J. L. Frink to Commanding General, Intermediate Section, October 23, 1944, Red Cross 1935–1946, NARA. Also "CBI Clubs" in Monthly Report— September 1944, 900.08 CBI, Reports, Statistics, Surveys, and Studies—General 1942–1944, Red Cross 1935–1946, NARA; also William E. Stevenson to Robert E. Bondy, January 15, 1944, 900.61 All Theaters, Service to Servicewomen, Red Cross 1935–1946, NARA; Bremner, Hutcheson, and Greenberg, *The History of the American National Red Cross*, 13:285.

124. Marie Barry to Robert F. Eaton, January 22, 1945, 900.61 All Theaters, Service to Servicewomen, Red Cross 1935–1946, NARA.

125. Jordan, "Let It Not Be Forgot," quote on 4, also 5.

126. Appel, *Dancing with GIs*, 5.

127. Elma Ernst Fay, "Through a Donut Hole," foreword, Elma Ernst Fay, box 2, folder 6, Clubmobile Collection.

128. Bright, interview by Trojanowski.

129. Norwalk, *Dearest Ones*, 14.

130. Harvey D. Gibson to All American Personnel, C.O. 71, August 23, 1943, 900.341 All Theaters, Marriage Policy, Red Cross 1935–1946, NARA; Hoslett, "Personnel Administration," 243–245.

131. Outgoing cablegram to London, April 19, 1944, and Richard F. Allen to Middle East, Australia, Iceland, Pacific Ocean Area, India, June 13, 1944, both in 900.341 All Theaters, Marriage Policy, Red Cross 1935–1946, NARA; Aaron Weinstein to Lt. McDonald, "Marriage of Red Cross Personnel," December 8, 1944, decimal .080 1943–1945 ARC Policy, General Correspondence, Special Services Section, CBI, NARA.

132. Wesley J. Gritton to Theater Special Service Section, May 9, 1945, decimal .080 1943–1945 ARC Policy, General Correspondence, Special Services Section, CBI, NARA.

133. Statements of Policy Applicable to American Red Cross Personnel Overseas, 9, 344.01 Overseas Personnel 1942–45, Statements of Policy Applicable to, Red Cross 1935–1946, NARA; "Uniforms—Services to the Armed Forces."

134. "A Guide for Your Trip," Nancy Bastien Chase folder, Clubmobile Collection; Hoslett, "Personnel Administration," 235–236. Also see Raymond D. Jameson, *The History of the American National Red Cross*, vol. 14, *The American Red Cross during World War II in the Pacific Theater* (Washington, DC: The American National Red Cross, 1950), 208–209, in 494.2 General—History of the ANRC (Monographs), Red Cross 1935–1946, NARA.

135. That number reflects officials' best recollections before October 1945, and a record of actual cases since then. Warren Stearns to Harry A. Wann, April 8, 1946, 370.1 Confidential Services to Returnees, Red Cross 1935–1946, NARA. For other estimates, see Hill to Smith; Ruth S. Searle to Warren Stearns, March 27, 1946, 370.1 Confidential Services to Returnees, Red Cross 1935–1946, NARA.

136. Alma Geist Cap, interview by Tara Kraenzlin and Barbara Tomblin, May 6, 1997, Rutgers Oral History Archives of World War II, http://oralhistory.rutgers.edu/interviewees/853-cap-alma-geist, accessed June 18, 2014.

137. Verda F. Hickcox to Virginia Dunbar, October 2, 1945, 370.1 Confidential Services to Returnees, Red Cross 1935–1946, NARA.

138. Ruth Hill to Robert E. Bondy, January 19, 1945; Ruth Hill to Don C. Smith, March 4, 1946; William L. Gower to C. Bolles Rogers, September 28, 1945; Charlotte Johnson to Area Directors, February 27, 1946; all in 370.1 Confidential Services to Returnees; Presnell K. Betts to Frank Cleverley, November 8, 1946, 900.37 All Theaters, Health and Welfare; Margaret Colt to Dick [Richard F. Allen], May 21, 1944, 900.3 All Theaters, Female Personnel; all in Red Cross 1935–1946, NARA.

139. Hill to Smith.

140. Sargent, *Runway towards Orion*, 35.

141. Frances Langford, interview by William O. Oldson, May 19, 1998, transcript, quote on 21, also 20–21, Frances Langford Collection 99.0274, World War II Institute.

142. Marion Bradley to My dears, August 26, 1945, Marion Bradley, World War II Veterans Survey, MHI.

143. Genevieve Reynolds, "Ingenuity Seen as Prime Asset for Red Cross Women Overseas," *Washington Post*, March 25, 1944.

144. Ernest O. Hauser, "Darling of the Tigers," *The Saturday Evening Post*, December 4, 1943, 17.

145. Langford, interview by Oldson, 18.

146. Louise Buckley to the People, Thanksgiving Day 1944, in Annual Report, 1944, 20, USO Camp Shows—Annual Report 1944, Series II—Reports and Office Files, Camp Shows.

147. Madison, *Slinging Doughnuts for the Boys*, 194.

148. Sargent, *Runway towards Orion*, 108–109.

149. Hazel Bowman to parents, November 22, 1943, Bowman Collection.

150. Hazel Bowman to parents, January 17, 1944, Bowman Collection.

151. Hazel Bowman to parents, February 4, 1944, Bowman Collection.

152. Hazel Bowman to parents, January 17, 1944, Bowman Collection.

153. Hazel Bowman to parents, June 20, 1944, Bowman Collection.

154. Bowman to parents, November 27, 1944.

155. Hazel Bowman to parents, September 29, 1944; Hazel Bowman to family, July 31, 1945, Bowman Collection.

156. Jordan, "Let It Not Be Forgot," 135–136.

157. Marcia Ward Behr, *Coffee and Sympathy: World War II Letters from the Southwest Pacific, April 1943–January 1945* (Indianapolis: 1st Books, 2002), quote on 127, also 126.

158. Norwalk, *Dearest Ones*, 135.

159. Wiesner, *Between the Lines*, quote on 10, also 7–10.

160. Behr, *Coffee and Sympathy*, 69.

161. Appel, *Dancing with GIs*, 23–24.

162. Norwalk, *Dearest Ones*, 116–118.

163. Appel, *Dancing with GIs*, 23–24.

164. Jameson, *The History of the American National Red Cross*, 14:291–292.

165. Norwalk, *Dearest Ones*, 79–81.

166. White, interview by Elliott.

167. Behr, *Coffee and Sympathy*, 157, 11.

168. G. Ott Romney to All Club Directors and Assistant Club Directors, Club Division Circular No. 119, March 30, 1943, 900.031 ETO, Club Division Circulars; H. Crump to All Club Directors, Club Division Circular No. 187, July 14, 1943, 900.52 All Theaters, Establishment of VD Prophylactic Stations in Red Cross Clubs; Incoming Cablegram from London, received February 12, 1943, 900.52 All Theaters, Establishment of VD Prophylactic Stations in Red Cross Clubs, all in Red Cross 1935–1946,

NARA. Although the pro stations were ostensibly for the GIs' use, a sign in the women's restroom at the largest Red Cross club in England, London's Rainbow Corner, advised that prophylactics were available at the reception desk. Presumably, both Red Cross women and local British guests would have used the restroom and seen the sign. See Gardiner, *"Overpaid, Oversexed, and Over Here,"* 121.

169. Not all GIs and officers believed the women to be sexually loose, of course. Many men genuinely appreciated the women's visits and the chance to think about something other than war. See, for example, "Censorship Summary and Morale Report-B.C.O. #7," Period 1–15 August 1944, section III, 1–2, decimal 319.1, Troop Information and Education Division Decimal File, ETO, Records of the Chief of Staff G-4, Army Staff, NARA.

170. Red Cross hospital workers were specifically directed to follow dating regulations for military nurses, who as officers, could date only fellow officers. "Uniforms— Services to the Armed Forces." See also Statements of Policy Applicable to American Red Cross Personnel Overseas, 7–9.

A Red Cross official in New Guinea ordered that Red Cross girls not date enlisted men, despite some protests that the policy would be a public relations problem. See Assistant Director of Operations, APO 50e to All American Red Cross Personnel in New Guinea, AH 15, May 29, 1944, 900.341 All Theaters, General Rules and Regulations and Robert F. Eaton to Nyles I. Christensen, June 2, 1944, 900.341 All Theaters, Marriage Policy, both in Red Cross 1935–1946, NARA.

On instructions to date officers at training, see Hariette Saeltzer to D. K. Baldwin, March 10, 1944, 900.341 All Theaters, General Rules and Regulations, Red Cross 1935–1946, NARA; Chase, *Never Too Late,* 52.

171. Richard F. Allen to Mr. Dinsmore, May 7, 1943, 421.1 SAF & V-Women's Uniform 1941–1943, Red Cross 1935–1946, NARA.

172. Gale A. Mathers, "The Special Service Officer in the European Theater," 7, Decimal 319.1, General Records, 1941–1945, Special Services Division, RG 160 Records of Headquarters, Army Service Forces, NARA.

173. Morale Services Division Research Unit, "What Soldiers in Alaska Think about Recreation and Special Service," Report #13, August 1944, 13, "Enlisted Men's Criticisms of the Red Cross in MTOUSA," Report No. MTO 38, June 19, 1945, 3, both in Attitude Reports of Overseas Personnel 1942–1953, Research Division, Assistant Secretary of Defense (Manpower, Personnel, Research), RG 330 Records of the Office of the Secretary of Defense 1921–2005, NARA; Gerald F. Linderman, *The World within War: America's Combat Experience in World War II* (New York: Free Press, 1997), 190–191.

174. Mayer, "Report to the Chairman of the Red Cross in China-Burma-India," 13.

175. Nyles I. Christensen to Robert F. Eaton, June 5, 1944, 900.341 All Theaters, Marriage Policy, Red Cross 1935–1946, NARA. Prohibition against dating enlisted men: Assistant Director of Operations, APO 50e to All American Red Cross Personnel in New Guinea, AH 15, May 29, 1944, 900.341 All Theaters, General Rules and Regula-

tions, Red Cross 1935–1946, NARA; Robert F. Eaton to Nyles I. Christensen, June 2, 1944, 900.341 All Theaters, Marriage Policy, Red Cross 1935–1946, NARA.

176. "Mr. Fesler's Recommendations to Major John Nixon for presentation to the A.R.C. Headquarters in Washington," in Don C. Smith to Mr. Dinemore, Mr. Romney, Dr. Wann, Miss Ryan, June 19, 1944, 900.08 CBI, Reports, Statistics, Surveys, and Studies—General 1942–1944, Red Cross 1935–1946, NARA.

177. Smith to Dinemore, Romney, Wann, Ryan. In a postwar *New York Times* article, the Red Cross defended itself against rumors that the women were "brass happy" by noting that it did not interfere with the women's dating preferences. See "Red Cross Defended against 'GI Gripes,'" *New York Times*, May 10, 1946.

178. Foster, *Letters Home*, 56, 40.

179. Rexford, *Battlestars & Doughnuts*, 80.

180. Sargent, *Runway towards Orion*, 83.

181. Chase, *Never Too Late*, 125, also 52.

182. Madison, *Slinging Doughnuts for the Boys*, 55. Red Cross officials agreed with Richardson's assessment of the significance of class. An official in the China-Burma-India theater reported: "Girls do not have to be snobbish or overly impressed by brass to gravitate towards the officers as companions for the evening. As a class they are apt to be more closely identified with the social milieu and past associations of most of our women. With jeeps, clubs and liquor they are far better equipped than GIs to offer entertainment." See Mayer, "Report to the Chairman of the Red Cross in China-Burma-India," 13.

183. Louise Buckley to the People, 25.

184. Appel, *Dancing with GIs*, 102.

185. Langford, interview by Oldson, 25.

186. Eleanor (Bumpy) Stevenson with Pete Martin, "I Knew Your Soldier," *Saturday Evening Post*, November 4, 1944, 109. The women's experiences are similar to those of women office workers who were expected to arbitrate advances from men in the workplace. See Julie Berebitsky, *Sex and the Office: A History of Gender, Power, and Desire* (New Haven, CT: Yale University Press, 2012), esp. 141–158.

187. Hoslett, "Personnel Administration."

188. Olewiler, *A Woman in a Man's War*, 69; "What Enlisted Men in China, India and Burma Think about the Red Cross," Report CBI-12, December 7, 1944, 23, HD: 730 (Neuropsychiatry) Morale Surveys Enlisted Men in India and Burma, World War II Administrative Records, ZI, OSG, NARA.

189. "Enlisted Men's Criticisms of the Red Cross in MTOUSA," 5.

190. "What Enlisted Men in China, India and Burma Think about the Red Cross," 23.

191. Mayer, "Report to the Chairman of the Red Cross in China-Burma-India," 2.

192. Leisa D. Meyer, *Creating G.I. Jane: Sexuality and Power in the Women's Army Corps during World War II* (New York: Columbia University Press, 1996), 136–147; Barbara Tomblin, *G.I. Nightingales: The Army Nurse Corps in World War II* (Lexington: The University Press of Kentucky, 1996), 51–52; Kathi Jackson, *They Called*

*Them Angels: American Military Nurses of World War II* (Westport, CT: Praeger, 2000), 147–149.

193. Jameson, *The History of the American National Red Cross,* 14:103.

194. Sargent, *Runway towards Orion,* 108.

195. Chase, *Never Too Late,* 100.

196. Hazel Bowman to family, January 9, 1945, Bowman Collection.

197. Virginia C. Claudon Allen, interview by Patricia A. Kuentz, August 4, 2005, transcript, Virginia C. Allen Collection (AFC / 2001 / 001 / 33674), VHP.

198. Hazel Bowman to family, April 20, 1944, Bowman Collection.

199. Appel, *Dancing with GIs,* 13, 24, 13.

200. Chase, *Never Too Late,* 83, 59, 49.

201. Jane Anne McKee Jack to husband, August 24, 1942, Jane Anne McKee Jack, box 4, folder 7, Clubmobile Collection.

202. Jane Anne McKee Jack to husband, May 8, 1943, Jane Anne McKee Jack, box 4, folder 7, Clubmobile Collection.

203. C. M. Fesler to Nathan H. Kaufman, "Shangra Lodge—APO 690," November 8, 1944, 900.118 CBI, Club and Recreation Service Field Supervisors Monthly Narrative Report, 1942–1944, Red Cross 1935–1946, NARA.

204. Kathleen Crandall to Beatrice Lynch, September 30, 1945, 900.11 / 6161 CBI (China), "Victory Club" Hostel III Kunming, China APO 627, Red Cross 1935–1946, NARA.

205. Wiesner, *Between the Lines,* 27, 25–27. Her account quoted here appeared as: Elizabeth Q. Phenix, "Critic Doffs Hat to 'Glamour Girls' in Africa," *New York Herald Tribune,* September 19, 1943.

206. Mary Rexford noted that soldiers "who stepped out of line" were "usually chastised by his buddies, not by us." Rexford, *Battlestars & Doughnuts,* 3. Also see Enoch P. Waters Jr., "Five-Foot Girl Is 'Goddess' to Soldiers in New Guinea," *Chicago Defender,* September 16, 1944.

207. Stevenson with Martin, "I Knew Your Soldier," October 28, 1944, 70.

208. Rexford, *Battlestars & Doughnuts,* 3, 80.

209. Maxene Andrews and Bill Gilbert, *Over Here, Over There: The Andrews Sisters and the USO Stars in World War II* (New York: Zebra Books, 1993), 52, 94.

210. Rexford, *Battlestars & Doughnuts,* 3, 4–5, 37.

211. See Phil Goodman, "'Patriotic Femininity': Women's Morals and Men's Morale during the Second World War," *Gender & History* 10, no. 2 (August 1998): 287.

212. Buszek, *Pin-Up Grrrls,* 231.

213. Despina Kakoudaki, "Pin-up: The American Secret Weapon in World War II," in *Porn Studies,* ed. Linda Williams (Durham, NC: Duke University Press, 2004), 361.

### 3. THE DIFFERENCE BETWEEN SAVAGERY AND CIVILIZATION

1. Jean Moore Fasse, *My Journey Wasn't Easy: From Farm to City to an International Career,* ed. Charles R. George (Chapel Hill, NC: Chapel Hill Press, 2001), 45.

2. "204 Negroes Now in Red Cross Jobs," *Chicago Defender,* March 17, 1945.

3. Fasse, *My Journey Wasn't Easy,* 58; M. Jean Moore Fasse, interview by Beth Carmichael, March 13, 2007, transcript, Fasse Papers.

4. Fasse, *My Journey Wasn't Easy,* 59.

5. Fasse, interview by Carmichael.

6. "Red Cross Girls Work Near Front," *New York Times,* December 22, 1944.

7. Oscar Whitelaw Rexford, *Battlestars & Doughnuts: World War II Clubmobile Experiences of Mary Metcalfe Rexford* (St. Louis, MO: The Patrice Press, 1989), 64.

8. "Suggested Principles for the Establishment and Operation of American Red Cross Clubs Abroad," August 22, 1942, 4, 900.616 All Theaters, in Recreation 1942–1943, Red Cross 1935–1946, NARA.

9. Thomas H. Evans to Joseph Gralnik, Narrative Report for July 1944, Newtown Park Leave Camp, 900.118 FETO, Red Cross 1935–1946, NARA; Frederick H. Osborn, "Morale Activities of the Special Services Branch," *The Army and Navy Chaplain* 12, no. 4 (April–May 1942), in Morale (Gen. Osborn) General Subject Files, JANCWR, JANBC, NARA.

10. Clubmobile uniform: "Directive No. P-1," August 1, 1944, Virginia Wilson Cook Osgood, box 11, folder 2, Clubmobile Collection. The Red Cross provided to women their basic uniforms, though the women had to purchase their own supplies and extra clothing, at a cost of up to $500. "American Red Cross Uniforms for Overseas Personnel—Women," Schuyler Papers; "Uniforms—Services to the Armed Forces," March 16, 1944, Virginia Storts Hall, box 2, folder 10, Clubmobile Collection. Red Cross Clubmobile worker Mary Lou Pearce Hart noted that she spent $500 on the required supplies. See Mary Lou Pearce Hart, "This Is the Way It Was: A World War II Love Story," 18, Mary Lou Pearce Hart, Box 3, Folder 9, Clubmobile Collection. For a broader discussion of women's uniforms, see Melissa A. McEuen, *Making War, Making Women: Femininity and Duty on the American Home Front, 1941–1945* (Athens: University of Georgia Press, 2011), chap. 4.

11. "Uniforms—Services to the Armed Forces."

12. William E. Katzenbach to Ralph A. Brandt, June 27, 1944, 900.616 CBI, Canteen Activities, Red Cross 1935–1946, NARA.

13. Hazel Bowman to parents, August 8, 1945, Bowman Collection. Conversely, USO performer Louise Buckley found that, while on tour in the South Pacific, although women were told to wear GI pants and long sleeves to protect them from mosquito bites, they defied the rules and wore dresses because they were there to raise morale. Louise Buckley to the People, Thanksgiving Day 1944, in Annual Report, 1944, 22, USO Camp Shows—Annual Report 1944, Series II—Reports and Office Files, Camp Shows.

14. Jean Holdridge Reeves to parents, April 4, 1945, Reeves Papers.

15. Nancy Jobson Foster, *Letters Home: The American Red Cross and the 8th Air Force* (Nashville, TN: Turner Publishing Company, 2006), 22.

16. Foster, *Letters Home,* 57.

17. Hazel L. Bowman V-Mail to parents, January 12, 1944; Hazel L. Bowman to family, March 27, 1944; both in Bowman Collection.

18. Rosalie Campbell Jordan, "Let It Not Be Forgot: A Memoir of World War II," 119, Rosalie Campbell Jordan, box 10, folder 7, Clubmobile Collection.

19. Jordan, "Let It Not Be Forgot," 157.

20. Richard F. Allen to Thomas M. Dinamore, March 31, 1943, 900.3 All Theaters, Female Personnel, Red Cross 1935–1946, NARA.

21. "Guide to the Foxhole Circuit," 32, 33, in "Camp Shows, Inc., a / k / a USO-Camp Shows, Inc. Records, 1941–1957," vol. 7, 3513, Records of Special Services Division, Records of Camp Shows, AGO, NARA. Some Red Cross women wore flowers in their hair as well. See Rexford, *Battlestars & Doughnuts,* 99.

22. Lynn O'Neal Heberling, "Soldiers in Greasepaint: USO-Camp Shows, Inc. during World War II" (PhD diss., Kent State University, 1989), 212, 213.

23. W. K. B., "Ann Sheridan's Tour of Army Camps Should be Banned by War Department," April 3, 1942, in "USO Camp Shows, Inc. Report of Activities for Six Weeks Ended April 16, 1942," 12, 13, United Service Organizations, Camp Shows Reports 1942 April, Weil Papers.

24. Lawrence Phillips to the Editor, *Carmel Cymbal,* April 30, 1942, in "USO Camp Shows, Inc. Report of Activities for Six Weeks Ended April 16, 1942," 11. Phillips later made the same point in a letter to the Executive Director of member agency the National Catholic Community Service when he insisted that women's costumes were "designed both for colorful effect and facility of action." See Lawrence Phillips to James J. Norris, November 6, 1943, Decimal File 1920–1945, 250.1 Morals & Conduct, vol. 1 (Entertainment), Chaplains, NARA.

25. "American Red Cross China Burma India Clubmobile Manual," Club Operations Department, 1943, 4, 900.43 All Theaters (CBI), Clubmobile Manual, Red Cross 1935–1946, NARA.

26. Marcia Ward Behr, *Coffee and Sympathy: World War II Letters from the Southwest Pacific, April 1943–January 1945* (Bloomington, IN: 1st Books, 2002), 160.

27. Robert Bremner, Minna Adams Hutcheson, and Lucille Stein Greenberg, *The History of the American National Red Cross,* vol. 13: *American Red Cross Services in the War against the European Axis, Pearl Harbor to 1947* (Washington, DC: The American National Red Cross, 1950), 283.

28. As historian Ann Elizabeth Pfau argues, pilots often understood their work as sexualized. Initially, many saw their planes extensions of their masculinity and anticipated combat as a masculine a rite of passage comparable to losing their virginity. The dangers of air missions, however, soon gave way to a profound sense of vulnerability and a dependence on the planes they decorated with suggestive nose art and named in ways that revealed both their preoccupations with female sexuality and their reverence for devoted women at home. Ann Elizabeth Pfau, *Miss Yourlovin: GI, Gender, and Domesticity during World War II* (New York: Columbia University Press, 2008), chap. 4, www .gutenberg-e.org/pfau, accessed July 1, 2018. John Costello similarly argues that the prospect of death heightened the sex drive, particularly among bomber crews who risked death daily. See John Costello, *Virtue under Fire: How World War II Changed Our Social and Sexual Attitudes* (Boston: Little, Brown, and Company, 1985), 91–92.

29. Turner Catledge, "Red Cross Clubs Havens of Fliers," *New York Times,* March 19, 1944.

30. "Club Report for the Month of January 1944," 900.6161 Brazil Office, "On Post" Club Parnamirim Field Natal, Brazil APO 604, Red Cross 1935–1946, NARA.

31. Katzenbach to Brandt. Also see "Report of Red Cross Activities at Adjacento Field, Fortaleza, Ceara, Brasil," June 1944, 900.6161 Brazil Office, Enlisted Men's Club Adjacento Field Fortalega, Ceara, Brazil APO 619, Red Cross 1935–1946, NARA.

32. Eleanor (Bumpy) Stevenson with Pete Martin, "I Knew Your Soldier," *Saturday Evening Post,* October 21, 1944, 11.

33. Katharine Harris van Hogendorp, *Survival in the Land of Dysentery: The World War II Experiences of a Red Cross Worker in India* (Fredericksburg, VA: Sergeant Kirkland's, 1998), 108–109; Stevenson with Martin, "I Knew Your Soldier," October 21, 1944, 11.

34. Elizabeth Williams, interview by Eric Elliott, March 29, 1999, transcript, WV0058 Elizabeth Williams Papers, WVHP.

35. The General Board, United States Forces, European Theater, "Report on Leaves, Furloughs, and Passes," Study Number 4, [1945–46], 12, MHI.

36. "Army Rest Camps a Boon Overseas," *New York Times,* January 31, 1944.

37. "Red Cross Cheers Troops in Britain," *New York Times,* June 21, 1943; "Early Narrative Report on Rest Homes," September 1943, 900.616 ETO, Rest Homes and Convalescent Centers, Red Cross 1935–1946, NARA.

38. "Early Narrative Report on Rest Homes."

39. Remarks of Mr. Norman H. Davis at Central Committee Meeting, September 27, 1943, 900.06 All Theaters, Visits and Inspection Trips, Red Cross 1935–1946, NARA.

40. The General Board, "Report on Leaves, Furloughs, and Passes," 12.

41. Lucile B. Brown to William Stevenson and Thomas W. Irving, August 17, 1943, 900.11 / 616 MTO (North Africa), Canteens, Clubs, Clubmobile, Rest Centers, Hostels, etc., Red Cross 1935–1946, NARA.

42. Williams, interview by Elliott.

43. Adelaide Kerr, "Experiences Overseas Will Help U.S. Girls, Mrs. Colt Believes," *Washington Post,* July 13, 1943.

44. R. B. Smith to Thomas W. Irving, September 27, 1943, 900.11.6161 MTO (North Africa), Showmobiles, Red Cross 1935–1946, NARA.

45. For studies of the military's regulation of soldiers' contact with and marriage to women in various theaters, see Susan Zeiger, *Entangling Alliances: Foreign War Brides and American Soldiers in the Twentieth Century* (New York: New York University Press, 2010), chaps. 3 and 4; Barbara G. Friedman, *From the Battlefront to the Bridal Suite: Media Coverage of British War Brides* (Columbia: University of Missouri Press, 2007), 58–66; Juliet Gardiner, *"Overpaid, Oversexed, and Over Here": The American GI in World War II Britain* (New York: Canopy Books, 1992), chap. 12; Lillian Jones Dowling, *One of the Boys but Always a Lady: The Life of a Red Cross Recreation Worker in Combat Troop Camps in Australia during the War with Japan* (New York:

Vantage Press, 1998), 25–26; George Korson, *At His Side: The Story of the American Red Cross Overseas in World War II* (New York: Coward-McCann, 1945), 48. The British Welcome Club program, which arranged for American GIs to visit the homes of British families, did not coordinate visits for African American soldiers but instead ran a segregated program called the Silver Birch Clubs. See Graham Smith, *When Jim Crow Met John Bull: Black American Soldiers in World War II Britain* (New York: St. Martin's Press, 1988), 84–85.

46. F. H. Osborn to Chester I. Barnard, August 27, 1942, United Service Organizations, 1942 Aug–Sept., Weil Papers.

47. Josephine Callisen Bresnahan, "Dangers in Paradise: The Battle against Combat Fatigue in the Pacific War" (PhD diss., Harvard University, 1999), quote on 126n72, also 123–126.

48. Minutes, Club Directors Conference, Recreation Section, July 8, 1943, 900.04 FETO, Conference of Club Directors, Red Cross 1935–1946, NARA.

49. Bremner, Hutcheson, and Greenberg, *The History of the American National Red Cross,* 13:75–77.

50. Tim H. Kirk to Edward R. Eichholzer, "Report on Club Activities for May," May 29, 1943, 4, 900.118 CBI, Club and Recreation Service Monthly Narrative Reports 1942–1943, Red Cross 1935–1946, NARA.

51. Alma B. Kerr to Tim H. Kirk, "Monthly Progress Report for Club Operations—August 1943, 6, 900.118 CBI, Club and Recreation Service Monthly Narrative Reports 1942–1943, Red Cross 1935–1946, NARA. See also Enoc P. Waters, "Red Cross Worker in Australia Gets Hundreds of Proposals from Soldiers," *Chicago Defender,* October 30, 1943.

52. Michael Malkin, "Yearly Report Clubmobile Department," 1943, 900.11 CBI, Clubmobile Service, Red Cross 1935–1946, NARA. Also see Clubmobile report, October 1945, 900.11 All Theaters, Club Department; and P. Yandell to Harvey D. Gibson, March 15, 1943, 900.118 ETO, Clubmobile Department Reports; both in Red Cross 1935–1946, NARA; Rosalie Campbell Jordan, "Let It Not Be Forgot."

53. Statements of Policy Applicable to American Red Cross Personnel Overseas, 38, 344.01 Overseas Personnel 1942–45, Statements of Policy Applicable to; "American Red Cross National Employment Service Recruiting Manual for Positions in S.A.F. Foreign and Domestic," June 1, 1943, 10, 494.2 Recruiting Manual (SAF), both in Red Cross 1935–1946, NARA. On USO citizenship requirements, see Francis Steegmuller, OWI Release on USO-Camp Shows, Inc., April 14, 1943, 6, USO Camp Shows—Press Releases 1943–1945, Series II—Reports and Office Files, Camp Shows. For Red Cross citizenship requirements, see ARC 831: General Guide for Selecting Assistant Club Directors, 494.1 ARC 831 General Guide for Selecting Assistant Club Directors; ARC 830a: General Guide for Selecting Assistant Program Directors, 494.1 ARC 830a General Guide for Selecting Assistant Program Directors; ARC 828: General Guide for Selecting Staff Assistants, 494.1 ARC 828 General Guide for Selecting Staff Assistants for Overseas Club and Recreation Centers; all in Red Cross 1935–1946, NARA.

54. "American Red Cross, "National Employment Service Recruiting Manual for Positions in S.A.F. Foreign and Domestic," June 1, 1943, 10, 494.2 Recruiting Manual (SAF), Red Cross 1935–1946, NARA.

55. "Yanks Relax as Tourists de Luxe while Exploring Britain on Leave," *New York Times,* August 6, 1942.

56. H. Crump to All Club Directors, Club Division Circular No. 169, May 28, 1943, 900.031 ETO, Club Division Circulars, Red Cross 1935–1946, NARA.

57. Korson, *At His Side,* 48, 52; Beatrice Lynch to Tim H. Kirk, "Report of Activities—July 17–July 24, 1942," July 27, 1942; both in 900.118 CBI, Club and Recreation Service Monthly Narrative Reports 1942–1943, Red Cross 1935–1946, NARA.

58. Quote in Alma B. Kerr to Edward R. Eichholzer, "Summary Report of Red Cross Club Activities in APO 629 and APO 689," April 30, 1943; also see Beatrice Lynch to Tim H. Kirk, "Report of Activities—July 24–July 31, 1942," August 1, 1942; both in 900.118 CBI, Club and Recreation Service Monthly Narrative Reports 1942–1943, Red Cross 1935–1946, NARA. Thanks to Brandon Marsh for helpful information on British tea planters and tea dances in India.

59. "Outline of Club Program, Natal, Brasil" and "Club Report for the Month of March 1944," both in 900.6161 Brazil Office, "On Post" Club Parnamirim Field Natal, Brazil APO 604, Red Cross 1935–1946, NARA.

60. Quotes in Ann D. Hill, "Recreation Report—May 1945," 900.6161 Brazil Office, Enlisted Men's Recreation Club-Val de Cans Field Belem, Brazil APO 603; also see "Report of Red Cross Activities at Adjacento Field, Fortalega, Ceara, Brasil," June 1944, 900.6161 Brazil Office, Enlisted Men's Club Adjacento Field Fortalega, Ceara, Brazil APO 619; Lolita Warner, "Narrative Report on Club Mais-o-Menos," April 30, 1944, 900.6161 Brazil Office, Club Mais-o-Menos Ibura Field Recife, Brazil APO 675; all in Red Cross 1935–1946, NARA. Officials even believed the dances worked as constructive foreign relations between the United States and Brazil. When one club planned a dance for January 29, President Franklin D. Roosevelt's birthday, organizers requested that the president send a cable to be read at the event. "These dances do a great deal to cement friendship between the two countries," they explained, "and a gesture like that would make a great impression on the Brazilians." See "Club Report for the Month of January 1945," 900.6161 Brazil Office, "On Post" Club Parnamirim Field Natal, Brazil APO 604, Red Cross 1935–1946, NARA. A Red Cross official stationed at Ibura Field in Recife, Brazil similarly described an enlisted men's dance in April 1944 as "a real gesture toward Pan-American friendship." Lolita Warner, "Narrative Report on Club Mais-o-Menos," April 30, 1944, 900.6161 Brazil Office, Club Mais-o-Menos Ibura Field Recife, Brazil APO 675, Red Cross 1935–1946, NARA.

61. Edward Mead Earle, "Memorandum Regarding Problems of Morale, Recreation, and Health in Connection with American Naval and Air Bases in the Caribbean Area," 2–5, Morale—June 1, 1941, General Subject Files, JANCWR, JANBC, NARA.

62. Howard, *"No Drums, No Trumpets,"* 10.

63. Jean M. Bright, interview by Hermann Trojanowski, April 2, 2004, transcript, WV0295 Jean M. Bright Collection, 1944–1946, 2004–2005, WVHP. At another French colony in the Pacific, Bora Bora, an American commander expressly noted that he did not want his soldiers dancing with native women. See H. M. Batezel to Stanford Oksness, February 24, 1944, 900.01 FETO, General Plans, Policies and Programs, Red Cross 1935–1946, NARA.

64. Margaret Chase, *Never Too Late* (San Francisco: Ausonia Press, 1983), 50.

65. Beth Bailey and David Farber, *The First Strange Place: The Alchemy of Race and Sex in World War II Hawaii* (New York: Free Press, 1992), 50–53, 178–180, 191–205; Julia M. H. Carson, *Home away from Home: The Story of the USO* (New York: Harper & Brothers, 1946), 151–152. Similar to the situation in Hawaii, clubs in China had to rely on a local population of women who did not neatly fit American binary views of race. There, the Red Cross recruited "acceptable" Chinese women to serve as dance partners for GIs. See Ralph A. Brandt to Robert C. Lewis, "Monthly Report of Club Operations, November 1943," 900.118 CBI, Club and Recreation Service Monthly Narrative Reports; Tim H. Kirk to Edward R. Eichholzer, "February Report," March 1, 1943, 900.118 CBI, Club and Recreation Service Monthly Narrative Reports 1942–1943, both in Red Cross 1935–1946, NARA.

66. Fashion Hints from GIs in the South Pacific, n.d., USO Camp Shows—Press Releases 1943–1945, Series II—Reports and Office Files, Camp Shows.

67. Robert Westbrook, "'I Want a Girl, Just Like the Girl That Married Harry James': American Women and the Problem of Political Obligation in World War II," *American Quarterly* 42, no. 4 (December 1990): 587–614, quote on 599.

68. Mr. Allen to Mr. Bondy, Mr. Don Smith, Mr. Wesselius, March 3, 1944, 900.616 All Theaters, Recreation 1944–1945; Don C. Smith to Mr. Bondy, March 3, 1944, in 900.01 All Theaters, General Plans, Policies and Programs; both in Red Cross 1935–1946, NARA.

69. Bess Furman, "Red Cross Praised on Burma Road Job," *New York Times*, February 19, 1945.

70. John M. Noelke to William S. Hepner, July 27, 1945, 340.03 Appointments and Assignments (Overseas Personnel), Red Cross 1935–1946, NARA.

71. Korson, *At His Side,* 121. Also see General Board, United States Forces, European Theater, "American Red Cross Activities in the European Theater," Study No. 5, [1945–1946], 17, MHI; Clubmobile report, October 1945, 900.11 All Theaters, Club Department, Red Cross 1935–1946, NARA.

72. Raymond D. Jameson, *The History of the American National Red Cross,* vol. 14: *The American Red Cross during World War II in the Pacific Theater* (Washington, DC: The American National Red Cross, 1950), 6, in 494.2 General—History of the ANRC (Monographs), Red Cross 1935–1946, NARA.

73. Jameson, *The History of the American National Red Cross,* 14:102.

74. Allen to Bondy, Smith, Wesselius.

75. Behr, *Coffee and Sympathy,* "abnormality of life" and "handful of girls" on 116, "scratch the surface" and "abnormal place" on 143.

76. Jameson, *The History of the American National Red Cross,* 14:7, 6.

77. Irma C. Bradford Bantjes, *"Utah": Angel in Disguise, World War II* (Orem, UT: privately printed, 1992), 89.

78. As Donna B. Knaff writes about the dangers members of the Women's Army Corps (WAC) faced in the Southwest Pacific, "Ultimately, the women themselves were the cause; thus the men must be protected from the women, and the women must be protected from themselves." See Donna B. Knaff, *Beyond Rosie the Riveter: Women of World War II in American Popular Graphic Art* (Lawrence: University Press of Kansas, 2012), 103.

79. Noelke to Hepner. Barbara Brooks Tomblin notes that Army nurses' and WACs' quarters in New Guinea were also enclosed by barbed wire and the women required to travel with armed escorts. Two chief nurses in the area offered explanations for the restrictions: one suggested that they were because of "colored" troops in the area, while the other pointed to a few white prowlers. See Barbara Brooks Tomblin, *G.I. Nightingales: The Army Nurse Corps in World War II* (Lexington: University Press of Kentucky, 2003), 51–52.

80. Memorandum No. 15, April 8, 1944, 900.341 All Theaters, General Rules and Regulations, Red Cross 1935–1946, NARA; White, interview by Elliott.

81. For Guam, see Memorandum 3-45 Security Measures for Service Women, January 4, 1945, 900.341 All Theaters, General Rules and Regulations, Red Cross 1935–1946, NARA; on Brisbane and the quotation, see "The American National Red Cross Welcomes You to the South-West Pacific Theater," 900.494 All Theaters (FETO), American National Red Cross Welcomes You to the South-West Pacific Theater, Red Cross 1935–1946, NARA.

82. Hazel Bowman to parents, December 2, 1945, Bowman Collection.

83. Mary Ferebee Howard, *"No Drums, No Trumpets": Red Cross Adventure* (Rocky Mount: North Carolina Wesleyan College Press, 1992), 41.

84. Judy Barrett Litoff and David C. Smith, eds., *We're in This War, Too: World War II Letters from American Women in Uniform* (New York: Oxford University Press, 1994), 195.

85. Janet MacCubbin, interview by Sharon Brown, May 14, 2009, transcript, MacCubbin Papers.

86. White, interview by Elliott; Chase, *Never Too Late*, 132.

87. Bantjes, *"Utah,"* 43. Dances, as they had in World War I, could prove especially frightening and troublesome for the women expected to manage the crowds, devote personal attention to GIs, and guard their shins and toes from the uncoordinated feet of eager soldiers. See Dowling, *One of the Boys but Always a Lady*, 25–26, and Behr, *Coffee and Sympathy*, 75.

88. Van Hogendorp, *Survival in the Land of Dysentery*, 133–134.

89. Van Hogendorp, *Survival in the Land of Dysentery*, 76.

90. Libby Chitwood Appel, *Dancing with GIs: A Red Cross Club Worker in India, World War II* (Cornelius, NC: Warren Publishing, 2004), 123, 147–151.

91. Richard F. Allen to S. G. Henry, February 10, 1945, decimal 330.11, 1 Oct 44–30 Oct 44, G-1 Personnel General Correspondence 1942–1948, RG 165 Records of the War Department General and Special Staffs, NARA.

92. C. B. Webster, Notes on Mr. Allen's Meeting the Morning of February 6 [1945], 900.06 All Theaters (CBI), Mr. Allen's Report of Inspection Visit of CBI, Red Cross 1935–1946, NARA.

93. Quoted in Furman, "Red Cross Praised on Burma Road Job."

94. Allen to Henry.

95. Bremner, Hutcheson, and Greenberg, *The History of the American National Red Cross,* 13:255.

96. Richard F. Allen, "The Chairman," February 10, 1945, 900.3 All Theaters, Female Personnel, Red Cross 1935–1946, NARA.

97. Webster, Notes on Mr. Allen's Meeting the Morning of February 6 [1945].

98. "The right sort," in Webster, Notes on Mr. Allen's Meeting the Morning of February 6 [1945]; "well-behaved" and "millions of such women" in Allen, "The Chairman."

99. John C. Smith, appointed to Red Cross national headquarters to advise on race, was unable to effect much progressive change, a problem he attributed to the organization's unwillingness to confront the military on racial matters. To any proposal he made, the Red Cross responded that the Army imposed limitations and encouraged discrimination, a response Smith believed to be "an escape avenue, and does in fact represent the fundamental attitude of officials of the American Red Cross." See Jesse O. Thomas to Files, November 30, 1944, 900.3 All Theaters, Negro Personnel, Red Cross 1935–1946, NARA. Dick Campbell, cofounder of the Negro Actors Guild and a lifelong advocate for African American actors, pressured the USO to recruit black entertainment units so that black actors would have an opportunity to contribute to the war effort. Once the USO began sending black women abroad, he called for black women to do as the "glamour girls of Hollywood and Broadway" had done, to "lay aside their luxuries, carry as little as they must, and . . . do their bit to raise the morale of the boys overseas." The *Chicago Defender* heralded their work as a sign that "once again, black America displayed its mettle." Izzy, "USO to Send Six Sepia Show Units Overseas," *Pittsburgh Courier,* March 18, 1944; Joe Bostic, "Navy's Discrimination of Negro USO Shows Finally Leaks Out," *Chicago Defender,* August 17, 1946. This article also boasted that some black performers had sacrificed higher wages to tour for soldiers "because they believed in the worthiness of the effort," though other articles differ on the question of wages. An earlier article in the *Chicago Defender* cited Dick Campbell as saying that African American performers earned salaries equal to the salaries they made in commercial entertainment, which was the USO's policy. Another article suggested that some people speculated that because of a shortage of "colored talent" those performers made equal or even more money than white artists. See "Negro Artists Score Overseas," *Chicago Defender,* August 11, 1945; "Sepians Contribute Share to USO Shows," *Pittsburgh Courier,* January 27, 1945.

100. Channing H. Tobias, "The U.S.O. Services to Negroes," *Opportunity* 20 (May 1942): 132–134; "A Review of the Race Relations Policy of the American Red Cross," November 1948, 3–4, American Red Cross, Service Clubs in England and Foreign Stations 1942–1944 Reel 2, Group II, Series A, General Office File, Part 15: Segrega-

tion and Discrimination, Complaints and Responses, 1940–1955, Series B: Administrative Files, NAACP. This review refers to Walter White, *A Rising Wind* (New York: Doubleday, Doran and Company, 1945), 19–20; Walter White, "People, Politics and Places: The Truth about Red Cross," *Chicago Defender,* December 29, 1945.

101. Jesse O. Thomas to Basil O'Connor, March 16, 1945, 900.616 All Theaters, Recreation 1944–1945, Red Cross 1935–1946, NARA; Summary of Conference with Negro Leaders Held July 15, 1942, American Red Cross, Service Clubs in England and Foreign Stations 1942–1944 Reel 2, Group II, Series A, General Office File, Part 15: Segregation and Discrimination, Complaints and Responses, 1940–1955, Series B: Administrative Files, NAACP. Also see Norman H. Davis to Harold L. Ickes, July 22, 1942, 900.61, All Theaters, ARC Service to Colored Troops and Questions of Discrimination, Red Cross 1935–1946, NARA.

102. Quote in Brandt to Lewis, "Monthly Report of Club Operations, November 1943." Also "Statement made by Mr. Harvey D. Gibson, American Red Cross Commissioner," No. 16, September 8, 1942, decimal 353.81, General Correspondence 1941–1945, Special Services Division, Office of Director of Personnel, RG 160 Records of Headquarters Army Service Forces; L. P. Yandell to Harvey D. Gibson, January 5, 1943, 900.118 ETO, Clubmobile Department Reports, Red Cross 1935–1946; Ralph A. Brandt to Robert C. Lewis, "Monthly Report for March 1945," April 17, 1945, 900.118 CBI, Club and Recreation Service Monthly Narrative Summary, Red Cross 1935–1946; Richard F. Allen to Stirling Tomkins, September 11, 1944, 900.3 All Theaters, Negro Personnel, Red Cross 1935–1946, all at NARA.

103. Roy Wilkins to S. Ralph Harlow, October 22, 1943, American Red Cross, Service Clubs in England and Foreign Stations 1942–1944 Reel 2, Group II, Series A, General Office File, Part 15: Segregation and Discrimination, Complaints and Responses, 1940–1955, Series B: Administrative Files, NAACP; Gene Lusty, "Report on American Red Cross Clubs in Australia as of November 15, 1943," 900.118 FETO, Club and Recreation Service Reports—Jan. 1942–1943; H. D. Gibson to Negro Staff Members of the American Red Cross Commission to Great Britain, C.O. 90, November 15, 1943, 900.3 All Theaters, Negro Personnel; Nyles I. Christensen to Walter Wesselius, December 3, 1943, 900.61 All Theaters, ARC Service to Colored Troops and Questions of Discrimination; all in Red Cross 1935–1946, NARA; Deton J. Brooks, "Negro GI's Jim Crowed in India; Red Cross Worker Quits in Protest," *Chicago Defender,* July 14, 1945.

104. Norman H. Davis to Walter White, January 6, 1943; "Memorandum to Mr. White from Mr. Wilkins, August 20, 1943; Walter White to Elsie Austin, August 12, 1943; Elsie Austin to Walter White, August 9, 1943; George W. Goodman to Walter White, July 26, 1943; all in American Red Cross, Service Clubs in England and Foreign Stations 1942–1944 Reel 2, Group II, Series A, General Office File, Part 15: Segregation and Discrimination, Complaints and Responses, 1940–1955, Series B: Administrative Files, NAACP; Jesse O. Thomas to Walter Davidson, August 23, 1943, 900.61 All Theaters, ARC Service to Colored Troops and Questions of Discrimination, Red Cross 1935–1946, NARA; Mayer, "Report to the Chairman of the Red

Cross in China-Burma-India," 12. The Red Cross explained that its "negro supervisor of colored clubs" approved of naming the clubs after prominent African Americans because the "colored troops take a good deal of pride in knowing that the name of a prominent distinguished member of their race is associated with the American Red Cross." It also noted that changing the club names after they had already been named would "create a rather serious problem." Christensen to Wesselius. Also see Richard F. Allen to Charles K. Gamble, January 10, 1944, 900.61 All Theaters, ARC Service to Colored Troops and Questions of Discrimination, Red Cross 1935–1946, NARA.

105. Jesse O. Thomas and H. E. Downey to L. M. Mitchell, December 7, 1944, 300.1 Negro personnel, 1935–1943, Red Cross 1935–1946, NARA; "Red Cross Needs 80 Workers for Overseas Duty," *Chicago Defender,* January 29, 1944; Jesse O. Thomas to L. M. Mitchell, October 20, 1943, 300.1 Negro personnel, 1935–1943, Red Cross 1935–1946, NARA. In March 1945, the Red Cross had 204 African American workers overseas, including 119 club workers. It sent nineteen more African American women by September. See "204 Negroes Now in Red Cross Jobs," *Chicago Defender,* March 17, 1945, and "15 More Red Cross Workers Go Overseas," *Atlanta Daily World,* September 16, 1945.

106. H. D. Gibson to Negro Staff Members of the American Red Cross Commission to Great Britain, C.O. 90, November 15, 1943, 900.3 All Theaters, Negro Personnel; Arthur Mayer, "Report to the Chairman of the Red Cross in China-Burma-India," 11, 900.06 All Theaters, Visits and Inspection Trips; both in Red Cross 1935–1946, NARA.

107. *USO Field Service Manual: A Manual of Policies and Procedures Prepared Primarily for National Agency Operations of USO* (New York: USO, 1944), 28. Maryann Lovelace argues that the primary financiers of the Philadelphia USO club struggled to adapt to wartime changes in race, gender, and class and used the club to maintain traditional values and social mores in these areas. See Maryann Lovelace, "Facing Change in Wartime Philadelphia: The Story of the Philadelphia USO," *The Pennsylvania Magazine of History and Biography* 123, no. 3 (July 1999): 143–175. The USO also backed down in the face of white opposition to its distribution of a progressive pamphlet, *The Races of Mankind,* which advanced scientific and anthropological arguments undermining biologically based claims of racial superiority. See Tracy Teslow, *Constructing Race: The Science of Bodies and Cultures in American Anthropology* (New York: Cambridge University Press, 2014), 253–254.

108. Pamela Bloom, "Jim Crow Entertainment: The Segregated USO during World War II" (MA thesis, Hunter College of the City University of New York, 2003), 29–34, 59–60, 78. By January 1945 the USO had hired 414 "colored performers" for 212 acts, about ten percent of the total hired. "Sepians Contribute Share to USO Shows." See "Stage Stars, Active in War, to Continue Entertainment for GIs," *Chicago Defender,* May 12, 1945, for a list of many of the African American troupes that toured overseas for USO Camp-Shows. Stephen Tuck argues that African American entertainers ultimately had little effect on the overall black image in popular culture. Although well-known entertainers such as Duke Ellington or Joe Louis advanced the image

of African Americans as patriotic citizens, Tuck maintains that "the association of African American high achievement with jazz and sports actually underscored the idea of innate racial difference—and black primitiveness and lack of intelligence." See Stephen Tuck, "'You Can Sing and Punch . . . But You Can't Be a Soldier or a Man': African American Struggles for a New Place in Popular Culture," in *Fog of War: The Second World War and the Civil Rights Movement,* ed. Kevin M. Kruse and Stephen Tuck (New York: Oxford University Press, 2012), 118.

109. Rexford, *Battlestars & Doughnuts,* 6.

110. Jean Holdridge Reeves, interview by Kim Adkins, February 14, 2007, transcript, Reeves Papers.

111. Angela Petesch, *War through the Hole of a Donut* (Madison, WI: Hunter Halverson Press, 2006), 84–86.

112. Alma Geist Cap, interview by Tara Kraenzlin and Barbara Tomblin, May 6, 1997, Rutgers Oral History Archives of World War II, http://oralhistory.rutgers.edu /interviewees/853-cap-alma-geist, accessed June 18, 20104.

113. See Smith, *When Jim Crow Met John Bull,* esp. chap. 8. Jane Dailey argues that the potential for interracial sex lay at the heart of wartime resistance to racial integration and explains the prevalence of segregation in USO clubs. One notable exception was the Stage Door Canteen in New York City, where servicemen of all races could dance with Junior Hostesses of all races. See Jane Dailey, "The Sexual Politics of Race in World War II America," in *Fog of War,* 145–170. Similarly, as Meghan K. Winchell and Kimberley L. Phillips suggest, dancing was a particularly troublesome activity for officials worried about interracial attraction. Many USO clubs in the United States banned the jitterbug, for example, because of its roots in African American culture and its presumed sexual underpinnings. See Meghan K. Winchell, *Good Girls, Good Food, Good Fun: The Story of USO Hostesses during World War II* (Chapel Hill: University of North Carolina Press, 2008), 136–137, 144–146, 152, 154; Kimberley L. Phillips, *War! What is it Good For? Black Freedom Struggles and the U.S. Military from World War II to Iraq* (Chapel Hill: University of North Carolina Press, 2014), 50.

114. George H. Roeder Jr., *The Censored War: American Visual Experience during World War II* (New Haven, CT: Yale University Press, 1993), 57.

115. Remarks of Mr. Norman H. Davis at Central Committee Meeting.

116. Rosemary Norwalk, *Dearest Ones: A True World War II Love Story* (New York: John Wiley & Sons, 1999), 69–70; Angela Petesch letter to Daddy, August 8, 43, Angela Petesch, box 11, folder 3, Clubmobile Collection.

117. Owen L. Crecelius to Theater Censor, ETOUSA, "Special Report on Negro Troops—16 to 31 March 44," April 1, 1944; also Torger Skabo to Theater Censor, ETOUSA, "Special Report (Negro Troops, Mar. 16–31, 1944)," March 31, 1944, both in decimal 319.1, Troop Information and Education Division Decimal File, ETO, Records of the Chief of Staff G-4, Army Staff, NARA. White GIs in Australia expressed similar displeasure at seeing African American soldiers with white Australian women. See Sean Brawley and Chris Dixon, "Jim Crow Downunder? African American Encounters with White Australia, 1942–1945," *Pacific Historical Review* 71, no. 4 (November 2002): esp. 621–623.

118. J. L. Fenton to G-2, Censorship Branch, "Special Report—Negro Troops—15–31 March 44," March 31, 1944, decimal 319.1, Troop Information and Education Division Decimal File, ETO, Records of the Chief of Staff G-4, Army Staff, NARA.

119. Onas F. Lowery, "Censorship Summary and Morale Report," August 16, 1944, decimal 319.1, Troop Information and Education Division Decimal File, Pacific Ocean Areas, Records of the Chief of Staff G-4, Army Staff, NARA.

120. William E. Stevenson to Richard F. Allen, August 2, 1942, 900.11 ETO, Club and Clubmobile Departments, Red Cross 1935–1946, NARA; Leisa D. Meyer, *Creating G.I. Jane: Sexuality and Power in the Women's Army Corps during World War II* (New York: Columbia University Press, 1996), 48; Brenda L. Moore, *To Serve My Country, to Serve My Race: The Story of the Only African American WACs Stationed Overseas during World War II* (New York: New York University Press, 1996), 80–82; Smith, *When Jim Crow Met John Bull,* 191–193; Pfau, *Miss Yourlovin,* chap. 2.

121. Sherrie Tucker, *Swing Shift: "All-Girl" Bands of the 1940s* (Durham, NC: Duke University Press, 2000), 238.

122. Ostensibly, the unit dances were enforced as a way to limit the number of men in attendance. Thomas W. Irving to Colonel Sears, April 6, 1944, 900.11 / 616 MTO (North Africa), Canteens, Clubs, Clubmobile, Rest Centers, Hostels, etc.; Stirling Tomkins to Walter Wesselius, October 28, 1944, 900.616 All Theaters, Recreation 1944–1945; Gerald J. Donovan to Bowen McCoy, May 21, 1945, 900.61, All Theaters, ARC Service to Colored Troops and Questions of Discrimination; all in Red Cross 1935–1946, NARA; Smith, *When Jim Crow Met John Bull,* 102–107. In March 1946, the Red Cross commissioner in Italy praised several integrated clubs as "models of working and racial harmony" because they had found a solution to the "headache" of interracial dancing. The club provided Italian hostesses for African American servicemen, while white soldiers danced with African American women. Though integrated to some degree, there is no record that the dances involved white women dancing with black men. See "Interracial Red Cross Naples Staff Praised," *Atlanta Daily World,* April 10, 1946; "headache" in P. L. Prattis, "The Horizon: Democracy Can Thrive, If Given a Chance, Even in the Red Cross Service," *Pittsburgh Courier,* June 1, 1946.

123. Deton J. Brooks, "Negro GI's Jim Crowed in India; Red Cross Worker Quits in Protest," *Chicago Defender,* July 14, 1945. After an investigation of the incident, Jesse O. Thomas concluded that the Red Cross should have advised the Army about the situation more fully and informed the military that it was harming morale instead of boosting it. See Jesse O. Thomas to Walter Wesselius, July 13, 1945, 900.3 All Theaters, Negro Personnel, Red Cross 1935–1946, NARA.

124. Mayer, "Report to the Chairman of the Red Cross in China-Burma-India," 12.

125. Elaine S. Gorham to Frank K. Tweedy, "Club Report—December 15 to 31st, 1944," 2, 12, 900.118 CBI, Club and Recreation Service Field Supervisors Monthly Narrative Report, 1942–1944, Red Cross 1935–1946, NARA.

126. Deton J. Brooks, "No Color Problem in India Red Cross Club," *Chicago Defender,* December 2, 1944.

127. Ralph A. Brandt to Robert C. Lewis, "Monthly Report for February 1945," March 16, 1945, 900.118 CBI, Club and Recreation Service Monthly Narrative Summary, Red Cross 1935–1946, NARA; Brandt to Lewis, "Monthly Report for March 1945."

128. Megan Taylor Shockley, *"We, Too, Are Americans": African American Women in Detroit and Richmond, 1940–1954* (Urbana: University of Illinois Press, 2004), 41–47; Winchell, *Good Girls, Good Food, Good Fun.*

129. On the use of light-skinned black women as symbols of black womanhood during the war, see Megan E. Williams, "The *Crisis* Cover Girl: Lena Horne, the NAACP, and Representations of African American Femininity, 1941–1945," *American Periodicals* 16, no. 2 (2006): 200–218; McEuen, *Making War, Making Women,* 23–30; Lena Horne and Richard Schickel, *Lena* (New York: Limelight Editions, 1986), 172–177; Bloom, "Jim Crow Entertainment," 50–51. Joanne Meyerowitz shows that black women's opinions split over pinups. Some saw the images as beautiful and signs of racial progress in their appeal to many audiences, while others viewed them as dangerous symbols steeped in historical sexualized images of black women. See Joanne Meyerowitz, "Women, Cheesecake, and Borderline Material: Responses to Girlie Pictures in the Mid-Twentieth-Century U.S.," *Journal of Women's History* 8, no. 3 (Fall 1996): 18–21.

130. Enoc P. Waters, "Red Cross Worker in Australia Gets Hundreds of Proposals from Soldiers," *Chicago Defender,* October 30, 1943.

131. "Life on Alcan Highway Described by First Race Woman to Serve There," *Chicago Defender,* July 3, 1943.

132. Enoch P. Waters Jr., "Five-Foot Girl is 'Goddess' to Soldiers in New Guinea," *Chicago Defender,* September 16, 1944.

133. Tucker, *Swing Shift,* 233.

134. See, for example, Enoc P. Waters Jr., "Red Cross Girls Come as Xmas Gift to Doughboys," *Chicago Defender,* December 25, 1943; Enoch P. Waters Jr., "Deplores Shortage of Red Cross Workers Overseas," *Chicago Defender,* May 13, 1944; Tucker, *Swing Shift,* 234.

135. Enoch P. Waters Jr., "Woman Red Cross Worker is Idol of 10,000 Soldiers," *Chicago Defender,* August 12, 1944.

136. Quote in Walter White to Norman Davis, December 19, 1942; also Walter White to Norman Davis, August 18, 1942; Norman Davis to Walter White, August 24, 1942, all in American Red Cross, Service Clubs in England and Foreign Stations 1942–1944 Reel 2, Group II, Series A, General Office File, Part 15: Segregation and Discrimination, Complaints and Responses, 1940–1955, Series B: Administrative Files, NAACP. The NAACP saw segregation in Red Cross clubs and its segregation of blood plasma as connected problems. See Roy Wilkins to Ella Mae Vanderboget, March 2, 1943, American Red Cross, Service Clubs in England and Foreign Stations 1942–1944 Reel 2, Group II, Series A, General Office File, Part 15: Segregation and Discrimination, Complaints and Responses, 1940–1955, Series B: Administrative Files, NAACP; also Thomas A. Guglielmo, "'Red Cross, Double Cross': Race and America's World

War II–Era Blood Donor Service," *Journal of American History* 97, no. 1 (June 2010): 63–90.

137. Brooks, "Negro GI's Jim Crowed in India."

138. "Life on Alcan Highway Described by First Race Woman to Serve There."

139. Marjorie Lee Morgan, ed., *The Clubmobile: The ARC in the Storm* (St. Petersburg, FL: Hazlett Printing and Publishing, 1982), 46–47; Petesch, *War through the Hole of a Donut*, 19–20, 92–93.

140. Petesch, *War through the Hole of a Donut*, 50.

141. Petesch, *War through the Hole of a Donut*, 30.

142. Gretchen Schuyler to Dad, August 22, 1944, Schuyler Papers.

143. Gretchen Schuyler to family, June 7, 1944, Schuyler Papers.

144. Hazel Bowman to parents, November 27, 1944, Bowman Collection.

145. Norwalk, *Dearest Ones*, 190.

146. Norwalk, *Dearest Ones*, 7.

147. Jane Weir Phillips Scott to Mother and Dad, April 24, 1944, Jane Weir Phillips Scott, box 11, folder 8, Clubmobile Collection.

148. Appel, *Dancing with GIs*, 107–110.

149. Gretchen Schuyler to Dad, May 15, 1944, Schuyler Papers.

150. Gretchen Schuyler to Katie, June 20, 1944; Gretchen Schuyler V-mail to family, May 30, 1944; Gretchen Schuyler V-mail to Katie, July 27, 1944; all in Schuyler Papers.

151. Enoch P. Waters Jr., "La. Red Cross Girl in New Guinea 'Makes Good,'" *Chicago Defender*, September 9, 1944.

152. Jane Anne Jack to husband, March 17, 1943, Jane Anne McKee Jack, box 4, folder 7, Clubmobile Collection.

153. Jane Anne Jack to husband, May 16, 1943, Jane Anne McKee Jack, box 4, folder 7, Clubmobile Collection.

154. Jane Anne Jack to husband, July 13, 1944, Jane Anne McKee Jack, box 4, folder 7, Clubmobile Collection.

155. Jane Anne Jack to husband, August 6, 1944, Jane Anne McKee Jack, box 4, folder 7, Clubmobile Collection.

156. Elizabeth Phenix Wiesner, *Between the Lines: Overseas with the Red Cross and OSS in World War II* (Chevy Chase, MD: Posterity Press, 1998), 27, also 25–27. Wiesner's account of this experience appeared as Elizabeth Q. Phenix, "Critic Doffs Hat to 'Glamour Girls' in Africa," *New York Herald* Tribune, September 19, 1943.

157. Nathalie Fallon Chadwick, memoir, 89, Nathalie Fallon Chadwick, box 1, folder 8, Clubmobile Collection.

158. "War-Zone Wedding," *Life* 18, no. 6 (February 5, 1945): 32–33.

159. Angela Petesch to family, [February 1945], Angela Petesch, box 11, folder 4, Clubmobile Collection.

160. Gretchen Schuyler to family, March 5, 1945, Schuyler Papers.

161. Louise Buckley to the People, 24.

162. Jeanne Devereaux Perkins, interview by Laura Marrone, December 5, 2003, transcript, Jeanne Perkins Collection (AFC / 2001 / 001 / 11146), VHP.

163. Williams, interview by Elliott.

164. Hazel Bowman to parents, September 24, 1945, Bowman Collection.

165. Morgan, *The Clubmobile*, 81.

166. Gretchen Schuyler to Katie and all the rest, January 14, 1945, Schuyler Papers. See also Gretchen Schuyler to Katie, May 24, 1945, Schuyler Papers.

167. Elma Ernst Fay, "Through a Donut Hole," chap. 25, Elma Ernst Fay, box 2, folder 6, Clubmobile Collection.

168. Anne Ferguson Boy to family, September 7, 1944, in Boy, "The Experiences of One American Red Cross Clubmobiler," 138.

169. Wiesner, *Between the Lines*, 89, 88–89.

170. Hazel Bowman to parents, August 12, 1945, Bowman Collection.

171. Gretchen Schuyler to Dad, May 15, 1944, Schuyler Papers.

172. Williams, interview by Elliott.

173. Rexford, *Battlestars & Doughnuts*, 135, 115.

174. Margaret Greene, interview by Eric Elliott, June 25, 1999, Margaret Greene Papers, WVHP.

175. Reeves, interview by Adkins.

### 4. DANCING FOR DEMOCRACY

1. Quoted in Kathleen A. Stewart, "Coffee, Doughnuts, and a Witty Line of Chatter. The Korean War Letters of Helen Stevenson Meyner" (MA thesis, Lehigh University, 1998), 19, also 3–24.

2. Quoted in Stewart, "Coffee, Doughnuts, and a Witty Line of Chatter," 3.

3. Helen Stevenson Meyner diary, October 29, 1950, Subseries 1: Biographical and Personal, Meyner Papers.

4. Helen Stevenson Meyner diary, November 8, 1950, Subseries 1: Biographical and Personal, Meyner Papers; Helen Stevenson Meyner letters to family, November 8 and 18, 1950, Subseries 2: Correspondence, Meyner Papers.

5. Helen Stevenson Meyner letter to family, November 29, 1950, Subseries 2: Correspondence, Meyner Papers.

6. Helen Stevenson Meyner diary, December 4, 1950, Subseries 1: Biographical and Personal, Meyner Papers.

7. Helen Stevenson Meyner letters to family, December 17, 1950, and February 18, 1951, Subseries 2: Correspondence, Meyner Papers.

8. Helen Stevenson Meyner letter to family, April 16, 1951, Subseries 2: Correspondence, Meyner Papers.

9. Helen Stevenson Meyner letters to family, April 16 and 17, 1951, Subseries 2: Correspondence, Meyner Papers.

10. Helen Stevenson Meyner letters to family, April 22 and May 22, 1951, Subseries 2: Correspondence, Meyner Papers.

11. Helen Stevenson Meyner letter to family, April 30, 1951, Subseries 2: Correspondence, Meyner Papers.

12. Remarks by Thomas D. Kinton, USO Overseas Conference, November 29 and 30, and December 1, 1954, NCCS Historical Information (1940–1954), Box 24, Series 3: General Subject Files, 1940–1975, NCCS.

13. Arthur Mayer, "Report to the Chairman of the Red Cross in China-Burma-India," 8, 900.06 All Theaters, Visits and Inspection Trips, Red Cross 1935–1946, NARA.

14. "What Enlisted Men in China, India and Burma Think about the Red Cross," Report CBI-12, December 7, 1944, HD: 730 (Neuropsychiatry) Morale Surveys Enlisted Men in India and Burma, World War II Administrative Records, ZI, OSG; "Memorandum for General Lanham: Director, Information and Education Div.," December 7, 1945, Entertainment Council-General, General Subject Files, JANCWR, JANBC, both at NARA.

15. See W. O. Thompson Memorandum to Mr. John M. Russell, November 27, 1945, Entertainment Council-General, General Subject Files, JANCWR, JANBC, NARA; General Board, United States Forces, European Theater, "Report on Live Entertainment," Study No. 117, n.d., 3, MHI; "USO Camp Shows, Inc. (Stage, Radio and Screen) Report on Year of 1945," January 1, 1945–December 31, 1945, United Service Organizations Camp Shows Reports 1945, Weil Papers; "Permanent Agency Similar to USO to Give Camp Shows Advocated," *New York Times*, February 5, 1947.

16. Sporting equipment numbers in Earl F. Ziemke, *The U.S. Army in the Occupation of Germany, 1944–1946* (Washington, DC: US Government Printing Office, 1975), 332, http://www.history.army.mil/books/wwii/occ-gy/ch18.htm, accessed November 13, 2015.

17. James T. Nicholson to the Chairman, August 30, 1946, 900.616 All Theaters, Recreation—Reports, Red Cross 1935–1946, NARA.

18. "What Enlisted Men in China, India and Burma Think about the Red Cross."

19. "What Enlisted Men in China, India and Burma Think about the Red Cross," 15.

20. "What Enlisted Men in China, India and Burma Think about the Red Cross," 7. Some GIs opposed the use of Red Cross women at all in the clubs, though their recorded comments in opinion surveys are not always extensive enough to gauge their rationale. While some men might have believed women had no place in a war zone, others clarified that they wanted to keep women out of the clubs because they paid too much attention to officers. One GI proposed that keeping women out of the clubs would reduce "friction between officers and EM [enlisted men] over Red Cross women." Others explained that they believed Red Cross women unfairly dated officers who had the "exclusive use of the nurses." At least one GI felt the perceived slight was worth it. "It's good to see a white woman," he reasoned, "even if they are bags and cater to high-ranking officers." See "What Enlisted Men in China, India and Burma Think about the Red Cross," 7–18, quotes on 7, 18, 15.

21. Nicholson to Chairman, August 30, 1946; James T. Nicholson to William A. Stephens, August 26, 1946, 900.616 All Theaters, Policies and Agreements Regarding Red Cross Club Program, Red Cross 1935–1946, NARA; Historical Division, Euro-

pean Command, "Morale and Discipline in the European Command, 1945–1949," Occupation Forces in Europe Series, 1945–1949 (Karlsruhe, Germany, 1951), 114; *An Introduction to the Army Service Club Program*, Department of the Army Pamphlet No. 21-59 (Washington, DC: Department of the Army, October 19, 1953), 13.

22. Between January 1, 1946 and December 31, 1947, Camp Shows sent 1912 performers. Number derived from two reports: "USO Camp Shows, Inc. (Stage, Radio and Screen) Report on Year of 1945," 7; "Operation USO: Report of the President," January 9, 1948, 33, USO—Printed Material—Press Releases, Series P Welfare—General, OMR, Rockefeller Archive.

23. Quotes in "Truman Hails USO, Ending War Effort," *New York Times,* January 10, 1948. Also see "USO Shows Quit Europe," *New York Times,* January 19, 1947.

24. "An Introduction to the Army Service Club Program"; Office of the Chief Historian, European Command, "Recreation and Welfare," Occupation Forces in Europe Series, 1945–46 (Frankfurt-am-Main, Germany, 1947), 78–80.

25. Office of the Chief Historian, European Command, "Recreation and Welfare," 78–80.

26. M. Jean Moore Fasse, interview by Beth Carmichael, March 13, 2007, transcript, Fasse Papers; "Etta Barnett Now with Red Cross in Germany," *Atlanta Daily World,* December 28, 1947.

27. Alice H. Washington, "Atlantan Enthusiastic about Army Overseas Work," *Atlanta Daily World,* May 5, 1949; Grace L. Hewell obituary, *Washington Post,* April 10, 2008.

28. "They're the CATS," *New York Times,* May 15, 1949; Agee in "Army Seeks CATs to Plan Shows in Japan," *New York Times,* September 28, 1948; also see "Army Seeks Actresses," *Atlanta Constitution,* November 4, 1945.

29. Anne Bruyere, "100 Pinup Girls at $4,680 a Year Stir WAC Wrath," *Chicago Daily Tribune,* September 6, 1945.

30. "Entertainers Are Sought by Far East Command," *New York Times,* September 30, 1949; "Recreation Experts to Sail for Germany," *New York Times,* January 1, 1950; "Women Civilians Sought by Army," *New York Times,* January 25, 1959.

31. For the committee's recommendations that the USO be charged with military welfare, see Russel B. Reynolds to Basil O'Connor, February 1, 1949, and Maurice T. Moore et al. to James Forrestal, December 27, 1948, both in American National Red Cross, 1948–1949, Weil Papers. For the Red Cross's perspective, see Supplemental Recreation Activities Overseas, February 20, 1953, 900.616 AT, SRAO General, 1952–1953, Red Cross 1947–1964, NARA and Basil O'Connor to Russel B. Reynolds, January 17, 1949, Basil O'Connor to James Forrestal, February 21, 1949, and Basil O'Connor to James Forrestal, October 28, 1948, all in American National Red Cross, 1948–1949, Weil Papers.

32. "USO Reactivated by Truman Order," *New York Times,* February 20, 1949; "USO to Seek $4,650,000," *New York Times,* August 17, 1948; "U.S.O. to Close up for Lack of Funds," *New York Times,* January 25, 1950; "Others Take over U.S.O.'s Activities," *New York Times,* January 26, 1950; Lawrence Phillips, "Report of the Executive Vice-President on Operations of USO-Camp Shows Fiscal Year Ended December 30,

1951," 2683–2701, in "Camp Shows, Inc. a / k / a USO-Camp Shows, Inc. Records, 1941–1957," vol. 5, Records of Camp Shows, Inc., 1941–1957, Special Services Division, AGO, NARA; Robert Dechert to Thomas B. Knowles, August 10, 1950, Associated Services for the Armed Forces, Inc. Minutes 1950–1951; Meeting of Inter-Agency Representatives, February 17, 1950, Associated Services for the Armed Forces, Inc. Minutes 1950–1951; Resolution of ASAF Board to be Acted on Finally at its Meeting on Thursday, November 9th, November 3, 1950, Associated Services for the Armed Forces, Inc. 1950, all in Weil Papers.

33. President's Committee on Religion and Welfare in the Armed Forces, "Free Time in the Armed Forces," 9.

34. Quoted in William A. Taylor, *Every Citizen a Soldier: The Campaign for Universal Military Training after World War II* (College Station: Texas A&M University Press, 2014), 93. Also see Michael Hogan, *A Cross of Iron: Harry S. Truman and the Origins of the National Security State, 1945–1954* (Cambridge: Cambridge University Press, 1998); John Sager, "Universal Military Training and the Struggle to Define American Identity during the Cold War," *Federal History Journal* 5 (January 2013), http:// heinonline.org/HOL/P?h=hein.journals/fedhijr15&i=59, accessed January 26, 2018; Michael S. Sherry, *Preparing for the Next War: American Plans for Postwar Defense, 1941–1945* (New Haven, CT: Yale University Press, 1977), esp. 65–90; Mark R. Grandstaff, "Making the Military American: Advertising, Reform, and the Demise of an Antistanding Military Tradition, 1945–1955," *Journal of Military History* 60, no. 2 (April 1996): 299–324.

35. "Statement by the President Making Public a Report on Moral Safeguards for Selective Service Trainees," September 16, 1948, Harry S. Truman Library, http:// trumanlibrary.org/publicpapers/viewpapers.php?pid=1806, accessed November 9, 2015; The President's Committee on Religion and Moral Welfare and Character Guidance in the Armed Forces news release, December 21, 1948, President's Committee on Religion and Welfare in the Armed Forces Misc. 1948, Weil Papers. Truman established the President's Committee on Morals, Welfare, and Character Guidance in the Armed Services in October 1948 to advise and assist the military in providing this guidance. It was later renamed the President's Committee on Religion and Welfare in the Armed Forces. Executive Order 10013 of October 27, 1948, Establishing the President's Committee on Religious and Moral Welfare and Character Guidance in the Armed Forces, online by Gerhard Peters and John T. Woolley, The American Presidency Project, http://www.presidency.ucsb.edu/ws/?pid=78229, accessed November 9, 2015. The Fort Knox experiment also illustrates increased attention to soldier welfare in the era. See "Kid Gloves Ready for New Draftees," *New York Times,* October 23, 1948; Taylor, *Every Citizen a Soldier,* 109.

36. Donna Alvah, *Unofficial Ambassadors: American Military Families Overseas and the Cold War, 1946–1965* (New York: New York University Press, 2000).

37. "An Introduction to the Army Service Club Program," 7.

38. "USO Reactivated by Truman Order," *New York Times,* February 20, 1949.

39. "There's Still a Job for the USO," *Saturday Evening Post* 219, no. 15 (October 12, 1946): 160; President's Committee on Religion and Welfare in the Armed Forces, "Community Responsibility to our Peacetime Servicemen and Women," March 24, 1949, 1, President's Committee on Religion and Welfare in the Armed Forces Misc. 1949–1950, Weil Papers; "The U.S. Army Now: Younger, Soberer," *New York Times*, April 16, 1949.

40. "Back Them up Again! A Preliminary Statement of Information Concerning the United Service Fund for the Armed Forces," December 1950, Associated Services for the Armed Forces, Inc. Minutes 1950–1951, Weil Papers.

41. Grandstaff, "Making the Military American," 303.

42. President's Committee on Religion and Welfare in the Armed Forces, "Free Time in the Armed Forces," 10.

43. Penicillin became available in the military in 1944. Allan M. Brandt, *No Magic Bullet: A Social History of Venereal Disease in the United States since 1880* (New York: Oxford University Press, 1985), 161, 170–174. See also Grandstaff, "Making the Military American," 319–321. The military continued to try to rein in an alarming venereal disease rate by monitoring German women and supplying prophylaxis to soldiers. See Maria Höhn, "'You Can't Pin Sergeant's Stripes on an Archangel': Soldiering, Sexuality, and U.S. Army Policies in Germany," in *Over There: Living with the U.S. Military Empire from World War Two to the Present*, ed. Maria Höhn and Seungsook Moon (Durham, NC: Duke University Press, 2010), 118–122.

44. Mark A. McCloskey, "Visit to European Installations, June 1–July 3, 1949," President's Committee on Religion and Welfare in the Armed Forces 1939–1949, Weil Papers.

45. Lt. John G. Morris, "VD since VE Day," *Army Information Digest* 3, no. 4 (April 1948): 26. Also see Historical Division, European Command, "Morale and Discipline in the European Command, 1945–1949," 77–87; *The Secretary of the Army's Brochure for the President's Committee on Morals, Welfare, and Character Guidance in the Armed Services*, n.d., and *Program for Recreation, Career Planning, and Education in the Navy*, n.d., both in President's Committee on Religion and Welfare in the Armed Forces Misc. 1949–1950, Weil Papers; Taylor, *Every Citizen a Soldier*, 111.

46. Quoted in "Changing Attitude of the Army with Regard to Venereal Diseases," *American Journal of Public Health* 38, no. 8 (August 1948): 1151.

47. There is a vast literature on sexuality and the Cold War. See especially Elaine Tyler May, *Homeward Bound: American Families in the Cold War Era* (New York: Basic Books, 2008); Joanne Meyerowitz, *Not June Cleaver: Women and Gender in Postwar America, 1945–1960* (Philadelphia: Temple University Press, 1994).

48. Morris, "VD since VE Day," 27.

49. Quoted in Brandt, *No Magic Bullet*, 172.

50. The National Ad Hoc USO Survey Committee, "Survey of Voluntary Civilian Services for Military Personnel," 36, USO.

51. Morris, "VD since VE Day."

52. The President's Committee on Religion and Welfare in the Armed Forces news release, July 24, 1949.

53. Historical Division, European Command, "Morale and Discipline in the European Command, 1945–1949," 78, 79.

54. Quoted in Ann Elizabeth Pfau, *Miss Yourlovin: GIs, Gender, and Domesticity during World War II* (New York: Columbia University Press, 2008), chap. 3, para 1, www.gutenberg-e.org/pfau, accessed July 1, 2018. Dates from Susan Zeiger, *Entangling Alliances: Foreign War Brides and American Soldiers in the Twentieth Century* (New York: New York University Press, 2010), 155; Pfau, *Miss Yourlovin*, chap. 3, para. 5. On the ban, see also Höhn, "'You Can't Pin Sergeant's Stripes on an Archangel,'" 109–145; Petra Goedde, *GIs and Germans: Culture, Gender, and Foreign Relations, 1945–1949* (New Haven, CT: Yale University Press, 2003), chap. 3.

55. Quoted in Ziemke, *The U.S. Army in the Occupation of Germany*, 320–327.

56. Historical Division, European Command, "Morale and Discipline in the European Command, 1945–1949," 115.

57. The fraternization ban was lifted in October 1945, though a marriage ban held until December 1946. See Zeiger, *Entangling Alliances*, 150–160.

58. Margaret (Bettie) Gearhart Brodie to Rosie, September 22, 1945, Margaret Gearhart Brodie, box 1, folder 7, Clubmobile Collection. See also Rexford, *Battlestars & Doughnuts*, 95, 105.

59. Gretchen Schuyler to Katie, June 30, 1945, 2006-M174, Schuyler Papers.

60. "Minutes of a Special Meeting of the Talent Committee of the Hollywood Victory Committee," July 10, 1945, in "USO Camp Shows, Inc. (Stage, Radio, and Screen) Report on Year of 1945," 130.

61. Nicholson to Chairman, August 30, 1946, 3.

62. *The Secretary of the Army's Brochure for the President's Committee on Morals, Welfare, and Character Guidance in the Armed Services*, 13.

63. "Women 'Take Over' in Army Zones Abroad," *Chicago Defender*, April 17, 1948.

64. President's Committee on Religion and Welfare in the Armed Forces, "Free Time in the Armed Forces," February 28, 1951, 4. See also Office of the Chief Historian, European Command, "Recreation and Welfare," 73; Zeiger, *Entangling Alliances*, 150–162. For Germans' perspective on relations with the American forces, see Maria Höhn, *GIs and Fräuleins: The German-American Encounter in 1950s West Germany* (Chapel Hill: University of North Carolina Press, 2002). Recreation clubs were also used to promote good relations between soldiers and local populations in other countries. USO officials called for clubs in England in 1952 to "assist our troops in meeting the right people and in fostering better relations," while the Department of Defense approved the opening of a Red Cross club in Verdun in 1958 "to provide a place for relaxation of service people and their dependents away from their military environment and to promote closer Franco-American relationships." See Minutes, USO—Overseas Committee Meeting, May 5, 1952, United Service Organizations Reports 1952–1956 (scattered), Weil Papers; "Summary of Major Events and Problems (CSHIS-6 (R1)), Special Services Division, TAGO, July 1, 1958 to June 30, 1959,

A-8, Historical Summaries of Major Events and Problems, 55–60, Special Services Branch, Special Services Division, AGO, NARA.

65. Office of the Chief Historian, European Command, "Recreation and Welfare," 91; "The U.S. Army Now"; Höhn, "'You Can't Pin Sergeant's Stripes on an Archangel,'" 119–120.

66. *The Secretary of the Army's Brochure for the President's Committee on Morals, Welfare, and Character Guidance in the Armed Services,* 13.

67. Laurene (Pat) Bulkley Drane, "My Service with the American Red Cross in France and Germany, 1945–1946," 19, Laurene Bulkley Drane Papers, World War II Institute.

68. "The U.S. Army Now."

69. Howard Beresford and Harold Williams, Report, Special Services Study, October 16–November 3, 1950, President's Committee on Religion and Welfare in the Armed Forces 1950 Nov.–Dec., Weil Papers, Marcus Center. Also see Howard C. Beresford, "Observations on Special Services," November 15, 1950, President's Committee on Religion and Welfare in the Armed Forces 1950 Nov.–Dec., Weil Papers; President's Committee on Religion and Welfare in the Armed Forces, "Free Time in the Armed Forces," vii.

70. Grandstaff, "Making the Military American," 316.

71. Fasse, interview by Carmichael.

72. Jean Moore Fasse, *My Journey Wasn't Easy: From Farm to City to an International Career,* ed. Charles R. George (Chapel Hill, NC: Chapel Hill Press, 2001), 65–96.

73. "Red Cross Girl: Myrtle Gross Finds Fun and Work in Germany," *Ebony* 2, no. 6 (April 1947): 48–50.

74. Yasuhiro Okada, "Negotiating Race and Womanhood across the Pacific: African American Women in Japan under U.S. Military Occupation, 1945–1952," *Black Women, Gender, and Families* 6, no. 1 (Spring 2012): 77–79.

75. Ethel Payne interview by Kathleen Currie, September 8, 1987, 26, also August 25, 1987, 17, Washington Press Club Foundation, beta.wpcf.org/oralhistory/payn.html, accessed March 9, 2016; James McGrath Morris, *Eye on the Struggle: Ethel Payne, the First Lady of the Black Press* (New York: Amistad, 2015), 9–16, 58–59.

76. Helen Stevenson Meyner letter to family, November 4, 1950 and December 10, 1950, Subseries 2: Correspondence, Meyner Papers.

77. Helen Stevenson Meyner letter to family, January 27, 1951, Subseries 2: Correspondence, Meyner Papers; also Helen Stevenson Meyner diary, January 26, 1951, Subseries 1: Biographical and Personal, Meyner Papers.

78. "Afro Readers Say," *Baltimore Afro-American,* May 11, 1946.

79. Executive Order No. 9981, *Code of Federal Regulations: Title 3—The President, 1943–1948 Compilation* (Washington, DC: Government Printing Office, 1957), 722; Kimberley L. Phillips, *War! What Is It Good For? Black Freedom Struggles and the U.S. Military from World War II to Iraq* (Chapel Hill: University of North Carolina Press, 2012), chaps. 2–3; Bernard C. Nalty, *Strength for the Fight: A History of Black Americans in the Military* (New York: The Free Press, 1986), chaps. 15–17.

80. "USO Shows Nix Segregation of Acts," *Pittsburgh Courier,* April 14, 1951.

81. "General Summary Report American Red Cross Club Program—Korea, November 1950–June 1952," 2, Subseries 3: Organizations, Box 10 Folder 47a American Red Cross, Meyner Papers.

82. "Atlanta U. Grad Leaves for Korea," *Atlanta Daily World,* September 17, 1950; "Red Cross Club Worker Tells of Trip to Korean Front Lines."

83. "Red Cross Club Worker Tells of Trip to Korean Front Lines."

84. Helen Stevenson Meyner letter to family, January 14, 1951, Subseries 2: Correspondence, Meyner Papers.

85. Helen Stevenson Meyner letter to family, January 27, 1951, Subseries 2: Correspondence, Meyner Papers.

86. Helen Stevenson Meyner letter to family, February 18, 1951, Subseries 2: Correspondence, Meyner Papers.

87. Harry McAlpin, "Says Red Cross Practices Bias in Pacific," *Atlanta Daily World,* October 27, 1945.

88. Margaret V. Scott to Constance B. Motley, August 11, 1948, Soldier Complaints, 1942–1948, Reel 11, Group II, Series G Veterans Affairs Department, Part 9 Discrimination in U.S. Armed Forces, 1918–45, Series C Veterans Affairs Committee 1940–1950, NAACP (hereafter NAACP Soldier Complaints). Scott subsequently brought the matter to the attention of Jesse O. Dedmon, secretary of Veterans' Affairs for the NAACP, in an attempt to "lessen the chances for such incidents to happen in the future." Quote in Margaret V. Scott to Jesse O. Dedmon, September 25, 1948, also Memorandum to Jesse O. Dedmon from Marian W. Perry, August 30, 1948, and [Jesse O. Dedmon] to Margaret V. Scott, September 23, 1948, all in NAACP Soldier Complaints. Unfortunately, the files do not indicate a resolution to Scott's quest to be reimbursed for her travel expenses. See Margaret V. Scott to Jesse O. Dedmon, September 29, 1948; Thomas C. Cassady to Murray N. Goodrich, September 2, 1948; and Margaret V. Scott to Jesse O. Dedmon, November 29, 1948, and January 12, 1949; all in NAACP Soldier Complaints.

89. "GI's Puzzled over Red Cross Attitude," *Atlanta Daily World,* September 23, 1945.

90. "Merge Red Cross Clubs in Italy; Staffs Interracial," *Chicago Defender,* March 30, 1946.

91. P. L. Prattis, "The Horizon: Democracy Can Thrive, If Given a Chance, Even in the Red Cross Service," *Pittsburgh Courier,* June 1, 1946; "Interracial Red Cross Naples Staff Praised," *Atlanta Daily World,* April 10, 1946.

92. Helen Stevenson Meyner letter to family, December 10, 1950, Subseries 2: Correspondence, Meyner Papers.

93. Helen Stevenson Meyner letter to family, December 18, 1950, Subseries 2: Correspondence, Meyner Papers.

94. Helen Stevenson Meyner letter to family, January 27, 1951, Subseries 2: Correspondence, Meyner Papers.

95. Helen Stevenson Meyner letter to family, November 27, 1951, Subseries 2: Correspondence, Meyner Papers.

96. Helen Stevenson Meyner letter to family, December 11, 1951, Subseries 2: Correspondence, Meyner Papers.

97. Helen Stevenson Meyner letter to family, January 27, 1951, Subseries 2: Correspondence, Meyner Papers.

98. The National Ad Hoc USO Survey Committee, "Survey of Voluntary Civilian Services for Military Personnel," 41.

99. Requests for USO Services Overseas, [1956], United Service Organizations Reports 1952–1956 (scattered), Weil Papers.

100. Margaret Flora Macdonald, "A History of the American Red Cross Mobile Recreation Program in Korea, 1953–1956" (MA thesis, University of Oregon, June 1957), 89.

101. Ethel Payne, "Says Japanese Girls Playing GIs for Suckers," *Chicago Defender,* November 18, 1950, and November 25, 1950 (two-part series). See also L. Alex Wilson, "Why Tank Yanks go for Japanese Girls," *Chicago Defender,* November 11, 1950; Payne interview by Currie, August 25, 1987, 20, 31–33.

102. Quoted in Macdonald, "A History of the American Red Cross Mobile Recreation Program in Korea," 80.

103. Nelson J. Riley, "Red Cross Clubmobiles Roll in Korea," *Army Information Digest* 9, no. 2 (1954): 14.

104. American National Red Cross Supplemental Recreational Activities Overseas, April 1, 1953, 900.616 AT, SRAO General, 1952–1953, Red Cross 1947–1964, NARA; Macdonald, "A History of the American Red Cross Mobile Recreation Program in Korea," 19–23, 51, Appendix C, 147; "General Summary Report American Red Cross Club Program—Korea, November 1950–June 1952," 1, Meyner Organizations, Box 10 Folder 47a American Red Cross, Meyner Papers; Riley, "Red Cross Clubmobiles Roll in Korea," 14, 16. At least one Red Cross club in Pusan was temporarily evacuated in late 1950. See "Red Cross Club Worker Tells of Trip to Korean Front Lines," *Atlanta Daily World,* January 30, 1951.

105. "General Summary Report American Red Cross Club Program—Korea, November 1950–June 1952," 2–3; Macdonald, "A History of the American Red Cross Mobile Recreation Program in Korea," 23–30; Riley, "Red Cross Clubmobiles Roll in Korea," 14–15. Also see "Red Cross to Add Korea Units," *New York Times,* May 23, 1951; Stewart, "Coffee, Doughnuts, and a Witty Line of Chatter."

106. The July 1953 cease-fire changed the arrangement of recreation services in Korea. The congressional charter that governed the Red Cross's work with the military gave it the authority to act during times of war, not peace, which meant that the organization had no authorization to work with the military after the armistice was signed. Moreover, while military and civilian officials hoped to provide as much entertainment for as many troops as possible, they also wanted to avoid duplicating each other's services. Thus, with the USO providing live entertainment and Special Services able to assume operation of all service clubs in June 1952, Red Cross leaders contemplated if and how the organization could remain involved in military recreation. Despite the cease-fire, the military predicted an extended presence in Korea,

among other places, and in July 1953 Congress expanded the president's authority to work with the Red Cross whenever he believed its services would be useful. See Brief Summary of Supplemental Recreational Activities Overseas, American Red Cross Clubmobile Service in Korea, October 1953–October 1954, 900.616 All Theaters, Recreation, Red Cross 1947–1964, NARA; Macdonald, "A History of the American Red Cross Mobile Recreation Program in Korea," 25–30; Riley, "Red Cross Clubmobiles Roll in Korea," 14–15; Memorandum of Understanding between the Department of Defense and the United Service Organizations, Inc., March 27, 1951, United Service Organizations Reports 1952–1956 (scattered), Weil Papers; *An Act to Provide for the Use of the American National Red Cross in Aid of the Armed Forces, and for Other Purposes,* Public Law 131, *U.S. Statutes at Large* 67 (1953): 178–179.

107. Brief Summary of Supplemental Recreational Activities Overseas; Macdonald, "A History of the American Red Cross Mobile Recreation Program in Korea," 3–5, 35; "Red Cross Requires Workers for Korea," *New York Times,* September 10, 1953.

108. Macdonald, "A History of the American Red Cross Mobile Recreation Program in Korea," 55.

109. The Red Cross states that 899 women served as Donut Dollies in Korea from 1953 to 1973. http://embed.widencdn.net/pdf/plus/americanredcross/uvz9xq0szm /history-korean-war.pdf?u=oa0rmr, accessed May 9, 2018.

110. G. C. Marshall to Harvey S. Firestone Jr., December 19, 1950, President's Committee on Religion and Welfare in the Armed Forces 1939–1949, Weil Papers. The renewed USO revived the World War II–era organization and merged it with the Associated Services for the Armed Forces, an organization that melded the efforts of the Jewish Welfare Board, the YMCA, and the National Catholic Community Service. These three agencies had been members of the USO during World War II and had pledged to continue their work with the armed forces after the USO discontinued its work. See United Service Organizations, Inc. and Associated Services for the Armed Forces, Inc., President's Committee on Religion and Welfare in the Armed Forces 1951–1954 and Memorandum of Understanding between the Department of Defense and the United Service Organizations, Inc., March 27, 1951, United Service Organizations Reports 1952–1956 (scattered), both in Weil Papers; Department of Defense Press Release No. 493-50, April 30, 1950, H&W Organizations-Associated Services for the Armed Forces, Assistant Secretary of Defense (MPR) Office of Personnel Policy, Military Personnel Policy Division, Morale and Welfare Branch General File 1949–1952, RG 330 Records of the Office of the Secretary of Defense, NARA; "U.S.O. Returning to Serve Soldiers," *New York Times,* January 12, 1951.

111. "Show being Prepared for Troops in Korea," *New York Times,* May 9, 1951; Lawrence Phillips, "Report of the Executive Vice-President on Operations of USO-Camp Shows Fiscal Year Ended December 28, 1952," in "Camp Shows, Inc. a / k / a USO-Camp Shows, Inc. Records, 1941–1957," 5:2709, and James Sauter to Board of Directors, April 30, 1953, "Camp Shows, Inc. a / k / a USO-Camp Shows, Inc. Records, 1941–1957," 5:2675–2676, both in Records of Camp Shows, Inc., 1941–1957, Special Services Division, AGO, NARA; Lawrence Phillips, "Report of the Executive Vice-

President on Operations of USO-Camp Shows Fiscal Year Ended December 28, 1952"; "Camp Shows to Go on," *New York Times*, August 11, 1951; "U.S.O. Need Seen Rising," *New York Times*, July 27, 1953; "Wall Street Views a U.S.O. Camp Show before Troupe Starts for Tour of Far East," *New York Times*, August 12, 1953.

112. "43 from Hollywood Set for Holiday Camp Tours," *Los Angeles Times*, December 7, 1953; "Summary of Major Events and Problems (CSHIS-6)," Special Services Division, TAGO, July 1, 1957 to June 30, 1958, A-22–23, D-2, Historical Summaries of Major Events and Problems, 55–60, Special Services Branch, Special Services Division, AGO, NARA. The USO restructured its services in the wake of the armistice. Since the reorganization of the USO in 1951, Camp Shows had been a separate, affiliated entity that depended on the umbrella organization for its funding. In early 1957, the Department of the Army granted the USO permission to establish clubs in large overseas metropolitan areas, and though Camp Shows continued to send shows abroad that year, the USO's growing focus on clubs led Camp Shows to conclude its work at the end of the year. The USO created a new division called USO Shows to organize live entertainment. Thereafter, the USO attempted to balance its desire to open clubs with the Department of Defense's pleas for more professional entertainment. See "Summary of Major Events and Problems (Reports Control Symbol CSHIS-6)," Special Services Division, TAGO, July 1, 1955 to June 30, 1956, D-3; "Summary of Major Events and Problems (CSHIS-6)," Special Services Division, TAGO, July 1, 1956 to June 30, 1957, A-29, 30, D-1–2; and "Summary of Major Events and Problems (CSHIS-6 (R1))," Special Services Division, TAGO, July 1, 1958, to June 30, 1959, A-4–8, all in Historical Summaries of Major Events and Problems, 55–60, Special Services Branch; "Camp Shows, Inc. a/k/a USO-Camp Shows, Inc. Records, 1941–1957," 1:xiv–xv, Records of Camp Shows, Inc., 1941–1957, all in Special Services Division, AGO, NARA; "New U.S.O. Troupe to Entertain G.I.'s," *New York Times*, November 1, 1957; "Camp Shows Face December Finale," *New York Times*, July 17, 1957.

113. Maria Höhn and Seungsook Moon, "The Politics of Gender, Sexuality, Race, and Class in the U.S. Military Empire," in Höhn and Moon, *Over There*, 18.

114. "A Non-Statistical Evaluation of Live Entertainment for United States Armed Forces Personnel in Alaska, the Far East, Islands of the Pacific, Europe, North Africa, Northeast Air Command," 1957, in "Camp Shows, Inc. a/k/a USO-Camp Shows, Inc. Records, 1941–1957," 7:3613, Records of Camp Shows, Inc., 1941–1957, Special Services Division, AGO, NARA.

115. A similar situation occurred in Japan, where the Japanese government organized the Recreation and Amusement Association to provide sexual services for the occupation army. The Japanese feared that US forces would rape local women and offered "comfort facilities" in an attempt to protect "good" women from harm. See John W. Dower, *Embracing Defeat: Japan in the Wake of World War II* (New York: W. W. Norton, 1999), 123–132; Michiko Takeuchi, "'Pan-Pan Girls' Performing and Resisting Neocolonialism(s) in the Pacific Theater: U.S. Military Prostitution in Occupied Japan, 1945–1952," in Höhn and Moon, *Over There*, 78–89; Yuki Tanaka,

*Japan's Comfort Women: Sexual Slavery and Prostitution during World War II and the US Occupation* (New York: Routledge, 2002).

116. Seungsook Moon, "Regulating Desire, Managing the Empire: U.S. Military Prostitution in South Korea, 1945–1970," in Höhn and Moon, *Over There,* 39–77, quote on 54; Zeiger, *Entangling Alliances,* 206–214. Naoko Shibusawa discusses how American soldiers stationed in Japan during the occupation were attracted to Japanese women's exotic beauty and their submissive behaviors. She notes that GIs in Korea were fans of a collection of "semi-pornographic" cartoons featuring Japanese women. See Naoko Shibusawa, *America's Geisha Ally: Reimagining the Japanese Enemy* (Cambridge, MA: Harvard University Press, 2006), 34–47, quote on 36. For a longer history of sexualized images of Asian women, see Jeffrey A. Keith, "Producing Miss Saigon: Imaginings, Realities, and the Sensual Geography of Saigon," *Journal of American–East Asian Relations* 22 (2015): 243–272.

117. Moon, "Regulating Desire, Managing the Empire," 54.

118. The National Ad Hoc USO Survey Committee, "Survey of Voluntary Civilian Services for Military Personnel," 44.

119. "A Non-Statistical Evaluation of Live Entertainment for United States Armed Forces Personnel," 3616. See also Edwin E. Bond, "USO Services in the Far East: An Address to USO Board of Governors," June 21, 1956, 4, United Service Organizations Reports 1952–1956 (scattered), Weil Papers.

120. "SRAO Staff Orientation for New Arrivals in Korea," 900.616 AT (FEA), SRAO 1958–, Red Cross 1947–1964, NARA.

121. Helen Stevenson Meyner letter to family, April 30, 1951, Subseries 2: Correspondence, Meyner Papers.

122. Moon, "Regulating Desire, Managing the Empire," 48; Sandra Lockney Davis, *So, What's a Nice Girl Like You Doing in a Place Like This? Seoul to Saigon* (Gulf Breeze, FL: East Bay Publishers, 2011), 60–61.

123. Lawrence Phillips, "Report of the Executive Vice-President on Operations of USO-Camp Shows Fiscal Year Ended December 28, 1952," in "Camp Shows, Inc. a/k/a USO-Camp Shows, Inc. Records, 1941–1957," 5:2713, Records of Camp Shows, Inc., 1941–1957, Special Services Division, AGO, NARA.

124. Lawrence Phillips, "Instructions to All Paid or Sponsored Entertainers," n.d. [1950s], in "Camp Shows, Inc. a/k/a USO-Camp Shows, Inc. Records, 1941–1957," 7:3686, Records of Camp Shows, Inc., 1941–1957, Special Services Division, AGO, NARA.

125. Minutes, USO Special Meeting of Operation Policy Committee, February 15, 1956, United Service Organizations Reports 1952–1956 (scattered), Weil Papers.

126. "Cute, but controversial" in "Film Artist is Ordered from Korea," *News-Sentinel* (Lodi, CA), December 26, 1952; "little Santa Claus" in Stan Carter, "Terry Moore Packs Away Her Controversial Bathing Suit," *Gettysburg Times,* December 26, 1953. Also see "Terry's Korea Suit Chills Her, but Warms Up GIs," *Los Angeles Times,* December 25, 1953.

127. Cover, *Life,* July 6, 1953.

128. Hedda Hopper, "Terry Didn't Tarry on the Road to Success!," *Chicago Tribune Magazine,* January 17, 1954, 21.

129. Carter, "Terry Moore Packs Away Her Controversial Bathing Suit."

130. "Terry Packs Her Swim Suit and Gets Out of Hot Water," *Chicago Daily Tribune,* December 27, 1953.

131. See "Marilyn Monroe Wows Servicemen in Korea," *Deseret News and Telegram,* February 16, 1954; "GI Trampled as 6,000 Surge to View Marilyn," *Chicago Daily Tribune,* February 19, 1954; "40th GIs Stampede at Sight of Marilyn," *Los Angeles Times,* February 1, 1954; "Whistles Greet Marilyn on Tour of Korea Front," *Sarasota Herald-Tribune,* February 15, 1954; C. Robert Jennings, "The Strange Case of Marilyn Monroe vs. the U.S. Army," *Los Angeles Magazine* (August 1966): 31–33, 58–63; Kristi Good, "Marilyn Monroe: Soldier in Greasepaint," *Theatre History Studies* 33 (2014): 209–225.

132. "40th GIs Stampede at Sight of Marilyn."

133. "New Pinup Queen Says She Prefers Books," *Pittsburgh Post-Gazette,* January 6, 1951; "The Pin-Up Takes Shape," *Life,* March 1, 1954, 29.

134. Hugh Hefner chose featured the photograph as the centerfold in the inaugural December 1953 issue of *Playboy.* Marilyn Monroe and Ben Hect, *My Story* (Lanham, MD: Taylor Trade Publishing, 2007), 157. On her popularity among GIs in Korea, see also "Star Poses for Airmen," *Eagle* (Reading, PA), February 19, 1954; Marilyn Monroe, "I'll Always Remember . . . My Trip to Korea," *Parade,* July 22, 1956; Donald Spoto, *Marilyn Monroe: The Biography* (New York: HarperCollins, 1993), 192, 264; Lois Banner, *Marilyn: The Passion and the Paradox* (New York: Bloomsbury, 2012), 158, 175–176.

135. When an Air Force colonel showed her his copy of the calendar, she insisted that she was "very pleased to have my picture hanging in a place of honor." See "The Pin-Up Takes Shape"; "Marilyn Stirs Korean Front to Wild Action," *Pittsburgh Post-Gazette,* February 17, 1954; Jennings, "The Strange Case of Marilyn Monroe vs. the U.S. Army," 59; Banner, *Marilyn,* 158, 175–76, 219–220.

136. "Marilyn Monroe Wows Servicemen in Korea"; "40th GIs Stampede at Sight of Marilyn."

137. "Star Poses for Airmen."

138. Monroe and Hect, *My Story,* 183. For videos of her performances, see "Rare Footage of Marilyn Monroe Entertaining the Troops on Stage in Korea 1954," uploaded by the Marilyn Monroe Video Archives, YouTube, https://youtu.be/DDAo084gZWc, accessed December 9, 2015. Biographer Donald Spoto notes that her version of the song was widely known for its sexual innuendo. She had performed the song at Camp Pendleton in California in 1952 and caused "a riot of applause and a stampede toward the stage" on that occasion as well. See Spoto, *Marilyn Monroe,* 209.

139. Monroe, "I'll Always Remember . . . My Trip to Korea." Also see "GI Trampled as 6,000 Surge to View Marilyn." The word had apparently been well known among soldiers in Korea for some time. In 1947, soldiers at a Red Cross club dressed in feminine attire for a cross-dressed beauty contest. One of the entries was named

"Miss Eddie Whau," which the Red Cross translated as meaning "Come Here in G.I. Korean." See Quadrangle Club Monthly Narrative Report, April 1947, 4, in Russell Blair Papers collection, World War II Institute.

140. "The Pin-Up Takes Shape."

141. Mrs. J. Broadus Haynes and James F. Orlay, letters to the editor, *Life,* March 22, 1954, 19.

142. "McCarthy and the Army," *New York Times,* February 21, 1954. The Italian weekly *La Domenica del Corriere* ran a back-cover illustration that showed American GIs climbing over top of each other to reach a seductively posed Marilyn Monroe. Illustration by Walter Molino, March 7, 1954.

143. Edward M. Flanagan, Jr., "Hollywood Can't Make Soldiers," *Army Combat Forces Journal* 6 (December 1955): 22–24.

144. "Soldiers, Not 'Cowboys,'" *Pittsburgh Post-Gazette,* February 25, 1954; Robert A. Javens, C. A. Henderson, and David W. Frank, letter to the editor, *Pittsburgh Post-Gazette,* March 24, 1954.

145. "An Introduction to the Army Service Club Program," 20.

146. "An Introduction to the Army Service Club Program," 14, 22, 25.

147. Mary Louise Dowling to Robert C. Lewis, January 31, 1961, and August 26, 1959, 12–13, both in 900.616 AT (FEA), SRAO 1958–, Red Cross 1947–1964, NARA.

148. May, *Homeward Bound.*

149. "Summary of Major Events and Problems (Reports Control Symbol CSHIS-6), Special Services Division, TAGO, July 1, 1955 to June 30, 1956, Historical Summaries of Major Events and Problems, 55–60, Special Services Branch, Special Services Division, AGO, NARA; "Army Seeking Women Leaders for Special Services Program," *New York Times,* November 8, 1959; "Service Clubs in Drive." On underemployed servicemen's wives, see Alvah, *Unofficial Ambassadors,* 87.

150. "An Introduction to the Army Service Club Program," 21.

151. "An Introduction to the Army Service Club Program," 17, 22.

152. "Army Seeking Hostesses in Pacific Bases," *Chicago Daily Tribune,* December 8, 1947.

153. "An Introduction to the Army Service Club Program," quote on 19, also 23.

154. "They're the CATS."

155. "Women Civilians Sought by Army."

156. Fasse, interview by Carmichael.

157. Macdonald, "A History of the American Red Cross Mobile Recreation Program in Korea," 104. Of the first one hundred SRAO in Korea, seventeen resigned to marry (ten before completing their term of service). See Mary Louise Dowling to Norman Durfee, August 25, 1955, 900.616 AT, SRAO General 1954–, Red Cross 1947–1964, NARA.

158. "Sp Service Club Miss Typical is Trim, Educated," January 13, 1956, news clipping in FY 1956 Inclosures, in "Summary of Major Events and Problems (Reports Control Symbol CSHIS-6), Special Services Division, TAGO, July 1, 1955 to June 30, 1956, Historical Summaries of Major Events and Problems, 55–60, Special Services Branch, Special Services Division, AGO, NARA.

159. "Marries in Germany," *Pittsburgh Courier,* April 9, 1949.

160. Payne interview by Currie, August 25, 1987, quote on 18, also 17–18.

161. Norman W. Drescher, "Briefing Information," in "Camp Shows, Inc. a / k / a USO-Camp Shows, Inc. Records, 1941–1957," 7:3523A, 7:3524, Records of Camp Shows, Inc., 1941–1957, Special Services Division, AGO, NARA.

162. General Board, United States Forces, European Theater, "Special Services Clubs," Study No. 121, [1945 or 1946], 7, MHI.

163. "The U.S. Army Now." See also Mary Louise Dowling to Norman A. Durfee, September 26, 1961, 900.616 AT, SRAO General 1954–, Red Cross 1947–1964, NARA.

164. President's Committee on Religion and Welfare in the Armed Forces, "Community Responsibility to our Peacetime Servicemen and Women," 17.

165. In 1947, applicants for hostess positions in Germany still had to be between twenty-five and thirty-five years of age. "Army Seeks Hostesses for Reich," *New York Times,* May 25, 1947. By the mid-1950s, women had to be twenty-three for the entry level position of recreation leader, twenty-six to be an assistant club director, and thirty to be a club director. "Summary of Major Events and Problems (Reports Control Symbol CSHIS-6), Special Services Division, TAGO, July 1, 1955 to June 30, 1956, Historical Summaries of Major Events and Problems, 55–60, Special Services Branch, Special Services Division, AGO, NARA; "Red Cross Seeks Aides," *New York Times,* January 30, 1955. Another source suggests the Red Cross imposed an age ceiling of thirty for the Korean War. See Ella T. Cruise, "Recreation on the Move—in Korea," *Recreation* 49 (January 1956): 15–17. It does appear that the Red Cross allowed some women to serve who were below the age requirement. Helen Stephenson Meyner joined the service in October 1950 when she was twenty-two years old. See Helen Stevenson Meyner diary, October 29, 1950, Subseries 1: Biographical and Personal, Meyner Papers.

166. The Army increased its standard in the mid-1950s from two years of college to a four-year degree, preferably in a recreation-related field. The Red Cross required a college degree but on occasion admitted women without one, provided they exhibited other desired qualities. See "Summary of Major Events and Problems (Reports Control Symbol CSHIS-6), Special Services Division, TAGO, July 1, 1955 to June 30, 1956, Historical Summaries of Major Events and Problems, 55–60, Special Services Branch, Special Services Division, AGO, NARA; John H. Thompson, "Army Seeking 350 Hostesses for Overseas," *Chicago Daily Tribune,* May 5, 1955; "Women Civilians Sought by Army"; "Army Seeking Women Leaders for Special Services Program," *New York Times,* November 8, 1959; "Service Clubs in Drive," *New York Times,* February 19, 1961; Norman A. Durfee to Mr. Herbert et al., February 14, 1958, and Norman A. Durfee to Mr. Herbert et al., December 9, 1959, both in 900.616 AT, SRAO personnel 1953–59, Red Cross 1947–1964, NARA.

167. In November 1958, for example, the average Donut Dolly recruit was twenty-four. Mary Louise Dowling to Norman A. Durfee, November 20, 1958, 900.616 AT, SRAO Personnel 1953–59, Red Cross 1947–1964, NARA.

168. Grace Swank Alexander, interview by Hermann Trojanowski, January 20, 1999, transcript, Grace Alexander Oral History, WV0018.5.001, WVHP.

169. Morris, *Eye on the Struggle,* 67.

170. "Summary of Major Events and Problems (Reports Control Symbol CSHIS-6), Special Services Division, TAGO, July 1, 1955 to June 30, 1956, "Service Club Personnel" pages, Historical Summaries of Major Events and Problems, 55–60, Special Services Branch, Special Services Division, AGO, NARA; also "Women Civilians Sought by Army."

171. "Report by Manager of Overseas Unit #1023 in the Far-East and Mid Pacific, April 21 through August 4, 1952," in USO-Camp Shows, Inc. 1951 and 1952 Report to the Board of Directors and the Advisory Council, April 30, 1953, 15, 701-01 Special Service Instr Files USO, Inc.—USO Camp Shows, 1951–1952, Army Education and Morale Support Directorate Executive Office, Selected Permanent Subject Files, 1953–1968, AGO, NARA.

172. "Philly Singer Charms Weary GIs in Japan," *Chicago Defender,* August 30, 1952.

173. Thompson, "Army Seeking 350 Hostesses for Overseas"; "Service Clubs in Drive."

174. Thompson, "Army Seeking 350 Hostesses for Overseas."

175. "Sp Service Club Miss Typical is Trim, Educated."

176. Linda Witt, Judith Bellafaire, Britta Granrud, and Mary Jo Binker, *"A Defense Weapon Known to Be of Value: Servicewomen of the Korean War Era* (Hanover, NH: University Press of New England, 2005), 52–55.

177. "An Introduction to the Army Service Club Program," quote on 28, also 29–30. D'Armitage company in "Summary of Major Events and Problems (CSHIS-6), Special Services Division, TAGO, July 1, 1957 to June 30, 1958, C-29 and "Summary of Major Events and Problems (CSHIS-6 (R1))," Special Services Division, TAGO, July 1, 1958 to June 30, 1959, C-23, both in Historical Summaries of Major Events and Problems, 55–60, Special Services Branch, Special Services Division, AGO, NARA.

178. "An Introduction to the Army Service Club Program," quotes on 28, also 29–30.

179. Employment Inquiry for Miss Crane, October 19, 1959, 262 Exit Interview Files (1959), Army Education and Morale Support Directorate Executive Office Selected Permanent Subject Files, 1953–1968, AGO, NARA.

180. Davis, *So, What's a Nice Girl Like You Doing in a Place Like This?,* 27.

181. "An Introduction to the Army Service Club Program," 28.

182. Norman W. Drescher, "Briefing Information," 3524, and Lawrence Phillips to John Leo Fogarty, March 24, 1947, 3486, both in "Camp Shows, Inc. a / k / a USO-Camp Shows, Inc. Records, 1941–1957," vol. 7, Records of Camp Shows, Inc., 1941–1957, Special Services Division, AGO, NARA.

183. "Summary of Major Events and Problems (Reports Control Symbol CSHIS-6)," Special Services Division, TAGO, July 1, 1955 to June 30, 1956, A-6, Historical Summaries of Major Events and Problems, 55–60, Special Services Branch, Special Services Division, AGO, NARA.

184. "Summary of Major Events and Problems (Reports Control Symbol CSHIS-6)," Special Services Division, TAGO, July 1, 1955 to June 30, 1956, A-39-A-41, C-5; "Summary of Major Events and Problems (CSHIS-6)," Special Services Division, TAGO, July 1, 1956 to June 30, 1957, A-39-A-45; "Summary of Major Events and Problems

(CSHIS-6)," Special Services Division, TAGO, July 1, 1957 to June 30, 1958, Inclo-sures A-3R-A6R; "Summary of Major Events and Problems (CSHIS-6 (R1))," Spe-cial Services Division, TAGO, July 1, 1959 to June 30, 1960, B-4-B10; all in Historical Summaries of Major Events and Problems, 55–60, Special Services Branch, Special Services Division, AGO, NARA; "Army Needs 100 Women," *New York Times,* No-vember 10, 1953; "Recreation Aides Leave for Europe," *New York Times,* December 1, 1957; "Army Seeking Women Leaders for Special Services Program," *New York Times,* November 8, 1959; "Service Clubs in Drive."

185. "Summary of Major Events and Problems (Reports Control Symbol CSHIS-6)," Special Services Division, TAGO, July 1, 1955 to June 30, 1956, A-6, Historical Sum-maries of Major Events and Problems, 55–60, Special Services Branch, Special Services Division, AGO, NARA.

186. "Summary of Major Events and Problems (CSHIS-6)," Special Services Division, TAGO, July 1, 1956 to June 30, 1957, A-43, Inclosure A-8R, Historical Summaries of Major Events and Problems, 55–60, Special Services Branch, Special Services Divi-sion, AGO, NARA.

187. Thompson, "Army Seeking 350 Hostesses for Overseas."

188. "Recreation Aides Sought by Army," *New York Times,* January 20, 1957.

189. Army Special Services advertisement, *Mademoiselle,* October 1957, 68; "2 Area Women Cheer Selves, GIs Overseas," *Chicago Daily Tribune,* December 30, 1956.

190. Washington, "Atlantan Enthusiastic about Army Overseas Work."

191. "Red Cross Seeks Aides," Average women's salaries in U.S. Department of Com-merce, "Current Population Reports Consumer Income," Series P-60, no. 23 (No-vember 1956), 1, http://www2.census.gov/prod2/popscan/p60-023.pdf, accessed February 26, 2016.

192. "Women Civilians Sought by Army." Average women's salaries in U.S. Department of Commerce, "Current Population Reports Consumer Income," Series P-60, no. 35 (January 5, 1961), 2, http://www2.census.gov/prod2/popscan/p60-035.pdf, accessed February 26, 2016. For salaries in other years see "Army Seeks Hostesses for Reich"; "Summary of Major Events and Problems (Reports Control Symbol CSHIS-6), Special Services Division, TAGO, July 1, 1955 to June 30, 1956, Historical Summaries of Major Events and Problems, 55–60, Special Services Branch, Special Services Di-vision, AGO, NARA; "Recreation Aides Sought by Army."

193. Army Special Services advertisement, *Mademoiselle,* December 1957, in "Summary of Major Events and Problems (CSHIS-6)," Special Services Division, TAGO, July 1, 1957 to June 30, 1958, Inclosure A-8R, Historical Summaries of Major Events and Problems, 55–60, Special Services Branch, Special Services Division, AGO, NARA; Winona Franklin Walker, interview by Hermann Trojanowski, July 9, 2003, transcript, Winona Franklin Walker Papers, WV0284.5.001, WVHP.

194. Alexander, interview by Trojanowski. See also "Recreation Aides Leave for Europe."

195. Payne, interview by Currie, August 25, 1987, 17.

196. Morris, *Eye on the Struggle,* 40.

197. Davis, *So, What's a Nice Girl Like You Doing in a Place Like This?,* 15–18.

198. Quote in Shirley J. Horning to family, September 11, 1953; also Shirley J. Horning to family, May 25, 1959, both in Service Club Manager Family Correspondence, Horning Papers, MHI.

199. Shirley J. Horning to family, August 22, 1953, Horning Papers, MHI.

200. Shirley J. Horning to family, September 11, 1953, Horning Papers, MHI (ellipses in original).

201. Shirley J. Horning to family, May 25, 1959, Horning Papers, MHI.

202. Shirley S. Horning to family, February 16, 1953, Horning Papers, MHI.

203. Shirley S. Horning to family, August 24, 1953, Horning Papers, MHI.

204. Shirley S. Horning to family, May 25, 1959, Horning Papers, MHI.

205. Shirley S. Horning to family, May 20, 1959, Horning Papers, MHI.

206. Helen Stevenson Meyner, letters to family, December 10 and November 20, 1950, Subseries 2: Correspondence, Meyner Papers.

207. Helen Stevenson Meyner, letter to family, January 23, 1951, Subseries 2: Correspondence, Meyner Papers.

208. The average age at which women married hovered between twenty and twenty-one in the 1950s. See "Estimated Median Age at First Marriage, by Sex: 1890 to the Present," US Census Bureau Families and Living Arrangements, https://www.census.gov/hhes/families/data/marital.html, accessed May 17, 2016.

209. Helen Stevenson Meyner, letter to family, December 10, 1950, Subseries 2: Correspondence, Meyner Papers.

210. Email correspondence with Diane W. Shaw, Director of Special Collections and College Archivist, Skillman Library, Lafayette College, May 18, 2016.

211. Helen Stevenson Meyner, letter to family, November 20, 1950, Subseries 2: Correspondence, Meyner Papers.

212. Helen Stevenson Meyner, letter to family, January 27, 1951, Subseries 2: Correspondence, Meyner Papers.

213. Helen Stevenson Meyner, letter to family, December 5, 1950, Subseries 2: Correspondence, Meyner Papers; Helen Stevenson Meyner diary, January 11, 1951, Subseries 1: Biographical and Personal, Meyner Papers.

214. Helen Stevenson Meyner diary, December 31, 1950, Subseries 1: Biographical and Personal, Meyner Papers.

215. Helen Stevenson Meyner, letter to family, January 27, 1951, Subseries 2: Correspondence, Meyner Papers.

216. Helen Stevenson Meyner, letter to family, February 18, 1951, Subseries 2: Correspondence, Meyner Papers.

217. Helen Stevenson Meyner, letter to family, January 23, 1951, Subseries 2: Correspondence, Meyner Papers.

218. Helen Stevenson Meyner, letter to family, February 18, 1951, Subseries 2: Correspondence, Meyner Papers.

219. Helen Stevenson Meyner, letter to family, May 22, 1951, Subseries 2: Correspondence, Meyner Papers.

220. Thompson, "Army Seeking 350 Hostesses for Overseas."

221. Davis, *So, What's a Nice Girl Like You Doing in a Place Like This?*, 24.
222. Davis, *So, What's a Nice Girl Like You Doing in a Place Like This?*, 57.
223. Davis, *So, What's a Nice Girl Like You Doing in a Place Like This?*, 61.
224. Davis, *So, What's a Nice Girl Like You Doing in a Place Like This?*, quote on 80, also 79–80.
225. Davis, *So, What's a Nice Girl Like You Doing in a Place Like This?*, quotes on 83, also 81–83.
226. Davis, *So, What's a Nice Girl Like You Doing in a Place Like This?*, 84.
227. Davis, *So, What's a Nice Girl Like You Doing in a Place Like This?*, 85.
228. Double underlines in original. Helen Stevenson Meyner letter to family, December 16, 1951, Subseries 2: Correspondence, Meyner Papers.
229. "Helen S. Meyner," The Robert B. and Helen S. Meyner Center, Lafayette College, https://meynercenter.lafayette.edu/about-the-center-meyners/helen-s-meyner/, accessed September 29, 2016.
230. Morris, *Eye on the Struggle*, 263.
231. Alexander, interview by Trojanowski.

### 5. LOOK, BUT DON'T TOUCH

1. All quotations come from Debby Alexander Moore, interview by Kara Dixon Vuic, July 25–28, 2016, telephone interview. Many thanks to TCU graduate student Sarah Miller for transcribing this lengthy interview.
2. See William H. Orrick, "Shut it Down! A College in Crisis: San Francisco State College, October 1968–April 1969, A Report to the National Commission on the Causes and Prevention of Violence," July 1969, https://archive.org/stream/shutitdowncollegooorririch/shutitdowncollegooorririch_djvu.txt, accessed February 9, 2017.
3. On conscription and the makings of the Vietnam War military, see Christian G. Appy, *Working-Class War: American Combat Soldiers and Vietnam* (Chapel Hill: University of North Carolina Press, 1993), 28–37. Dependents were evacuated from Vietnam in February 1965. See George S. Eckhardt, *Command and Control, 1950–1969* (Washington, DC: Department of the Army, 1991), 54, https://history.army.mil/html/books/090/90-8-1/index.html, accessed February 1, 2018.
4. Creighton W. Abrams to Deputy Commanding General, May 16, 1970, Morale and Welfare Activities, Headquarters USARV, DCSPER Military Personnel Policy Division Morale and Welfare Branch General Records, USFSEA, NARA.
5. Quote in USO 1966 Annual Report, Item 3710103003, Frizzell Collection; USO 1972 Annual Report, Item 3710103010, Frizzell Collection; Frank Coffey, *Always Home: 50 Years of the USO* (Washington, DC: Brassey's, 1991), 91; "U.S.O. Expanding to Wartime Basis at Johnson Behest," *New York Times*, September 12, 1965; "Three Women Enroute to Viet Nam to Serve as USO Staff Directors," *Chicago Daily Defender*, December 4, 1965; "USO's 16 Clubs Serve U.S. Forces," *Pacific Stars and Stripes*, MACV Orientation Edition (Summer–Fall 1968), 15, Item Number 13100201002, Willis F. Marshall Collection, TVA.

6. "U.S.O. Expanding to Wartime Basis at Johnson Behest"; *USO Annual Report* (New York: USO, 1965); Coffey, *Always Home*, 92; *USO Annual Report* (New York: USO, 1969); *USO Annual Report* (New York: USO, 1970); *USO Annual Report* (New York: USO, 1971); *USO Annual Report* (New York: USO, 1972); *USO Annual Report* (New York: USO, 1973); "Orientation Information for Armed Forces Professional Entertainment Units Touring the Republic of Vietnam" (revised), July 1970, Orientation Instructions for Professional Entertainers Touring Vietnam 1967–1971, Headquarters, EBGA, USFSEA, NARA.

7. Robert C. Lewis to James F. Collins, June 4, 1965, 2, 900.16 SEASIA-SRAO, DOD request for, 5 / 26 / 65 Regulations and Guidelines folder, Red Cross 1965–1979, NARA.

8. "Cross Reference Sheet" (no title or date on document), 900.3 SEASIA-SRAO, Personnel; "Red Cross Clubmobile Girls Coming Home from Vietnam," press release, May 26, 1972, 020.101 SRAO, both in Red Cross 1965–1979, NARA.

9. Organization and Functions Manual, March 2, 1970, General Historical Records Relating to the Entertainment Branch, 1970–1972, Headquarters, EBGA, NARA; Meredith H. Lair, *Armed with Abundance: Consumerism and Soldiering in the Vietnam War* (Chapel Hill: University of North Carolina Press, 2011), esp. 116–144.

10. The Armed Forces Professional Entertainment Office, a joint services organization under the Army, coordinated much of the live entertainment between organizations and agencies in the United States and Special Services in Vietnam. See Special Services Agency Conference, July 14, 1970, Records Relating to Entertainment Conferences within Vietnam 1970; MACV Directive 28-6: Welfare, Recreation, and Morale Entertainment Program, June 30, 1970, USO / CMTS Project Officer Instructions, 15 March 1971; and "Historical Background," Organization and Functions Manual, March 2, 1970, General Historical Records Relating to the Entertainment Branch, 1970–1972, all in EBGA, USFSEA, NARA. On CMTS, see untitled history in Correspondence and Memoranda Pertaining to Command Military Touring Shows 4 Jan 70–12 Jan 1972, EBGA, USFSEA, NARA; Michael Kramer, *The Republic of Rock: Music and Citizenship in the Sixties Counterculture* (New York: Oxford University Press, 2013), part 2.

11. "Historical Background," Organization and Functions Manual, March 2, 1970 and "US Forces Vietnam Basic Commercial Entertainment Agreement—RVN Agencies," both in General Historical Records Relating to the Entertainment Branch, 1970–1972, EBGA, USFSEA, NARA; MACV Directive 28-6; Douglas Robinson, "U.S. Entertainers Find Audiences and Enemy Fire," *New York Times*, July 17, 1968. See also "Over There," *Time* 89, no. 1 (January 6, 1967): 75; Roy Harris, "Singer Hurt in Ambush Was Scared," *Los Angeles Times*, July 7, 1968; Wayne Warga, "A Promotor's Entertainment War in Vietnam," *Los Angeles Times*, August 4, 1968. Performers complained about corruption among booking agents, whom they accused of breaking payment contracts, and among club custodians, whom they alleged were receiving kickbacks for contracts. See "Entertainer's Kickback Charges Under Study," *Los Angeles Times*, September 12, 1969; Robert M. Smith, "Booking Agent Describes Army

Club 'Kickbacks,'" *New York Times*, October 10, 1969; Bobbi Jo Pettitt, in Keith Walker, *A Piece of My Heart: The Stories of Twenty-Six American Women Who Served in Vietnam* (New York: Ballantine Books, 1985), 116–117; Peter Arnett, "Entertainers Risk Lives in Vietnam," *Los Angeles Times*, July 16, 1968; Reuben Noel and Nancy Noel, *Saigon for a Song* (Phoenix: UCS Press, 1987).

12. Regulations quoted in Directive Number 28-7: Welfare, Recreation, and Morale Commercial Entertainment in RVN, April 16, 1969, 3 and 7, 206-02 Morale and Welfare (USO / Entertainment) (1969), MACV Secretary of the Joint Staff-Military History Branch Background Materials, USFSEA, NARA; Special Services director quoted in Arnett, "Entertainers Risk Lives in Vietnam."

13. Robert A. "Bob" Bratt, *Four Stars on a Blue Shield* (Indianapolis: 1st Books, 2001), 19, 17–19.

14. "Topless Go-Go Girls for Vietnam Soldiers," *Panama City News*, March 2, 1967. Australian entertainers similarly traveled to Vietnam in both official and unofficial ways. See Ann-Mari Jordens, "Not *Apocalypse Now*: Government-Sponsored Australian Entertainers in Vietnam 1965–1971," *Labour History* 58 (May 1990): 65–75.

15. Draft: Special Services Conference Entertainment Branch, November 4–5, 1970, Records Relating to Entertainment Conferences within Vietnam 1970, EBGA, USFSEA, NARA.

16. Carol A. Hunter, "'A Touch of Home': Red Cross Recreation Workers in the Vietnam War" (MA thesis, University of New Mexico, 1994), 81–82.

17. William C. Westmoreland, *A Soldier Reports*, new ed. (Garden City, NY: Doubleday, 1976; New York: Da Capo, 1989), 187, 295. Citations are to the Da Capo edition.

18. Lair, *Armed with Abundance*, chap. 2.

19. Lawrence H. Glaab, "Special Services in a Cold War Setting," [1963], 719–01 Special Services Prog Files (64) Service Clubs, Army Education and Morale Support Directorate Executive Office Selected Permanent Subject Files, 1953–1968, AGO, NARA.

20. J. C. Lambert to Jerome B. Coray, October 18, 1965, 203-05 Review and Analysis Files—Entertainment Requirements, Army Education and Morale Support Directorate Executive Office, Selected Permanent Subject Files, AGO, NARA.

21. Red Cross Press Release, SEA #88 "Red Cross Girls Boost Morale of American GI's in Vietnam," February 1969, Red Cross Archives.

22. John Dittmann, Press Release, Public Information Office, HQ 25th ID [n.d.], 25th Infantry Division Cu Chi, 900.6161 SEASIA-Vietnam, Red Cross 1965–1979, NARA.

23. "SRAO'er BARBARA LYNN," press release to *Ebony* magazine, 020.281 Ebony folder, Red Cross 1965–1979, NARA.

24. "Red Cross Clubmobile Girls Coming Home from Vietnam," press release, May 26, 1972, 020.101 SRAO, Red Cross 1965–1979, NARA; "Vietnam Clubmobile," *New York Times*, March 2, 1967, 8.

25. Emily Strange in Ron Steinman, *Women in Vietnam* (New York: TV Books, 2000), 214.

26. "U.S. Army Special Services: Where the Action Is," MF 28 5426, produced by the Army Pictoral Center, 1970, https://youtu.be/piyqtiosYYw, accessed February 9, 2017.

27. LTC Robert J. Kelvit, interview by Col Robert G. Sausser, 1984, 8; LTC Terrence M. Wallace, interview by LTC Thomas M. Montgomery, 1985, 18, both in Senior Officer Oral History Program, MHI.

28. LTC John C. Truesdell, interview by LTC Jerry W. Felder, 1985, 11, Senior Officer Oral History Program, MHI.

29. LTC Richard F. Timmons, interview by LTC Wesley L. Fox, 1984, 14–15, Senior Officer Oral History Program, MHI.

30. PACOM Professional Entertainment Coordinator unclassified message to RUEPBA / DA, November 12, 1965, 203-05 Review and Analysis Files—Entertainment Requirements, Army Education and Morale Support Directorate Executive Office Selected Permanent Subject Files, AGO, NARA.

31. Military History Branch Office of the Secretary, Joint Staff, MACV, Command History 1969 vol. 3, 14–45, MACV Command History 1969 Final Determination, Headquarters, MACV Secretary of the Joint Staff-Military History Branch Annual Command Histories 1964–1973, USFSEA, NARA.

32. "USO after 30 Years: More than Coffee and Donuts," [1971], 1, 610.02 United Service Organizations, Red Cross 1965–1979, NARA.

33. Westmoreland, *A Soldier Reports*, 187.

34. Jacques Nevard, "U.S. and Vietnam Form Councils to Avert Incidents in Saigon," *New York Times,* June 10, 1965.

35. Operation MOOSE deemed Saigon off limits to soldiers and moved them instead to the burgeoning army post at Long Binh. See Susan Zeiger, *Entangling Alliances: Foreign War Brides and American Soldiers in the Twentieth Century* (New York: New York University Press, 2010), 215; Jeffrey A. Keith, "Producing Miss Saigon: Imaginings, Realities, and the Sensual Geography of Saigon," *Journal of American-East Asian Relations* 22 (2015): 263; Sue Sun, *"Where the Girls Are:* The Management of Venereal Disease by United States Military Forces in Vietnam," *Literature and Medicine* 23, no. 1 (Spring 2004): 66–87.

36. Military History Branch Office of the Secretary, Joint Staff, MACV, Command History 1966, 173, MACV Command History 1966 Final Determination, Headquarters, MACV Secretary of the Joint Staff-Military History Branch Annual Command Histories 1964–1973, USFSEA, NARA. Both locations had nearby areas where GIs solicited prostitutes. In Da Nang, the area was known as the "Dog Patch," while Cam Ranh Bay had the "Meat Market." See Heather Marie Stur, *Beyond Combat: Women and Gender in the Vietnam War Era* (New York: Cambridge University Press, 2011), 91–92.

37. Amanda Boczar, "Uneasy Allies: The Americanization of Sexual Policies in South Vietnam," *Journal of American-East Asian Relations* 22 (2015): 187–220; Stur, *Beyond Combat*, 48–61, Keith, "Producing Miss Saigon," 256–267.

38. Official Department of Defense policy was to suppress prostitution, declare places where GIs could access prostitutes to be off-limits, and to work with local au-

thorities to suppress prostitution. See Jerome H. Greenberg, "Venereal Disease in the Armed Forces," *Medical Aspects of Human Sexuality* (March 1972): 197–198. Sue Sun argues that the military's sex education film *Where the Girls Are—VD in Southeast Asia* presented contradictory messages that GIs should abstain from sexual relations and that Vietnamese women were sexually alluring and available. See Sun, "*Where the Girls Are.*"

39. See Andre J. Ognibene and O'Neill Barrett Jr., eds., *Internal Medicine in Vietnam,* vol. 2: *General Medicine and Infectious Diseases* (Washington, DC: Office of the Surgeon General and Center of Military History, 1982), 233–236, http://history.amedd.army .mil/booksdocs/vietnam/GenMedVN/CH09.html, accessed July 25, 2016; Spurgeon Neel, *Medical Support of the U.S. Army in Vietnam, 1965–1970,* Vietnam Studies (Washington, DC: Department of the Army, 1973), 34.

40. Jerome H. Greenberg, "Venereal Disease in the Armed Forces," *Medical Clinics of North America* 56, no. 5 (September 1972): 1087, 1096. An extended version of this article was originally printed in *Medical Aspects of Human Sexuality* in March 1972. Data on venereal disease suggests he was right. Incidence rates of soldiers with venereal disease in Vietnam far outpaced rates of soldiers from prior wars in the twentieth century. See Ognibene and Barrett, *Internal Medicine in Vietnam,* 233.

41. Paulette "Pat" Smith Sweeney, interview by Therese Strohmer, October 29, 2013, WV0553.5.001, Paulette "Pat" Sweeney Papers, WVHP.

42. Boczar, "Uneasy Allies," 187–220.

43. Ognibene and Barrett, eds., *Internal Medicine In Vietnam,* 236; Greenberg, "Venereal Disease in the Armed Forces," 1096.

44. LTC Jesse H. Denton, interview by LTC Allan R. Wetzel, 1983, L-54–L-59, Senior Officer Oral History Program, MHI. See also LTC Ted A. Cimral, interview by Samuel J. Dennis, 1985, 5, Senior Officer Oral History Program, MHI.

45. R. W. Apple, Jr., "Four G.I.'s Are Accused of Possessing Narcotics— 20 Under Inquiry," *New York Times,* January 27, 1966.

46. Boczar, "Uneasy Allies," 187–220; Moore, interview by Vuic; Gloria Glover Gates, interview by Anna Snipes, November 17, 2015, recording, TVA; Lair, *Armed with Abundance,* 207.

47. Sydney Gruson, "R&R Tours on Taiwan," *New York Times,* February 14, 1968; Sun, "*Where the Girls Are*"; Zeiger, *Entangling Alliances,* 220–21; Lair, *Armed with Abundance,* 207–208.

48. "How Madam and Her 400 Girls Laid Siege to U.S. Army HQ," *Los Angeles Times,* March 5, 1971. See Stur, *Beyond Combat,* 171–176.

49. Jeanne (Bokina) Christie, in Kathryn Marshall, *In the Combat Zone: An Oral History of American Women in Vietnam, 1966–1975* (Boston: Little, Brown and Company, 1987), 178.

50. Heather Marie Stur offers an insightful examination of the ways that Donut Dollies were utilized as symbols of a supportive domesticity that was under threat during the Vietnam War era. See Stur, *Beyond Combat,* chap. 2.

51. Rex Bowman, "GIs' Plea: Get Us the Playmate, Sir," *Richmond Times-Dispatch,* November 10, 2002. Thanks to Amber Batura for sharing Bowman's articles. See also

Christian G. Appy, *Patriots: The Vietnam War Remembered from All Sides* (New York: Viking, 2003), 28–30.

52. Rex Bowman, "Amid a War's Horrors, Soldiers Met an Angel," *Richmond Times-Dispatch,* November 11, 2002; "Playmate First Class: Jo Collins in Vietnam," *Playboy* (May 1966): 144–151, 198–200. See also "'Bunny' Project Officer visited by 'Playmate,'" *Eugene Register-Guard,* January 11, 1966. Special Services "staff . . . agreed that the show should be sent into Vietnam" in September 1966. Special Services Director Jack Edwards accompanied Collins, served as liaison with the military, and coordinated press coverage. See L. H. Glaab, Memo for record, September 15, 1966, 719–03 Rec & Entertainment Case Files GA-278 (67) "Martha Raye Show," Army Education and Morale Support Directorate Executive Office Selected Permanent Subject Files, 1953–1968, AGO, NARA.

53. Quoted in Elizabeth Fraterrigo, *Playboy and the Making of the Good Life in Modern America* (New York: Oxford University Press, 2009), 42.

54. Armed Forces Professional Entertainment Consolidated Attendance and Final Itinerary Report, December 11, 1970, Colorado Kappa Pickers Christmas Special—December 11, 1970, EBAAR, USFSEA, NARA.

55. "Colorado Kappa Pickers Christmas Special to Visit the Troops in Vietnam during the Holidays," press release, Colorado Kappa Pickers Christmas Special—December 11, 1970, EBAAR, USFSEA, NARA.

56. Armed Forces Professional Entertainment Consolidated Attendance and Final Itinerary Report, December 11, 1970, Colorado Kappa Pickers Christmas Special—December 11, 1970, EBAAR, USFSEA, NARA.

57. Entertainment Evaluation, December 27, 1970, Colorado Kappa Pickers Christmas Special—December 11, 1970, EBAAR, USFSEA, NARA.

58. Sherry Taylor, interview by Kara Dixon Vuic, March 24, 2009, telephone interview. Also see Bobbie Keith, in Steinman, *Women in Vietnam,* 168.

59. Ursula Vils, "Santa Ana Mother Boosts Troop Morale in Vietnam," *Los Angeles Times,* June 19, 1969.

60. Margaret Mary Kelly, interview by Rebecca Winters, May 29, 2003, Margaret Mary Lynd Kelly Collection (AFC / 2001/001/07981), VHP.

61. "Fourth Annual Miss America–USO Show to Entertain Troops in Vietnam," press release, and Albert B. Myers to Irene Bryant, September 23, 1970, both in Miss America 1970—August 12, 1970, EBAAR, USFSEA, NARA.

62. Performers with USO and commercial shows had to be eighteen, though there was no upper limit on their ages. Women and men who performed or toured Vietnam were of a wide age range, and included young college girls, middle-aged mothers, and well-known women in the twilight of their careers. See Armed Forces Overseas Touring Shows Program (Washington, DC: Department of the Army, September 1975), 10.

63. Mary Louise Dowling to Norman A. Durfee, August 4, 1965, 900.3 SEASIA, SRAO Personnel folder, Red Cross 1965–1979, NARA. See also James A. Purdue to Norman A. Durfee, August 13, 1965, 900.3 SEASIA, SRAO Personnel folder, Red

Cross 1965–1979, NARA; "For the Best Year of Your Life," ARC 873, rev. April 1969, item 16450113004, Young Collection. Of the 125 women who trained for Red Cross work in Vietnam and Korea in 1970, 15 were twenty-one years old, 57 were twenty-two, 35 were twenty-three, and 18 were twenty-four. See 1970 Training Period, Training-Basic Orientation, NHQ Records Relating to Service to Armed Forces, Red Cross 1965–1979, NARA.

64. Moore, interview by Vuic. "Summary of Major Events and Problems (Reports Control Symbol CSHIS-6), Special Services Division, TAGO, July 1, 1955 to June 30, 1956, Historical Summaries of Major Events and Problems, 55–60, Special Services Branch, Special Services Division, AGO, NARA.

65. "For the Best Year of Your Life," ARC 873, rev. April 1969; Harriet Rice, "Army Morale Welfare Recreation" (US Army Community and Family Support Center, ca. 1987), 43, MHI; Harriet Rice, interview by Kara Dixon Vuic, July 3, 2017, telephone interview; Marcy Stennes, interview by Kara Dixon Vuic, June 30, 2017, telephone interview; Appy, *Working-Class War,* 25–27.

66. Jennifer Young, interview by Richard Burks Verrone, November 7, 2002, OH0235, Young Collection; Jennifer Young, in Michele Turk, *Blood, Sweat and Tears: An Oral History of the American Red Cross* (Robbinsville, NJ: E Street Press, 2006), 81; Jill York, interview by Kara Dixon Vuic, March 19, 2009, telephone interview; Sue C. Behrens to Mary Louise Dowling, August 26, 1967, 900.3 SEASIA, SRAO Personnel folder, Red Cross 1965–1979, NARA; Jeanne Christie, interview by Kelly Crager, October 13–16, 2014, Item OH0896, Christie Collection.

67. Leah O'Leary, "The G.I.s Called Us Donut Dollies," in *Time It Was: American Stories from the Sixties,* ed. Karen Manners Smith and Tom Koster (Upper Saddle River, NJ: Pearson, 2008), 46.

68. Summary Report: Unit Directors' Meeting, April 13, 1968; Quinn Smith to Unit Directors, SRAO #55, February 12, 1969, both in 900.031 SEASIA-SRAO, SRAO Letters 1–111 May 1968–July 1970, Red Cross 1965–1979, NARA; Taylor, interview by Vuic; J. V. Mullins, Memorandum for USO Show Personnel Staying at the China Beach R&R Center, March 3, 1971, Orientation Instructions for Professional Entertainers Touring Vietnam 1967–1971, EBGA, USFSEA, NARA; Letter of Instruction to USARV Escort Officers for USO / Professional Shows, December 30, 1970, USO Escort Officer Instructions—30 December 1970–April 1972, EBGA, USFSEA, NARA.

69. Jenny Young letter to family, November 2, 1969, Young Collection.

70. Johnny Grant After-Action Report, July 13, 1969, Johnny Grant—22 June 1969, EBAAR, USFSEA, NARA.

71. The Silk and Soul Show After-Action Report, December 9, 1969, Silk and Soul—Oct. 31, 1969, EBAAR, USFSEA, NARA.

72. The Tony Diamond Show After-Action Report, December 29, 1969, Tony Diamond Show—Nov. 6, 1969, EBAAR, USFSEA, NARA. Also see Janet Olson Fortune diary, Fortune Collection. Date as on folder

73. Jan Morehead, interview by Kara Dixon Vuic, July 30, 2009, telephone interview.

74. Mary Louise Dowling to Pete Upton and Roy Popkin, February 3, 1969, 494.1 ARC 873 Recruitment Brochure folder, Red Cross 1965–1979, NARA.

75. Notes on three women in training session, n.d., 900.3 OA-SRAO, Staff folder, Red Cross 1965–1979, NARA.

76. Mary Louise Dowling to Meyer Mathis et al., January 24, 1966, 421.1 Supplemental Recreational Activities Overseas folder, Red Cross 1965–1979, NARA.

77. See Susan Conklin, interview by Kara Dixon Vuic, March 30, 2009, telephone interview; Taylor, interview by Vuic; Penni Evans, in Walker, *A Piece of My Heart*, 338.

78. Moore, interview by Vuic; Stennes, interview by Vuic.

79. Moore, interview by Vuic.

80. Mary Louise Dowling to Frances P. Douglass and Sue C. Behrens, February 5, 1971, 421.1 Supplemental Recreation Activities Overseas; Summary Report: Unit directors' Meeting, April 13, 1968, 900.031 SEASIA-SRAO, SRAO letters 1–111 May 1968–July 1970, both in Red Cross 1965–1979, NARA.

81. Mary Louise Dowling to Mr. Thomas F. Lavelle, January 22, 1971, 421.1 Supplemental Recreation Activities Overseas, Red Cross 1965–1979, NARA.

82. "Articles for USO Girls to Bring to Viet-Nam," n.d., 1–2, Orientation Instructions for Professional Entertainers Touring Vietnam 1967–1971, EBGA, USFSEA, NARA.

83. Wilbur W. Evans, "Information of Special Importance to USO Shows Personnel Touring in South Vietnam," n.d, Orientation Instructions for Professional Entertainers Touring Vietnam 1967–1971, EBGA, USFSEA, NARA.

84. "USO Shows Information for Tour Republic of Vietnam," n.d., 2, Orientation Instructions for Professional Entertainers Touring Vietnam 1967–1971, EBGA, USFSEA, NARA.

85. "USO Shows Information for Tour Republic of Vietnam," n.d., 2; "pant dresses" in Minutes, Entertainment Directors' Meeting, April 3, 1970, Records Relating to Entertainment Conferences within Vietnam 1970, EBGA, USFSEA, NARA.

86. Information for Vietnam-Bound SRAO Personnel, January 1969, 6, Christie Papers.

87. Quinn Smith to Mary Louise Dowling, July 2, 1965, 900.3 SEASIA-SRAO, Personnel folder; "Information for Vietnam-Bound SRAO Personnel," May 1970, 900.3 OA-SRAO, Staff folder, both in Red Cross 1965–1979, NARA.

88. "Three Lovely Models to Visit Troops in Vietnam and Korea," press release, The Going Thing—August 8, 1970, EBAAR, USFSEA, NARA.

89. "The American Style," newsclipping, Entertainment Vietnam-Tours—Aug. Dec. 1970, EBGA, USFSEA, NARA.

90. "The American Style," newsclipping; Photographs and Photography Work Order, July 25, 1970, The Going Thing—August 8, 1970, EBAAR, USFSEA, NARA.

91. "Johnny Grant and His Hollywood Pinups" press release, Johnny Grant—Dec. 19, 1971, EBAAR, USFSEA, NARA.

92. Notes on three women in training session.

93. Red Cross Press Release, SEA #88.

94. Winzola McLendon, "It's Not Paradise, But the Men Are There," *Washington Post*, January 13, 1966.

95. McLendon, "It's Not Paradise, But the Men Are There."

96. "For the Best Year of Your Life," ARC 873, rev. April 1969.

97. "Supplemental Recreational Activities Overseas" Service Goals for 1966–1967, 140.11 SRAO Objectives & Goals, Red Cross 1965–1979, NARA. Also see Mary Louise Dowling to Quinn Smith March 28, 1969, 900.616 SEASIA-SRAO, July 1968–1972 and Mary Louise Dowling to Office of Personnel and Office of Publications, February 4, 1969, 494.1 ARC 873 Recruitment Brochure folder, both in Red Cross 1965–1979, NARA.

98. "U.S. Army Special Services: Where the Action Is."

99. Morehead, interview by Vuic.

100. Jeanne 'Sam' Bokina Christie, in Walker, *A Piece of My Heart*, 70; O'Leary, "The G.I.s Called Us Donut Dollies," 45–46. See also Christie, in Marshall, *In the Combat Zone*, 171.

101. Evans in Walker, *A Piece of My Heart*, 338.

102. O'Leary, "The G.I.s Called Us Donut Dollies," 46–47.

103. Taylor, interview by Vuic.

104. Mary Blanchard Bowe, in Olga Gruhzit-Hoyt, *A Time Remembered: American Women in the Vietnam War* (Novato, CA: Presidio Press, 1999), 204.

105. Nancy Smoyer, interview by Kara Dixon Vuic, December 15, 2007, telephone interview.

106. Sweeney, interview by Strohmer.

107. Young, interview by Verrone.

108. Christie, in Walker, *A Piece of My Heart*, 69. Also Christie, interview by Crager.

109. Conklin, interview by Vuic.

110. Frederic S. Laise to Mr. Solverud et al., June 25, 1965, 900.616 SEASIA-SRAO, DOD request for, 5/26/65 Regulations and Guidelines folder, Red Cross 1965–1979, NARA. Also James A. Purdue to Norman A. Durfee, August 13, 1965 and Information for SRAO Trainees Concerning Assignment to Vietnam, n.d. [probably late 1965–early 1966], both in 900.3 SEASIA-SRAO, Personnel folder, Red Cross 1965–1979, NARA.

111. J. Holley Watts, interview by Therese Strohmer, March 9, 2008, transcript, WV0407 J. Holley Watts Oral History, WVHP.

112. Susan Bradshaw McLean, in Steinman, *Women in Vietnam*, 199.

113. Linda K. Morgan Maini, interview by Therese Strohmer, March 8, 2008, transcript, WV0406.5.001, Linda K. Morgan Maini Papers, WVHP.

114. Maureen "Mo" Nerli, in Walker, *A Piece of My Heart*, 153.

115. Gloria Glover Gates, interview by Anna Snipes, November 17, 2015, OH0915, TVA.

116. See Morehead, interview by Vuic; Young, in Turk, *Blood, Sweat and Tears*, 73–74.

117. Kelly, interview by Winters.

118. O'Leary, "The G.I.s Called Us Donut Dollies," 42.

119. O'Leary, "The G.I.s Called Us Donut Dollies," 47.

120. O'Leary, "The G.I.s Called Us Donut Dollies," 44.

121. O'Leary, "The G.I.s Called Us Donut Dollies," 47.

122. Mary Louise Dowling to Norman A. Durfee, August 4, 1965, 900.3 SEASIA-SRAO, Personnel folder, Red Cross 1965–1979, NARA.

123. James A. Purdue to Norman A. Durfee, August 13, 1965, 900.3 SEASIA-SRAO, Personnel folder, Red Cross 1965–1979, NARA. Also see Letter to Miss Quinn Smith from Mary Louse Dowling, April 27, 1966, 900.11[8] SEASIA-SRAO and Mary Louise Dowling to Sue Behrens and Quinn Smith, September 27, 1968, 900.3 SEASIA-SRAO, Personnel folder, both in Red Cross 1965–1979, NARA.

124. Mary Louise Dowling to Norman A. Durfee, December 9, 1968, 900.3 SEASIA-SRAO, Personnel folder, Red Cross 1965–1979, NARA. Also see Mary Louise Dowling to Norman A. Durfee, August 9, 1967, 900.16 SEASIA-SRAO, 1967–June 1968; Mary Louise Dowling to Sue Behrens and Quinn Smith, October 3, 1968 and December 17, 1968, both in 900.3 SEASIA-SRAO, Personnel folder, all in Red Cross 1965–1979, NARA.

125. R. C. Breasley to Ralph R. Springer, November 9, 1965, 403–07 News media and release files AFPEB Program, Army Education and Morale Support Directorate Executive Office Selected Permanent Subject Files, 1953–1968, AGO, NARA.

126. "Theater: Hollywood Discovers Viet Nam—Belatedly," *The Sunday Star* (Washington, DC), May 8, 1966, newsclipping in 403–07 News Media and Release Files AFPE Program, Army Education and Morale Support Directorate Executive Office Selected Permanent Subject Files, 1953–1968, AGO, NARA.

127. Ethyl L. Payne, "GIs Lament Lack of U.S. Entertainment in Vietnam," *Chicago Daily Defender,* January 25, 1967.

128. J. Anthony Lukas, "This is Bob (Politician-Patriot-Publicist) Hope," *New York Times Magazine,* October 4, 1970, 28ff. Also "Historical Resume, Entertainment Activities," Organization and Functions Manual, March 2, 1970, General Historical Records Relating to the Entertainment Branch, 1970–1972, EBGA, USFSEA, NARA.

129. Emily Strange, in Steinman, *Women in Vietnam,* 212.

130. Cherie Rankin, in Marshall, *In the Combat Zone,* 62–64.

131. Sharon Vander Ven Cummings, in Turk, *Blood, Sweat and Tears,* 59.

132. Taylor, interview by Vuic. Also Vander Ven Cummings, in Turk, *Blood, Sweat and Tears,* 59.

133. Judy Jenkins, in Marshall, *In the Combat Zone,* 130.

134. Smoyer, interview by Vuic.

135. Christie, interview by Crager.

136. Strange, in Steinman, *Women in Vietnam,* 216.

137. "Red Cross Clubmobile Girls Coming Home from Vietnam," press release, May 26, 1972, 2, 020.101 SRAO, Red Cross 1965–1979, NARA.

138. Christie, interview by Crager; Bowe, in Gruhzit-Hoyt, *A Time Remembered,* 209.

139. Christie in Walker, *A Piece of My Heart,* 77–78, quote on 78.

140. York, interview by Vuic.

141. Jennifer Young, in Gruhzit-Hoyt, *A Time Remembered,* 185.

142. Historian Heather Stur calls these the gentle warrior, the gunslinger, and the sexual aggressor. See Stur, *Beyond Combat,* chaps. 4 and 5.

143. Henry J. Thomas letter to the editor, *Ebony* 21, no. 9 (July 1966): 14, 16.

144. Ed Madison letter to the editor, *Ebony* 21, no. 9 (July 1966): 14. Madison referred to unnamed "twins" who performed in the Bob Hope tour. The Nicolas Brothers (who were not twins) were an acrobatic tap dancing duo whose style became known as "flash dancing." They performed with the 1965 Bob Hope Christmas tour.

145. Mary Louise Dowling to Robert C. Lewis, August 11, 1966 and Norman A. Durfee to John H. Johnson, September 1, 1966, both in 020.281 Ebony folder, 200-85-17, Red Cross 1965–1979, NARA.

146. On recruitment efforts, see Mary Louise Dowling to Sue Behrens and Quinn Smith, October 3, 1968 and Robert C. Lewis to John F. Higgins, July 31, 1968, both in 900.3 SEASIA-SRAO, Personnel folder, Red Cross 1965–1979, NARA; Mary Louise Dowling to George E. Hand, January 25, 1971, 900.616 SEASIA-SRAO, July 1968–1972, Red Cross 1965–1979, NARA. For numbers, see Quinn Smith to Charles P. Stone, August 15, 1968, 900.3 SEASIA-SRAO, Personnel folder; Mary Louise Dowling to Sue C. Behrens, January 8, 1971, 900.3 OA, Negro Personnel folder, both in 200-85-35, Red Cross 1965–1979, NARA.

147. James D. Dorsey to Commanding General US Army Support Command Cam Ranh Bay, January 22, 1972, General Correspondence and Memoranda of the Entertainment Branch, January 1, 1972–April 4, 1972, EBGA, USFSEA, NARA.

148. On African Americans and the Vietnam War, see James E. Westheider, *Fighting on Two Fronts: African Americans and the Vietnam War* (New York: New York University Press, 1999); Kimberley L. Phillips, *War! What Is It Good For? Black Freedom Struggles and the U.S. Military from World War II to Iraq* (Chapel Hill: University of North Carolina Press, 2012), chaps. 5 and 6.

149. Charles P. Stone to Quinn Smith, August 7, 1968, 900.3 SEASIA-SRAO, Personnel folder, 200-85-35, Red Cross 1965–1979, NARA.

150. Quinn Smith to Charles P. Stone, August 15, 1968, 900.3 SEASIA-SRAO, Personnel folder, Red Cross 1965–1979, NARA.

151. Suzanne Martony letter to the editor, *Ebony* 26, no. 7 (May 1971): 18.

152. Ethel L. Payne, "Crowded Saigon is Lonely, Black GIs Find," *Chicago Daily Defender,* February 7, 1967. Also James McGrath Morris, *Eye on the Struggle: Ethel Payne, the First Lady of the Black Press* (New York: Amistad, 2015), 263.

153. Kathy Ormond letter to mother, July 28, 1968, Ormond Papers.

154. Oscar Colbert to Kathy Ormond, September 17, 1969 and September 16, 1969, both in Ormond Papers.

155. Although Special Services worker Harriet Rice recalled no explicit policies on interracial relationships, when one of her white colleagues in Germany began dating an African American enlisted man in 1968, her supervisors instructed her to end the relationship. She refused, and the couple married. Rice, interview by Vuic.

156. Young, interview by Verrone; Smoyer, interview by Vuic.

157. "Fort Pierce Girl Home from Red Cross Duty in Korea; Vietnam Next," *Fort Pierce News Tribune,* April 11, 1971.

158. Barbara Lynn, "Good Samaritan in Vietnam: Red Cross Girl Brings Cheer to Men at Front," *Ebony* 23, no. 12 (October 1968): 179.

159. "Mississippi Girl Aiding Troops in Vietnam," press release, July 16, 1968, 020.101 SRAO folder, Red Cross 1965–1979, NARA.

160. Sweeney, interview by Strohmer.

161. "Mississippi Girl Aiding Troops in Vietnam."

162. Hunter, "'A Touch of Home,'" 149.

163. Wesley's political awareness grew during the war, and she became very concerned about drug problems among soldiers, the plight of Vietnamese women and orphans, and the postwar future of Vietnam. After finishing her year as a Donut Dolly, she stayed for another year with Special Services, then worked with other agencies after the military withdrew in 1973. She died during the initial Operation Babylift flight, which was an attempt to evacuate Vietnamese orphans shortly before the war's end. Reesa Eisler to Janice Christie, April 15, 1985, Christie Papers; Christie, interview by Crager.

164. John E. Christian to Commanding Officer, Qui Nhon Sub-Area Command, December 9, 1971, General Correspondence and Memoranda of the Entertainment Branch, 1 January 1972–4 April 1972, EBGA, USFSEA, NARA.

165. James D. Dorsey to Commanding General US Army Support Command Cam Ranh Bay, January 22, 1972, General Correspondence and Memoranda of the Entertainment Branch, 1 January 1972–4 April 1972, EBGA, USFSEA, NARA.

166. "The Miss Black America Show to Entertain the Troops in Vietnam," press release, Miss Black America—January 5, 1970, EBAAR, USFSEA, NARA.

167. "Miss 'Black America' Takes Soul to Vietnam," *Ebony* 25, no. 7 (May 1970): 89, 90.

168. Armed Forces Professional Entertainment Consolidated Attendance and Final Itinerary Report, January 20, 1971, Miss Black America Show—Jan. 20, 1971, EBAAR, USFSEA, NARA.

169. Miss Black America Show After-Action Report, February 26, 1971; Miss Black America Show—Long Binh Post 9 February 1971, February 10, 1971, both in Miss Black America Show—January 20, 1971, EBAAR, USFSEA, NARA.

170. "Miss Black America Show a Breath of Fresh Air," *Seventh Air Force News*, February 24, 1971, news clipping, Miss Black America Show—Jan. 20, 1971, EBAAR, USFSEA, NARA.

171. J. C. Pennington to the DCS P&A, RE: The Miss Black America Show, February 7, 1971, and George J. Harold to Joseph W. Smith, April 8, 1971, both in Miss Black America Show—Jan. 20, 1971, EBAAR, USFSEA, NARA. See also Robert C. Lueders to George J. Harold, March 22, 1971, in Miss Black America Show—Jan. 20, 1971, EBAAR, USFSEA, NARA.

172. John O. Ensor to Commanding General COMUSMACV, October 7, 1971, USARV-IG Investigative Files (FY 72) Case #72-64 Activities of Miss Millie Majette Cam Ranh Bay USO, USFSEA, NARA. See also Stanley Lenard, Summary-Fact Sheet: Activities of Miss Millie Majette, October 7, 1971; Report of Inquiry Concerning the Activities of Miss Millie Majette, September 3, 1970; Dallas W. Clark to Commanding General United States Army Support Command, September 3, 1971, all in USARV-IG Investigative Files (FY 72) Case #72-64 Activities of Miss Millie

Majette Cam Ranh Bay USO, USFSEA, NARA; Richard R. Moser, *The New Winter Soldiers: GI and Veteran Dissent during the Vietnam Era* (New Brunswick, NJ: Rutgers University Press, 1996), 59–62.

173. Quote in Clark to Commanding General United States Army Support Command; Norman E. Trask to Commanding General, US Army Support Command Cam Ranh Bay, January 20, 1972 and Richard N. Shiremann to Mildred Majette, January 13, 1972, both in 701-07 Discipline, Law and Order, Headquarters, USARV DCSPER Military Personnel Policy Division Morale and Welfare Branch General Records, USFSEA, NARA.

174. McLendon, "It's Not Paradise, But the Men Are There."

175. *USO Annual Report* (New York: USO, 1967), 16.

176. Conklin, interview by Vuic.

177. Maini, interview by Strohmer.

178. Sweeney, interview by Strohmer.

179. Evans in Walker, *A Piece of My Heart*, 345.

180. Sandra Lockney Davis, *So, What's a Nice Girl Like You Doing in a Place Like This? Seoul to Saigon* (Gulf Breeze, FL: East Bay Publishers, 2011), 236–237.

181. Women also found that wartime stresses induced personal attachments. See Joann Puffer Kotcher, *Donut Dolly: An American Red Cross Girl's War in Vietnam* (Denton: University of North Texas Press, 2011), 127.

182. Rankin in Marshall, *In the Combat Zone*, 71, 72.

183. Hunter, "'A Touch of Home,'" 112–113.

184. Evans in Walker, *A Piece of My Heart*, 345.

185. "Haute Couture," *The Red Cross Newsletter*, 19, no. 1 (January 1970): 1, 491 Newsletter, 1970–71, Volume 19, No. 1–4, January 1970–April 1970, Red Cross Archives. Also see Davis, *So, What's a Nice Girl Like You Doing in a Place Like This?*, 189.

186. Rankin, in Marshall, *In the Combat Zone*, 76, 75–76.

187. Stennes, interview by Vuic.

188. "Famous French hair stylist" and "pretty girl models" in "Daniel to tour Vietnam with Three Lovely Models," press release; "extremely well received" in "Daniel & Friends" After-Action Report, February 8, 1970, both in Daniel and Friends—Jan. 18, 1970, EBAAR, USFSEA, NARA.

189. Entertainment Evaluation, January 28, 1971, Daniel and Friends—Jan. 18, 1971, EBAAR, USFSEA, NARA.

190. Skip Young After Action Report, May 6, 1969, Skip Young Show—9 April 1969, EBAAR, USFSEA, NARA.

191. "Interview with Bobbie Keith the Weathergirl," HistoryNet, www.historynet.com /interview-with-bobbie-keith-the-weathergirl.htm/print, accessed July 17, 2009.

192. The phrase comes from "An Introduction to the Army Service Club Program," Department of the Army Pamphlet No. 21–59 (Washington, DC: Department of the Army, October 19, 1953), 21.

193. "GIs Defend Visits of Cuties," *The Evening Star* (Washington, DC), March 24, 1966, news clipping, 403-07 News Media and Release Files AFPE Program, Army Education and Morale Support Directorate Executive Office Selected Permanent Subject

Files, 1953–1968, AGO, NARA; LTC Clyde W. Glosson, interview by LTC Leonard P. Wice, 1984, 23, Senior Officer Oral History Program, MHI.

194. After Action Report, Miss America USO Show 1971, August 24, 1971, Miss America Pageant 71—Aug. 11, 1971, EBAAR, USFSEA, NARA; Critique, Miss America–USO Show 1970, September 9, 1970, Gen. Records Relating to USO / Professional Shows, 30 March 1970–11 Jan. 1972, EBGA, USFSEA, NARA; Brad [Arrington] to Al [Myers], August 24, 1972, Miss America 1972—Aug. 8, 1972, EBAAR, USFSEA, NARA.

195. O'Leary, "The G.I.s Called Us Donut Dollies," 50. Also see Christie, interview by Crager; Jenny Young letter to family, July 3, 1969, 16450102014, Young Collection; Davis, So, What's a Nice Girl Like You Doing in a Place Like This?, 166–167; Kotcher, Donut Dolly, 224.

196. Christie, interview by Jones. Also see Taylor, interview by Vuic.

197. Jenny Young letter to family, April 25, 1969, 16450102004, Young Collection.

198. Saltwater Express & The Mack Sisters; Escort Officer After Action Report (Extracts), Saltwater Express and the Mack Sisters—Aug. 26, 1971, EBAAR, USFSEA, NARA.

199. Skip Young After Action Report, May 6, 1969, Skip Young Show—9 April 1969, EBAAR, USFSEA, NARA.

200. "Harrison-Tyler Show" After-Action report, March 27, 1970, Harrison & Tyler, March 1, 1970, EBAAR, USFSEA, NARA.

201. Entertainment Evaluation, [March] 18, [1970], Harrison & Tyler, March 1, 1970, EBAAR, USFSEA, NARA. Also see W. Don Chandler to Staff Entertainment Director, March 20, 1970, Harrison & Tyler, March 1, 1970, EBAAR, USFSEA, NARA.

202. Rankin in Marshall, In the Combat Zone, 71, 72.

203. Christie, interview by Crager. Also in Jeanne M. Christie, interview by Timothy H. Jones, July 1, 2008, Jeanne B. Christie Papers, VHP2008 / 10. Veterans History Project, Central Connecticut State University, Center for Public Policy and Social Research, http://content.library.ccsu.edu/cdm/ref/collection/VHP/id/5554, accessed June 1, 2016.

204. Sherry Alberoni After-Action Report, August 21, 1969, Sherry Alberoni—July 22, 1969, EBAAR, USFSEA, NARA. See also Christie, interview by Crager; Christie, interview by Jones.

205. Jenny Young letter to family, April 11, 1969, 16450102002, Young Collection.

206. Rankin in Marshall, In the Combat Zone, 68–70.

207. Military Police Report, June 14, 1969, Complaint: Entertainment and Club Irregularities, Criminal Investigations Reports, March–December 1969, Headquarters, USARV Special Services Agency (Provisional) Entertainment Branch Criminal Investigations Reports (hereafter SSAEB CIR), USFSEA, NARA.

208. K. V. John to Chief, Commercial Entertainment Office, September 30, 1969, Criminal Investigations Reports, March–December 1969, SSAEB CIR, USFSEA, NARA.

209. Jill Russell Witness Statement, November 1, 1969 and Elmer Cooke Witness Statement, December 2, 1969, both in Criminal Investigations Reports, March–December 1969, SSAEB CIR, USFSEA, NARA.

210. O'Leary, "The G.I.s Called Us Donut Dollies," 48, 59, 52.

211. Military nurses endured similar expectations from men that they were available sexually. See Kara Dixon Vuic, *Officer, Nurse, Woman: The Army Nurse Corps in the Vietnam War* (Baltimore: Johns Hopkins University Press, 2009), 138–154.

212. Young, in Turk, *Blood, Sweat and Tears*, 80.

213. O'Leary, "The G.I.s Called Us Donut Dollies," 54.

214. Jeanne Marie Christie, "The Basic Premise of the 'Donut Dolly' Program was Simple," *Vietnam* (October 1998): 66.

215. Christie, interview by Crager.

216. Christie in Marshall, *In the Combat Zone*, 180–181.

217. Christie, "The Basic Premise of the 'Donut Dolly' Program was Simple," 64; Christie in Marshall, *In the Combat Zone*, 180.

218. Christie, interview by Crager.

219. Davis, *So, What's a Nice Girl Like You Doing in a Place Like This?*, 156–161.

220. Strange, in Steinman, *Women in Vietnam*, 216.

221. Kathy Ormond letter to mother, November 17, 1968, Ormond Papers.

222. Conklin, interview by Vuic.

223. Cummings in Turk, *Blood, Sweat and Tears*, 61.

224. Christie in Marshall, *In the Combat Zone*, 179.

225. Jenkins in Marshall, *In the Combat Zone*, 134, 135.

226. Christie, interview by Crager.

227. Christie in Marshall, *In the Combat Zone*, 183.

228. Cummings in Turk, *Blood, Sweat and Tears*, 62.

229. Nerli in Walker, *A Piece of My Heart*, 160–162.

230. Christie, interview by Crager.

231. Maini, interview by Strohmer.

232. Conklin, interview by Vuic.

233. Linda Johnson Jones, interview by Hermann Trojanowski, April 14, 2011, wv0291.5.001, WV0291 Linda Jones Papers, WVHP.

234. Shirley Ann Hines collection, catalog record, VHP, http://memory.loc.gov /diglib/vhp/bib/loc.natlib.afc2001001.19147, accessed July 1, 2018.

235. "No More Miss America!," August 22, 1968, http://www.redstockings.org/index .php/no-more-miss-america, accessed July 21, 2016.

236. York, interview by Vuic.

237. Christie, interview by Crager.

238. Christie, interview by Crager.

239. Young, interview by Verrone.

240. Rankin in Marshall, *In the Combat Zone*, 78.

241. O'Leary, "The G.I.s Called Us Donut Dollies," quotes on 59 and 60, also 56–60.

242. Bowe in Gruhzit-Hoyt, *A Time Remembered*, 209.

243. Young, interview by Verrone. Another Donut Dolly described their work as "therapy." See Cindy Randolph (alias) in Marshall, *In the Combat Zone*, 235, 242.

### 6. NO BEER, NO BOOZE, NO BABES

1. Gina Lee, interview by Kara Dixon Vuic, March 23, 24, and 29, 2017, telephone interviews. On the expectations of Army wives to perform nonpaid volunteer work, see Jennifer Middlestadt, *The Rise of the Military Welfare State* (Cambridge, MA: Harvard University Press, 2015), 120–147, 174–179; John Sloan Brown, *Kevlar Legions: The Transformation of the U.S. Army, 1989–2005* (Washington, DC: Center for Military History, 2011), chap. 8.

2. Jackie Walters, email to the author, July 25, 2017.

3. Deployments more than tripled in the 1990s, then "increased again by an order of magnitude" after 2003. See Brown, *Kevlar Legions*, 355.

4. Marianne Lester, "A Gathering of Patriots," *The Times Magazine*, May 31, 1976, 22–24, 610.02 United Service Organization, Red Cross 1965–1979, NARA.

5. Beth Bailey, *America's Army: Making the All-Volunteer Force* (Cambridge, MA: Belknap Press of Harvard University Press, 2009), 133, 147, 154–155; Jeanne M. Holm, *Women in the Military: An Unfinished Revolution*, rev. ed. (New York: Presidio Press, 1992), 246–380.

6. Peter A. Morrison, Georges Vernez, David W. Grissmer, and Kevin F. McCarthy, *Families in the Army: Looking Ahead*, Santa Monica, CA: RAND, R-3691-A, June 1989, 6–7, 11, 33–34.

7. Bailey, *America's Army*, chap. 1.

8. Lester, "A Gathering of Patriots."

9. "Blue Ribbon Study Committee Report on the Needs of U.S. Armed Services Personnel for Continued Voluntary Social Services," February 1975, quote on 4, also 18, United Services Organizations, John Marsh Files, Gerald R. Ford Presidential Library, https://www.fordlibrarymuseum.gov/library/document/0067/1563223.pdf, accessed June 9, 2017.

10. Barbara Campbell, "U.S.O. Read Voices Hope on Finances," *New York Times*, May 1, 1975. See also Executive Committee of the Board of Governors minutes, May 8, 1974, USO Board of Governors Minutes, 6/13/1974, Series 1 USO Records, 1943–1978, NCCS. Scandals involving the USO during the Vietnam War were already leading to a decline in public contributions. See Public Relations Committee, December 7, 1972, USO Public Relations Committee, 1972, Series 1 USO Records, 1943–1978, NCCS.

11. "Blue Ribbon Study Committee Report," 4. The USO secured the charter in 1979. Frank Coffey, *Always Home: 50 Years of the USO* (Washington, DC: Brassey's, 1991), 137.

12. "Blue Ribbon Study Committee Report," 14–15.

13. *Hearing before the Subcommittee on Administrative Law and Governmental Relations of the Committee on the Judiciary*, House of Representatives, 94th Cong., 1st sess., on HR 7462, HR 7463, HR 7464, and HR 7537 to Incorporate United Service Organizations, Incorporated, December 9, 1975, Serial No. 28, 19.

14. Public Relations Committee minutes, September 20, 1973, 2, Board of Governors 1973 (2), Series 1 USO Records, 1943–1978, NCCS.

15. "Blue Ribbon Study Committee Report," 6.

16. Michael E. Menster, Remarks before Blue Ribbon Study Committee, October 16, 1974, 7, Board of Governors Blue Ribbon Study Commission 1974 (2), Series 1 USO Records, 1943–1978, NCCS.

17. William Aramong to Local United Way Executives, June 7, 1974, 2, USO Board of Governors Minutes, 6 / 13 / 1974, Series 1 USO Records, 1943–1978, NCCS.

18. Menster, Remarks before Blue Ribbon Study Committee, 2–3.

19. "Blue Ribbon Study Committee Report," 15.

20. "Blue Ribbon Study Committee Report," 7–8.

21. USO 1972 Annual Report, Item 3710103010, Frizzell Collection.

22. Moe Hoffman, "Military Family Problems and USO," June 1972, Military Family Problems and USO, Series 3 General Subject Files, 1940–1975, NCCS.

23. Leo Ellingson, "Program Presentation," Board of Governors Ad hoc Study Committee 1974, Series 1 USO Records, 1943–1978, NCCS.

24. "Reaching Out to Today's Armed Forces," USO Board of Governors 1976, Series 1 USO Records, 1943–1978, NCCS. Also see USO Fact Sheet in George M. Elsey to Mrs. Waite, January 19, 1978, 610.02 United Service Organization, Red Cross 1965–1979, NARA.

25. National Program Committee minutes, June 9, 1976, USO Board of Governors, 1976, Series 1 USO Records, 1943–1978, NCCS.

26. Junior Volunteer Manual, January 1972, 16 and 18, also 17, Junior Volunteer Program 1974, Series 3 General Subject Files, 1940–1975, NCCS. Delegates to the 1974 national conference of Junior Volunteers took up the problem of how better to integrate servicewomen into Center programs as a main topic of discussion. See USO JV Conference, March 28–31, 1974, 2, Junior Volunteer Program 1974, Series 3 General Subject Files, 1940–1975, NCCS.

27. National Program Committee minutes, June 9, 1976.

28. "Wholesome" in *Hearing before the Subcommittee on Administrative Law*, 20; "link" in National USO Shows Committee minutes, September 11, 1975, Board of Governors Minutes, Standing Committees, 1973–1975, vol. 12, USO; "warmth" in *Hearing before the Subcommittee on Administrative Law*, 16.

29. Quote and numbers in National USO Shows Committee minutes, September 11, 1975; also see Board of Governors Meeting minutes, September 12, 1975, USO Board of Governors Minutes, 9 / 12 / 1975, Series 1 USO Records, 1943–1978, NCCS.

30. National USO Shows Committee minutes, March 12, 1975, Board of Governors Minutes, Standing Committees, 1973–1975, vol. 12, USO.

31. National USO Shows Committee minutes, September 20, 1973, 3, Board of Governors 1973 (2), Series 1 USO Records, 1943–1978, NCCS. Even in 1986, the USO was short of funds to finance its celebrity tours. That year, the organization had a $20 million operating budget but was $1.16 million in debt. USO President Charles Hagel said corporate sponsors and annual fund raisers would erase the debt. See Laurence Jolidon, "USO Show Goes On and On Over There," *USA Today*, November 27, 1987.

32. Fact Sheet: Armed Forces Entertainment, www.armedforcesentertainment.com /fact-sheet, accessed March 16, 2017; Army Regulation 215-6/OPNAVINST 1710.4B/ AFR 215-10/MCO 1710.23B Morale Welfare and Recreation: Armed Forces Professional Entertainment Program Overseas, January 15, 1987, http://usahec.contentdm .oclc.org/cdm/ref/collection/p16635coll11/id/1122, accessed July 1, 2018.

33. USO Annual Report, 1975, USO Board of Governors, 6/10/1976, Series 1 USO Records, 1943–1978, NCCS.

34. McKay quotes in Karen McKay letter to editor, *Soldiers* 27, no. 5 (May 1972): 4; Lane quotes in Robert A. Dobkin, "Troops Reject Female Pinups," *The Free Lance-Star* (Fredericksburg, VA), September 8, 1972. Responders favored the continuation of cheesecake until the last reporting of the unofficial poll in August 1972. See "More Baring the Bod," *Soldiers* 27, no. 8 (August 1972): 5. The magazine continued to print the pinups through the late 1970s, and in the July 1979 issue featured what appears to be its first male pinup, a midriff-baring Bucky Dent, star shortstop for the New York Yankees.

35. Controversies about images of women increased in the mid-1990s in debates about the sale of pornography in military PXs and shops. Many of the extant records on military recreation and entertainment remain unavailable to researchers. Following the Vietnam War, as oversight for Special Services decentralized, records that would have documented program changes were held by local commanders, not at a central headquarters. Additionally, records were often lost as Special Services became known by other names and was overseen by various Army agencies. In 2008, the Family Morale, Welfare, and Recreation (FMWR) command located in Washington, DC, hired a professional historian and archivist, Maria Christina Mairena, to collect as many records as she could. Those records—gathered from individuals who had worked in Army morale programs since the 1970s—were transferred to Fort Sam Houston, Texas when the FMWR command downsized and became part of the Installation Management Command. As of July 2017, the records Mairena gathered are sealed and waiting transfer to the planned Army Museum, where they will be processed by the staff of the Center for Military History. In the absence of a more substantial archival collection, I have relied heavily on oral history interviews with individuals who worked in Special Services and its later iterations, a few personal collections held in various archives, and newspaper coverage of the events in question.

36. Amy L. Culbertson, Patricia J. Thomas, and John P. Harden, *The Role of Recreation in Facilitating Gender Integration in the Navy,* TN-98-12 (San Diego, CA: Navy Personnel Research and Development Center, March 1998), 81.

37. Record of Interview with Margaret Hodge, December 3, 1971, Margaret Hodge papers, in possession of the author. Hodge filed an official complaint against Special Services when denied a job near her husband.

38. Harriet Rice, interview by Kara Dixon Vuic, July 3, 2017, telephone interview; Kim Mills, interview by Kara Dixon Vuic, June 27, 2017, telephone interview.

39. Service Club Council minutes, May 14, 1971, 5; Debby Alexander Moore, interview by Kara Dixon Vuic, July 25–28, 2016.

40. Marcy Stennes, interview by Kara Dixon Vuic, June 30, 2017, telephone interview.

41. Joan Capella, interview by Kara Dixon Vuic, July 12 and 13, 2017, telephone interview.

42. Rice, interview by Vuic.

43. "Uniform for Special Services Civilian Personnel," [1969]; Josephine M. Kovacek to Kay Johnson, August 11, 1972, both in Kay Johnson "Project Ugly" files, in possession of the author. Implementation of the new policy seems to have taken even longer. Most women note that they were no longer required to wear the uniform by 1973, though Barbara Clemens, who worked in arts and crafts, did not have to wear one when she began in October 1972 at Fort Benjamin Harrison. Joan Capella, who joined Special Services in 1974, noted that women were forbidden from wearing jeans as part of their civilian attire, on or off duty. According to Nick Credgington, some "lifers" in Special Services continued to wear the blue uniform even after they were no longer required to do so. Barbara Clemens, interview by Kara Dixon Vuic, June 27, 2017, telephone interview; Credgington, interview by Vuic; Capella, interview by Vuic; Judy Max, interview by Kara Dixon Vuic, April 13 and May 1, 2017, telephone interviews; Vanita Rae Smith, interview by Kara Dixon Vuic, May 5, 2017, telephone interview; Stennes, interview by Vuic; Mills, interview by Vuic.

44. Kay Johnson, interview by Kara Dixon Vuic, July 7, 2017, telephone interview.

45. Capella, interview by Vuic.

46. Max, interview by Vuic.

47. Capella, interview by Vuic.

48. Max, interview by Vuic.

49. Mills, interview by Vuic.

50. Reed, interview by Vuic.

51. Max, interview by Vuic.

52. Robert Hollis, "Navy Joins Trend, Bans Topless at Clubs," *Honolulu Advertiser,* March 19, 1980.

53. L. Emmett Lewis Jr., "Ban on Dancers Blamed for Clubs' Business Slump," *Stars and Stripes* (Europe), July 31, 1984, 9.

54. Norman Black, "Shows at Clubs Must Observe Modesty Rules, Navy Decrees," *Stars and Stripes* (Europe), August 5, 1988, 4.

55. Quote in Black, "Shows at Clubs Must Observe Modesty Rules"; also see Hollis, "Navy Joins Trend."

56. Quote in "Male Dancers New to Circuit" inset in L. Emmett Lewis Jr., "Ladies' Night Out," *Stripes Magazine* (Europe), April 19, 1984, 11; Nancy Ross, interview by Kara Dixon Vuic, March 23, 2017, telephone interview.

57. L. Emmett Lewis Jr., "VII Corps Bans 'Suggestive' Entertainers," *Stars and Stripes* (Europe), July 31, 1984, 9. One deputy community commander stipulated that no "strip / go-go dancing, male or female" would be permitted without prior approval.

However, it is hard to determine how effectively such a policy was enforced across the military. Male strippers performed at Camp Casey in Korea in the early 1990s, prompting a similar command-level review of policies on dancers and subsequent cancellation of the practice. Credgington, interview by Vuic.

58. DOD Instruction 1015.10, Programs for Military Morale, Welfare, and Recreation (MWR), November 3, 1995, http://ndri.org/docs/DoDI%201015.1%20 Programs%20for%20Military%20Morale,%20Welfare,%20and%20Recre.pdf, accessed July 1, 2018.

59. Unclassified Memo "Army Recreation Programs for Dependents of Military Personnel" [early 1960s], 719-01 Special Services Program Files 66: Establish Dependent Recreation Program, Selected Permanent Subject Files, 1953–1968, Army Education and Morale Support Directorate, AGO, NARA.

60. Army Regulation No. 28-17 Welfare, Recreation, and Morale: Army Dependent Youth Activities Program, March 19, 1968, 3, Regulations, USARV Adjutant General Section / Special Services Section General Records, USFSEA, NARA. Youth Activities became a dedicated component of Special Services in 1968. Mady Wechsler Segal and Jesse J. Harris, "What We Know about Army Families," US Army Research Institute for the Behavioral and Social Sciences, September 1993, 45.

61. See Kathy Sawyer, "Military's Single Parents," *Washington Post*, June 21, 1981. Problems continued for many years. See Molly Moore, "New Lifestyles Undercut Readiness, Strain Facilities," *Washington Post*, September 25, 1989.

62. John A. Wickham, "White Paper 1983: The Army Family," HathiTrust.org, quote on 1, also 14, http://hdl.handle.net/2027/uiug.30112037802268, accessed July 1, 2018. See also Middlestadt, *The Rise of the Military Welfare State*, 136–145.

63. William Joe Webb et al., *Department of the Army Historical Summary Fiscal Years 1990 and 1991* (Washington, DC: Center of Military History, 1997), 46, http://www.history .army.mil/books/DAHSUM/1990-91/cho4.htm#C4N2, accessed May 25, 2017.

64. Segal and Harris, "What We Know about Army Families," 17, 23–24, 30–31.

65. Mills, interview by Vuic.

66. Stennes, interview by Vuic.

67. Max, interview by Vuic.

68. Karl E. Cocke, *Department of the Army Historical Summary Fiscal Year 1974* (Washington, DC: Center for Military History, 1978), 119; Karl E. Cocke, *Department of the Army Historical Summary Fiscal Year 1978* (Washington, DC: Center for Military History, 1980), 139; Segal and Harris, "What We Know about Army Families," 84. Nick Credgington, who had a career in Army entertainment and worked for a time in the Community and Family Support Center (CFSC) at the Department of the Army headquarters, noted that until the CFSC was formalized, programs were decentralized, with local commanders controlling the nature and the name of morale programs. Even afterward, much of the funding and decision making was determined by commanders instead of centralized directives. Credgington, interview by Vuic.

69. U.S. Army MWR, "About Us: History," www.armymwr.com/about-us/history, accessed March 16, 2017; Brown, *Kevlar Legions*, 342–343.

70. Lee, interview by Vuic.

71. *Hearing before the Subcommittee on Manpower and Personnel of the Committee on Armed Services*, U.S. Senate, 100th Cong., 1st sess., October 9, 1987, on Morale, Welfare, and Recreation Programs, 5, 2. Also see Susan Way-Smith, Edward G. Keating, Peter A. Morrison, and Michael T. Childress, *Army Morale, Welfare, and Recreation Programs in the Future: Maximizing Soldier Benefits in Times of Austerity* (Santa Monica, CA: RAND, 1994); Randy Pruitt, "MWR Managers Challenged to Maintain Viable Programs," *Stars and Stripes* (Europe), September 17, 1991, 7; Pat Harden, "Armed Forces Recreation Services: Our Hallowed Ground Raison d'etre," *Parks & Recreation* 29, no. 12 (December 1994): 24. MWR programs continue to be prioritized by category and receive some appropriated funding based on level of importance. See DOD Instruction 1015.10. While demands for support services expanded exponentially in the 1980s, it was also a time of reorganization. Women who staffed Special Services clubs (as well as libraries and arts and crafts programs) had always been civilians, but until the 1980s some other positions had been designated military occupational specialties, especially administrative and sports positions. With the formation of CFSC and other Army restructuring, however, most Army positions were phased out. The Air Force similarly civilianized MWR positions, even to the extent that officials worried if the change would hamper their ability to quickly deploy MWR personnel to wartime positions. The Navy kept some military positions in MWR through the 1990s. See William Bradner, "MWR: Caring for Soldiers and Families," *Soldiers* 63, no. 1 (January 2008): 11; Weldon B. Durham, *Liberty Theatres of the United States Army, 1917–1919* (Jefferson, NC: McFarland and Company, 2006), 168; Gary C. Bradham, "Integrating AF Services and MWR Organizations: Impacts, Assessments, and Recommendations," Executive Research Project A71 (Industrial College of the Armed Forces, National Defense University, 1992), 51; David A. Kennett, "Mission Essential Service: Evaluation and Enrichment of Afloat MWR Initiatives" (MS thesis, Naval Postgraduate School, 1996), 17–21.

72. Capella, interview by Vuic; Coleen Amstein, interview by Kara Dixon Vuic, July 6 and 10, 2017, telephone interviews; Clemens, interview by Vuic; Credgington, interview by Vuic.

73. Webb et al., *Department of the Army Historical Summary Fiscal Years 1990 and 1991*, 49–50; US Army MWR, "B.O.S.S.," https://www.armymwr.com/programs-and -services/boss/about-boss/, accessed June 14, 2017; Theodore C. Fox III, *The Single Soldier Dilemma* (Carlisle, PA: Army War College Study Project, 1992), 11–12, 21; Mills, interview by Vuic; Amstein, interview by Vuic; Cole, interview by Vuic.

74. Statement of Rear Admiral Annette E. Brown, U.S. Navy Assistant Commander, Navy Personnel Command Personal Readiness and Community Support, Before the Oversight Panel on Morale, Welfare and Recreation, March 12, 2002, http://www .navy.mil/navydata/testimony/qol/aebrown020312.txt, accessed July 10, 2017; also see Kennett, "Mission Essential Service," 239–240.

75. Douglas Jehl, "There'll Be No Low Morale, Marines Told," *Los Angeles Times*, September 27, 1990.

76. Mary Jordan, "Troops Older, More Likely To Be Married Than in Past," *Washington Post,* February 8, 1991; David H. Marlowe, *Psychological and Psychosocial Consequences of Combat and Deployment with Special Emphasis on the Gulf War* (Santa Monica, CA: RAND Corporation, 2001), 124, https://www.rand.org/pubs/monograph_reports/MR1018z11.html, accessed June 17, 2017.

77. Michael R. Gordon, "The Troops Are in the Desert, and in More Ways than One," *New York Times,* September 3, 1990.

78. Robin Wright, "GIs Find Parched, Eerie Outpost," *Los Angeles Times,* August 10, 1990.

79. H. Norman Schwarzkopf with Peter Petre, *It Doesn't Take a Hero: The Autobiography* (New York: Bantam Books, 1992), 312, also 332. Even *Sports Illustrated* was banned for showing too much skin. Douglas Jehl, "For Troops, It's Diet of Boredom," *Los Angeles Times,* October 10, 1990. Frederic L. Borch further specifies that the order forbid any images that even hinted at genitalia, and thus banned body-building, swimsuit, lingerie, and underwear magazines and catalogs. See Frederic L. Borch, *Judge Advocates in Combat: Army Lawyers in Military Operations from Vietnam to Haiti* (Washington, DC: Office of the Judge Advocate General and Center of Military History, 2001), 131–132.

80. "Censored: Saudis Screen GI Mail for Pinups, Bibles," *The Pittsburgh Press,* September 12, 1990.

81. Schwarzkopf with Petre, *It Doesn't Take a Hero,* 336. Schwarzkopf recalled that he had a lot of military planners but "I was the only one who could assure the Saudis that the Dallas Cowgirls were not going to come over and corrupt the kingdom" (334).

82. James Ledbetter, "Deadlines in the Sand," *Village Voice,* February 5, 1991.

83. Schwarzkopf with Petre, *It Doesn't Take a Hero,* 312.

84. Kim Murphy, "Saudi Complaints Shut down Variety Show for American Troops," *New York Times,* September 16, 1990; Schwarzkopf with Petre, *It Doesn't Take a Hero,* 336–337. Aramco had been the locus of American and Saudi conflicts over cultural sensibilities for many years. See Chad H. Parker, *Making the Desert Modern: Americans, Arabs, and Oil on the Saudi Frontier, 1933–1973* (Amherst: University of Massachusetts Press, 2015).

85. Murphy, "Saudi Complaints Shut down Variety Show."

86. Schwarzkopf with Petre, *It Doesn't Take a Hero,* 338.

87. Robert Reinhold, "Policewoman in Denim is Betty Grable of Gulf," *New York Times,* February 15, 1991; Fara Warner, "Utah Police Officer's a Pinup," February 16, 1991, http://www.apnewsarchive.com/1991/Utah-Police-Officer-s-a-Pinup-Wearing-Clothes-and-Packing-a-Gun/id-5e33dbe95cc92371d3d32f99a57c6bb9, accessed June 30, 2017.

88. Jehl, "There'll Be No Low Morale"; "Entertaining Soldiers in Gulf Area Is 'Ludicrous,' General Says," *Los Angeles Times,* September 19, 1990.

89. Keith L. Thomas, "With the Gulf Crisis, USO is Having a Busy 50th Anniversary," *Detroit Free Press,* November 25, 1990.

90. Douglas Jehl, "He Can't be 'Wild and Crazy Guy,'" *Los Angeles Times,* October 17, 1990.

91. Phil McCombs, "USO's Desert No-Show," *Washington Post,* November 16, 1990; "Don't Send Brooke, Saudis Tell US," *Los Angeles Times,* December 7, 1990; Schwarzkopf with Petre, *It Doesn't Take A Hero,* 388.

92. "Hope to Tame USO Tour for Gulf," *Los Angeles Times,* October 24, 1990. Hope was joined by Ann Jillian, Marie Osmond, and the Pointer Sisters when the tour continued in Bahrain. See Schwarzkopf with Petre, *It Doesn't Take a Hero,* 396–397.

93. Al Martinez, "Calling Bunnies to War," *Los Angeles Times,* November 1, 1990.

94. "'Operation Playmate' Returns," *Daily Reporter* (Greenfield, IN), November 23, 2001.

95. Schwarzkopf with Petre, *It Doesn't Take a Hero,* 332; James Le Moyne, "Army Women and the Saudis: The Encounter Shocks Both," *New York Times,* September 25, 1990; Tracy Wilkinson, "In Alcohol-Free Gulf, GIs Stayed out of Hot Water," *Los Angeles Times,* March 29, 1991; *Hearing before the Morale, Welfare and Recreation Panel of the Readiness Subcommittee of the Committee on Armed Services,* House of Representatives, 101st Cong., 2nd sess., October 10, 1990, on "Military Exchange Operations during Mobilization, including Operation Desert Shield," 43.

96. "Well-Dressed Bunnies," *Palladium-Item* (Richmond, IN), October 31, 1990.

97. Elaine Viets, "Playmates Lose Allure in Letters," *St. Louis Post-Dispatch,* November 7, 1990.

98. Memorandum for Jan Osthus, November 8, 1990, Desert Storm / Shield (2 of 5), Rice Papers.

99. James LeMoyne, "Where Cookies Are Manna and Mail Is Gold," *New York Times,* September 15, 1990.

100. Army Recreation Centers Information News Brief, 2nd Quarter FY 91, February 1991, 4, Army Recreation Centers—Info Brief Community Rec Imperatives, Rice Papers; "Civilian Recreation Professionals Sent to Support Soldiers in Saudi," Desert Storm / Shield (2 of 5), Rice Papers; Webb et al., *Department of the Army Historical Summary Fiscal Years 1990 and 1991,* 48; Jan Kaplan Osthus, interview by Kara Dixon Vuic, June 27, 2017, telephone interview; Bob McKeta et al., "Recreation under Fire," *Parks & Recreation,* October 1991, 30–37, 72.

101. Discussion Paper, November 28, 1990, 3–4, Desert Storm / Shield (2 of 5), Rice Papers; Stennes, interview by Vuic.

102. McKeta et al., "Recreation under Fire," 32, 33.

103. McKeta et al., "Recreation under Fire," 37, 30ff; Harriet Rice, "Army Morale Welfare Recreation" (U.S. Army Community and Family Support Center, ca. 1987), 22–23.

104. Douglas Jehl, "500 Weary Soldiers Get First Real Taste of R&R," *Los Angeles Times,* October 1, 1990.

105. Michael Wines, "U.S. to Rent Cruise Ship for Gulf G.I. Furloughs," *New York Times,* December 15, 1990; "Cruise Ship Chartered for R&R," *Los Angeles Times,* December 14, 1990; Charles P. Wallace, "'Love Boat' of the Gulf Offers Respite from War," *Los Angeles Times,* February 18, 1991; Bradham, "Integrating AF Services and MWR Organizations," 53. A twenty-two-year-old Army sergeant reported that she

was raped in her room on the cruise ship. Her assailant was never identified. See John Lancaster, "24 Women Assaulted on Gulf Duty," *Washington Post,* July 21, 1992.

106. *Field Manual 12-6: Personnel Doctrine* (Washington, DC: Headquarters Department of the Army, September 9, 1994), chap. 7, http://www.globalsecurity.org/military /library/policy/army/fm/12–6/Ch7.htm#top, accessed July 24, 2017; Harriet E. Rice, "Recreation Downrange: Army MWR Delivers," *Parks & Recreation* 33, no. 2 (December 1998): 45–49; Cole, interview by Vuic.

107. Henry Allen, "Gender Games in the Gulf," *Washington Post,* December 31, 1990.

108. Ann Bergstrom, "Plan, but Stay Flexible: The Key to Successful MWR Down-range," MWR Deployed: Bosnia Watch, Joint Endeavor / Bosnia Book (4 of 7), Rice Papers; Rice, "Army Morale Welfare Recreation," 23; DOD Overseas Shows Program 1996 Holiday Schedule and Stanley Adamus to Harriet Rice, et al., April 2, 1996 email, both in Joint Endeavor / Bosnia Book (2 of 7), Rice Papers.

109. Coffey, *Always Home.*

110. Kristie Lovelace letter to the editor, *Stars and Stripes* (Europe), July 24, 1997, 16.

111. Russell A. Cleveland letter to the editor, *Stars and Stripes* (Europe), August 7, 1997, Joint Endeavor / Bosnia Book (4 of 7), Rice Papers.

112. Keith Bennetts, "'We're Real People . . . Not Sexpots,'" *Stars and Stripes* (Europe), March 13, 1980, 2.

113. Cleveland letter to the editor.

114. Lovelace letter to the editor.

115. Capella, interview by Vuic.

116. James Sohre, interview by Kara Dixon Vuic, May 9, 2017, telephone interview.

117. Cole, interview by Vuic.

118. USO / DOD Dallas Cowboys Cheerleaders "Bosnia Tour" schedule and information, courtesy of Kathleen Cole, in possession of the author.

119. Sohre, interview by Vuic.

120. Cleveland letter to the editor.

121. Cole, interview by Vuic.

### EPILOGUE

1. Al Franken, "Tearaway Burkas and Tinplate Menorahs," *Mother Jones* 29, no. 2 (March / April 2004): 48, 49, 50. Video of the dance is available at https://youtu.be /TnJ6cKr8uek, accessed July 24, 2017.

2. Nicholas Fandos, "Al Franken Issues Apology after Accusation of Forcible Kissing and Groping," *New York Times,* November 16, 2017; Sheryl Gay Stolberg, Yamiche Alcindor, and Nicholas Fandos, "Franken, Bruised by Accusations, Will Quit Senate," *New York Times,* December 8, 2017.

3. Jay Rath, "Hooters Headliners: Madison Student-Waitress Recounts Tour to Entertain War-Zone Troops," *Wisconsin State Journal,* March 7, 2005; "Concord Hooters Girl Visits Troops in Iraq & Kuwait," PR Newswire, December 3, 2010, http://www .prnewswire.com/news-releases/concord-hooters-girl-visits-troops-in-iraq-kuwait

-111272289.html, accessed July 27, 2017; entries at www.MWROverseas.wordpress
.com, accessed July 24, 2017.

4. All overseas entertainment and recreation is defined as "mission sustaining" and
is therefore funded through appropriated monies. The USO supports its tours in part
through public and corporate funds, but all overseas shows operate with military
transportation, security, and logistical support, all of which is funded through appropriated funds. Tours operating through the Armed Forces Professional Entertainment Office are funded entirely by appropriated funds.

5. William Donnelly, *Department of the Army Historical Summary Fiscal Year 2002*
(Washington, DC: Center for Military History, 2011), 45.

# Illustration Credits

Every effort has been made to identify copyright holders and obtain their permission for the use of copyright material. Notification of any additions or corrections that should be incorporated in future reprints or editions of this book would be greatly appreciated.

*Page 16:*    Library of Congress.

*Page 31:*    Courtesy of Salvation Army National Archives.

*Page 41:*    Courtesy of Kautz Family YMCA Archives, University of Minnesota Libraries.

*Page 51:*    Courtesy of Kautz Family YMCA Archives, University of Minnesota Libraries.

*Page 65:*    Schlesinger Library, Radcliffe Institute, Harvard University.

*Page 74:*    Esther Gilbert Scrapbook (WV0297), Betty H. Carter Women Veterans Historical Project, Martha Hodges Special Collections and University Archives, University Libraries, The University of North Carolina at Greensboro.

*Page 112:*   Peter Stackpole / Getty Images.

*Page 118:*   Peter Stackpole / Getty Images.

*Page 126:*   National Archives (111-SC-329741).

*Page 153:*   National Archives and Records Administration, RG 200 Records of the American National Red Cross, Entry P82 Records

Relating to Service to the Armed Forces, Photos—Supplemental Recreation Activities Overseas (SRAO) Korea, 1950s–1970s (Folder 1).

*Page 164:*   Bettmann / Getty Images.

*Page 174:*   *Mademoiselle,* October 1975, page 68, reproduced from the holdings of Tredway Library, Augustana College.

*Page 190:*   Keystone Pictures / Alamy.

*Page 193:*   © The American National Red Cross 1968, Courtesy of The American National Red Cross. All rights reserved in all countries.

*Page 202:*   P. Lough O'Daly Papers, Sophia Smith Collection, Smith College.

*Page 213:*   © The American National Red Cross 1969, Courtesy of The American National Red Cross. All rights reserved in all countries.

*Page 225:*   National Archives and Records Administration, RG 472, Special Services Agency (Provisional), Entertainment Branch, After Action Reports RE: USO Tours in Vietnam.

*Page 270:*   John Moore / Getty Images.

# Acknowledgments

In May 1918, a young woman named Emma Young Dickson gave a speech to celebrate the opening of the YMCA canteen where she served hot chocolate and smiles to lonely doughboys. She had eagerly volunteered for wartime work but discovered that it was "a much bigger job than I ever dreamed it would be and I feel very little and incompetent measured up beside it." I think I know how she felt. While I love reading other people's acknowledgments, I feel quite intimidated at the prospect of writing my own. This book has been many years in the making, and I have accumulated many debts in the process. Nothing I can say here will adequately convey my thanks to the people who have been so generous with their time and talents.

I'll start with my husband, Jason, who knew there was a story here all along and kept up my morale as I tried to tell it. He has tracked down random sources, has been a somewhat willing assistant at archives, and has moved our family literally halfway across the country while writing his own books. He definitely provides the recreation and the entertainment in our family. Our children, Asher and Imogene, both came along while I was writing this book. They are still "reading" board books, but I hope that one day, if they read this one, they will recognize some of the goodness of humanity that can be found in its pages. They will, undoubtedly, recognize the goodness of our extended family, especially my parents, Kevin and Sarah Dixon, and my brother and his family, Tracy, Cindy, Riley, and Brady Dixon.

I began this project while at Bridgewater College, continued it at High Point University, and finished it at Texas Christian University (TCU). Along the way, I've had the privilege to work with great colleagues who have become dear friends, especially Richard Fogarty, Brandon and Anne Marsh, David Reis, Jean Hawk, Jenn Brandt, Matt and Rebekah Carlson, Shannon Campbell, and Fearghal O'Reilly. I owe Frederick C. Schneid many thanks for his unconditional support, mentorship, and friendship. I miss our walks across campus much more than the free coffee we set out to get.

TCU has quickly become home, due in no small part to my wonderful colleagues and students. From our initial meetings as I interviewed with a four-week-old infant in tow, my colleagues have gone beyond the call of duty to welcome me and my family to Fort Worth. I admire their generosity and commitment to our students, and I am lucky to have landed among them. For all sorts of help, including rocking my babies, hanging curtain rods, and serving as a day care emergency contact, not to mention having smart conversations about this book, I am especially grateful to Jodi Campbell, Gregg Cantrell, Alan Gallay, Max Krochmal, Bill Meier, and Rebecca Sharpless. Special thanks, as well, for the support—material and scholarly—of the Department of History and the AddRan College of Liberal Arts and its dean, Andy Schoolmaster. I am also lucky to work with our outstanding graduate and undergraduate students. In particular, Meraleigh Randle and Sadie Scott-Martinson—both of whom are set to begin careers as military officers—remind me every day that the history of gender and the military matters. They make me proud and give me hope.

I count myself very fortunate to have a great circle of colleagues who have made this a better book and me a better historian. I became a historian in part because of my first college history professor at Marshall University, David C. Duke. I have to admit I don't remember everything he taught me about intellectual history, but he showed me what it truly means to be a professor. I hope that my students see even a little bit of Duke in me. Beth Bailey probably had no idea that I was adopting her as my mentor and life coach when we first met, but I'm enormously grateful that she accepted both tasks. She has been a great support and sounding board and always provides sage advice and good humor, all while doing her own model work on the military and gender. She has offered invaluable commentary on nearly every iteration of this book, from the first conference paper to the final manuscript, and at all stages has made it a better product. Andrew Huebner also read the manuscript for Harvard University Press. His feedback, our many conversations about the book, and his own outstanding work on love and families in World War I all pushed me to think about the larger significance of military entertainment. I am also grateful for the helpful conversations with friends and colleagues who read portions or all of the manuscript, or who offered insight at conferences or other venues, including Chris Capazzola, Stephanie Cole, Richard Fogarty, Susan Grayzel, Karen Hagemann, Robin Henry, Jennifer Keene, Donna Knaff, Jennifer Koslow, Joanne Meyerowitz, Sarah Parry Myers, Michael Neiberg, Stephen Ortiz, Kurt Piehler, Tammy Proctor, Heather Stur, Charissa Threat, Janet Valentine, Leigh Ann Wheeler, and John Worsencroft. For answering some pretty odd questions or helping with research, I thank Amber Batura, Greg Daddis, Lt. Col. Darin Gregg, Sok Ju Kim, Meredith Lair, Francesca Lee, Ed Lengel, Jennifer McCutchen, Ron Milam, Sarah Miller, Jane Monson, Shannon and Lisa Porter, and Sierra Reis.

Research for this book took me to libraries across the country, where I benefited from the tireless help of archivists and historians who amazed me with their encyclopedic knowledge of their collections. Special thanks go to Richard Boylan, who, despite being retired, continued to assist me at the National Archives. Finding one's way through military and civilian records of several wars at the National Archives was a daunting task, but archivists Tab Lewis, Wil Mahoney, and Martin Gedra helped me find my way, even when the subject terms and decimal files did not easily answer my questions. Eric VanSlander did double duty by answering a number of questions and helping with image scans long after I'd left the archive. I am similarly indebted to librarians at a number of other archives, including Ryan Beam at the Kautz Family YMCA Archives; Susan Watson at the

American Red Cross Archives; Susan Mitchem at the Salvation Army National Archives; Michael Case at the USO; Maida Goodwin and Karen V. Kukil at Smith College; Diana Carey and Lynda Leahy at the Schlesinger Library; Monica Blank at the Rockefeller Archive Center; Kevin Proffitt and Gary P. Zola at the American Jewish Archives; Stephen Bye of the Military History Institute at Carlisle Barracks; Diane Shaw of the Lafayette College Library; William Donnelly at the Center for Military History; Janet Weaver at the University of Iowa Libraries; Shane MacDonald at the American Catholic Research Center and University Archives; Beth Koelsch at the Betty H. Carter Women Veterans Historical Project at the University of North Carolina at Greensboro; Sarah-Jane M. Poindexter at the University of Louisville Libraries; and G. Kurt Piehler, Anne Marsh, Vincent Kolb-Lugo, and Brianna McLean at the Institute on World War II and the Human Experience at Florida State University.

Librarians Robyn Reid and Linda Chenoweth at TCU, Bob Fitzgerald at High Point University, and Rob Tout at Bridgewater College tracked down every random and often weird request I made, always with great humor and speed. Dr. Maria Christina Mairena knows a thing or two about tracking down information, and she graciously shared her knowledge of the post–Vietnam War Special Services records with me. Ann Kelsey, whose career in Army Special Services began in Vietnam, not only shared her knowledge of the program's history with me but also put me in touch with many of the women I interviewed. Nick Credgington and Holley Watts also introduced me to people whose memories of working in military entertainment (including their own) proved invaluable for this project. I began this project by interviewing Vietnam War Donut Dollies, and I finished it by interviewing women and men who continued their work decades later. I appreciate their generosity in sharing their lives. In particular, I want to thank Debby Alexander Moore and Gina Cardi Lee. Their stories brought this history to life for me, and I hope they are pleased with the result.

Several grants supported my travel to visit archives and collections, and I am grateful for having received a Clarke Chambers Travel Grant from the University of Minnesota, a Schlesinger Library Research

Support Grant, a Grant-in-Aid from the Rockefeller Archives Center, the Loewenstein-Wiener Fellowship from the American Jewish Archives, a minigrant from the New Jersey Historical Commission, a Ridgeway Research Grant from the Military History Institute, an Albert J. Beveridge Grant from the American Historical Association, the Mednick Fellowship from the Virginia Foundation for Independent Colleges, and several Faculty Research Fund Awards from Bridgewater College. A fellowship from the Virginia Foundation for the Humanities provided a blissful year in which to write and think as this project took shape. The "Lady Fellows," especially Jasmin Darznik and Susan McKinnon, provided insightful feedback and support at this critical stage.

It has been a great pleasure to work with Harvard University Press on this book. I am especially grateful to my editor, Kathleen McDermott, for her unfailing support for this project at all its stages, even when those stages sometimes lasted a bit longer than she had expected. Thanks as well to John Donohue, Elizabeth Granda, and Julia Kirby for their careful editing, and to Stephanie Vyce for helping to navigate the image permissions.

Finally, I want to acknowledge a twenty-four-year-old young man I never met. Benjamin W. Schmidt was a TCU student who joined the US Marine Corps before finishing his degree in history. After a couple of years, and inspired by a love for military history, he decided to return to school and become a professor. Before he could do so, however, he deployed for a second time to Afghanistan, where he lost his life. His father and stepmother, David and Teresa Schmidt, along with countless family members and friends, endowed a professorship in his name so that TCU students would have the opportunity to study the relationships among war, conflict, and society in twentieth-century America. I am deeply honored and humbled to hold that position, though, like Emma, "I feel very little and incompetent measured up beside it." I am privileged to have the opportunity to spend my days with students, thinking about the ways wars and conflicts have shaped and continue to shape our world. I hope this book contributes to that conversation and honors the legacy of Benjamin W. Schmidt.

# Index

*Note:* Page numbers in *italics* indicate figures.